The Parish in Medieval and Early Modern Ireland

The Parish in Medieval and Early Modern Ireland

Community, Territory and Building

Elizabeth FitzPatrick and Raymond Gillespie

EDITORS

FOUR COURTS PRESS

for the Group for the Study of Irish Historic Settlement

This book was set in 10.5 on 12.5 point Ehrhardt by
Mark Heslington, Scarborough, North Yorkshire for
FOUR COURTS PRESS
7 Malpas Street, Dublin 8, Ireland
Email: info@four-courts-press.ie
and in North America for
FOUR COURTS PRESS
c/o ISBS, 920 N.E. 58th Avenue, Suite 300, Portland, OR 97213.

A catalogue record for this title
is available from the British Library.

ISBN 1-85182-947-4

SPECIAL ACKNOWLEDGMENT

This publication was grant-aided by the Heritage Council of Ireland
under the 2005 Publication Grant Scheme.

AN
CHOMHAIRLE
OIDHREACHTA

THE
HERITAGE
COUNCIL

Printed in Great Britain
by MPG Books Ltd, Bodmin, Cornwall.

Contents

PART III. PERSPECTIVES ON THE REFORMED PARISH

Illustrations

ROULSTON

Plates

Contributors

TOBY BARNARD is fellow and tutor in history at Hertford College, Oxford.

HELEN BERMINGHAM is a contract archaeologist currently working in the County Museum, Tralee.

EAMONN COTTER is a contract archaeologist working mainly in Co. Cork.

CHARLES DOHERTY is lecturer in early and medieval Irish history at UCD.

ROWENA DUDLEY is the author of a PhD thesis on the parochial system in Dublin, 1660–1750.

PATRICK J. DUFFY is associate professor of geography at NUI Maynooth.

COLMÁN ETCHINGHAM lectures in medieval Irish history at NUI Maynooth.

ELIZABETH FITZPATRICK lectures in medieval archaeology at NUI Galway.

RAYMOND GILLESPIE is associate professor of history at NUI Maynooth.

HENRY A. JEFFERIES is head of history at Thornhill College, Derry.

ROLF LOEBER AND MAGDA STOUTHAMER-LOEBER, Pittsburgh, have written extensively on early modern Irish settlement.

SINÉAD NÍ GHABHLÁIN is a senior archaeologist with ASM Affiliates in southern California.

PATRICK NUGENT is a geographer based at the Institute of Irish Studies, University of Liverpool.

TOMÁS Ó CARRAGÁIN lectures in archaeology in UCC.

TADHG O'KEEFFE lectures in archaeology at UCD.

WILLIAM ROULSTON is research officer with the Ulster Historical Foundation.

Abbreviations

Anal. Hib.	*Analecta Hibernica*
BAR	British Archaeological Report
BL	British Library
CBA	Council for British Archaeology
Cal. S.P. Ire.	*Calendar of the state papers relating to Ireland*, 24 vols (London, 1860–1911)
JRSAI	*Journal of the Royal Society of Antiquaries of Ireland*
NAI	National Archives of Ireland
NLI	National Library of Ireland
NMAJ	*North Munster Antiquarian Journal*
PRIA	*Proceedings of the Royal Irish Academy*
PRONI	Public Record Office of Northern Ireland
RCB	Representative Church Body Library
RIA	Royal Irish Academy
TCD	Trinity College Dublin
UCC	University College Cork
UCD	University College Dublin

Preface

One of the most significant developments in the study of medieval and early modern Europe has been the recognition of the importance of the parish as both a social and an ecclesiastical unit. The parish as an idea comprehends a very wide range of human activity. At the most basic level it is a physical space, often with well-defined boundaries. At another level it is a state of mind which creates shared values among its inhabitants who are connected through the provision of pastoral care. Finally, the parish has a material expression through its church, its furniture and fittings, as provided and maintained by the local community. Those within the medieval parish identified with it, since they were baptised at the parish font and buried in the parish graveyard. In Ireland after the sixteenth-century Reformation the entire parish may no longer have been baptised with a common rite at a common font, they all continued to be buried in the parish graveyard until the creation of separate Catholic burial grounds from the 1830s.

In the early medieval context John Blair and Richard Sharpe (eds), in *Pastoral care before the parish* (Leicester, 1992), have prompted a wider discussion as to the possible existence and function of the pre-Norman parish in Ireland. From a historical perspective Colmán Etchingham, principally in his *Church organisation in Ireland, 650–1000* (Maynooth, 1999), has re-evaluated a range of ecclesiastical sources from the perspective of the workings of the early Irish Church. Concurrently, from an archaeological perspective, Tomás Ó Carragáin in his 2002 doctoral thesis has examined the building fabric within which this early Irish Church worked noting the emergence of mortared stone churches from the mid-eleventh century onwards which he suggests, in this volume, may reflect shifts in the provision of pastoral activity.

By the early twelfth century what appears to be a more clearly identifiable parochial system comes into view. Some of this appears to be related to Hiberno-Scandinavian developments in Dublin and in Waterford as testified by the excavations at St Peter's parish church and graveyard by Maurice Hurley and Sarah McCutcheon. Whatever about the existence of a pre-Norman parish, Anglo-Norman settlement in the twelfth and thirteenth centuries with a concomitant definition of property rights, especially those of tithe, led to the diffusion of the parish in tandem with the manor. Beyond the regions of Anglo-Norman influence the question as to when the parish was formalised remains a subject of much debate. In Gaelic Ireland the property matrix, and particularly the right of tithe, was not regulated by the same legal mechanisms as in Anglo-Norman Ireland. However, the same principle of associating units of pastoral care and units of secular authority, which resulted in the manor and parish being co-terminous, in Gaelic Ireland led to links between secular units, generally the *tuath* but occasionally the *tríocha ceád*, and the parish. Inevitably, as geographers such as P.J. Duffy have pointed out, this gave rise to different parish morphologies across Ireland.

Of course, the pattern is much more nuanced than these generalisations suggest. For instance, in some parts of Ireland where Anglo-Norman settlement was short-lived, the parish church and pastoral care became a casualty of Gaelic resurgence, although the spatial entity, shorn of its ecclesiastical rationale, survived to be revitalised at a later date. Therefore, apparent spatial continuities between the medieval and modern parish may conceal real discontinuities within the historical process.

Some of these complexities become apparent in the western Irish dioceses. While the documentary evidence, as elucidated by Kenneth Nicholls in his seminal article 'Rectory, vicarage and parish in the western Irish diocese' in *JRSAI*, 101 (1971), 53–84, points to a very limited development of parochial structure before the mid-thirteenth century, the architectural evidence from the churches of the diocese of Kilfenora detailed by Sinéad Ní Ghabhláin in 'The origin of medieval parishes in Gaelic Ireland: the evidence from Kilfenora' in *JRSAI*, 126 (1996), 37–61, suggests that what appear to be parish churches had begun to be created, at least in that area, during the first half of the thirteenth century. By contrast, in colonial Ireland, the position is much clearer. By the beginning of the fourteenth century the papal taxation reveals an intricate network of well-formed parishes, some of which were impropriated to the larger religious houses. Many of the resulting churches were new thirteenth-century creations on greenfield sites designed to meet the needs of emerging towns and rural boroughs.

While these parishes have left architectural evidence in the form of their churches and chapels, and geographical evidence, in the form of their boundaries which persisted in the guise of the civil parish into the nineteenth century, they have left little by way of historical evidence. The earliest parochial archive for Ireland is that for the parish of St Werburgh but this does not commence before the late fifteenth century. Admittedly some earlier deeds do survive for the larger Dublin parishes but, while they tell us a good deal about property ownership, they say little about the dynamics of parochial life. Despite these evidential problems, Adrian Empey in his 'The layperson in the parish: the medieval inheritance, 1169–1536' in R. Gillespie and W.G. Neely (eds), *The laity and the Church of Ireland, 1000–2000: all sorts and conditions* (Dublin, 2002), 7–48, has demonstrated the engagement of local communities and parochial organisations by the fifteenth century.

Empey's insight about the vitality of the fifteenth-century parish is borne out by the architectural evidence for the re-building and refurbishment of parish churches in fashionable fifteenth-century style both in the church *inter Anglicos* and the church *inter Hibernicos*. This was not an exclusively Irish development. The work of Eamonn Duffy has suggested that religious life in later medieval England, and the involvement of the average layperson with their parish, was much more active than historians of the Reformation have previously believed. In particular, his *The voices of Morebath: Reformation and rebellion in an English village* (New Haven and London, 2001), has demonstrated the vitality of parish life both before and during the reform process. However, Duffy's contention that the transformation of the parish from a community-based religious association to a unit of local government by the late seventeenth century was a regressive move, is a disputed one.

From the sixteenth to the eighteenth centuries central government increasingly realised the potential of the parish as a way of governing Ireland. This is reflected in the dramatic growth of surviving historical evidence in the form of vestry books, churchwardens' accounts and parish registers. Such evidence suggests that in Ireland the parish did not become exclusively a unit of colonial government. At one level the fabric of parish churches decayed, as a result of war, changing landownership and the fact that those who worshipped within them became a minority. Yet, the parish as a social and governmental unit flourished. Catholics who were not prepared to worship within the church still retained familial connections with the parish, retaining for example burial rights and in some cases serving on the parish vestry. It is striking, for example, that across Cos. Kilkenny and Tipperary, Church of Ireland parish churches contain funerary monuments of this period with overtly Catholic symbolism reflecting the complex relationship between parish and people.

The majority of essays in this volume are based on the proceedings of a conference organised by the Group for the Study of Irish Historic Settlement in 2003. Additional contributors were invited to explore other aspects of the parish that had not been treated in the conference. Thus, this book attempts the first overview of the evolution of the Irish parish from early medieval to early modern times. Since the parish is a complex phenomenon linking community, territory and building, an interdisciplinary approach to its evolution is imperative. Reflecting the ethos of the Group for the Study of Irish Historical Settlement (GSIHS), the expertise of archaeologists, geographers and historians is deployed to explore the evolution of the parish. The book opens with three introductory essays, which provide an overview of the most significant aspects of the parish: the concept behind it, its shape and material world. The subsequent essays in the book are divided between medieval and early modern, the division reflecting the importance of the reform process of the sixteenth and seventeenth centuries in re-shaping the concepts, shapes and materiality of the parish.

ACKNOWLEDGEMENTS

The editors on behalf of GSIHS would like to thank those who have been part of this project for their enthusiasm and commitment and especially for their forbearance throughout the editorial process. Special thanks are due to Charles Doherty who was involved in the planning stages of this volume and Dáibhí Ó Cróinín who offered advice. As always we are grateful to Four Courts Press who have acted as publishers to the GSIHS over a number of years and on this occasion have produced a handsome volume with their customary efficiency. This publication was grant-aided by the Heritage Council under the 2005 publication grants scheme.

Finally the editors would like to express their sincere thanks to the committee of GSIHS for their support during this project, especially Bernadette Cunningham and Michael O'Hanrahan.

PART I

Introductions

The idea of the parish

CHARLES DOHERTY

There can be little doubt of our great debt to the inheritance of Greece and, more immediately, to that of Rome. Much of our ecclesiastical terminology, for instance, owes its origin to the Romans. It is useful to understand something of the context of the use of these terms since that may give us an idea of their meaning when adapted by Christians. The Roman empire looms large like an enormous monolithic structure, a great administrative machine the like of which has not been seen in western Europe until modern times. The recent work of Andrew Lintott, *Imperium Romanum, politics and administration* (1993), however, has shown just how diverse and pragmatic Roman administrative structures were. For example on the concept of the province he says:

> The term that the Romans came to use for the areas directly administered by their officials was *provincia*. The basic meaning of this word was 'appointment' or 'task'. Thus one of the quaestors in Italy had the treasury as his *provincia*. Overseas a *provincia* was originally the field of operations assigned to a magistrate. Some of these of course had clear natural geographical limits; for example, Sicily or Corsica and Sardinia which became the first permanent *provinciae* overseas in 241 and 227 BC respectively. However, the first evidence of an attempt to draw geographical boundaries over a large land mass relates to the year 197 BC, when two new praetors were created to be the regular governors of two Spanish *provinciae*.[1]

Lintott shows 'that by 101 BC the spatial concept of a *provincia* was firmly established, though only in the context of assigning specific functions to magistrates'.[2] He goes on to say, 'However, we should not infer that the Romans were thinking in terms of absolutely precise boundaries.'[3]

The flexibility of the concept of *provincia* even in the late Republic is illustrated by Cicero's own activities in Cilicia. Syme, when discussing the

---

1 A. Lintott, *Imperium Romanum: politics and administration* (London and New York, 1993), 22–3.
2 Ibid., 23. 3 Ibid., 24.

early history of that province, took it as a classic example of the word retaining its original sense of official duty. However, we need not deny the territorial sense, provided that is not interpreted too rigidly.[4]

The *provincia* in the late Republic had become more closely defined geographically but its borders, especially with hostile peoples, were imprecise, and it might be interspersed with districts belonging to free cities or the possessions of allied kings and dynasts.[5]

Here Lintott was speaking of the military assignment of a *provincia*. 'This was not admissible when it came to administration, justice and the collection of taxes. Yet even here a greater stability of organisation is sometimes assumed than is warranted by the evidence.'[6] This point is important because those engaged in the study of the earliest church structures may feel some sympathy with their Classical colleagues as they grapple with the problems of terminology.

Consider first the word diocese. Originally Greek *dioikesis* > Latin *dio(e)cesis* > French > English. This word comes from *dioikeein* 'to keep house' *di* for *dia* 'completeness' and *oikeein* 'to keep house' *oikos* 'house'. In the Roman empire it came to mean an administrative district within a province, the centre of an assize (a *conventus*) and taxation unit. Our word for parish also has an origin in the Greek language – *paroikia* > Latin *parochia* (*paruchia* in Hiberno-Latin), > Anglo-French *paroche* > English *parish*. The Greek word is made up of *para* 'beside' and *oikos* 'dwelling'. There was also another Greek word *paroche* that is a term for the compulsory provision of entertainment for travellers, associated with *kataluma* 'a lodging'. The *parochi*, those neighbouring the road, provided firewood and salt for the travellers.[7] There would seem to be confusion between these words. As with the *dio(e)cesis* the word *oikos* 'dwelling' lies at the heart of this word too. Both *paroikia* and *dio(e)cesis* contain the idea of paying a tax. The word *paruchia* gave us *pairche* (later *fairche*) in Old Irish as Cormac mac Cuillenáin points out in his glossary.[8] And Clonbur between Lough Mask and Lough Corrib in the west of Ireland is called An Fhairrche.

A second word, that for church, *ekklêsia*, is an element in the constitution of the cities of the ancient world. In this sense it means the 'assembly'. It was this word that gave us Latin *ecclesia*. As such it means the 'body of the faithful'. But, of course, it also gives us a word for the church building. In the course of time the *pagi*, the districts of Italy, North Africa and Gaul were incorporated in *municipia* as the empire became further urbanised.[9] In Gaul Celtic *oppida* were replaced by towns or new *civitas* capitals. In the north of Gaul these *civitates*

---

4 Ibid. 5 Ibid., 27. 6 Ibid., 28. 7 Ibid., 92. 8 See E.G. Quin et al. (eds), *Dictionary of the Irish language* (RIA, Dublin, 1984), s.v. *pairche*, s.v. *fairche*. 9 Lintott, *Imperium Romanum*, 130.

were much further apart than in the south. It was along this urban network that the early Church spread in the first few centuries AD. Its evolving administration borrowed the terminology of the Empire as I have indicated above. 'Roman domination under the Principate was usually elegantly clothed in ceremonies of the imperial cult, the *adventus* of proconsuls and the succession of the assizes.'[10] This too was taken over by the Church, as pointed out by Peter Brown.[11] As the power of Rome collapsed it was the Church that became her heir. By the late empire Rome was viewed as a world empire by Christians 'whose destiny it was to prepare the way for the kingdom of God. According to this perception, when, under Constantine, the Christian world and the Roman world became coterminous, *ipso facto* Christendom became a universal society.'[12] It was an ideal that was resurrected at various stages in the history of the Church but one that was never more than an aspiration.

There are a number of significant points in the history of the Church. The first is the freedom given to the Christian religion by Constantine in 312 following his victory over his co-emperor Maxentius on 28 October of that year. In 380 the Emperor Theodosius made Christianity the religion of the Empire. As early as 313 Christian clergy and laity were high in the administrative circles of Constantine's government. Many of them were aristocrats. It was these people who fostered the idea of Rome as a world empire. From this point onwards the Church was in a position to grow in power. Following the sack of Rome, however, at the beginning of the fifth century it fell more and more to the popes to provide not only spiritual but also political leadership, particularly since the centre of the Empire had switched to Constantinople. Beginning with Pope Damasus the papacy was increasingly identified with St Peter and the Church with Rome. This process was brought to its logical conclusion by Pope Leo the Great 440–61. In his words 'Rome has become the Head of the World through the Holy See of Saint Peter.'[13] A brief recovery in Italy initiated by Justinian from Constantinople was ended with the invasion of the Lombards in 568. The popes now emerged as temporal rulers of Rome and the surrounding territories. They now looked not to Byzantium but to the Frankish West.

Pope Gregory the Great (590–604) was the first of the medieval popes. He defended Rome against invasion, provided for public services, looked after the poor, maintained church estates, sent missionaries to the far north-west and kept up a massive correspondence (Columbanus had written to him in 603) as well as his theological work. No church was built during his pontificate. To the Irishman, Cummean and his compatriots, he was 'golden-mouthed'.[14] In relation to our theme one of his most important works was his *De cura*

---

10 Ibid., 191. 11 P. Brown, *The cult of the saints: its rise and function in Latin Christianity* (London, 1981), 98–100. 12 Lintott, *Imperium Romanum*, 193. 13 Quoted in T. Charles-Edwards, *Early Christian Ireland* (Cambridge, 2000), 206. 14 M. Walsh and D. Ó Cróinín (eds), *Cummian's letter* De Controversia paschali *and the* De ratione conputandi (Toronto, 1988), 82–3.

pastoralis, 'Pastoral care', a work written shortly after his election to the papacy that was the handbook of the Middle Ages and has been recommended in recent writings on pastoral care as *the* source. His ideas on pastoral care were expounded in his forty Homilies on the Gospels. They were read in Roman churches in 591–2. The American historian Thomas L. Amos has written:

> Among many other themes, Gregory developed in these homilies the idea of a universal audience for preaching and the need to extend Christianity to the unconverted peoples of Europe. In the homily for the Ascension, commenting on the text 'Preach the Gospel to all creatures', Gregory compared preaching to sowing seed and stated that no harvest of faith in this world would be possible if the seeds of preaching were not sown. Describing the Holy Ghost's gift of tongues to the Apostles on the first Pentecost, he asked: 'What does this miracle mean if not that Holy Church, filled with the same Spirit, should be a voice speaking to all peoples?' Belief in pastoral care and preaching led Gregory to the idea of a universal mission which would have an impact on the monastic world.[15]

Some of Gregory's ideas on pastoral care are found in the hymn, *Audite Omnes*, written in praise of Patrick, probably by Bishop Colmán Elo of Lynally (southwest of Durrow), who died in 611.[16] The preaching of the Gospel to all creatures is an echo of Prosper of Aquitaine's *De Vocatione Omnium Gentium*, 'The Call of All Nations', which may in turn have been inspired (at least in part) by the mission of Palladius to Ireland. As such this document is the first statement on mission in the Christian Church in a Europe that for a very long time was a mission area.[17]

As mentioned earlier, the papacy had increasingly turned towards the Frankish west. This eventually led to an alliance that was cemented with the coronation of Charlemagne in Rome on Christmas Day 800 AD. The papacy needed a new Roman emperor in the west as her protector. But Charlemagne's empire did not last long and power devolved to local lords. Church property and appointments fell under the control of these lords. The entire life of the Church fell into decline with abuses in all areas of church life. Even in Rome the popes became puppets of the local aristocracy. It was the revival of the tradition of Charlemagne by Otto I (936–73), when he went to Rome to be

---

15 Thomas L. Amos, 'Monks and pastoral care in the early Middle Ages' in T.F.X. Noble and John J. Contreni (eds), *Religion, culture, and society in the early middle ages: studies in honor of Richard E. Sullivan* (SMC XXIII, Medieval Institute Publications, Western Michigan University, Kalamazoo, MI, 1987), 165–80: 170. **16** Cf. Andy Orchard, '"Audite omnes amantes": hymn in Patrick's praise' in D.N. Dumville et al., *Saint Patrick, A.D. 493–1993* (Woodbridge, 1993), 153–73; C. Doherty, 'The cult of St Patrick and the politics of Armagh in the seventh century' in J.M. Picard (ed.), *Ireland and Northern France, AD 600–850* (Dublin, 1991), 53–94: 88–92. **17** See the important comments of T. Charles-Edwards on this document in Charles-Edwards, *Early Christian Ireland*, 207–14.

crowned emperor, that was to lead to the reform of the papacy in the following century. A series of popes in the eleventh century undertook a complete reform of the Church. It led one historian, Norman Cantor, to call this process one of the four great 'world-revolutions of Western history'.[18] The greatest of these popes was Hildebrand, Pope Gregory VII (1073–85). The papacy itself was reformed, churches were freed from secular control, moral reform of clergy and laity was sought, clerical celibacy was rigorously enforced, simony abolished and steps were taken to provide for an educated priesthood. It was Gregory's successor Urban II (1088–99) who applied these reforming principles to parish churches. Addelshaw points out that by this time:

> each diocese north of the Alps was well on the way to being organised on the basis of the parochial system in the generally accepted sense of the term, that is a system of pastoral care exercised through numerous small urban and rural units, each with its church, its endowment and its priest. In the northern half of Italy, however, the country areas of dioceses continued down to comparatively modern times to be organised round the country churches of the older type (such a church being called a *plebs* or *pieve*), each with a number of dependent chapels.[19]

The impact of all these reforms was felt in Ireland in the late eleventh century and the process of reform continued right into the last quarter of the twelfth century.

The greatest pope of the Middle Ages, if not in history, was Innocent III (1198–1215). During his pontificate the papacy had reached the zenith of its power. The papacy had by now the most sophisticated bureaucracy in the Western world. It had a system that placed a resident representative in each country. She also had papal ambassadors who went on particular missions to oversee the solution to problems and she had a taxation system, 'Peter's pence', that brought her revenue from throughout Christendom. Despite the collapse of the pretensions to temporal power during the pontificate of Boniface VIII at the beginning of the fourteenth century her machinery of government meant that nothing much happened throughout Christendom that Rome did not know of or had not something to say about. The final great turning point in the

---

18 Quoted among opinions of other historians by B. Tierney, *The crisis of Church and state, 1050–1300* (Englewood Cliffs, NJ, 1964), 47. 19 G.W.O. Addelshaw, *The development of the parochial system from Charlemagne (768–814) to Urban II (1088–1099)* (St Anthony's Hall Publications No. 6, Borthwick Institute of Historical Research, University of York, [1954] 2nd ed., 1970), 3. For more recent work on Italy see C. Violante, 'Pievi e parrocchie nell Italia settentrionale durante i secoli xi e xii' in *Le istituzioni ecclesiastiche della 'Societas Christiana' dei seculi xi–xii*, Atti della vi settimana internationale di studio a Mendola (Milan, 1977) and C. Violante, 'Le strutture organizzative della cura d'anime nella campagne dell'Italia centrosettentrionale (secoli v–x)' *Settimana di Studio Spoleto*, 28 (1980). See also C. Boyd, *Tithes and parishes in medieval Italy* (Ithica, 1952).

history of the Church, as far as this essay is concerned, is the Reformation and Counter-Reformation and the implications that that brought about for Church structures and organisation.

The structures of the Church are a reflection of the world of which they are a part. The world of Constantine was utterly different from that of any of the great turning points discussed above. This was a point that was emphasised by Monsignor Corish, writing of the early Irish Church:

> The first is that we must not take as our framework a juridico-theological system elaborated in the twelfth century. Rather, we must look to the earlier and contemporary world, and more particularly to the world as it existed after the pontificate of Gregory the Great. The second is that even within this earlier framework we must expect differences of emphasis. The popes will put things one way. Ecclesiastics of the Irish Church may put them another. What we may call 'the religious mind' – which, it may or may not be necessary to say explicitly, the clergy share with the laity – may well put them another way. There will be real tension between forms of expression that are juridical or theological, and forms of expression that are, for want of better words, 'community' and 'familial'. It has been noted that such forms of expression had their influence among the Christian communities of the Roman empire. They may be expected to be even more influential among the kin-societies of the Celtic and Germanic peoples.[20]

Much of what Monsignor Corish says here has relevance to any period in the history of the parish. My only slight disagreement with his statement is that the period *before* the pontificate of Gregory the Great has equal relevance in the early history of the Church in Ireland. After all, people were becoming Christian in Ireland during the fourth century when the Church had been given her freedom and some had probably accepted Christianity before it became the official religion of the empire. The Irish Church has old roots and the Irish themselves knew that.

In confronting the history of church structures, and particularly that of the parish, we are brought face to face with some of the most fundamental problems that beset historians. To take a simple point made by Marc Bloch, 'For, to the great despair of historians, men fail to change their vocabulary every time they change their customs.'[21] Terms can take on a life and certitude of their own. On the other hand we can impose *our* terminology on the past. And again as Bloch has said, 'A nomenclature which is thrust upon the past will always end by distorting it, whether by design or simply as a consequence of

20 P.J. Corish, 'The early Irish Church and the Western patriarchate' in P. Ní Chatháin and M. Richter (eds), *Ireland and Europe: the early Church* (Stuttgart, 1984), 9–15: 11–12. 21 M. Bloch, *The historian's craft* (Manchester, 1992), 28.

equating its categories with our own, raised, for the moment, to the level of the eternal.'[22] If we use the word parish in sixth-century Ireland what do we mean by it? What did contemporaries mean by the word *paruchia?*: a problem analysed in some detail by Colmán Etchingham.[23]

What do we know about the earliest parishes, or, to maintain a degree of neutrality, the earliest units of pastoral care? But before doing so the definition of the parish of the Middle Ages given by G.W.O. Addleshaw may reveal the complexity of the subject as it was at its fullest development in the High Middle Ages:

> Through the parish the Church's pastoral work is done. This unit consists of a certain geographical area, with a church, a priest (the parson or rector) and an endowment, the income from which belongs to the rector for the time being. But the parish does not function on its own. It is a subdivision of a wider unit, the diocese, ruled by a bishop, the ordinary. Without the bishop, no new rector can be appointed, no church consecrated, and no changes made in the disposal either of the endowment or of its income; nor without the bishop can the people receive the blessing of confirmation. If there is a lay patron he enjoys wide rights in the appointment of a rector. Often the rector is a religious house or a cathedral or collegiate church or the occupant for the time being of a canonry in such a church. In this case, while the rector is still the legal recipient of most of the income from the parish's endowment, the parish itself is cared for either by a vicar, appointed and paid under a deed known as an ordination of a vicarage, or by a curate, paid by the rector and removable at his will. Some parishes may stand outside the diocesan organisation altogether; ordinary jurisdiction being exercised either by another bishop or by a rector of the type just described. Such parishes are commonly known as 'peculiars', and in them acts requiring episcopal orders are performed when the ordinary is not a bishop, by either the diocesan bishop or a bishop of the ordinary's own choice, according to the extent of the peculiar jurisdiction in question.[24]

This is the best and most succinct description that I have found of the parish. The parishes described here, however, are a long way away from the country parishes of the fourth century. In Rome the earliest Christian communities met in private houses or apartments. Each *Domus ecclesiae* or 'House of the assembly of the faithful' was known by the name of the original owner of the title to the property – for example, *titulus Clementis*. By the fourth century there were

22 Ibid., 143. 23 C. Etchingham, *Church organisation in Ireland, AD 650-1000* (Maynooth, 1999). For slightly different emphasis see Charles-Edwards, *Early Christian Ireland*, 241–64; for Anglo-Saxon England as well as Ireland see J. Blair and R. Sharpe, *Pastoral care before the parish* (Leicester, 1992). 24 Addleshaw, *Beginnings of the parochial system*, 3.

twenty-five such places in Rome.[25] Just before 312 barn-like halls or community centres were built to hold larger congregations. The fabric of some of these buildings is still to be found in churches built on their sites. Under Constantine a spate of church building was begun with the erection of huge basilicas.

Up to the fourth century Christianity was essentially a religion of the city. The Christian communities in these cities were called a *parochia* and this was the primary unit of pastoral care. In the first few centuries this arrangement was felt to be temporary – Christians expected the second coming to be immanent. But from the fourth century onwards, following the freedom of the Church, more permanent structures began to emerge. In the cities it was the bishop who led the Christian community – the *parochia*. The word bishop in modern English comes from OE *biscop* < Latin *episcopus*, < Greek *episkopos* 'overseer', from *epi* 'upon' and *skopeein* 'to view'. And, of course, Latin *episcopus* gives us OI *epscop*. So essentially the bishop was the manager and leader of his flock. Jacques Fontaine has pointed out that 'The Latin verb *superinspicere* renders here, in an expressive but precise manner, the Greek verb *episkopein*, which from a very early date Christians had used to designate the function of supervision of the community – even before 'bishops' existed as the word is commonly understood.'[26] At first the bishop of the city went from church to church saying Masses, baptising, confirming and carrying out the general liturgical functions. As the population of the Church grew he needed assistants, priests, deacons and clerks in minor orders whose titles suggested their functions – sub-deacons (*diaconus*) < Greek *diakonos*, 'a servant'), acolytes (*akolouthos* 'an attendant', *akoloutheein* 'to follow'), exorcists (*exorkizein*, from *ex* 'out', *horkos* 'oath'), readers, and door-keepers. The chief deacon was the archdeacon whose job was to help the bishop in the management of the finances. The clergy could only exercise their function under the authority of the bishop. In fourth century Rome pastoral care was exercised through the twenty-five titular churches mentioned above. They were staffed by priests and clerks in minor orders who were appointed by the bishop, and upon whom they depended financially. The *parochia*, therefore, was what was later to be called the diocese.[27]

The urban church was territorially compact and, by contrast with the countryside, lay in densely populated areas. When the Church spread into the countryside the administrative unit of the diocese was chosen as the area of jurisdiction of the bishop and the sub-units within this area became ultimately the modern parishes. But this took a long time to evolve. In sixth-century Gaul the word *diocesis* stands for what we now call a 'parish'. In Anglo-Saxon England during the seventh century the whole area controlled by the bishop was his *parochia* 'parish'. In seventh-century Ireland the *paruchia* of Armagh is

25 Ibid., 5.   26 J. Fontaine, 'The bishop in the Western Church of the fifth century' in *Seanchas Ard Mhacha*, 16 (1995), 1–21: 5.   27 Addleshaw, *Beginnings of the parochial system*, 5.

the area within which her archbishop provided direct pastoral care but it is also used very cleverly (in the *Liber Angeli*) in the further sense in that all the peoples of Ireland as a 'community' (*in modum paruchiae* 'in the manner of a paruchia')[28] make up the *paruchia,* thus allowing Armagh claim jurisdiction over the entire island. It is not until the ninth century on the Continent that the words 'parish' and 'diocese' are used in the modern way. Indeed, it was to emphasise this that, I assume, John Blair and Richard Sharpe entitled their book *Pastoral care before the parish.*

At first the clergy went out from the cities to administer to the churches in the countryside but in time the country churches came to have a permanent staff. Landowners also had churches on their estates. In smaller cities and the countryside the clergy often lived with the bishop in a *domus ecclesiae* as in Merovingian Gaul. Is this the origin of the *domus / tech* in early Irish sources and placenames? The *tech* is a word for the shrine of a saint but its origin may lie in its function as a bishop's church of the missionary period. Such churches often had a school attached that laid the foundation for the next generation of priests. These early *parochia* covered a large area that was often ill-defined, and in these situations the church was (in the words of Addleshaw) 'more like a mission station than a modern parish church'.[29] These were the *monasteria,* 'old' minsters of Anglo-Saxon England.[30] The staff were called a *familia,* and might be secular clergy, or monks, or both. The head was called an *abbas* or *praepositus.* Some were double monasteries, that is a primary minster of nuns having clergy attached.[31]

The old debate as to whether the Church in Ireland was monastic or episcopal is not quite dead but there are difficulties still in finding terms to categorise that Church. It should be remembered that this is a problem for scholars in England and Europe as well. Although initially against monks serving outside their monasteries Pope Gregory the Great later became a patron of monks placing some in Roman churches. In fact there may have been a power struggle between monastic and clerical parties.[32] In the seventh-century churches of Britain and Ireland and the Continent we find both secular and monastic clergy. Although there were tensions contemporaries had less difficulty with this situation than the modern scholars who have tried to deal with the matter. Those who have relied on ecclesiastical legislation can point to councils of the Church that forbade monks from participating in pastoral care. By contrast hagiographical and other sources show clearly that monks did participate in such activity.[33] Quite apart from this, monasteries, as the treasure houses of relics, were centres of pilgrimage. As Peter Brown has shown, the

---

28 L. Bieler, *The Patrician texts in the Book of Armagh* (Dublin, 1979), 184.   29 Addleshaw, *Beginnings of the parochial system,* 9.   30 Sarah Foot, 'Anglo-Saxon minsters: a review of terminology' in Blair and Sharpe, Pastoral care, 212–25; John Blair, 'Anglo-Saxon minsters: a topographical review' in ibid., 226–66.   31 Addleshaw, *Beginnings of the parochial system,* 12.   32 Cf. Amos, 'Monks and pastoral care', 170.   33 Amos, 'Monks and pastoral care'.

holy man, the ascetic, was the focal point for individuals and communities with difficulties. And as part of the process of pilgrimage monks must have given pastoral care to the visitors to the shrines.[34]

The communities that surrounded Eusebius of Vercelli and Augustine of Hippo were both monastic and clerical. Fifth and sixth-century conciliar legislation has provisions for the ordination of monks for pastoral work with the permission of their abbots. Indeed some of the Gaulish monasteries were famous for supplying bishops. Lérins between 420 and 600 provided eight bishops for Arles, including Honoratus, Hilary, Caesarius, and Aurelian. And there were others. Slowly the idea of monk-priests gained acceptance but on the Continent there seems to have been very little direct monastic influence on pastoral work before the seventh century.[35] Irish monk-priests and bishops made an enormous contribution to the conversion of parts of Europe in the seventh and eighth centuries. Many of these enterprises were in co-operation with Anglo-Saxon and Frankish colleagues. Amos points out:

> Given the Irish fascination with number symbolism, it is hard to believe that when Columbanus or Killian came to the Continent as leaders of parties of twelve monk-priests and monks, they did not see themselves as following the model of the Apostles who went out to preach to the nations.
>
> In addition, the Irish who became bishops in newly-converted areas often served simultaneously as abbots of *Domklosters* in which the monks became a sort of cathedral chapter assisting the bishop in administering the diocese. Virgil of Salzburg is one of the better known examples of the bishop-abbots.[36]

Attempts to limit monastic involvement in pastoral care through legislation was largely ineffective. As the Saxons, Avars and other peoples were conquered bishops lacked the resources to provide sufficient clergy and monks continued to play a role as they continue to do. The modern parishes of the new urban town of Tallaght in west Co. Dublin, for instance, are almost entirely staffed by Dominicans who have their headquarters in Tallaght. Due to lack of secular clergy they were invited by the archbishop of Dublin some years ago to supply pastoral care for the area. Bishops also relied heavily on the educational resources of monasteries. They had libraries, schools, scriptoria and were in a better position to provide trained clergy. Monasteries too had their own parishes and many dependant churches. For example 'before 850, St Germain-des-Près owned thirty-six churches, St Remi of Rheims thirteen, and St Germain of Auxerre ten'.[37] They also increased their number from the Eigenkirchen (proprietary churches) granted by kings and lords.

34 Brown, *The cult of the saints*, 86–127.   35 Amos, 'Monks and pastoral care', 166–7.   36 Ibid., 168–9.   37 Ibid., 173.

The emergence of the territorial parish, as we know it, from the ninth-century onwards in Europe is a result of shifts within society. As we have seen the Church used secular units throughout its history. As long as kings and lords relied upon raiding and counter-raiding for tribute income was uncertain. As early Europe moved towards what has been called feudalism there emerged more stable political units that were sustained by an efficient system of taxation. All over the north of Europe there emerged taxable units such as the hundreds, ounce-lands, penny-lands, townlands (the *baile*, in Ireland), multiples of which provided the basis of lordship of the High Middle Ages. As this system stabilised during the course of the tenth and eleventh centuries it provided the basis for the Church's own system of taxation – the modern parochial system. Marc Bloch suggested that for solutions to some problems we ought to move from the known contemporary situation backwards in time.[38] The parish is one institution that allows us to do just that. In the case of Ireland it may very well allow us to map the pre-Norman lordships of the Irish, for as I have said elsewhere, when the Normans came to Ireland they slipped into structures like a hand into a glove.[39]

In a very interesting article John Contreni compared the ancient polis to the parish. Of course, he didn't push this idea too far – he was simply trying to make a point. That was that the parish came to be a local, self-contained unit to which people belonged and with which they were identified.

> The parish also dispensed social welfare in the form of poor relief and hospitality for travellers. The parish clergy were responsible for whatever formal education was available. Priests were even called upon to engage in civil functions such as the drawing up of wills and charters.[40]

He ends his comparison by saying:

> Nonetheless, the fact remains that the parishes, often overlooked in favour of powerful bishoprics, centralizing monarchies, and ambitious papal organizations, fulfilled a multifaceted role in early medieval society that stands them in good stead as significant sources of communal organization, identification, and inspiration, not unlike their classical predecessors.[41]

The sense of the parish as local community is embodied in some of the phrases we use in English. We talk of 'parish politics' or the 'politics of the parish pump'. We use the term 'parochial' in the sense of being 'inward-

---

38 Bloch, *The historian's craft*, 38.　39 C. Doherty, 'The Vikings in Ireland: a review' in H.B. Clarke, M. Ní Mhaonaigh and R. Ó Floinn (eds), *Ireland and Scandinavia in the early Viking age* (Dublin, 1998), 314–30.　40 J.J. Contreni, 'From polis to parish' in Noble and Contreni (eds), *Religion, culture, and society*, 155–64: 162.　41 Ibid., 162.

looking', 'small-minded', 'back turned to the outside world'. The parish is, we might say, 'tribal, – the majority are certainly rural, – internally, they are frequently socially hierarchical, – and they are familiar', if I may re-use (and abuse) a famous statement of Professor Binchy.[42] It is everything that suggests the small, local, self-contained community. That was one of the strengths of the unit and one of the reasons for its endurance over time. For instance it was one of the reasons that they were used as a unit of survey in the seventeenth century in Ireland. As such the investigation of its history in an Irish context is one of the most exciting challenges facing historians of all descriptions today.

---

42 D.A. Binchy, 'Secular institutions' in M. Dillon (ed.), *Early Irish society* (Dublin, 1954), 52–65: 54.

The shape of the parish

P.J. DUFFY

The territorial history of the parish in Ireland raises a number of issues. Not only is there the importance of territoriality and spatial coherence, as manifested in the parish, but also the implications for a territorial community, territorial allegiance and identity. In England, for instance, deeply-rooted parochialism and allegiance to the parish church are opposed to any kind of alteration in the boundaries or geographies of parishes.[1] In Ireland too modern changes in parishes are also resented and seldom fully implemented. The idea of the parish also raises isues about location, distance and accessibility. Pastoral care is the principal distinguishing feature of parochial organisation – what might be characterised in modern terms as the delivery of religious rites such as baptism, marriage, communion or burial. The relative frequency, or infrequency, of these services in the medieval period might be expected to have some bearing on territorial morphology, especially as it relates to early medieval Ireland, and later medieval Gaelic and English Ireland. Thus the geography of parishes and questions of relative centrality should relate to patterns of settlement and population. Up until the nineteenth century, people lived in a world where matters of distance and location were determined largely by walking ranges. The historical geography of the parish is further connected with processes of territorialisation or the spatial delineation of parishes and the evolution of boundaries. One could start with an assumption that geography (in the senses implied above) probably mattered as much a millennium and more ago as it does today. Questions of distance, space, belonging to place and territorial boundaries are enduring realities of life and landscape.

There is a growing consensus about the evolution over time of pastoral care and the management of the business of the Church, the distribution of revenues, property and personnel, though there remains an amount of ambiguity about the early medieval period. Considerable progress has been made in understanding the significance of churches and the evolution of their accompanying territories in medieval Ireland.[2] Many local historical studies,

---

1 S. Seymour and C. Watkins, 'The decline of the country parish: sixty years of parochial change in the dioceses of Lincoln and Southwell' in *The East Midland Geographer*, 17 (1994), 12–21; S. Seymour and C. Watkins, 'Church landscape and community: rural life and the Church of England' in *Landscape Research*, 20 (1995), 30–44. 2 See R. Sharpe, 'Churches and communities

however, tend to overstate the fluidity and flexibility of the medieval units, without paying more attention to topographical and territorial continuities.

GENEALOGY AND GENESIS OF THE PARISH

In examining the genealogy of the parish in Ireland, three main strands must be recognised. The first is the historic parish which emerged from the middle ages and the second and third are the Roman Catholic and Church of Ireland parishes of today that evolved from that older structure. In order to understand the genetic morphology of the parish, it is helpful to look initially at the geographies of parishes administered by both these Churches. The most immediate influence on the geography of parishes would be the requirements of pastoral care and the accompanying incomes from revenues and property accruing to ecclesiastical authorities in parochial territories. Changes in the patterns and size of population and settlement, in the numbers of pastors and in the jurisdictional authority of the Church might be expected to have some bearing on parish structure, as well as the conservative force of popular allegiance to the parochial territory and its church. The countervailing force in the management and arrangement of parishes, which acted as a brake on any radical modification of their geographies, was the revenue generated by tithes and other dues and fees. For much of the medieval period it is likely that there was more emphasis on property as a defining factor of the parish than on pastoral duties, which would tend to underline the endurance of territories and boundaries as priority considerations. For centuries, asserted Otway Ruthven, it was tithes which gave 'fixity and permanence' to parish boundaries, and which tended to cement for perpetuity the relationship between income from lands attached to particular churches which invariably became part of the parish and property of that church.[3] Others suggest that dues and renders predating tithes had a similar role in territorial consolidation.[4] The most common process of parish formation in recent centuries consisted of unions of historic parishes in response to some of these factors. For the Catholic Church, generally, unions took place in the seventeenth and eighteenth centuries as a consequence of problems with the supply of clergy. For the Church of Ireland

in early medieval Ireland: towards a pastoral model' in J. Blair and R. Sharpe (eds), *Pastoral care before the parish* (Leicester, 1992), 81–109; A. Empey, 'The layperson in the parish: the medieval inheritance, 1169–1536' in R. Gillespie and W.G. Neely (eds), *The laity and the Church of Ireland, 1000–2000* (Dublin, 2000), 7–48; S. Ní Ghabhláin, 'The origin of medieval parishes in Gaelic Ireland: the evidence from Kilfenora' in *JRSAI*, 126 (1996), 37–61; E. FitzPatrick and C. O'Brien, *The medieval churches of county Offaly* (Dublin 1998). **3** A.J. Otway-Ruthven, 'Parochial development in the rural deanery of Skreen' in *JRSAI*, 94 (1964), 111–22: 112. S. Ní Ghabhláin, 'Origins of medieval parishes', 37–61, looks at the continuities of tithes from the taxation of the early fourteenth century to the tithe applotment books of the early nineteenth century. **4** Sharpe, 'Churches and communities in early medieval Ireland', 104–5.

it was the size of congregation which largely dictated change, though revenue and preferment in appointments to benefices were also important.

CHURCH OF IRELAND PARISHES

The established Church of Ireland in the sixteenth century inherited the property and territorial structures of the pre-Reformation Church. In many regions the small Protestant congregations necessitated changes, and the buildings and burial grounds of the late medieval church were sometimes abandoned.[5] However, alterations to Church of Ireland parishes were complicated to implement, although the Cromwellian administration attempted some radical rearrangements in 1657.[6] From 1660, changes such as unions or divisions, or local exchanges of individual townlands, could only be made by order of the privy council in Dublin. Other statutory requirements throughout the eighteenth century inhibited alterations to parish boundaries, so that the possibility of radical change was limited even though there were serious problems with churches frequently being 'incommodiously' situated and some parishes described as 'ill-formed and ill-distributed.' The Church of Ireland maintained the historic extent, legal rights and especially ownership of tithes of existing diocesan and parochial structures. Indeed the researches and visitations of seventeenth-century bishops, such as Bishop Montgomery in Ulster, are important in establishing the extent of parochial properties and boundaries in many places. Early seventeenth-century inquisitions in Clogher diocese, for instance, carefully recorded the range of rents, refections and cosheries (during visitations), duties and proxies to which the bishop was entitled, as well as the share of tithe with vicars and pastors and obligations to maintain the fabric of the church.

In Ulster dioceses, where there was a substantial Protestant population, the old parish legacy generally continued to have demographic viability and social meaning locally. The operation of parish vestries by the Church of Ireland as a minimal form of local government in areas with significant Protestant populations in the seventeenth and eighteenth centuries, also kept alive a local awareness of the older parish framework. In Clogher diocese, for instance,

5 See W.J. Smyth, 'Ireland a colony: settlement implications of the revolution in military-administrative, urban and ecclesiastical structures, *c*.1550 to *c*.1730' in T.B. Barry (ed.), *History of settlement in Ireland* (London, 2000), 158–86. 6 See T.C. Barnard, *Cromwellian Ireland: English government and reform in Ireland 1649–1660* (Oxford, 1975), 160–6; P.J. Duffy, *Landscapes of south Ulster: a parish atlas of the diocese of Clogher* (Belfast, 1993), 5–6. According to the Church of Ireland bishop of Clogher in 1622, Drumully parish church 'standeth inconveniently' (J.E. McKenna, *Diocese of Clogher: parochial records*, 2 vols (Enniskillen, 1920), ii, 117). Sir William Petty, among his many interesting projects, had several proposals to rearrange parish boundaries in order to improve parishioners' access to churches. See J.H. Andrews, 'The making of Irish geography, 1: William Petty' in *Irish Geography*, 9 (1976), 100–3.

outlines of the older parish geography continued with a small number of new units created in the eighteenth century, and by the nineteenth century there were 50 parishes (with 29 perpetual curacies) compared with 47 older (civil) parishes. In much of Leinster and Munster, however, where the older parishes were too small for the pastoral needs of sparse Church of Ireland congregations, the crown facilitated parochial unions which usually respected earlier entities by aggregating complete older units. The circumstances of the Church of Ireland's ministry outside Ulster were well summarised for Kilkenny by a witness in 1802: '147 parishes are distributed at present into 55 benefices; some of which consist of parishes dispersed in various parts: that thirteen incumbents reside within their parishes in this county … Some clergymen reside near, though not in their parishes; some attend their parishes on Sundays from Kilkenny and other places; and it is not uncommon for incumbents in one parish to be curates in another.'[7] The result was that while the Ordnance Survey recorded 2,428 civil parishes in Ireland in the 1830s, the Church of Ireland had 1,518 parishes when it was disestablished in 1870 and this number was further reduced in the following decades.

CATHOLIC PARISHES

Over much of the seventeenth and eighteenth centuries, the Catholic Church was frequently an underground, and even a missionary, church where bishops had considerable freedom to make ad hoc changes within their dioceses to meet pastoral needs. Individual priests were often fairly independent within their own parishes – with friars often assisting at local ministry and laity accustomed to little outside interference in their parish. By the late eighteenth century, in parts of Meath, Clogher and other dioceses, bishops often had to re-assert their authority over recalcitrant local clergy and congregations. Stations (sometimes a response to penal conditions in the eighteenth century where masses took place in private houses) were adopted as a mandatory practice which helped to consolidate the coherence of parish identity.[8]

It has been suggested that following the loss of its parochial inheritance after the Reformation, and especially after the 1640s, Catholic Church administrative structures had collapsed, requiring it to set about reconstructing the 'shattered parish system' in the late seventeenth century, with little reference to the medieval legacy.[9] There is an assumption of dissonance between the

---

7 William Tighe, *Statistical observations relative to the county of Kilkenny made in the years 1800 and 1801*, (facsimile edition, Kilkenny 1998), 618.　8 See P. Mulligan, 'The life and times of Bishop Edward Kernan' in *Clogher Record* (1981), 323–48; T. O'Connor, 'Thomas Messingham (c.1575–1638?) and the seventeenth-century Church,' in *Riocht na Midhe*, 11 (2000), 86–102: 88, 95, 99.　9 P.J. Corish, *The Catholic community in the seventeenth and eighteenth centuries* (Dublin, 1981), 58–9.

Catholic parish and the older medieval parish, with suggestions of 'massive transformation' into 'radically new', 'roughly circular' parishes which maximised accessibility in response to local needs.[10] Parish administration was certainly seriously interrupted in the sixteenth and seventeenth century upheavals and new arrangements in parochial management had to be made. However, the eventual territorial organisation of parishes undertaken by the Catholic Church seems more conservative than radical for much of Ireland.[11] At the latter end of the eighteenth century, attachment to the older medieval structures had survived, ancient ecclesiastical sites and burial grounds continued to be revered, and local popular allegiance to and memory of the earlier entities had endured. Where the older parishes were comparatively extensive (as in Ulster) continuance of parish spaces into the modern period made geographical and social sense. Additionally, parochial tithes paid to the Established Church, though obviously unpopular with Catholics, probably helped maintain the continuity of older units in collective consciousness.

In Ulster, the Catholic parishes and the older parishes showed a high level of congruity. In Clogher diocese, for instance, the area of the 38 Catholic parishes in the nineteenth century were virtually all co-terminous with the 43 historical parishes.[12] In fact, in many cases the Catholic parishes re-established the older medieval geography in Fermanagh, where it had been departed from somewhat by the established Church of Ireland (fig. 1). In Cos. Donegal and Cavan, there is a similar close correspondence between the older parish boundaries and the Catholic units (fig. 2).[13] Further south, in the archdiocese of Cashel, where the older parishes were considerably smaller than those in Ulster, the correspondence between Catholic and civil parishes continues.[14] Catholic parishes in the main comprised a number of the smaller older units: there are 46 Catholic parishes in the diocese and 130 civil parishes. Approximately 21 Catholic parishes are composed of from one to nine civil parishes, and the boundaries of nearly all the others are coincident with civil parish boundaries. Minor adjustments were made by the Catholic authorities to some of the more unwieldy civil parishes to produce a more rational territorial unit, by re-allocating townlands singly or in small blocs or in a few cases by using the line of roads which post-

10 K. Whelan, 'The Catholic parish, the Catholic chapel and village development in Ireland' in *Irish Geography*, 16 (1983), 1–15: 4. See also Whelan, 'The Catholic church in county Tipperary 1700–1900' in W. Nolan and T. McGrath (eds), *Tipperary: history and society* (Dublin, 1985), 215–55. 11 Power in 1949, based largely on anecdotal personal experience, speculated that 'there is no great reason to think that many rectifications of parish boundaries ever took place': P. Power, 'The bounds and extent of Irish parishes' in S. Pender (ed.) *Féilscríbhinn Torna* (Cork, 1947), 218–24: 221. 12 Duffy, *Landscapes of south Ulster*, 6–8, 25. 13 *County atlas 2001*, Donegal county development board, 2001, map no. 82. In the archdiocese of Armagh, the Louth portion consists of multiple small civil parishes per Catholic parish, while in the Armagh portion Catholic and civil parishes are larger. 14 Based on *Pobal Áilbe: Cashel and Emly Atlas*, [1970]. Though Smyth, 'Ireland a colony', 175–6 refers to 'significant re-structuring' and 'massive trauma' in relation to the Catholic parishes.

Fig. 1: Civil and Catholic parishes in Clogher diocese

Fig. 2: Civil and Catholic parishes in Co. Cavan

dated the civil parishes as boundaries. In Co. Meath there is a very close correspondence between both civil parishes and Catholic parishes.[15] As can be seen
in fig. 3, the 46 Catholic parishes are effectively unions composed of 144 civil
parishes. The older civil parish boundaries in the overwhelming majority of
cases make up the boundaries of the Catholic unions which were emerging in
the late eighteenth century. This process of re-arrangement is well exemplified
in Meath where the objective was to provide pastoral care to large congregations with limited numbers of clergy in flexible unions of the smaller medieval
parishes.[16] For example, Ardsallagh was an early church which was constituted
as a parish after the Anglo-Norman colonisation. In 1690 a parish priest was
appointed to the parishes of Ardsallagh and Navan. In 1704 the priest was
registered as parish priest of the historic parishes of Ardsallagh, Navan, Bective
and Donaghmore. Later the Franciscan friars of Flower Hill in Navan were in
charge of Donaghmore and Dunmoe. Donaghmore was later permanently
united to Navan. In the early eighteenth century, Franciscans were also given
jurisdiction over the parishes of Clonmacduff, Bective, Rataine, Churchtown,
Moymet, Tullaghenoge and Kilcooly, which ultimately became the Catholic
parish union of Dunderry. The early Christian church of Kilmoon was created
a parish in the twelfth century and was united with Kilbrew under one parish
priest in 1690. In the 1704 registration of priests it was administered with
Kilbrew, Crickstown and Trevet, called the Curraha union in the eighteenth
century. Trevet was united to Skyrne parish in 1823 and Curraha union was
allotted the parishes of Kilmoon, Kilbrew, Crickstown, Primatestown,
Donaghmore and Greenoge.

In the midst of the disorder imposed on the Catholic Church in the seventeenth and eighteenth centuries, the older historic parishes may have
represented units of stability, places with a sense of allegiance and community
solidarity, as in Co. Limerick – although it has been suggested that in the early
modern Catholic Church the idea of the parish was more signficant as a
community than a precisely-defined territorial entity.[17] Indeed there was some
local friction within some of the ad hoc unions. The nineteenth century
historian Cogan's use of the term 'united to' instead of 'united with' may
suggest the maintenance of the integrity of the older units in Meath. In
Kilkenny, the term 'annexe' was used for these Catholic unions of contiguous
older parishes, which were flexible enough to allow for change as the population
and clergy increased in numbers.[18] Over time, as a result of settlement and

15 P.J. Duffy, 'Habitat and history: exploring landscape and place in Co. Meath' in *Riocht na
Midhe*, 11 (2000), 187–218.   **16** Based on A. Cogan, *The diocese of Meath, ancient and modern*, 3
vols (Dublin, 1867).   **17** T. Jones Hughes, 'The large farm in nineteenth century Ireland' in A.
Gailey and D. Ó hOgáin (eds), *Gold under the furze: studies in folk tradition* (Dublin, 1982), 93–100.
18 Tighe, *Statistical observations of Kilkenny*, 619–20. See also F. O Fearghail, 'The Catholic
Church in county Kilkenny 1600–1800' in W. Nolan and K. Whelan (eds), *Kilkenny: history and
society* (Dublin, 1990), 197–250: 202.

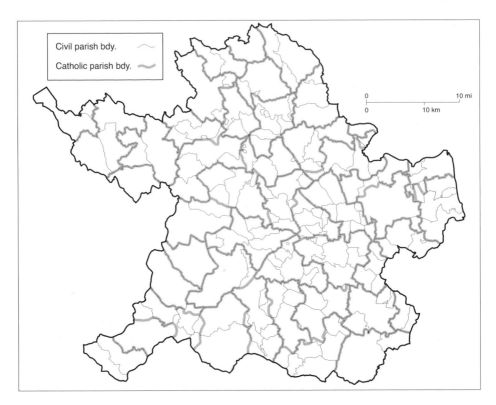

Civil parish bdy.

Catholic parish bdy.

0   10 mi

0   10 km

Fig. 3: Civil and Catholic parishes in Co. Meath

demographic change, new names and identities sometimes developed for some of the unions, though the Catholic Church was often anxious to retain the older parish name.

In Wexford, Kerry and elsewhere, the continuity of older boundaries is also evident in the new parochial arrangements of the Catholic Church.[19] Although Jones Hughes refers to 'new territorial frameworks' being developed in the eighteenth century to capitalise on emerging focal points and arterial communications in the landscape, in fact the older parochial entities normally endured and where they were small, as in parts of Munster and Leinster, they were mostly combined into Catholic parish unions. What most often did emerge, however, were new chapel villages located more centrally in these emerging unions. In general, therefore, it is within the medieval framework of parishes that we must look for whatever adjustments were made by the modernising Catholic Church authorities in the nineteenth century.

---

19 Based on ESB MSS maps of Catholic parishes, Russell Library, Maynooth and maps of civil parishes in B. Mitchell (ed.), *The new genealogical atlas of Ireland* (Baltimore, 1986).

CIVIL PARISHES

The common antecedent of the Catholic and Church of Ireland parishes was the late medieval parish. Seventeenth-century records of confiscation and administration used the barony, parish (and/or townland or its contemporary equivalent) as basic units of record – as, for example, in the Civil Survey, Down Survey, hearth money and poll tax returns of the 1660s. As a result the parish became the earliest convenient adminstrative unit, which eventually came to be called the civil parish. The seventeenth-century parish, therefore, might be taken as a reliable representation of the territorial structure of the late medieval parish. Civil parish linkages back to the thirteenth century can be uncovered in the documents relating to papal taxation of parishes from the late thirteenth and early fourteenth centuries.[20] In Clogher, for instance, the 1306 list of parishes matches the seventeenth-century lists in broad terms. In some instances there are records of the territorial extent of the parishes incorporating internal details on placenames. Local names and territorial units are listed in considerable detail for the Fermoy district of north Cork for the twelfth century, including the church of each tuath.[21] Complete lists of parishes for Cashel and Emly can be found in papal taxations of 1297 and 1302 and a visitation of 1437, which are virtually identical with the list of civil parishes. In the absence of comprehensive records of the territorial extent of parishes in the twelfth or thirteenth centuries, and acknowledging that there were many unions and subdivisions in the fourteenth and fifteenth centuries,[22] the Ordnance Survey civil parish maps of the 1830s exhibit the broad outline of the medieval parish framework. Maps are an important key to understanding more about medieval parish morphologies. There is a wealth of evidence to be excavated from the maps of civil parishes and townlands in Ireland. The most convenient sources for examining the detail of parish topographies are the indices to the townland survey (in one sheet per county) and townland indices (which detail the townlands in several sheets per county).

Historians have long been aware of the broad regional contrasts in parish geography – from the small parishes of the manorial regions colonised by the Anglo-Normans to larger parishes in Gaelic regions of medieval Ireland. There is an evident relationship between the map of Norman settlement and the distribution of smaller parishes in Ireland.[23] The Pale extending southwards through

20 H.S. Sweetman (ed.), *Calendar of documents relating to Ireland*, 5 vols (London, 1875–86), v, nos 693–729. **21** L. O Buachalla, 'Placenames of north-east Cork' in *Journal of the Cork Historical and Archaeological Society*, 54 (1949), 31–4 and 88–91; Sharpe, 'Churches and communities in early medieval Ireland', 96 citing P. Power (ed.), *Crichad an Chaoilli, being the topography of ancient Fermoy* (Cork, 1932). **22** There were also numbers of new parishes created in the eighteenth century, many of them reflecting pre-existing units. **23** See map of Norman settlement in F.H.A. Aalen, K. Whelan and M. Stout (eds), *Atlas of the Irish rural landscape* (Cork, 1997), 54. I am grateful to W.J. Smyth and the Geography Department, UCC, for permission to reproduce the map of civil parishes in Ireland.

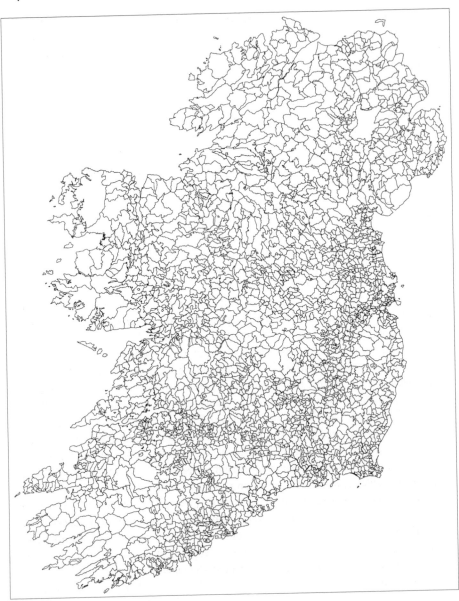

Fig. 4: Ireland: civil parishes

east Kildare, and districts through the Barrow valley to south Wexford, east Waterford, Kilkenny, Tipperary, east Cork, north Kerry, Limerick, east Galway, south Sligo, north Roscommon, Westmeath, Longford and east Down, all intensively or partially colonised landscapes of mottes and moated sites, clearly contain the smallest parishes. These contrast with much larger parish units in the Gaelic regions of Ulster, as well as the south midlands, Wicklow, south Kerry and much of Connacht. These contrasting patterns are evident across the south Ulster frontier with the Pale, where parishes range from 1,700 to 5,000 acres in Louth and 4,000 acres in Meath as compared with 17,000–30,000 in Armagh and Monaghan. There are clearly colonial connotations evident in the map, reflecting the cultural impact of Anglo–Norman settlement, associated with the topographical influence of favoured soils and better drainage in the rich lowlands and river valleys where small manorial parishes developed along European lines. Areas beyond the influence of the English colony exhibit a much coarser framework of parishes reflecting perhaps a pre-Norman process of terri-torialisation and a different approach to parish management and ministry. This larger parish matrix sometimes also coincides with thinly populated areas, or marginal undeveloped land, where parish support (via economic productivity of secular lands) called for more extensive districts. While the 'manorial' parishes are considerably smaller than those in the Gaelic regions, they also exhibit greater variations in size – some being very small, others considerably larger. Such wide ranges are much less evident in the Gaelic areas, which show greater uniformity and regularity in size. Indeed if mountain and waste land, as in the western dioceses,[24] are exluded these parishes show more areal uniformity than in the southern and eastern regions of the country.

The contrasting development of local ministry, pastoral care and management of church business across the frontier may also help to explain the contrasts in the geography and genesis of the parish. Empey depicts a vigorous parish church in Anglo-Ireland, especially after the Black Death (1348–50), with actively-involved laity and church building on orthodox European lines. This contrasts with the nature of parish life in Gaelic Ireland where kin branches of ruling families monopolised lands and office at local level and where parish organisation was generally haphazard in the sixteenth century.[25] Parish centres in the feudalised Ireland, usually focussed on church and manor house, were powerful centres of local community life.[26] Coarb and erenagh lands were taken over in Anglo-Norman areas and transferred to bishops or monastic foundations, or absorbed by new settlers. In Gaelic regions, their functions and landholdings continued in the post-reform dioceses in attenuated but still vigorous form which had an important defining role in parish geographies.

The genesis of the historic parishes has been traced back to the twelfth-century reform of the Church in Ireland, especially in the decades after the Anglo-Norman colonisation. The original development of parish territorial structures, as elsewhere in mainland Europe, was closely associated with secular

24 See K.W. Nicholls, 'Rectory, vicarage and parish in the western Irish dioceses' in *JRSAI*, 101 (1971), 53–84: 62. 25 C. Lennon, 'The sixteenth century' in R. Ó Muirí (ed.), *Irish church history today* (Armagh, nd [1990]), 27–41: 35. 26 See W.J. Smyth, 'Property, patronage and population: reconstructing the human geography of mid-seventeenth century county Tipperary' in Nolan and McGrath (eds), *Tipperary*, 104–38: 126–7.

territorial structures. From its earliest days the survival of the Christian Church depended on its ability to ally itself with secular authority.[27] The twelfth-century reforms in Ireland aimed at introducing mainstream European standards to the Irish church, by constructing dioceses which were synchronised with political order, and parish formation in colonial Ireland is most clearly associated with the Anglo-Norman manors. Regularisation of the tithing system led to parishes being constructed around tithe-paying tenants on the manor, as in Wexford where thirty-seven manors had the same name as the parishes in which they were situated, and in Skryne barony in Meath where parishes were developed by its military tenants.[28]

But how were these Anglo-Norman manors conjured up? On what territorial precedents were they based? Territorial structures often endure through social and political upheaval, especially, as with parishes, where property and associated revenues are implicated and embedded in a secular matrix of landholding. There was a strong driving force for territorial inertia and continuity within parochial structures which were meshed in a web of legal privilege, entitlement to revenues, perhaps duties of pastoral care, as well as local allegiances, tradition and custom. In England, twelfth-century parish boundaries were often based on those of early Saxon estates, which in turn were frequently based on Roman landholdings.[29] The connection between Anglo-Norman fiefs and pre-conquest territorial frameworks such as tuaths has been demonstrated in a number of places, with parishes being carved out of pre-existing units, as in the Tipperary manors, though Hennessy places most emphasis on the innovatory nature of the Anglo-Norman parish formations.[30] In the east midlands of Kildare and Meath, there are innumerable small parishes whose names are suggestive of an earlier genealogy, such as Kilmore, Kilmeague, Kilmessan, Kilbride or Donaghmore, Donaghcumper, Donaghpatrick, all representing important churches and indicating pre-parish, or proto-parish geographies from pre-Norman times; 78 per cent of the parish names in Meath suggest a pre-Norman origin; Smyth has calculated that 70 per cent of the parish names in Dublin county are early Christian in origin, indicating that the Normans 'were inheritors rather than creators of ecclesiastical structures.'[31]

27 See B. Millet, 'Dioceses in Ireland up to the fifteenth century' in *Seanchas Ard Mhacha*, 12 (1986–87), 2–3; P. Corish, *A history of Irish Catholicism* (Dublin, 1972) i, 3–4. **28** B. Colfer, *Arrogant trespass: Anglo-Norman Wexford 1169–1400* (Enniscorthy, 2002), 85–6; Ottway-Ruthven, 'Skyrne', 119–20. See also A. Empey, 'Conquest and settlement: patterns of Anglo-Norman settlement in north Munster and south Leinster' in *Irish Economic and Social History*, 13 (1986), 5–31: 19. **29** Seymour and Watkins, 'The decline of the country parish', 12. C. Taylor, *Village and farmstead: a history of rural settlement in England* (London, 1983), 120. See Blair and Sharpe's note on the fact of eighth-century ecclesiastical *regiones* being based on secular *regiones* in their *Pastoral care before the parish*, 6–7. **30** Empey, 'Conquest and settlement', 12–16, 30; M. Hennessy, 'Parochial organisation in medieval Tipperary' in Nolan and McGrath (eds), *Tipperary*: 60–70: 63; see also Dermot Gleeson (1949) cited in Otway-Ruthven, 'Skyrne', 114. **31** Duffy, 'Landscape and place in Co. Meath', 193–204; W.J. Smyth, 'Exploring the social and

Hereditary and family links of erenaghs and coarbs with associated church lands and pastoral functions lend further credence to the existence of territorial coherence between the more extensive parochial entities and sept lands in Ulster and elsewhere. Erenagh families in later medieval Clogher, for instance, were generally responsible for two-thirds of the cost of repairing the church from the revenues of the erenagh land in the parish (as well as usually paying rent to the diocese)[32] and churches appear to have been commonly sited on erenagh land. Simms has demonstrated the broad regional pattern of Gaelic erenagh and coarb parochial management and ministry from the synod of Kells in 1152, corresponding broadly with the broad regional dichotomy in the geography of civil parishes, especially in Ulster.[33] The relationship between lineage groups and the local church and parochial lands (erenagh and termon lands) extended back to early times when they had a more influential role. In this context it seems logical that parishes and their pre-parochial antecedents, under the control of coarbs and erenagh families (who often also provided the parochial or later diocesan clergy), should coincide with the political and economic extent of the secular authority of lordship.[34] In such a scenario, boundaries should remain comparatively stable. The nature of such an alliance is evident in the late medieval lordship of Airghialla, where the lucht tighe lands of MacMahons comprised a parish and all the ballybetaghs of the various sept branches were closely associated with the parish structure in 1591.[35] Ní Ghabhláin has suggested that the 1591 map of landownership may indicate a correlation between distinctive sept lands and parochial territories which probably endured for several generations.[36] Thus to what extent are the parishes which ultimately emerged as a

cultural topographies of sixteenth and seventeenth-century county Dublin' in F.H.A. Aalen and K. Whelan (eds), *Dublin city and county: from prehistory to present* (Dublin, 1992), 121–79: 150, 152. **32** See for instance, M.A. Costello (ed.), *De annatis Hiberniae, vol. 1, Ulster* (1909): Inishmacsaint parish from Inquisition of Ulster, Sept. 1603. See also Fermanagh Inquisition, 1609, *Inquisitionum in officio rotulorum cancellariae Hiberniae ... Ultoniae* (Dublin, 1829).Erenagh families customarily provided the parochial clergy as well, with duties of hospitality to travellers, wayfarers, and the poor, often involving the maintenance of a house or hostel for such purposes. See the comments in H. Jefferies essay below. **33** K. Simms, 'Frontiers in the Irish Church – regional and cultural' in T. Barry (ed.), *Colony and frontier in medieval Ireland* (London, 1995), 177–200: 182–5. In the plantation Inquisitions in Ulster, erenaghs represented themselves as descendants of original owners of these church lands who had been turned into rent payers after the twelfth-century reforms. See also A. Lynch, 'Religion in late medieval Ireland' in *Archivium Hibernicum*, 26 (1981), 3–15: 4, 7. **34** See, for example, S. Ó Dufaigh, 'The MacCathmhaoils of Clogher' in *Clogher Record*, 2 (1957), 25–46: 36–7 for a politically ascendant family who were ecclesiastically dominant as clerics and erenaghs in the south Tyrone area in the twelfth to sixteenth centuries. **35** P.J. Duffy, 'Social and spatial order in the MacMahon lordship of Airghialla in the late sixteenth century' in P.J. Duffy, D. Edwards and E. FitzPatrick (eds), *Gaelic Ireland, c.1250–c.1650* (Dublin, 2001), 115–37: 134–6; see also Muinterheny and Ballymore parishes in Armagh in C.F. McGleenon, 'The medieval parishes of Ballymore and Mullabrack' in *Seanchas Ard Mhacha*, 12 (1987), 46–7. M. Ní Loighnsigh notes that the 1609 Inquisition in Donegal identified parishes in the currency of ballybetaghs: 'An assessment of castles and landownership in late medieval north Donegal', *Ulster Journal of Archaeology*, 3rd series, 57, (1994), 104–150: 145. **36** Ní Ghabhláin, 'Origins of medieval parishes', 51–2, though the association

consequence of the twelfth-century reforms 'related to what existed previously'?[37] Both Sharpe and Empey refer to the reluctance of historians to look across the twelfth-century divide for antecedents of the later medieval parish, in 'proto parishes' or 'pre-parishes' instead of the widely-dispersed monastic federations of an earlier generation of historians.[38] This would represent a much more familiar north European structure perhaps of great and little 'parishes' akin to the minster parishes of England.

At a more global level, Dodgshon's comments on the nature of feudal and pre-feudal space and territory may have a bearing on the evolution of parochial territories in Ireland before and after the Anglo-Norman colonisation. Pre-feudal or tribal forms of territorialisation are ultimately based on kin and sept networks. Feudalism introduced notions of spatial order of land resources by measurement, extent and valuation, as part of a wider articulated world of economic integration.[39] In an Irish context generally one can see how in the Gaelic chiefdoms, space and territorial hierarchies were determined by kinship and lineage: distance from the centre, for instance, was genealogical as well as geographical. *Lucht tighe* lands, usually consisting of the best land at the centre of the territory, belonged to the chief's kin group, and other territorial units to branches of the sept. In the context of parochial development, erenagh and coarbial families were very much part of this local disarticulated world, arranged very much in tandem with secular and kinship-determined space.

Empey and others have highlighted the importance of tithe as markers of a parochial system, with possession of a baptismal font, for example, being a sign of parochial status.[40] The absence of disputes about ownership of tithes after the Anglo-Norman colonisation suggests the absence of a proper parish system in place in the twelfth century, though Katherine Simms considers that the newly-established diocesan bishops did not have the legal power to intervene with the incoming new settlers in the matter of tithes.[41] Richard Sharpe, however, has pointed to the existence of a regulated system of pastoral care in the early medieval period, which could only be administered territorially presumably. He has proposed the notion of a three- or four-tier hierarchy of churches coming into existence approximately by mid-seventh century, with local churches ministering to population groups in return for dues, in subdivisions linked to tuatha, subordinate to mother churches and supervised by a small number of greater churches, which he characterises as one of the most

with particular branches of the septs is not always clearcut in the map: P.J. Duffy, 'The territorial organisation of Gaelic landownership and its transformation in county Monaghan 1591–1640' in *Irish Geography*, 14 (1981), 1–26. **37** Sharpe, 'Churches and communities in early medieval Ireland', 84. **38** In a similar sense to the 'pre-village' of C. Doherty which shows less of the exceptionalism of earlier nationalist medieval histories, resembling much more the rest of Europe. See his 'Settlement in early Ireland: a review' in T.B. Barry (ed.), *A history of settlement in Ireland* (London, 2000), 50–80. **39** R.A. Dodgshon, *The European past: social evolution and spatial order* (London, 1987), 72, 126–130, 139, 166. **40** Empey, 'The layperson in the parish', 12–14. **41** Ibid., 13–14; Simms, 'Frontiers in the Irish Church', 184–5.

comprehensive pastoral organisations in northern Europe. Swan has suggested that the strong coincidence of parish units with early ecclesiastical sites in Westmeath supports the notion of a pre-Norman genesis of these territorial units, as does the clustering of such sites within the parish matrix in the Dingle penisula.[42] Much of the research on parishes derives from studies of ecclesiastical sites and parish centres containing suites of buildings and landscape features such as burial grounds. In most cases it does seem reasonable to assume that sites and centres are broadly indicative of territorial parishes, especially when the medieval church site name (the townland today) is the same as the parish name. One of the main problems in reading the geography of parishes is the contemporaneity of early churches and territorial districts. As in the case of Dingle, where a range of ecclesiastical sites are located in the civil parishes, they may reflect a gradual process of development over a long period of time, with some sites fading while others peaked.

Colmán Etchingham has noted that the payment of pastoral dues was an early practice, though not always necessarily universally observed. He has also emphasised the importance of territory and people in early medieval Ireland, with principal and subordinate churches where authority was spatially delineated in paruchia and episcopal jurisdiction extended over subject churches located in integrated geographical regions.[43] This early allegiance of place and people is reflected in many early church placenames where *domnach* is listed in conjunction with a definite area or people.[44] Many historians of Ireland's territorial structures have used the evidence of the twelfth-century *Crichad an Chaoilli* to emphasise the strong links between communities of kin groups and local churches as far back as the eighth century. Hogan's investigation of tricha céd in 1928 suggested a correspondence between parish and tuatha which has been identified by Ní Ghabhláin, FitzPatrick and comprehensively demonstrated for county Clare by Nugent, with in most cases *túatha* consisting of two or more of the later parishes.[45] Ní Ghabhláin's notion of primary parishes later subdividing into the medieval parishes resembles the process in many other places, with the detached portions of parishes in Kilfenora demonstrating the existence of earlier larger entities with rectorial tithes. This resembles the putative process of parish formation in Clogher diocese discussed in the following section. Recent studies in Cornwall, whose parochial development resembled early Ireland rather than manorial England, support this notion of territorial organisation of parishes being closely bound up with local commu-

42 D.L. Swan, 'The early Christian ecclesiastical sites of County Westmeath' in J. Bradley (ed.), *Settlement and society in medieval Ireland* (Kilkenny, 1988), 3–32; J. Cuppage et al., *Archaeological survey of the Dingle peninsula* (Ballyferriter, 1986), 363.   43 See C. Etchingham's essay below and his 'The implications of *paruchia*' in *Eriu*, 44 (1993), 147–152.   44 Sharpe, 'Churches and communities in early medieval Ireland', 95, 96–7. See also Doherty, 'Settlement in early Ireland: a review', 57–9.   45 James Hogan, 'The tricha cét and related land-measures' in *PRIA*, C37 (1928–9), 148–235: 184; Ní Ghabhláin, 'Origin of medieval parishes', 56; FitzPatrick and O'Brien, *The medieval churches of Offaly*, 12; See also P. Nugent's essay below.

nities and local identities, reflected especially in a highly developed context of epic tales of hero-saints.[46] Before the twelfth-century reform in Ireland many of the smaller local churches had been abandoned and were in ruins, but it is at the level of these local churches and their pastoral territories that the foundations of the medieval parishes reside. Taken together the ideas discussed above have the potential to shed additional light on the evolution of the modern parish. The next two sections of this essay will attempt to test some of these ideas by applying them to the problem of the shapes of the parishes of south Ulster.

THE PARISHES OF CLOGHER[47]

In the diocesan boundaries agreed at the synod of Rathbreasail in 1111, only the boundaries of the central districts of the eventual diocese of Clogher were agreed, based on early Uí Cremthain territories. The borders of the diocese were rapidly extended south eastwards towards the sea in modern Louth following the expansion of the Ó Cearbhaill kingdom, westwards to the sea at Donegal bay through the dominance of the Fir Manach and briefly northwards to Ardstraw which was traditionally associated with the Airgialla peoples. Much of the Louth lands were lost in face of Anglo-Norman expansion and Ardstraw was returned to Derry. The history of the MacCathmhaoils of Clogher in the twelfth century demonstrates the links between secular power and the diocesan boundary in the modern south Tyrone area.[48]

The obituary of Donnchadh Ó Cearbhaill (king of Airgialla who died 1168) credits him with helping to reform the church in the territory of Airgialla: 'by whom were made ... the chief books of the order of the year, and the chief books of the Mass ... by him the church throughout the land of Oirghiall was reformed ... In his time tithes were received, churches were founded, temples and cloichtheachs [belltowers] were made ...'.[49] Under his influence, his kingdom was made a diocese. From the thirteenth century, the territories of Airgialla and Lough Erne were consolidated by MacMahons and Maguires, with their subterritorial units being quickly organised as parishes. By 1306, the following parishes were listed for taxation purposes in correspondence with Rome[50] and are shown on figure 5.

---

46 D.C. Harvey, 'Landscape organization, identity and change: territoriality and hagiography in medieval west Cornwall' in *Landscape Research*, 25: 2 (2000), 201–12. 47 Based on H. J.Lawlor, 'The genesis of the diocese of Clogher' in *County Louth Archaeological Journal*, 4 (1916–20), 129–59; McKenna, *Diocese of Clogher*; P. Mulligan, 'The diocese of Clogher in brief' in J. Duffy (ed.), *Clogher Record album: a diocesan history* (Monaghan, 1975), 9–12; K. Simms 'The origins of the diocese of Clogher,' in *Clogher Record*, 10 (1980), 180–98; J. Duffy, 'Parish names and boundaries' in P.J. Duffy, *Landscapes of south Ulster*, 2–4; *Inquisitionum in officio rotulorum cancellariae Hiberniae ... Ultoniae*, appendix vi Fermanagh. 48 Ó Dufaigh, 'The MacCathmhaoils of Clogher', 31–5. 49 Quoted in Lawlor, 'The genesis of the diocese of Clogher', 138. 50 *Calendar of documents relating to Ireland* (1302–7), quoted in McKenna, *Diocese of Clogher*, i,

Fig. 5: Clogher diocese, *c.*1306

Bishop's Mensa: Clogher, Donagh; *Deanery of Lough Erne*: Termon Davog, Cúlmáine, Inis Muighe Samh, Devenish, Botha, Lisgoole, Inniskeen, Cleenish, Derryvullen, Derrybrusk, Aghavea, Aghalurcher; *Deanery of Clones*: Clones, Galloon, Kilmore with the chapel of Drumsnat, Tydavnet, Tyholland; *Deanery of Donaghmoyne*: Donaghmoyne, Ros Cluain, Inniskeen, Killanny, Muckno, Cremorne. Most of these listed parishes correspond with the map of later civil parishes and had roots in the earlier medieval period. Nearly all of them contained churches founded as far back as the sixth and seventh centuries. Individual histories will make this clearer.

Clogher, an extensive area with early associations with kings of the Airgialla in the sixth century, had an important church foundation associated with sixth-century Macartan and became the mensal parish of the newly established bishop of Clogher.

Donagh was another mensal parish of the bishop in 1306 which probably also included Errigle Trough. Domhnach and Aireagal Tríocha suggest a much earlier significance as pre-parochial territories. Errigle was first mentioned as a parish in 1532.[51]

16–17; Ó Dufaigh, 'MacCathmhaoils of Clogher', 47–8 and 'Parish names and boundaries', 2.
51 Hogan, 'The tricha cét', 206 identifies Trough as a remnant of an early *tricha céd*. See S. Ó

Termon Davog (Templecarn civil parish) was an early termon land on the borderland between Fir Manach and Tír Conaill territory which was focussed on the early Christian pilgrimage site at Lough Derg. In the later medieval period it was called Termonmagrath after the local coarbial family.

Cúlmáine (Magheraculmoney civil parish) had an early sixth-century church foundation.

Inis Muighe Samh (Inishmacsaint). Its early territorial morphology is traceable to the Cineal Cairbre territory of Túatha Rátha which by late twelfth century had affiliated to the Fir Manach. The important early Christian site of Domnach Mór Magh Ene at the western ocean point was part of the thirteenth-century parish.

Devenish was an important and extensive territorial parish with a large number of ecclesiastical centres within it, not least the sixth-century foundation of St Molaise on Devenish island which became the principal centre in the area.

Cleenish was an extensive borderland parish with Breifne, running from upper Lough Erne westwards, which had pre-parochial orgins in the sixth-century church foundation of St Sinell.

Lisgool was a monastic centre which was associated with the small surrounding district of Rossory and *Botha* (**Boho**) continued as a comparatively small medieval parish.

Inniskeen (Enniskillen civil parish) was associated with the *lucht tighe* lands of Maguires in the later medieval period. It was called Pubble (Pobal Phádraig) in the sixteenth century.

Derryvullan was an extensive parish comprising detached portions east of Lough Erne containing several church/chapel districts in Kilskeery and portions of Magheracross which emerged as separate parishes by the fifteenth century. Kilskeery however had a sixth-century church founded by St Scíre and a ninth-century church at Trillick (Trelic Mór).

Derrybrusk was a small parish listed in 1306 whose tithes were paid in toto to the erenagh.[52]

Aghavea and **Aghalurcher** had sixth-century foundations.

Clones was a large and important parish with a foundation tradition by St Tighernach in the sixth century.

Galloon (including the civil parishes of Galloon, Drumully, Currin, Killeevan, Aghabog and Ematris) incorporates much of the later barony of Dartree and was sometimes called Dartree parish. Although the later civil parishes were mostly created in the eighteenth century, they had a distinctive earlier existence. Drumully, mentioned in a papal document of 1428, included Currin.[53] Killeevan church had a strong early Christian foundation tradition.

Dufaigh, 'Medieval Monaghan: the evidence of the placenames' in *Clogher Record*, 16 (1999), 19–26 for evidence of Errigle as an early territorial name. **52** McKenna, *Diocese of Clogher*, ii, 195. **53** Ibid., ii, 115

Ematris, created in 1738, was a separate chapel district in the sixteenth century and was recorded as a parish in the mid seventeenth-century Down Survey and Book of Survey and Distribution.[54]

Kilmore & Drumsnat were important early Christian foundations.

Tedavnet was an early church foundation of St Damhnait.

Tehallen. The medieval parish was much bigger than the later small civil parish. In 1306 it included Tullycorbet and Monaghan which evolved from the later medieval lucht tighe lands of MacMahons. In 1428 papal correspondence refers to the rectory of *Teach Calan* (Tehallen) with the vicarage of Lucht tighe[55] which was probably endowed by the lordship as were similar districts in Fermanagh and Cavan. Tullycorbet (which is mentioned as a parish in 1415) had a distinctive earlier pre-parochial existence, as did Rackwallace (later Monaghan).

Donaghmoyne was an early and important church site and a large parish with several medieval church sites.

Ros Cluain. (Magheross, Magheracloone civil parishes). Its subdivision into the two later medieval parishes took place in the fourteenth and fifteenth centuries. Both parishes had many early Christian associations and a number of ecclesiastical sites.

Inniskeen, Iniscaoin Deagha after its founder St Daig, and **Killanny** were parishes on the southern borders of the diocese with small portions in Louth reflecting the remnants of Airgialla expansion in the twelfth century

Muckno comprised three ballybetaghs of termon lands in 1591 on the eastern boundary of the diocese.

Cremorne (Clontibret, Aghnamullen, Ballybay civil parishes). Like Galloon this was a large parish incorporating much of the territory (barony) of Cremorne. It had distinctive sub-districts in Clontibret and Aghnamullen which were formally noted as parishes in 1429 and 1530 respectively. Ballybay was a modern parish created in 1798 to take account of the modern town, similar to Belleek civil parish in the west of the diocese.

In this survey, it is possible to see how the map of civil parishes broadly corresponds with the outline of parochial territories in 1306. An agreement between the bishop of Clogher and Brian MacMahon, king of Airgialla, and his sub-lords in 1297 hints at the context of secular territories in the emerging diocese of Clogher within which the parochial re-organisation was occurring at the time.[56] While a number of changes were made in the later medieval period, mainly subdivisions of very large parishes from the 1306 list, it is also evident that many of these divisions and subdivisions already existed with important early medieval antecedents.

54 E.P. Shirley, *The history of the county of Monaghan* (London, 1879), 564–9. **55** Ó Dufaigh, 'Medieval Monaghan', 11. **56** K.W. Nicholls, 'The register of Clogher' in *Clogher Record*, 7 (1971–72), 413.

PRE-PAROCHIAL TERRITORIES BEFORE RÁITHBREASAIL[57]

Earlier medieval septlands and sub-kingdoms in the south Ulster borderlands suggest linkages with a pre-existing parochial territorialisation. Just as the civil parishes are not precise delineations of the medieval parishes, however, so the baronies are not maps of the actual political geography of medieval Ireland, but are approximate representations of the morphology of medieval territories as they were translated by inquisitions of the late sixteenth and early seventeenth centuries. The territories which emerged from the waxing and waning of the early medieval septs of Airgialla, Uí Cremthainn, Uí Fiachrach, Fir Manach, Uí Méith, Dartraige and Mugdorni were the *túatha* which find echoes in these baronies which were largely in the control of the later medieval septs of Maguires in the kingdom of Lough Erne (Fermanagh) and the MacKennas and MacMahons in Airgialla (Monaghan). The sixteenth-century baronies of Fermanagh had their origin in the seven *túatha* around Lough Erne which were originally carved out by a variety of peoples who were welded together by the Fir Manach in the eleventh century. At the same time the territories of the Uí Méith, Mugdorni and Fir Rois were emerging as the kingdom of Airgialla. From figure 6 it is clear that there was a broad tapestry of *túatha* in the south Ulster region, out of which the diocese of Clogher, and its neighbouring dioceses, were carved by the early thirteenth century. Preliminary analysis would suggest that parochial organisation within these territories reflected secular septlands belonging to various *sliochts*, *clanns* and branches of septs which were translated through the geometry of ballybetaghs in the landscape. The precedents for much of this process of territorial division and control (or territorialisation) can be found in the emerging geographies of the Airgialla and Fir Manach, and before them the Cinéal Cairbre, Cinéal Eoghan, Cinéal Fearadhaigh, Uí Fhearghail, Uí Méith and so on. It appears that these political geographies formed the basis for early pre-parish formations which pre-figured the later medieval parishes. (Fig. 6) Indeed, close examination of the map of baronies and parishes, suggests that in some instances the parishes may in fact reflect the original medieval extent of some of these tuatha territories.

Magheraboy coincides with the early medieval Túatha Rátha, which had been carved out by a Cinéal Cairbre people pushing northwards into south Ulster. The seventeenth-century surveys identified three sub-territories of Magheraboy, Túatha Ratha and Sliocht Redmond within it, which represented early versions of the parish territories of Inishmacsaint, Devenish and Rossory

57 Based on P. Mulligan, 'Notes on the topography of Fermanagh' in *Clogher Record;* 1 (1954), 24–34; *Inquisitionum in officio rotulorum cancellariae Hiberniae ... Ultoniae,* xxxiv–v. N. O Muraíle, 'The barony names of Fermanagh and Monaghan' in *Clogher Record,* 11 (1984), 387–402; Simms, 'Origins of the diocese of Clogher'; Ó Dufaigh, 'The MacCathmhaoils of Clogher' and 'Medieval Monaghan'; C. Devlin, 'The rise and fall of a dynasty: medieval west Tyrone as reported in the annals' in *Clogher Record,* 16 (1999), 71–85.

Fig. 6: Early pre-parishes of south Ulster

(Lisgool). St Ninnidh was the seventh-century founder of churches in Inis Muigh Samh and at Domhnach Mór in Magh Ene. Magheraboy also extended across to the eastern side of Lough Erne to include Devenish island and a narrow strip of land which later emerged as the civil parish of Trory.

Lurg barony was the territory of Fir Luirg. It was identified with the two 'countries of Lurg and Cooil McKernan' in 1603. Cúil Mhic Thighearnáin was the genesis of the parish of Derryvullan. Cúlmáine parish corresponded with the remainder of Lurg territory. This territory may also have lost a portion of land to the Cenel Eoghain, corresponding to the parish of Kilskeery in the later county of Tyrone.

Knockninny (Cnoc Ninnidh) and **Coole** (Cúil na nOirear) were territories or countries, equivalent to half baronies in the 1603 commission, lying on either side of upper Lough Erne. Ninnidh was a sixth-century saint founder of a church in Inis Muigh Samh. The Knockninny territory was absorbed into the lands of Bréifne and the diocese Kilmore in which lies the corresponding parish of Kinawley. Galloon was the parish coinciding with the Coole portion.

Tirkennedy barony contained two countries of Tír Cennfota and Cúil which had early Uí Cremthainn antecedents. These territories show evidence of links with the parishes of Derryvullan (southern portion), Magheracross and Iniskeen (later Enniskillen).

Clankelly corresponds with the territory of Clann Cheallaigh who were another early Uí Cremthain people. By 1603 three sub-territories belonging to Clann Cheallaigh Mac Dhonnchad, Clann MacDomhnaill and Clann MacMaolruanaigh were identified. A portion known as Sliocht Maolruanaigh corresponded with the parish of Clones in 1603. The other territories suggest links with parishes of Galloon and Aghalurcher.

Clanawley is from Clann Amhlaoibh who were connected with the Muinter Pheodachain whose Uí Cremthainn origins can be traced to the seventh century. The boundary of their lands in the medieval period was marked by the Arney river which delineates Cleenish parish and also marks the boundary with Breifne in which the parish of Killesher is located.

Magherastephana, Machaire Stefanach, in the medieval period contained a number of subdivisions which correspond with the parishes of Aghalurcher and Aghavea.[58]

Monaghan and **Trough** baronies originated in early medieval kingdom of the Uí Méith. Tehallan, Tullycorbet, Kilmore, Rackwallace and Tedavnet were early church districts of the Uí Méith in what became the territory of Monaghan which passed to the MacMahons in the twelfth century. Trough was the remnant of a more extensive early *trícha céd* in which the McKennas, Uí Méith descendants, continued through the later medieval period.[59] Donagh and Errigle parishes were ancient subterritories with early ecclesiastical links.

Cremourne, a legacy of the early seventh-century Mugdorni, who with the Fir Rois formed what later became Cremorne and Farney baronies. Críoch Mhughdorn was a large parish territory from the 1306 ecclesiastical taxation until the late sixteenth century which later subdivided. Its subdivision Sliabh Mughdorn, in the medieval period sometimes also called Owenagh, corresponds to the later parish of Aghnamullen, which with the other later parishes seems to coincide with sept branch lands of MacMahons.

Dartree, from the Dartraige people in the eighth century, was a large parish in 1306, but with the later medieval parishes corresponding with distinctive older subdivisions.

Farney, which extended into the midlands in the early medieval period, was called Donaghmoyne in the later medieval period. Originally part of the territory of Cremourne, it was called called Mugdorna Maigen, then Domhnach Maigen.

58 Mulligan, 'Topography of Fermanagh', 31–2.   59 Ó Dufaigh, 'Medieval Monaghan', 12–26.

Clogher (Clochar) contained parishes reflecting lands of Cinéal Fearadhaigh, MacCathmhaoils and septlands of O Neills in the fifteenth century. This was the remnant of a much more extensive territory in the early medieval period,

Before the Synod of Ráithbreasail outlined the first boundaries of a diocese for Clogher, figure 6 shows a set of territories and tuatha, which were remarkably equal in territorial extent, in which pre-parochial districts emerged in tandem with septlands and political allegiances and formed the basis for the parochial structure outlined in 1306. At a broad regional level, during the course of the twelfth century this political geography facilitated the emergence of dioceses which coincided with the kingdoms of Airghialla and the Fir Manach and Breifne. At the local territorial level, proto-parochial districts, sprinkled with early churches, were resolving themselves into subdivisions of tuatha that reflected the developing internal geographies of septlands.

Since the term 'parish' carries with it particular connotations of pastoral care and regulated ministry flowing from the twelfth-century reforms, is it possible to envisage a 'pre-parish' territorial entity existing without the seemingly well-ordered tithe system which characterised the post-reform Church? The arrangement of parishes under episcopal jurisdiction followed in the century after diocesan organisation, taking somewhat different directions in Anglo-Norman and Gaelic Ireland, reflecting the contrasting cultural and economic exigencies of feudal and lineage societies. However, the erection of such parishes did not necessarily mean extensive creation of parochial territories *de novo*. The reform of the parochial structures might more properly be seen as a regularisation of pre-existing territorial entities within the new dioceses. In this sense therefore the medieval parishes which are broadly represented in the civil parish boundaries are likely to have been essentially subdivisions (in some cases) of pre-existing territories into proto-parishes, evolving to deliver pastoral services more effectively and to reflect the income-generating capacity of local septlands. This resembled the process Nicholls refers to for the later thirteenth century rectorial subdivisions in which 'the tribal state or territory was taken to constitute a parish ...'[60] In Ulster, for instance, the seven *túatha* around Lough Erne may be seen as providing the primary territorial structures for the parishes which ultimately emerged.

Large districts with one parish church and additional dependent chapels were referred to as 'plebania' in the medieval records: Derryvullen and Galloon were such parochial territories in Clogher in which the pastor was called 'plebanus'.[61] Katharine Simms has noted that on some occasions this title attached to earlier medieval coarbs as ordained rectors of major parish churches with authority over minor churches in the neighbouring districts.[62] Many of

60 Nicholls, 'Rectory, vicarage and parish', 61–2.   61 McKenna, *Diocese of Clogher*, ii, 188.
62 Simms, 'Frontiers in the Irish Church,' 178

these church or chapel districts subsequently emerged as parishes in the later Middle Ages. It seems clear that the post-reform churches were not conjured up out of thin air but were foreshadowed in earlier secular and proto-parochial units whose existence should be the object of a concerted forensic enquiry by collaborating historians, medievalists, geographers, archaeologists and local historians.

MORPHOLOGY, BOUNDARIES AND RURAL CENTRALITY

Townland geographies are important in reading and understanding many of the processes which went into shaping the Irish landscape, in this case in providing clues to early ecclesiastical settlement. There are more than 62,000 of these units recorded by the Ordnance Survey in the 1830s. Understanding the language of townlands and other small territorial units helps to read the geography of larger units like baronies and parishes. These small units were units of landholding, which laced the countrysides of late medieval – early modern Ireland. They had different nomenclatures in separate lordships, either tates, ballyboes, polls, gneeves, quarters, sessiaghs and so on.[63] As elsewhere in Europe, this parcellation of the landscape formed the basis for landholding in medieval Gaelic and English Ireland – in many cases reaching back to the tribal septlands of pre-Norman Ireland. The medieval septlands or estates of kindred were fragmented into fractions (halves, quarters, sixths, sixteenths) of primary units such as ballybetaghs – a territorialisation which in detail and delineation mirrored local topographical diversity in environmental resources. As Hogan expressed it, the (Anglo-Norman) ploughland of 120 acres of arable in the rich land of Waterford, Tipperary or Limerick could support as much stock as perhaps 1,000 acres of poorer lands in west Mayo or Kerry.[64] This parcellation process probably developed within an initial broader framework of larger units which were progressivly subdivided by streams and other physical landmarks to accommodate increasing population, settlement and land clearance.

The ballybetagh units formed sub-territories of *túatha* within the Gaelic lordships. It is within the territorial hierarchy of *túath* and ballybetagh that the parish embedded itself. There may have been some instability of boundaries and territories, but it is more likely that many of the larger entities survived, with landholders, overlords and perhaps placenames simply changing. Historians tend to attribute the same fluidity and change to landscape territorial structures as to its peoples – a parallel expansion and contraction of places and people. In 1929 Hogan wrote about an 'elaborate territorial demarcation [which] connotes a degree of symmetry in the organisation of early Irish

---

63 T. McErlean, 'The Irish townland system of landscape organisation' in T. Reeves-Smyth and F. Hammond (eds), *Landscape archaeology of Ireland*, BAR 116 (Oxford, 1983), 315–39. 64 Hogan, 'The tricha cét', 189.

society, which is not easy to reconcile with the political instability commonly attributed to Irish institutions'.[65] In many ways, however, such social change (like changes in sept overlords or colonising immigration) was only possible within a framework of territorial continuity – places remain fixed with societies in flux.

All our ideas of territorial continuities are grounded in the significance of boundaries as natural and socially-produced lines in the landscape. It would be folly to suggest, however, that the precise, definitive lines of the civil parishes of the eighteenth and nineteenth centuries are exact replicas of medieval reality. There is a need to divest ourselves of our modern concern with finely-delineated units, like acres, roods and perches – the grammar of territorial order through which we read the landscape. We must go back to a much more loosely-arranged landscape, marked partly by natural features and partly by ill-defined boundary zones running through grazing land, common lands or wastelands – where landownership or control was ambiguous or non-existent.[66] Maps of the earl of Kildare's lands in the 1670s still contained many commons lying on the boundaries of two or more townlands.[67] This ambiguity was eventually to give way to reclamation or clearance which came with agrarian improvements of the early modern period, when land was mapped and measured more precisely.

Parish shapes and boundaries are associated with a secular landholding structure of septs and lordships of pre-modern Ireland which mirror the lie of the land in lowland, highland and watershed. In early seventeenth-century inquisitions, as the spatial order of septlands is dissolved, the parish geography survives. Boundary descriptions relied on selecting a number of well-known points such as hills close to the boundary line, on the basis that more detailed delineation was well-known at local level. The parish of Clonmany in Donegal, for instance, is described in the following terms in the Civil Survey of 1654

> on ye northside with ye great river of Strabregg running towards the southeast, with a bogg and a ditch upon the quarter of Carne and the quarter of alto Shane, ... and from thence through the mountaine of Drumkuny, on the south with a brooke running to a bogg called Milliverin and from thence to a mountaine called Abbernelorigg, which boundeth us south west from the parish of Disertnegee, and from thence westward through a gutter and a bogg, to the mountaine of Urbellreaugh, and from thence south-ward into a brooke which runeth into the river of Loghswilly, which boundeth us southward while we come to ye river of Strabregg, where we began our bounds.[68]

65 Ibid., 190. 66 J.H. Andrews, 'The mapping of Ireland's cultural landscape, 1550–1630' in Duffy et al. (eds), *Gaelic Ireland*, 178 talks about the ambiguity of boundaries on many sixteenth-century maps. See also Andrews' *Plantation acres: an historical study of the Irish land surveyor and his maps* (Belfast, 1985), chapter one, for discussion of boundaries and small area measurement. 67 A. Horner, 'Thomas Emerson's Kildare estates surveys 1674–1697' in *Journal of the Kildare Archaeological Society*, 18 (1996–7), 399–429. 68 R.C. Simington (ed.) *The civil survey: counties*

The parish of Kells in Co Meath is described as follows: '... bounded on the east with the river Rorah on the south with Pepperdstowne, Berfordstowne, Boolis, Scoulockstown, Dandelstowne, Redmore, both Ballanagons and Castlekenan, on the west with Dewleene & Knockleess & on the north with the river Rorah'.[69] An inquisition of 1614 outlines the boundaries of the granges of the abbey of SS Peter and Paul in Armagh in classic pre-cartographic terms:

> The said Granges lie within the following meares and bounds viz: From the ford of Altrapoigy near Carnavanaghan and along a small stream to Laeghtdonogh and along another stream to Bealananarine ford and through a marsh to Bealanaskelgach and thence in a valley through the middle of Altatessy ... and then through the bog beside Knockanroe and Belanabaridy and along a river between Foalee and Sigaghan to a small river running between Foalee and Ballymacnab and so through the middle of a great bog and along a stream through the middle of Altfinogeh and thence through the middle of a marsh as far as Barebane ford.[70]

Similarly an inquistion of 1609 outlined the parish of Magheraculmoney as being 'bounded on the north uppon the half barony of Coolemckernan, and from thence to a great rocke of stoane called Ardshanckie in bawagh on the north west, and from thence to the river of Termonmcgragh, which river is the auncient meere and bound of the said parishe, unto a mountaine called Urliewe on the north east, and on the east it is bounded by Mononvarrowe, and on the south by Lougherne.'[71] The boundaries followed streams, ditches, torrents, passing through the middle of bogs and marshes, over mountains, with particular locations registered by an intricate network of ballyboe and sub-ballyboe names. The parishes are based on this detailed template of townland boundaries, some of which in marginal areas only fully materialised in eighteenth and early nineteenth centuries but most of which are of long-standing antiquity.

Though many of these boundaries were frequently more zonal than linear, physical topography made it possible to be precise. Raven's maps of Monaghan in 1634 depicted a townland net quite finely delineated and Bodley's early plantation maps in Ulster, while impressionistic in outline, obviously derive from definitive boundaries based on intricate drainage networks.[72] The stream

of Donegal, Londonderry and Tyrone (Dublin, 1937), 3. **69** R.C. Simington (ed.), *The civil survey: county of Meath* (Dublin, 1940), 279. **70** McGleenon, 'The medieval parishes of Ballymore and Mullabrack', 23–24. **71** *Inquisitionum in officio rotulorum cancellariae Hiberniae ... Ultoniae,* appendix vi Fermanagh. See also P. Mulligan, 'Notes on the topography of Fermanagh' in *Clogher Record,* 1 (1954) for comments on various commissions as sources for Co. Fermanagh. **72** P.J. Duffy, 'Farney in 1634: an examination of Thomas Raven's survey of the Essex estate' in *Clogher Record,* 11 (1983), 245–56: 245 and J.H. Andrews, 'The maps of the escheated counties of Ulster, 1609–10' in *PRIA,* 74C (1974), 133–70. For reproductions of Bodley's maps see M. Swift, *Historical maps of Ireland* (London, 1999), 52–63.

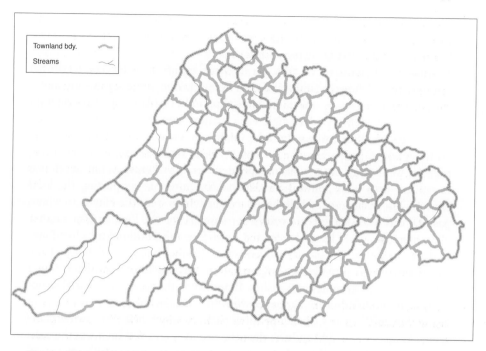

Fig. 7: Townlands of Errigal Truagh parish, Co. Monaghan

network in the Ulster drumlins, for example, afforded a natural template for
boundary evolution, where smaller streams echo the townland net and larger
streams frequently coincide with ballybetagh or parish boundaries, drumlins
forming the core of the small townlands. However, in areas of impeded
drainage like south Ulster, boundaries running through marshy low-lying areas,
or lakelands as in Fermanagh, were zonal in medieval times. Townlands and
parishes in many mountainous parts of the west reflect an upslope-downslope
morphology, frequently encompassing a range of land quality from upland to
shore, bordered by the template of streams flowing downslope as evidenced on
the southern slopes of the Dingle peninsula and in north Mayo. In Kildare and
Meath, by contrast, with a much less complex natural drainage network, early
socio-economic boundary markers are commemorated in the several names like
Blackditch and Blacktrench as boundary townlands. Indeed the more closely-
settled and humanised manorial landscapes of the Pale, south Leinster and
Munster contained many examples of man-made boundaries: the angularity of
townlands in much of Meath and Kildare reflect the presence of early ditch and
hedge boundaries.[73] In the late medieval and early modern seventeenth and
eighteenth centuries in most parts of the country there was a further layer of

73 Duffy, 'Landscape and place in Co. Meath', 196; P.J. Duffy, 'The territorial identity of county
Kildare' forthcoming in T. McGrath and T. O'Keeffe (eds), *Kildare: history and society.*

smaller denominations underneath the townland, many of which survived in local memory into the nineteenth century, but were largely ignored in estate leases and by the first Ordnance Survey maps.

Important boundaries if they are to have significance for the territorial community and future stability need to be marked in some significant way – either by nature or by the community: periodic walking or peregrination supported its memory. Although ecclesiastical boundaries may have been marked by standing stones, burial grounds or crosses, searching for some lasting mark of parish boundaries may be futile since, as has been suggested, parishes were never initiated as independent territorial entities, but developed in tandem with local political and landholding interests supporting the local church. The occupants of ballybetaghs or ballyboes were the clients to whom pastoral care was delivered in return for support for the local and/or mother church and clergy. The parish slotted itself into this landholding–chiefdom–lordship structure. So secular exigencies of landholding or lordship and the wealth or support provided by its population were the important determining influences on geographies of parishes. If and when the secular territorial structures were modified or, as happened with ballybetaghs of Gaelic lordships in the seventeenth century, abandoned, the parishes which had their own ecclesiastical *raison d'être* would endure: the tithe revenues ensured such was the case.

Churches, whether of wood or stone, were among the first significant central places in the Irish landscape – more so than the castles or the houses of lords. In pre-Norman Ireland or later medieval Gaelic Ireland, where towns were largely absent, parish churches possessed what might be characterised as rural centrality – either in larger ecclesiastical settlements, or local churches with burial grounds. Burial grounds, which from the eighth and ninth centuries became mandatory for Christian inhumation, in particular gave parishes and pre-parishes lasting significance more or less as central places for local districts. 'Historically parish centres were powerful settlement foci and community anchors,' says Smyth, who has highlighted the endurance of the centralising function of parish centres after the Reformation in Dublin, Kilkenny and Tipperary counties.[74] Parish centres were also occasional meeting places, often revered sites, places of sanctuary, frequently marking earlier pre-Christian sites. If pastoral care was rudimentary in Gaelic and pre-Norman Ireland, or occasional in its delivery (as with baptism and burial), and Mass-going not a weekly requirement as in the post-Tridentine church, this may have some bearing on parish size and accessibility and may help to explain the large parish territories and subsequent subdivision in some places. The petition of the parish of Ferceall to Rome *c.*1400 complaining about accessibility to their church at eight miles distant, especially during winter rains and times of war,

---

74 Smyth, 'Property, patronage and population', 126; Smyth, 'Sixteenth- and seventeenth-century county Dublin', 153–8.

resulted in it being elevated to parish status (with font and fenced burial ground) above its surbordinate local churches.[75] During the upheavals of the Tudor period – and periodic disturbances in earlier centuries – parish life and pastoral services were severely disrupted and churches in many places were ruined and abandoned.[76] Do references to the collapse of the parish system[77] mean that the system of pastoral care by properly appointed priests, tithe collection and church repair had failed? The idea of the parish, in contrast to its buildings and possessions, was virtually indestructible: its burial grounds, sites and boundaries were indelible in the landscape and embedded in local memory.

75 FitzPatrick and O'Brien, *The medieval churches of county Offaly*, 123. **76** See Andrews, 'Mapping Ireland's cultural landscape' on roofless ruins, though Andrews also considers that this may have been a stylistic convention by surveyors. **77** FitzPatrick and O'Brien, *Medieval churches of Offaly*, xiv. See also Smyth, 'Sixteenth- and seventeenth-century county Dublin', 153–8 for references to the survival of Catholic pastoral care in Dublin in the first half of the seventeenth century.

The material world of the parish

ELIZABETH FITZPATRICK

An understanding of the physical appearance of Irish parish churches has advanced over the last twenty years as a result of published regional studies conducted in Co. Dublin,[1] in Co. Offaly,[2] in the diocese of Kilfenora[3] and more recently in Co. Meath.[4] The field data accrued and published by the Archaeological Survey of Ireland has also, in some instances, served to highlight the regional identities of groups of parish churches, as indeed did some of the earlier observations of Leask on particular medieval parish churches,[5] and de Breffny and Mott on post-Reformation churches.[6] In addition postgraduate students have also been making contributions to this field.[7] But there is still quite some distance to go before sustainable overviews, like those available for English parish churches and their associated features by Platt,[8] Blair,[9] Morris,[10] and Fawcett,[11] can be presented for the medieval and early modern parish churches of Ireland.

One of the questions frequently asked by students of buildings-archaeology and the Irish church is how one identifies a parish church in the landscape from the thirteenth century through to the eighteenth century. In contrast to the situation in Britain and in continental Europe, the opportunity to readily identify the physical remains of parish churches in Ireland is greatly reduced

1 M. Ní Mharcaigh, 'The medieval parish churches of south-west County Dublin' in *PRIA*, 96C (1997), 245–96; M. McMahon, *Medieval church sites of north Dublin* (Dublin, 1991); B. O'Brien, 'Churches of south-east County Dublin' in G. Mac Niocaill and P.F. Wallace (eds), *Keimelia: studies in medieval archaeology and history in memory of Tom Delaney* (Galway, 1988), 504–24. 2 E. FitzPatrick and C. O'Brien, *The medieval churches of County Offaly* (Dublin, 1998), 111–48. 3 S. Ní Ghabhláin, 'Church and community in medieval Ireland: the diocese of Kilfenora' in *JRSAI*, 125 (1995), 61–84; 'The origin of medieval parishes in Gaelic Ireland: the evidence from Kilfenora' in *JRSAI*, 126 (1996), 37–61. 4 M. O'Neill, 'The medieval parish churches in County Meath' in *JRSAI*, 132 (2002), 1–56. 5 H.G. Leask, *Irish churches and monastic buildings, iii* (Dundalk, 1966), passim; H.G. Leask, 'The collegiate church of St Nicholas, Galway' in *Journal of the Galway Archaeological and Historical Society*, 17 (1936), 1–23. 6 B. de Breffny and G. Mott, *The churches and abbeys of Ireland* (London, 1976), 115–41. 7 See S. Scully, 'Medieval parish churches and parochial organisation in Muintir Eolais', unpublished MA (NUI, Galway, 1999). 8 C. Platt, *The parish churches of medieval England* (London, 1981). 9 J. Blair (ed.), *Minsters and parish churches: the local church in transition 950–1200*, Oxford University Committee for Archaeology, Monograph 17 (Oxford, 1988). 10 R. Morris, *Churches in the landscape* (London, 1989). 11 R. Fawcett, *Scottish medieval churches: architecture and furnishings* (Stroud, 2002).

Pl. 1: Baptismal font at Clonfert cathedral, Co. Galway

by their ruinous condition and the poor survival of items that clearly communicate parish status. The primary indicators of parochial status are a baptismal font (pl. 1) and a fenced graveyard – a parish church is actually defined by these two features. Other items that hint at parish status, but some of which are also associated with chapels, include defined liturgical space constituting a chancel and a nave, a stone chancel arch or beam-holes indicating the former position of a timber rood screen that separated laity from celebrant, an attached sacristy, a bell-tower, belfry or bellcote, a chantry chapel, priest's quarters, medieval graveslabs and a graveyard cross, a piscina, a stoup and a sacrament house or aumbry. Church furnishings such as stone altars, church fittings like timber rood screens and wooden or stone rood crosses, and church plate such as chrismatories for the holy oils and censers, have seldom survived outside of the Pale. Statuary and statue niches are also rare survivals.

While attention is now being paid to the architecture of the parish churches and the symbols of their parochial status, their landscape contexts have been largely overlooked. Features denoting parish headquarters, for instance, are not confined to the church itself. They may also be present as an attached or a freestanding priest's residence, a tithe barn, defined glebeland, roadways, and as secular buildings in the form of mote castles, moated sites or tower houses, and indications of village settlement that grew up in the vicinity of the church, whether of colonial or Gaelic origin. Within the greater parish there are daughter chapels, with and without cure, to be found, and of course more traditional elements of parish religion in the form of penitential sites associated with local saints – such as holy wells, sacred trees and groves, stone 'chairs', 'beds' and 'footprint' stones.

In this book the principal focus is on the parish church itself. Seven scholars deal with the buildings that provided pastoral care for communities, from the early medieval period up to and including the eighteenth century, spanning about eleven centuries. What emerges is the fact that the churches and material world of the parish community throughout Ireland, in the period concerned, afford some of the best insights into the provision of pastoral care and often reveal when parishes were created and altered. The churches themselves reflect changes in liturgical practice over time and they bear witness to the resources of their patrons. They manifest cultural nuances, both in terms of the Anglo-Norman and Gaelic perspectives and the post-Reformation and early modern Protestant and Catholic traditions. The parish church in the rural landscape is also a reminder that settlement once converged there.

PRE-NORMAN CHURCHES AND PASTORAL CARE

The more difficult challenge of providing evidence for early medieval pastoral ministry through an analysis of church buildings is taken up by Ó Carragáin. The issue of pastoral care, and whether or not the pre-twelfth-century Church in Ireland provided it, has served to highlight the variety of functions that churches of that period served. Ó Carragáin notes variation in the dry-stone churches of peninsular Kerry. While he concedes that church size is related to function, he argues that the area of a church building (with the obvious exception of tiny shrine chapels or feretories designed to house relics) does not always automatically tell us whether that church provided pastoral care. Factors like the size of the resident community and the pilgrim population, and perhaps most importantly the resources available to a lay patron, were more critical in determining the eventual size of a church building. He notes that the second phase church on Church Island, Co. Kerry, which could have housed four times as many people as its counterpart on Illaunloughan, must be viewed as having been congregational. This he sees as strongly contrasting with the tiny dry-stone church on Illaunloughan (that replaced the earlier sod-built church there) which perhaps served a small resident male community of monastic character as outlined by White Marshall and Walsh in their recently published *Illaunloughan Island*.[12]

A significant number of early church sites seem to have gone out of use before the parish system was formally established in Ireland. Ó Carragáin

12 J. White Marshall and C. Walsh, *Illaunloughan Island: an early medieval monastery in County Kerry* (Bray, 2005), 125–34.

argues that these were replaced by mortared pre-Romanesque churches, which date to the eleventh or early twelfth century with the majority dating from the mid-eleventh century onward. Ultimately he attempts to correlate the advent of viable tithing units and pastoral ministry with the building of these mortared stone churches in the second half of the eleventh century. But, perhaps the emergence of pastoral care coincided with the construction of large 'barn' churches, generally referred to as *damliac mór*, under royal patronage in the tenth century? The expansion of church building in the eleventh century, which both the essays by Ó Carragáin and O'Keeffe emphasise, might also represent a proliferation of dependant chapels or daughter chapels under the care of the larger 'mother-churches', some of which later became parish churches. The large pre-Reform *damliac*, such as Clonfert, Clonmacnoise and Glendalough, are uniquely large buildings relative to the majority of pre-Norman Irish churches. The architecture of some *damliac mór*, namely those at Clonmacnoise and Glendalough, has been the subject of thorough analysis.[13] Despite the fact that they had royal benefactors (and in this book Ó Carragáin refers to Clonmacnoise as 'a post-Carolingian episcopal-monastic church), the function of these buildings in their pre-Reform contexts has not been questioned. Is the large size of these buildings simply the outcome of ostentation on the part of their royal patrons, or could they represent mother-churches something like the large minster churches of Anglo-Saxon Britain, where local communities attended for the cure of souls? It is believed that a system of minsters or mother-churches providing parochial care began to emerge in Anglo-Saxon Britain from the end of the seventh century. The territories, called *parochiae*, served by these mother-churches, were coterminous with royal and episcopal estates, and the creation of the mother-churches was frequently the outcome of royal policy. When the estates served by the mother-churches were broken up into smaller, independent units, there was a proliferation of manorial churches within these newly formed areas. However, the mother-churches assumed authority over the manorial churches, thereafter termed daughter chapels, and claimed, among other rights, sole right to burial.[14] Over time, the functions of these daughter chapels developed. Some became independent and others dependent parochial chapels[15] while several became oratories attached to households and chantries dedicated to prayer for departed souls.

Could it then be the case that Ireland, before the formal establishment of parishes, had a system of mother-churches that provided pastoral care to a large

13 C. Manning, 'Clonmacnoise cathedral' in H. King (ed.), *Clonmacnoise studies 1: seminar papers 1994* (Dublin, 1998), 57–86; C. Manning, 'The nave of Glendalough cathedral' in *Bulletin of the Irish Association of Professional Archaeologists*, 22 (1996), 6.   14 T.A. Hall, *Minster churches in the Dorset landscape*, BAR British Series 304 (Oxford, 2000), 1.   15 Hall, *Minster churches*, 5, explains that 'the status of chapels was not fixed and many grew into fully fledged parish churches, technically known as independent parochial chapels. Some chapels took on all the characteristics of parish churches but did not gain independence: the dependent parochial chapels'.

area commensurate in some instances with a *tríocha céad* and more commonly with the *túath*?[16] Also, might it be that this arrangement was fossilised in some of the Gaelic parishes formed from the thirteenth century onwards whereby the very large size of the parishes reflected the earlier areas of pastoral ministry? This would certainly explain some of the impossibly large parishes in Gaelic areas such as Kinawley which constituted 51,000 statute acres,[17] commensurate with the *tríocha céad* of Clann Amhlaoibh and the later barony of Clanawley in Mag Uidhir's (Maguire) lordship of Fir Manach, and Muintir Eolais, the small lordship of Mac Raghnaill (Reynolds) in south Leitrim which constituted a rural rectory in itself.[18] Nicholls has suggested that the great rectories like Muintir Eolais, which covered a group of parishes, might represent 'a survival not so much of a pre-parochial stage of organisation as of an intermediate stage in which the tribal state or territory was taken to constitute a parish and acquired, therefore, an incumbent, the predecessor of the later rector'.[19]

EARLY PARISH CHURCHES

The provision of pastoral care and the formal establishment of a tithe-based network of parishes in Ireland are two different but related things. While a church could have provided some form of pastoral ministry to a community in pre-Norman Ireland, it does not necessarily follow that evidence of pastoral care implies the existence of a tithe-based parish. O'Keeffe is unconvinced that any of the eleventh-century churches in Ireland functioned as formally established parish centers. He agrees with Ó Carragáin that what are generally described as pre-Romanesque churches are in fact constructions of the eleventh century. But with their unicameral plan and scanty interior room he deems them unlikely candidates as parish churches. They are quite different to their counterparts in eleventh-century England, which are uniformly bicameral and clearly divided into nave for laity and chancel for celebrant. Size of church and clearly defined liturgical space within a church are therefore viewed by O'Keeffe as prerequisites of parish status, an opinion which he shares with British parish church scholars such as Platt who has written that 'The parish church ... is designed for a very clear purpose. It must accommodate a congregation, which may enlarge or contract according to the fortunes of the settlement, and it must make some provision for liturgical space – for the unencumbered celebration of the Mass.'[20]

O'Keeffe sets out to find pre-Norman churches in Ireland comparable to the

16 These units are explained in Table 1 of Pat Nugent's essay in this volume. 17 P. Walsh, *Ancient Westmeath* (Mullingar, 1985), 7. 18 K.W. Nicholls, 'Rectory, vicarage and parish in the western Irish dioceses' in *JRSAI*, 101 (1971), 53–84: 60. 19 Ibid., 61. 20 Platt, *The parish churches*, 13.

bicameral structures of eleventh-century Britain. He finds a handful in Hiberno-Scandinavian settlements (pp. 128–30), such as the early twelfth-century St Peter's church at Waterford and the churches at Clondalkin, Killiney and Palmerstown, Co. Dublin, that he dates to *c*.1120, possibly pre-dating St Peter's. Both Ó Carragáin (pp. 103–104) and Nugent (p. 188) also allude to Viking communities as the focus of early parishes in Ireland. O'Keeffe points out that, remarkably these bipartite buildings with differentiated nave and chancel do not appear to have exerted any influence on eleventh- and early twelfth-century church building in Ireland. It would be at least the third decade of the twelfth century before chancels began to be tacked on to existing churches and chancel arches inserted, and still later before newly built nave and chancel churches appeared on the landscape.

Neither can the advent of Romanesque, and its perceived links with the twelfth-century Reform movement, be viewed as the catalyst and hallmark of parochial formation and the emergence of parish churches in Ireland. The presence of Romanesque architecture and architectural sculpture in a church does not predicate early parish status. Indeed, O'Keeffe observes that most Romanesque churches post-date the reforming synod of 1111 by several decades. Ultimately he sees the Anglo-Normans as the builders of the first true parish churches, the earliest of which, albeit small in number, include St Nicholas's in Carrickfergus dated to the late 1100s and the church at Bannow, Co. Wexford. The paucity of new Anglo-Norman churches in the early colonial period leads him to suggest that the private chapels of Anglo-Norman castles could have provided pastoral ministry for manorial tenants in the late 1100s.

But the Anglo-Normans initially engaged in the pragmatic process of creating their parish churches out of existent Gaelic churches too. Citing the Co. Dublin and Co. Meath examples of St Doulagh's and Cannistown, which are early medieval churches refurbished under Anglo-Norman patronage in the thirteenth century, de Breffny and Mott make the point that 'Of the parish churches built, not all were innovations'.[21] This Anglo-Norman expediency in the early colonial period can be seen in several parts of Ireland. Take Kilkenny for example, where Anglo-Norman settlement was long lasting and Offaly where Anglo-Norman colonisation was short-lived. The early medieval monastic site at Tullaherin, Co. Kilkenny, with its enclosure, early church, round tower, ogham stone and cross (the cross-base survives) was adopted as an Anglo-Norman manorial church.[22] Indeed it became the settlement centre of the parish, as witnessed by the extensive remains of a deserted medieval village extending over the fields north of the church. In Offaly, St Barrind's church on the north bank of the Camcor River, in the foothills of the Slieve Bloom Mountains, became St John's Anglo-Norman manorial church, possibly under

---

21 De Breffny and Mott, *The churches*, 78.　22 C. Manning 'Some notes of the early history and archaeology of Tullaherin' in *Shadow of the Steeple*, 6 (1998), 19–39.

the patronage of Meiler fitzHenry.[23] It was situated within view of a sizeable motte and bailey castle. This church lost its status as a centre of pastoral care for the manorial community after the failure of Anglo-Norman colonisation in this area, and it does not appear again as a parish church in documentary records until the late fifteenth/early sixteenth century.

St Barrind's, alias St John's, raises another important point in the debate about the correlation between Romanesque and the advent of parish churches. While newly built Romanesque parish churches attributed to Anglo-Norman patronage are rare, Romanesque additions to earlier Gaelic churches may well have been made under Anglo-Norman patronage in particular regions of Ireland. There is a compelling case to be made for the correlation of Romanesque and Anglo-Norman patronage at manorial churches in the Slieve Bloom district at the end of the twelfth and turn of the thirteenth century. It is difficult to avoid making an association between the patronage of Meiler fitzHenry and the voussoir with lateral chevron and scrolling foliage tendril that once formed the springer of the head of a Romanesque doorway at St Barrind's manorial church. It is equally impossible to preclude the patronage of Adam de Hereford, *c.*1200, from an understanding of the late Romanesque scalloped capital with scrollwork that once graced either a chancel arch or the doorway of the manorial church at Clonfert Molua on the Laois side of Slieve Bloom.[24]

By the thirteenth century when the parish network was advancing and consolidating in colonial Ireland, the Anglo-Norman community had begun to build sometimes elaborate parish churches from scratch. Typically, these tended to conform to the long nave and long chancel plan beloved of the Benedictines. The parish churches in Anglo-Norman towns such as St Nicholas's, Carrickfergus; St Multose, Kinsale; St Mary's, New Ross and the early fourteenth-century St Nicholas's in Galway (1320) typify this genre. O'Keeffe discusses the rural examples of Wells, Co. Carlow; Faithlegg, Co. Waterford; and St Finghin's at Quin, Co. Clare. Other thirteenth-century rural new-builds that are known are Loughmoe, Co. Tipperary, constructed under Purcell patronage (pl. 2), Newtown, Co. Kilkenny, patronised by Baldwin de Hamptonsford,[25] Claregalway in the borough of that name, Co. Galway,[26] and Holywood, Co. Down, on the south side of Belfast Lough, opposite Carrickfergus.[27] The defensive features of some of these churches, such as the base batter and machicolation at Claregalway parish church, remind us too that

23 FitzPatrick and O'Brien, *The medieval churches*, 122.   24 The Romanesque capital was first noted by Helen Roe and described in the typescript of her unpublished history of Co. Laois which is housed in Laois County Library; See also E. FitzPatrick, 'On the trail of an ancient highway: rediscovering Dála's Road' in J. Fenwick (ed.), *Lost and found: discovering Ireland's past* (Bray, 2003), 165–71: 167, pl. 40.   25 L. Shine, 'The manor of Earlstown, county Kilkenny: an interdisciplinary approach' in J. Lyttleton and T. O'Keeffe (eds), *The manor in medieval and early modern Ireland* (Dublin, 2005), 40–69: 43, 55–61.   26 N. Keary, 'The medieval borough and manor of Claregalway: a study of an archaeological landscape', unpublished MA (NUI, Galway, 2004), 55–7.   27 DOENI, *Historic monuments of Northern Ireland* (Belfast, 1983), 54.

Pl. 2: Loughmoe parish church, Co. Tipperary

early Anglo-Norman parish-manorial centres felt the need to protect themselves in the less hospitable frontiers of the colony.

Moving from colonial to Gaelic Ireland, the built evidence for the emergence of high medieval parish churches is quite clear-cut in Kilfenora. Ní Ghabhláin notes tremendous continuity in the use of pre-Reform church sites as parish church centres. However, she found no evidence for the refurbishment of those older churches, or for the construction of parish churches serving pastoral care, before the middle of the twelfth century. Her methodical masonry survey informs our view of the construction date of church buildings and it challenges historical opinion about the date of the establishment of parishes in Connacht. She identifies three different masonry styles in the Kilfenora group and concludes that the majority of parish churches (nine out of thirteen) in the diocese of Kilfenora were built anew or, more usually, created out of old church fabric in the late twelfth to early thirteenth century. Most churches in the diocese had been provided with a chancel by the beginning of the thirteenth century. The results of Ní Ghabhláin's Kilfenora study are important. Nicholls' argument for parish formation in Connacht generally (although he does cite exceptions) being, at the earliest, a mid-thirteenth-century development,[28]

28 Nicholls, 'Rectory, vicarage and parish', 62.

must now be modified, since this event could in fact have occurred at the end of the twelfth century and during the first half of the thirteenth century in the diocese of Kilfenora. The intensity of church building and refurbishment there, in that period, must surely be viewed as formative evidence of parish church creation.

SITE PEDIGREE AND THE GAELIC PARISH CHURCH

The use of antique church sites as parish centres is a feature that is of course standard in the story of the creation of parish churches throughout Ireland. While newly built parish churches were more common than we think from the thirteenth century to the fifteenth century, continuity of building on older sites is the more usual story, especially in Gaelic lordships. In fact, most Gaelic parish churches of the thirteenth, fourteenth and even the fifteenth century are piecemeal additions to pre-twelfth-century Reform churches. A classic case is St Colman's at Lynally in the lordship of Fir Cheall in Offaly. Fir Cheall lacked a parish church until the fifteenth century and the population were obliged to travel to their designated parish church of St David's at Ardnurcher in the adjoining lordship of Cineál bhFiachach. In 1424 Fir Cheall was granted a parish church of its own at Lynally (pl. 3), complete with cemetery, font and all requisite parochial insignia.[29] The fabric of the building reveals pre-Norman, fifteenth-century and later periods of building. In Kilfenora, Ní Ghabhláin notes that despite the fifteenth-century renewal of church fabric and fittings, which is evident throughout the churches of her study area, as it is in Ireland generally, there was no attempt to build brand new churches or to abandon long-established church sites in fifteenth-century Kilfenora. Rather, the new accommodated the old: standing buildings were refurbished in fashionable fifteenth-century style.

While the use of existing churches by Anglo–Norman manorial lords was, it seems, a very practical response to the problem of providing a parish church serving pastoral care for their tenants, the re-use of a long-established church as a parish centre was a cultural imperative for Gaelic lords. It is virtually impossible to identify a parish church in Gaelic Ireland that is not either the result of a re-fabrication of an older church or, less usually, a newly built late medieval structure at a hallowed early medieval monastic site. In general, periodic building on the same site defines the built environment of the parish centre in Gaelic Ireland. Lemanaghan in Co. Offaly, reputedly founded by St Manchan in the seventh century, demonstrates the predilection of the Mic Chochláin (MacCoghlans) chiefs of Dealbhna Eathra for creating their parish centres at early medieval monasteries in their lordship. Lemanaghan presents a

---

29 *Calendar of entries in the papal registers relating to Great Britain and Ireland: papal letters*, 17 vols (London, 1893–1994), iv, 314; vol. vii, 179, 352.

Pl. 3: Lynally church and graveyard, Co. Offaly

remarkable array of medieval features including the multi-period church and graveyard, the remains of a possible priest's residence to the north-west of the church, graveslabs, a bullaun stone and holy well, a baptismal font and a graveyard cross, in addition to the pre-Norman 'St Mella's Cell' and its stone enclosure. This is connected to St Manchan's church by a stone causeway. The 'cell' is likely to have functioned as a shrine chapel, perhaps accommodating the twelfth-century St Manchan's shrine maintained throughout the medieval period by its hereditary keepers, the Uí Mhaonaigh. St Manchan's church had acquired the status of a parish church by 1426.[30] Prior to the fifteenth-century alterations to the building, it consisted of an eleventh- or twelfth-century masonry church, 12m by 6m, with a late twelfth-century Romanesque west doorway and a round-headed late twelfth- or early thirteenth-century window in the east gable.[31] In order to create the necessary liturgical space to facilitate its new status, the eastern end of the existing church was lengthened by 4m and a new window was set into the east gable and the south wall of the chancel. A nave and chancel were thereby created and other parochial insignia were acquired in the fifteenth century including a baptismal font with octagonal bowl and a graveyard cross with openwork cross-head.

A clear instance of building a new church on an older site, in order to augment the status of the place, can be seen on Loch an Oileáin or

30 M.A. Costello (ed.), *De annatis Hiberniae*, i (Dundalk, 1909), 144. 31 FitzPatrick and O'Brien, *The medieval churches*, 63–5.

Loughinisland in the small Mac Artáin (MacCartan) lordship of Cineál Faghartaigh (barony of Kinelarty) in south-east Co. Down. There, three churches and a graveyard stand on the island ecclesiastical site patronised by the Mic Artáin lords whose stronghold overlooked the lake and who reserved the right of burial in the island graveyard. The churches include the so-called Middle church, which has thirteenth-century features and may be the parish church referred to in 1306; the north church which is the largest and was constructed in the fifteenth century as the new parish church, and the south church or MacCartan's church patronised by Phelim MacCartan whose initials and the date 1636 feature on the west doorway.[32]

The pedigree of a site was all-important in its choice as a Gaelic parish centre, as indeed was the visible continuity in the coarbship of a site by particular families. Consider the case of Clonfert Molua in Ossory, which was allegedly founded by Molua in the sixth century. It became a parish church *c.*1200 under Anglo-Norman influence, and as late as 1622 still functioned as the parish church served by the Uí Dhuibhgeannáin (Duignans), who were the hereditary coarbs of the church and keepers of the Mionn Molua.[33] In her study of regional and cultural frontiers in the Irish Church, Simms found that in Gaelic lordships 'the clergy tended to be hereditary, recruited from the erenagh families who occupied the church's lands or from cadet branches of the ruling dynasties'. Her accompanying distribution map of locations at which coarbs and erenaghs were noted in records of clerical appointments between 1250 and 1633 shows the remarkable persistence of these officials and hereditary incumbencies in Gaelic parishes well into the seventeenth century.[34]

A point that field archaeologists seeking parish churches in Gaelic Ireland might also need to be aware of is that pastoral ministry was quite often provided at religious houses, especially in the late medieval period. For instance, papal letters of 1438 and 1451 indicate that either the transept or the side chapel adjoining the east end of the north wall of the Augustinian priory church at Gallen in Co. Offaly, run by Malachy Mac Coghlan, prior, was at that time in use as a parish church in Dealbhna Eathra.[35]

PARISH SETTLEMENT

Many of the deserted and lost villages of Ireland can be traced through their upstanding medieval parish churches. Nucleated settlements and rural boroughs of Anglo-Norman Ireland, such as Bunratty, Co. Clare, and Jerpoint

32 DOENI, *Historic monuments*, 104–5. 33 P. Dwyer (ed.), *The diocese of Killaloe from the Reformation to the eighteenth century* (Dublin, 1878), 144. 34 K. Simms, 'Frontiers in the Irish Church: regional and cultural' in T. Barry, R. Frame and K. Simms (eds), *Colony and frontier in medieval Ireland: essays presented to J.F. Lydon* (London, 1995), 177–200: 178–80. 35 *Calendar of entries, 1447–55*, 527.

church, Co. Kilkenny, and dispersed settlement in the parish-manor, are especially identifiable.[36] In this book, Nugent raises the important issue of secular settlement at late medieval parish centres. The symbiotic relationship between manor and parish is echoed in the mostly mutual identity of *túath* and parish in Gaelic Ireland. Nugent expresses the opinion that once a *túath* became a parish one of its church sites was singled out and prioritised as the parish centre – a process that attracted secular settlement. He notes that there was a tendency to locate the principal tower house of the parish-*túath* at the parish centre around which additional settlement also converged over time. In Anglo-Norman founded parish-manor centres there is also, in some instances, a very discernible continuity of associated secular settlement well into the late medieval period. Examples of the proximity of tower houses to parish church centres can be seen at the O'Dea headquarters of Dysert O'Dea and the O'Grady village of Tuamgraney Co. Clare; at Mac Coghlan's Lemanaghan in Co. Offaly; at Newtown, Co. Kikenny where the tower house was constructed for the Sweetman family;[37] and in Co. Wexford at Tomhaggard and on Lady's Island where the parish church lay on the island, joined to the mainland by a causeway which was defended by a tower house and double curtain wall.[38]

Settlements in the form of house platforms and enclosures can be distinguished too in the vicinity of Carran parish church in the Burren, Co. Clare, at Cannakill in Offaly next to the O'Connor tower house and parish church,[39] and around the fifteenth-century Burke of Clanricard tower house at Dunkellin, near Killeely parish church, Co. Galway.[40]

Accommodation for the parish priest and a tithe barn are two features that one would also expect to find at a parish centre. In this book, Bermingham recognises four types of priests' residences in later medieval Ireland. These include quarters mostly incorporated into the west end of the church or attached externally to one long wall or gable end. The residential tower is common in the Pale but not exclusively so, as the fine example from Cross East, Co. Mayo, illustrates. The freestanding priest's house in stone, like Banagher, Co. Londonderry,[41] Howth, Co. Dublin, and Graffan, Co. Offaly,[42] are a rarity but they are also unusual in Britain, and Bermingham makes the important

36 See T. O'Keeffe, *Medieval Ireland: an archaeology* (Stroud, 2000); K.D. O'Conor, *The archaeology of medieval rural settlement in Ireland* (Dublin, 1998), 41–71; T.B. Barry, 'Rural settlement in Ireland in the middle ages: and overview' in *Ruralia*, 1 (1996), 134–41; B.J. Graham, 'Anglo-Norman manorial settlement in Ireland: an assessment' in *Irish Geography*, 18 (1985), 4–15; R.E. Glasscock, 'The study of deserted medieval settlements in Ireland (to 1969)' in M.W. Beresford and J.G. Hurst (eds), *Deserted medieval villages: studies* (London, 1971), 279–301. 37 Shine, 'The manor of Earlstown', 65. 38 M. Moore, *Archaeological inventory of County Wexford* (Dublin, 1996), 133. 39 C. O'Brien and P. D. Sweetman, *Archaeological inventory of County Offaly* (Dublin, 1997), 135. 40 E. FitzPatrick, 'Assembly and inauguration places of the Burkes in late medieval Connacht' in P. J. Duffy, D. Edwards and E. FitzPatrick (eds), *Gaelic Ireland: land, lordship and settlement, c.1250–c.1650* (Dublin, 2001), 357–74: 369. 41 D.M. Waterman, 'Banagher Church, County Derry' in *Ulster Journal of Archaeology*, 3rd series, 39 (1976), 25–39. 42 O'Brien and Sweetman, *Archaeological inventory*, 175.

point that some priest's residences were probably timber built. The use of timber for some of the more diagnostic buildings at the parish centre may also be applicable to the tithe barn. With the exception of fine masonry examples like that at Annamult, Co. Kilkenny, upstanding remains of tithe barns in the Irish parish landscape are an uncommon sight.

PARISH CHURCHES AFTER THE
SIXTEENTH-CENTURY REFORMATION

The view of Irish parish churches as dilapidated and ruinous due to the privations of the late sixteenth and seventeenth centuries is well known.[43] In this book, three authors demonstrate that this is not the entire picture. The parish church did not enter a period of unrelenting stasis nor did the parish lose its vitality in Irish life. There is much evidence for alterations to existing parish churches and for the construction of new parish churches throughout the early modern period.

Loeber and Stouthamer-Loeber uncover the details of the lost Jesuit complex of Kildare Hall, which opened at Back Lane near Dublin Castle, in the parish of St Audeon's, *c.*1628, and included a chapel, novitiate, sodality and the private residence of its founder, the countess of Kildare. They reconstruct the interior of the Catholic Counter-Reformation chapel providing a virtual reality tour of that unique liturgical space where Mass was celebrated, sermons preached and confessions heard until its final destruction during Cromwell's siege of Dublin in 1650.

Moving from Dublin city to rural Cork in the seventeenth and eighteenth centuries, Cotter explores the evidence for alterations to existing medieval parish churches and the building of new ones by Protestant communities. The creation of a sense of continuity was important to seventeenth-century Protestants who tended to re-use an existing medieval church or build their new church on the foundations of, or adjacent to, a medieval church. Tell-tale signs of alterations to medieval churches for Protestant worship include inserted south wall windows, which was usually done to emit more light. It also reflects a significant liturgical change whereby all partitions and differentiation between the space used by minister and people were to be removed. More tangible evidence of this re-ordering of church space in tandem with liturgical requirements is the removal of chancel screens and even stone chancel arches. The contraction of space for worship, whereby the chancel was kept in repair and the nave closed up, is also a diagnostic feature of the re-use of medieval parish churches by seventeenth-century rural Protestant communities.

---

43 W.L. Renwick (ed.), *A view of the present state of Ireland by Edmund Spenser* (Oxford, 1970), 163.

The Catholic and Protestant traditions declared their parish church style throughout the late seventeenth, eighteenth and nineteenth centuries. Roulston investigates the dialogue between parishioners and Church of Ireland parish churches in the north of Ireland 1660–1740 focusing on the nature of building works and how that work was organised and financed. What comes across clearly is the industry and dedication of the ordinary parishioners in ensuring that churches were provided in the first instance and thereafter maintained and repaired.

As new Protestant churches were being constructed in Ulster of the late seventeenth and eighteenth centuries, new Catholic Mass houses were appearing on the Cork landscape in the same period. Cotter notes the use of private houses for Catholic worship in Cork in the period immediately after the Reformation and the subsequent construction of Mass houses, radically different from their medieval antecedents, having variously T-shaped and even Greek-cross shaped plans, in the late seventeenth and eighteenth centuries. The turning away from the medieval tradition and declaration of a new Catholic architectural tradition in rural Cork stands somewhat in contrast to the tendency in Tipperary in the same period which is a reminder that responses to building in the parish were quite nuanced. The progression of the revitalised Catholic chapel in Tipperary from the Mass house to the barn-chapel through to the Gothic revival church has been traced.[44] In this progression there was an atavism that expressed itself in the re-occupation of some of the medieval parish church sites in Tipperary, among them Loughmoe which, ironically, had been one of those Anglo-Norman manorial churches built as new by the Purcells in the thirteenth century.

Amidst all of these changes, cult sites of traditional religious practices continued to form the link with the earliest Christian past within many parishes. While new Mass houses were being erected, places like the Struell wells in Co. Down remained popular destinations for Catholics. In 1744 Walter Harris wrote of Struell – 'Vast throngs of rich and poor resort on Midsummer-eve and the Friday before *Lammas* [1st of August], some in hopes of obtaining health, and others to perform penances enjoined them by the Popish priests from the water blessed by St Patrick.'[45]

Perhaps one of the most enduring themes of the material world of the parish, over the long period served in this book, is that of continuous innovation in response to liturgical and pastoral needs, especially during periods of critical change. Yet there was also an abiding desire to maintain or, if necessary, to create connections with the perceived earliest Christian landmarks of the parish.

44 K. Whelan, 'The Catholic Church in County Tipperary 1700–1900' in W. Nolan and T.G. McGrath (eds), *Tipperary: history and society* (Dublin, 1985), 215–55: 230, 236.   45 Cited in J. O'Laverty, *An historical account of the diocese of Down and Conor, ancient and modern*, 5 vols (Dublin, 1878–80), i, 42, fn. p.

PART II

Perspectives on the Medieval Parish

Pastoral provision in the first millennium: a two-tier service?

COLMÁN ETCHINGHAM

Pastoral care is a vital part of the story of the Irish Church in the first millennium, as it is in other periods of Irish ecclesiastical history. Several contributions to these conference proceedings treat of this earliest period of Christian ministration. Accordingly, it may seem rather banal to begin by stressing the importance of pastoral provision. Yet it is appropriate, because it has only recently been recognised that there is a story to tell about the pastoral ministry of the early Irish Church. Remarkably, pastoral care as offered by the pre-Norman Irish Church is a matter first seriously considered only a generation ago, by P.J. Corish.[1] Corish wrote as an early modernist, without specialist expertise in the period. Disinterested and perceptive, however, he found the account of the early Irish Church in the published literature wanting. One might expect that the nature of pastoral ministration would be central to any investigation of the role of the Church in early Irish society (the subject of Katherine Hughes' survey[2] that had appeared a few years before Corish's study). Yet Hughes and her predecessors gave very little attention to the subject.[3] In retrospect, this is a startling omission. It is the major defect of the 'monastic' model of early Irish church organisation. This model was arguably spawned by Reeves, influentially espoused by Ryan and Kenney and endorsed in the final third of the twentieth century by Hughes' standard textbook.[4]

The chief value of Corish's observations was simply to highlight in general terms the inadequate account of pastoral ministration current in the 1970s. More specifically, although he regarded *Ríagal Phátraic* ('The Rule of Patrick'), in particular, as attesting to a ministry to the laity in general, he proposed that

1 P.J. Corish, 'The pastoral mission in the early Irish Church' in *Léachtaí Cholm Cille*, 2 (1971), 14–25; idem, *The Christian mission* (Dublin, 1972). 2 K. Hughes, *The Church in early Irish society* (London, 1966). 3 Hughes, *The Church*, 140 did cite *Ríagal Phátraic* as evidence of a ministry to the Church's *manaig*. 4 W. Reeves, *The life of Saint Columba, founder of Hy: written by Adamnan* (Dublin, 1857), 336 n.; J.F. Kenney, *Sources for the early history of Ireland: 1 ecclesiastical* (New York, 1929), 291–2, 329; idem, 'St Patrick and the Patrick legend' in *Thought*, 8 (1933–4), 5–34, 213–39: 215–21; J. Ryan, *Irish monasticism: origins and early development* (London, 1931); Hughes, *The Church*; cf. C. Etchingham, *Church organisation in Ireland, AD 650 to 1000* (Maynooth, 1999), 13, 15–17, 19–20.

canon lawyers' attempts to introduce tithes were unrealistic and that the level of religious practice in early Irish society at large was minimal.[5] In the early 1980s Ó Corráin offered passing comments on pastoral ministration and payment of dues, in the guise of tithes and the like. He maintained that the system envisaged in Old Irish (i.e. pre-900) prescriptive texts, such as *Ríagal Phátraic* and *Córus Bésgnai*, is likely to have been restricted in practice to the particular dependants of the Church known as *manaig*.[6] A few years later, Ó Corráin again invoked *Córus Bésgnai*, but this time as evidence that the system of pastoral care and dues was intended to apply to the populace at large. His earlier and contrary opinion was passed over in silence, and his apparent change of view was not explained.[7]

In the same volume in which the latter interpretation appeared, Richard Sharpe presented a fundamental critique of the 'monastic' model of early Irish church organisation in its entirety.[8] Sharpe expressly acknowledged his debt to Corish, whom he credited with drawing attention to previously neglected elements of the primary sources that bear on pastoral ministration.[9] Sharpe professed to detect, in the Ireland to which *Ríagal Phátraic* is a witness, 'one of the most comprehensive pastoral organizations in northern Europe'.[10] Clancy made a similarly positive assessment of early medieval Scotland.[11] It should be noted, on the other hand, that Sharpe also wondered if religious practice was regular among the general public in early medieval Ireland.[12] In the 1990s the present writer re-examined in detail the evidence relating to pastoral care and dues and re-appraised the impact on the laity in general. My judgment was that the operation of a system of regular pastoral ministration and payment of reciprocal dues is likely to have been limited in practice to 'paramonastic'

---

5 Corish, *Christian mission*, 32–41; see also idem, 'Pastoral mission', passim. 6 D. Ó Corráin, 'The early Irish churches: some aspects of organisation' in D. Ó Corráin (ed.), *Irish antiquity: essays and studies presented to Professor M.J. O'Kelly* (Cork, 1981), 327–41: 334; previously Hughes, *The Church*, 140 and C. Doherty, 'Exchange and trade in early medieval Ireland' in *JRSAI*, 110 (1980), 67–89: 75 cited *Ríagal Phátraic* for a ministry to *manaig*; cf. Ó Corráin's remarks on strict regulation of marriage and sexual mores for *manaig* and devout laity in his 'Women in early Irish society' in D. Ó Corráin and M. MacCurtain (eds), *Women in Irish society: the historical dimension* (Dublin, 1978), 1–13: 7. 7 In D. Ó Corráin, L. Breatnach and A. Breen, 'The laws of the Irish' in *Peritia*, 3 (1984), 382–438: 410. 8 R. Sharpe, 'Some problems concerning the organisation of the Church in early medieval Ireland' in *Peritia*, 3 (1984), 230–270; cf. idem, 'Churches and communities in early medieval Ireland: towards a pastoral model' in J. Blair and R. Sharpe (eds), *Pastoral care before the parish* (Leicester, 1992), 81–109. 9 Sharpe, 'Some problems', 252 and n. 6; *pace* D. Ó Cróinín, who stated recently, with reference to Sharpe's comments on *Ríagal Phátraic*, that he was 'seemingly unaware that Professor Patrick Corish had discussed it more than ten years previously ... as I pointed out in my *Early medieval Ireland, 400–1200* in 1995' (Review of Etchingham, *Church organisation*, in *Peritia*, 15 (2001), 413–20: 417); cf. C. Etchingham, 'Early medieval Irish history' in K. McCone and K. Simms (eds), *Progress in medieval Irish studies* (Maynooth, 1996), 123–53: 151. 10 Sharpe, 'Churches and communities', 108–9. 11 T.O. Clancy, 'Annat in Scotland and the origins of the parish' in *Innes Review*, 46 (1995), 91–115: 93–5; cf. Etchingham, *Church organisation*, 249, 256, 429. 12 Sharpe, 'Churches and communities', 82.

manaig-dependants of the Church.[13] I proposed that such ministration had a limited impact on the wider laity. Accordingly, on this matter I found myself in closer agreement with Corish and Ó Corráin of 1981, than with Ó Corráin of 1984 and Sharpe.

If the evidence has been variously interpreted since the 1970s, there is widespread agreement that pastoral ministration requires serious consideration in any new account of the early Irish Church. Such agreement is not entirely unanimous, however. Ó Cróinín rejected the fundamental revision that was prompted by Corish and taken up by Sharpe and myself. This is exemplified by his treatment of *parochia* or, in Hiberno-Latin spelling, *paruchia*. This term has pastoral connotations, of course, and gives rise to the vocabulary of parochial organisation. Much of the traditional model of early Irish Church organisation depends, however, on an understanding of *paruchia* as a peculiarly monastic, dispersed jurisdictional entity, rather than a spatially defined, clerico-pastoral one. Ó Cróinín invoked the concept of the so-called 'monastic *paruchia*', 'a *paruchia* of far-flung dependencies',[14] as disseminated by Kenney and Hughes. His confidence in the authority of these writers' ideas, as against the results of a painstaking examination of the primary sources, was apparently unshaken, but unfortunately no actual evidence, old or new, was adduced in support in support of this position.

Ó Cróinín did offer what appears to be a new theory, however. He stated that 'the term *paruchia* (in that spelling) has always existed in Ireland as a separate concept from *parochia*, and its technical definition "monastic federation" (coined by Kenney, not Kathleen Hughes), in the sense of a non-territorial unit of jurisdiction was clear to contemporaries, whatever about modern scholars'.[15] This is indeed a singular claim, made in response to what the present writer had deduced from the primary sources about the connotations of *parochia*/*paruchia*. Unfortunately, Ó Cróinín did not support the novel dichotomy he proposed between the two spellings with any alternative assessment of the data on *parochia*/*paruchia* in these primary sources. Textual scholars and others have hitherto regarded the opposition *parochia*/*paruchia* as merely ortho-graphic.[16] They will doubtless be surprised but perhaps not necessarily persuaded by Ó Cróinín's proposition. While Okham's razor is generally a blunt instrument in the hands of a historian, it is not always without merit.

To rehearse the evidence of the relevant Irish primary sources would be out of place here.[17] Suffice it to reiterate that, where these elucidate the meaning of

---

13 C. Etchingham, 'The early Irish Church: some observations on pastoral care and dues' in *Ériu*, 42 (1991), 99–118; Etchingham, *Church organisation*, 239–318.   14 Ó Cróinín, 'Review of Etchingham', 416.   15 Ibid., 419; in point of fact Reeves seems to have been the first to propose this meaning for the term, for which he used the conventional spelling *parochia* (see Etchingham, *Church organisation*, 13).   16 See Etchingham, *Church organisation*, 125–6 n.; Ó Cróinín was evidently displeased by this note, but did not spell out his reasons (op. cit., 419).   17 Etchingham, *Church organisation*, 106–30.

parochia/paruchia, it is evidently a sphere of pastoral jurisdiction over people or territory. *Pace* Ó Cróinín, one must repeat that the 'monastic *paruchia*' is altogether elusive in early medieval texts and is merely a conceit of modern scholarship.[18] Sharpe's judgement that the use of the term *paruchia* 'by recent historians … has crept further and further from that found in the early sources'[19] seems thoroughly justified. A contrary view will surely carry more conviction if founded in counter argument from the sources, than if it consists of mere assertion. With particular reference to the theme of this volume, it should be noted that *parochia/paruchia* in an early medieval Irish context does not denote jurisdiction at the (proto-) parochial level of the priest. Instead, in Ireland as elsewhere in the early centuries of the Church's history, the term refers to the larger sphere of jurisdiction pertaining to the bishop.

Ó Cróinín chided writers such as Sharpe and myself for what he termed an 'obsessive concern with an imagined pastoral role for the early Irish churches'.[20] Earlier writers were doubtless guilty of neglecting the Church's pastoral role, but none, to my knowledge, went so far as to suggest that it had no such role in reality. In the absence of evidence presented in support of the proposition, one can only assume that it was not Ó Cróinín's intention to seem to espouse such a view, but that he was misrepresented by a less than happy choice of words. The sources that shed light on the pastoral ministration of the early Irish Church are not abundant, but they have been highlighted by recent work and their existence is undeniable. In truth, it would seem, rather, that an obsession with the supposedly all-embracing 'monasticism' of the early Irish Church explains previous scholarly neglect of the pastoral ministry. Thus the remnants of the exclusively 'monastic' model of organisation are still to be seen in the vocabulary of some contemporary writers.

If evidence for the pastoral ministry of the early Irish Church is limited in quantity, it is also, as we have seen, open to various (and varying) interpretations. This is obviously neither the time nor the place to restate the case made in my book in a manner that, I gather, some have found to be exhaustive, in at least one sense of the word.[21] I make no claim to have uttered the last word on the subject, but the point to be emphasised is the ambiguity of the evidence. There are, on the one hand, statements that seem to imply a system of pastoral care and dues that is all embracing, involving the whole of the populace. On the other hand, there are apparent indications that a regular application of the

18 Much of what modern scholarship has portrayed as characteristic of the 'monastic *paruchia*', including its supposedly 'monastic' essence and the dispersed distribution of its components, is associated in the contemporary sources with *familia*, not *paruchia*. My efforts to chart carefully the real distinctions between these terms and the extent to which they overlap (Etchingham, *Church organisation*, 126–30, 223–37) were not discussed by Ó Cróinín. 19 Sharpe, 'Some problems', 243. 20 Ó Cróinín, 'Review of Etchingham', 414. 21 See, for example, reviews and short notices by R. Roche in *Irish Times*, 1 July 2000; by Ó Cróinín, 'Review of Etchingham'; by T.M. Charles-Edwards in *English Historical Review*, 116 (2001), 920–21; by P. Ó Néill in *Éigse*, 33 (2002), 243–5.

system was restricted in practice to the *manaig*-dependants of the Church. This essential ambiguity has been detected in a range of sources, but it is most starkly exhibited in *Ríagal Phátraic*.[22] As we have already seen, this is a crucial text for all modern writers about the ministry.

Ó Cróinín makes the valid point that the precise provenance, status and date of *Ríagal Phátraic* – and, indeed, of other vernacular prescriptive texts – are not certain.[23] If, however, we were to disallow all texts that are open to such an objection on one or more grounds, the body of source-material for early Irish history would be greatly reduced. Presumably such an outcome would not be welcome in any quarter. In particular, we should hardly wish to revert to an environment in which historians did not trouble to study the vernacular laws, in the apparent belief that they did not illuminate early medieval Ireland so much as prehistoric Indo-European institutions.[24] In truth, the exercise of a proper critical methodology requires no such excessive positivism. First-hand familiarity with the actual contents of vernacular prescriptive texts, including *Ríagal Phátraic*, should prove the best antidote to misgivings about their value.[25]

In the case of *Ríagal Phátraic*, the text can be dated, at least broadly, on linguistic grounds, as we shall see. There are further considerations that illuminate its purpose and provenance. Responsibility for observing its prescriptions 'is incumbent upon the souls of the men of Ireland (*fir Érenn*) in virtue of Patrick's injunction'. The latter remark points to involvement by Armagh or, conceivably, by other churches that identified with the Patrician cult.[26] Those who framed this blueprint for pastoral ministry accordingly invoked the highest saintly authority and evidently aspired to an island-wide implementation, although the identification of *Ríagal Phátraic* with *Cáin Phátraic* of the annals, recently advocated by Kelly, may be questioned.[27] Kelly re-assessed the textual character of *Ríagal Phátraic* in a valuable and thought provoking commentary. Noteworthy is her suggestion of a ninth-century (i.e. late Old Irish) date, as against the widespread assumption heretofore that *Ríagal Phátraic* is a product of the eighth century.[28] Her reasons for this re-dating were not spelled out, but a

---

22 The fullest discussion is at Etchingham, *Church organisation*, 250–8.   23 Ó Cróinín, 'Review of Etchingham, 417–18.   24 Etchingham, 'Early medieval Irish history', 124–7.   25 On Ó Cróinín's view of the vernacular legal material and of the modern secondary literature thereon, see Etchingham, 'Early medieval Irish history', 150–1.   26 Etchingham, *Church organisation*, 198–9, 251; that the promotion of the cult of Patrick should not automatically be identified with the interests of Armagh is shown by C. Swift, 'Tírechán's motives in compiling the *Collectanea*: an alternative interpretation' in *Ériu*, 45 (1994), 53–82.   27 P. Kelly, 'The Rule of Patrick: textual affinities' in P. Ní Chatháin and M. Richter (eds), *Ireland and Europe in the early Middle Ages: texts and transmission* (Dublin, 2002), 284–95; cf. D.A. Binchy (ed.), *Corpus iuris Hibernici*, 6 vols (Dublin, 1978), i, x. Among objections to this identification are that *Ríagal Phátraic*, at least as it stands, does not treat of the killing of clerics (cf. Etchingham, *Church organisation*, 202; Kelly, 'Rule of Patrick' 288), while other references in the vernacular laws to *Cáin Phátraic* suggest that *Ríagal Phátraic* is not the referend (see e.g. Etchingham, *Church organisation*, 203).   28 Kelly, 'Rule of Patrick', 287.

ninth-century date, if sustainable, would add a further dimension to the context. *Riagal Phátraic* would then testify to the continued relevance, after 800, of the bishop's jurisdiction over a system of regular pastoral care that was, as I have argued, geared in practice primarily to the Church's *manaig*-dependants. Also of significance here is Kelly's case that a variant version of the text is a Middle Irish reworking of a putative Latin original, in support of which she adduced textual evidence.[29] This would imply the continuing relevance of the provisions of *Riagal Pháraic* after the ninth century. Whenever precisely, within the Old Irish period, the earlier extant version of *Riagal Phátraic* was composed (perhaps most likely between about 750 and 850), there is no reason to question the value of its contemporary testimony about the operation of the pastoral ministry.

With particular reference to the theme of this paper, *Riagal Phátraic* may illuminate a little the spatial range of a priest's pastoral activity. It declares that the scarcity of priests 'in the (lay) communities' (*lasna túatha*) may require that three or four churches be in the care of a single priest. The minimum service expected of a priest serving such churches is 'communion and baptism for the souls of all and mass on solemn days and feast-days on their altars'. Seemingly he need not attend each church every Sunday, but only on major feast days. The next paragraph accordingly prescribes as a key element of his fee 'a meal for four (*pruind cethrair*) at Christmas, Easter and Pentecost'. Even this minimal frequency of pastoral ministration appears, from the context, to be provided not for the generality of the laity, but for the churches' peculiar dependants known as *manaig*.[30] The churches concerned must have been relatively proximate, if each could be visited on the same day, even on an infrequent basis, and even assuming the priest travelled on horseback or by carriage. This passage may be considered alongside various indications that the *túath* or *plebs*, in the sense of the minimal polity or 'petty kingdom' of early Ireland, might be the typical sphere of activity either of a priest, or of a cleric of episcopal rank.[31] Unfortunately, research has not as yet clarified the spatial dimensions of the minimal polity to which *túath/plebs* sometimes refers. Accordingly, one cannot be sure as to how extensive a priestly sphere of pastoral ministration might be in reality.

Riagal Phátraic finds an echo in a revealing anecdote in the early (perhaps eighth-century) *Vita* of Colmán of Lynally, Co. Offaly. Here an individual, described both as a *monachus* of the saint and a *laicus fidelis* 'faithful layman', repaired to the saint to receive the sacrament only *diebus solempnibus* 'on solemn days'. Even such a level of religious practice was thought remarkable and distinguished the practitioner from the generality of the laity. One is reminded of the account, in *Bethu Brigte* (the Old Irish 'Life of Brigit'), of the Easter-week visitation of Kildare by bishop Mel. Brigit and her virgins pay him a fee for preaching and celebrating mass and also provide for a feast to celebrate the

---

29 Ibid., 291.   **30** Etchingham, *Church organisation*, 254–5.   **31** Ibid., 134–45.

pastoral visitation.[32] This literary reconstruction, in the eighth century or perhaps the ninth,[33] of the formative era of the Irish Church, assumes that even committed Christians might enjoy no more than an intermittent pastoral ministry. This is an assumption that accords well with that of the *Vita* of Colmán of Lynally, while *Ríagal Phátraic*, a text of roughly the same period, reflects a similarly limited expectation. As Swift points out to me, an anecdote recounted by Adomnán in the late seventh century may also bespeak such a context. Here the Eucharist was rarely available and it might be put to relatively unusual spiritual purposes. Columba instructed his disciple Silnán to bring the sacred bread, blessed by the saint, to the region north of Dublin, not for distribution to the faithful in conventional fashion, but there to be dipped in water for use to cure men and beasts afflicted by pestiferous rain.[34]

I have interpreted elsewhere references in a variety of sources as indicating that quite a limited pastoral ministry obtained in practice, alongside the notion that the ministry was of general benefit to society. Moreover, I have also argued that such a scenario makes sense of evidence pointing to the existence, in early medieval Ireland, of an elective Christian elite, whom I have termed 'paramonastics', and who are distinguished from the rest of society by their permanently repentant status.[35] A pastoral ministry that was itinerant and intermittent, even for some of this elite, is reminiscent of the model of the English minster churches, a model that originally inspired Sharpe in his critique of the prevailing orthodoxy regarding Irish church organisation.[36] An example from Bede may be mentioned: he lauded Cuthbert for visiting outlying communities that rarely if ever saw a minister.[37]

A possible indicator of the operation of pastoral 'mother-churches' or minster-churches in the Gaelic world is the distribution of stone carving associated with the subsidiary churches of both Iona and Clonmacnoise. Swift discusses such material in a recent paper, for access to which in advance of publication I am grateful. She has studied grave-slabs and other stone carving at church sites on Islay and in Cos. Offaly and Westmeath. These churches are otherwise connected with Iona and Clonmacnoise, respectively, whose styles of stone carving were apparently followed by their subsidiaries.

---

32 For all of this see conveniently Etchingham, *Church organisation*, 254–5, 263–4. **33** See discussion of the date of the Life by D. Ó hAodha (ed.), *Bethu Brigte* (Dublin, 1978), xxv–xxvii, and the linguistic data presented ibid., 66–87. **34** M.O. Anderson, *Adomnán's Life of Columba* (revised edn, Oxford, 1991), 98–101 (II § 4). **35** Etchingham, *Church organisation*, chapters 6 and 7; Ó Cróinín, 'Review of Etchingham, 419, suggests that chapter 7 should have been 'jettisoned'; cf. Ó Corráin's term 'para-clerical', used of the 'church tenants', 'Marriage in early Ireland' in A. Cosgrove (ed.), *Marriage in Ireland* (Dublin, 1985), 5–24: 18. **36** See e.g. Blair and Sharpe (eds), *Pastoral care before the parish*, passim. **37** B. Colgrave (ed.), *Two lives of Saint Cuthbert* (Cambridge, 1940), 184–7 § 9, drawn to my attention by Swift; cf. Ó Cróinín's statement that the Northumbrian situation conforms to the model of an Irish 'monastic *paruchia*' (op. cit., 416–17), beside alternative interpretations (such as the 'minster' model), canvassed by the present writer and others (e.g. Etchingham, *Church organisation*, 459).

Swift conjectures that links between superior and subsidiary churches involved not only stone carving, but also pastoral ministration, so that the subsidiaries might be envisaged as 'proto-parochial' churches. The evidence is insufficient to demonstrate this beyond doubt, but Swift remarks that food- and other renders paid by the subsidiaries could be likened to those payable by *manaig* for priestly services in *Ríagal Phátraic*. It may be significant that the Islay sites are recorded later as medieval parochial churches or chapels, while Bealin/ Twyford (of high cross fame) was a rectory of Clonmacnoise in the early fourteenth century.[38]

The limits of pastoral ministration in early medieval Ireland, as I would see it, are exemplified by the continuing burial of laity in unconsecrated ground. This particular matter is one to which I referred briefly on a previous occasion.[39] I should like to take this opportunity to comment further, especially in the light of evidence newly come to light. Some years ago Charles-Edwards recognised that the eighth-century Irish canon law collection, known as the *Hibernensis*, attests to the practice of burial in unconsecrated ground. Sharpe too was aware of evidence that burial did not necessarily take place in church precincts.[40] This evidence sits well with *Córus Bésgnai*'s prescribing a fee for burial in consecrated ground, a fee that amounts to the deceased's 'honour-price', or quantification of status. *Córus Bésgnai* also insists that any bequest/ burial payment (*imnae*) must be from the individual's personal resources and must leave no charge upon his/her kindred's estate.[41] These regulations indicate a potential tension between obligations to kin and provision for full Christian burial. It may be envisaged that, in such a socio-legal climate, there might be a real disincentive to burial in church precincts. In recent times, striking new evidence that there was a positive preference for burial elsewhere has been provided by archaeologists.

Noteworthy is the work of O'Brien, who has drawn together archaeological and documentary evidence to argue for the persistence up to about AD 700 of burial other than in consecrated Christian cemeteries. Archaeologically, this practice manifests itself as isolated burials, circular enclosures and kindred/ familial cemeteries. O'Brien relates this to documentary evidence that, in the late seventh century, the Church sought to encourage burial in Christian cemeteries.[42] In the light of the documentary evidence, O'Brien interpreted dated archaeological material as being consistent with a turning point around AD 700, after which burials in unconsecrated contexts are not found. This

38 C. Swift, 'Grave-slabs of Clonmacnoise and the people they commemorate' in H. King (ed.), *Clonmacnoise studies*, 2 (Dublin, 2003), 105–24.   39 Etchingham, *Church organisation*, 269, 273.   40 T. M. Charles-Edwards, 'The pastoral role of the Church in the early Irish laws' in Blair and Sharpe (eds), *Pastoral care*, 63–80: 76 n. 74; Sharpe, 'Churches and communities', 82. 41 Etchingham, *Church organisation*, 244–5, 272–4.   42 E. O'Brien, 'Christian burial in Ireland: continuity and change' in N. Edwards and A. Lane (eds), *The early Church in Wales and the west* (Oxford, 1992), 130–7.

analysis was borne out by O'Brien's recent excavations at Ballymacaward, Co. Donegal, where she detected a 'seventh-century horizon [which] represents the final stage of use for burial purposes of the monument at Ballymacaward, probably because it was in this period that the Church started to urge Christians to abandon burial among their pagan ancestors and to bury instead among the 'saints'.[43]

Granted the importance of O'Brien's archaeological discoveries, one wonders if the postulated change of practice at the end of the seventh century is well founded. In fact, it would seem that the documentary evidence for 'non-Christian' burial practices reflects the eighth century as well as the seventh. This is the period to which belongs the *Hibernensis*, one of the key documentary sources for such practices, cited by Charles-Edwards, Sharpe and O'Brien. In vernacular law, the ritualised procedure of legal entry to establish title to land involved crossing *fert*/*fertae* 'mound(s)' at the boundary of the estate. The indications are that these were burial-mounds, presumed to be those of the landowners' ancestors, and the law-text in which the practice is mentioned forms a component of the eighth-century *Senchas Már*. In establishing a claim to land as a kindred heir, the symbolic significance of thus traversing the graves of reputed ancestors is obvious. Indeed, it seems reasonable to draw a general connection with another phenomenon attested in the law-tracts, that is, in the period extending into the eighth century. Ogam stones could prove title to land, presumably as the memorials of claimed ancestors, if not as actual burial markers, for which archaeological evidence is lacking.[44] To refer the symbolism of traversing ancestors' graves to pagan beliefs, as Charles-Edwards did, perhaps prejudges the issue. Conversely, reluctance on the part of McManus to allow ogam inscriptions as boundary markers anything other than the 'practical' function of 'communicating information … in a straightforward way' bespeaks, perhaps, an unduly utilitarian preconception.[45]

Considerable interest attaches to the recently published excavation by Charles Mount of a site at Knoxspark, near Ballysadare, Co. Sligo. This seems to be a cemetery, but without apparent ecclesiastical associations. Here, Mount uncovered no less than 185 inhumation-burials, and he estimated the existence of about 100 more such burials. The inhumations were accompanied by a single cremation-burial, which was deposited in one of two stone cairns on the site.

43 E. O'Brien, 'Excavation of a multi-period burial site at Ballymacaward, Ballyshannon, Co. Donegal' in *Donegal Annual*, 51 (1999), 56–61: 60–1. 44 For all of this see Binchy, *Corpus iuris*, i, 206.21, 207.23; ii, 596.8; v, 1566.6–7; vi, 2019.16; see T. Charles-Edwards, 'Boundaries in Irish law' in P. Sawyer (ed.), *Medieval settlement: continuity and change* (London, 1976), 83–7: 83 n. 3; idem, *Early Irish and Welsh kinship* (Oxford, 1993), 259–65; F. Kelly, *A guide to early Irish law* (Dublin, 1988), 186, 204; D. McManus, *A guide to ogam* (Maynooth, 1991), 163–6; C. Swift, 'Pagan monuments and Christian legal centres in early Meath' in *Ríocht na Midhe*, 9 (1996), 1–26: 13–18; cf. Binchy, *Corpus iuris*, i, 24.2, 7–9, where *fert* is explained as an ecclesiastical enclosure; for archaeological evidence on the function of ogam stones see C. Swift, *Ogam stones and the earliest Irish Christians* (Maynooth, 1997), 42–4. 45 McManus, *Ogam*, 165.

Remarkably, the burials, including the cremation, produced a number of radio-carbon dates that are consistent with deposition between the eighth and the tenth centuries. An eighth- or ninth-century gold filigree disk was found in the cairn containing the cremation. The inhumations have an east-west orientation, which would seem to suggest the adoption of a Christian-influenced practice in an apparently non-ecclesiastical cemetery. Possible evidence of decapitation has been detected in the case of some of the inhumation-burials, one of which is also associated with a socketed spear-head.[46] The excavator resorted to the model of burial in a period of pagan-Christian transition in the early centuries of the historic era, as envisaged by O'Brien and others.[47] The archaeological dates provided by his findings, however, would appear to require more radical interpretation as indicating the persistence of communal burial in a non-ecclesiastical environment in the last quarter of the first millennium.

It is plausible, therefore, that burial of the general laity in ecclesiastical precincts, far from being normal, may well have been relatively unusual in the first millennium. The evidence accords with Swift's study of the persons commemorated on grave-slab inscriptions, especially at Clonmacnoise. Notwithstanding literary and annalistic references to royal burials at Clonmacnoise, Swift makes the case that the vast bulk of extant inscriptions commemorate ecclesiastical professionals, especially those in higher clerical orders, together with those whom we may describe as 'committed Christians' or the 'paramonastic' Christian elite. There is very little evidence that surviving inscribed cross-slabs commemorate the generality of the laity.[48]

In sum, then, we may fairly observe that there is now widespread, if not universal agreement that pastoral ministration by the early Irish Church must be considered seriously. There is no consensus as to how the relevant evidence is to be interpreted, however. Ó Corráin has held to the position he first adopted in print in 1984, namely, that pastoral provision for the general laity was extensive and intensive. The present writer clearly shares neither that perspective, nor Ó Corráin's optimistic conviction that a proto-parochial structure for pastoral care existed in Ireland in the first millennium. There is obviously much scope for debate. It would surely be folly, however, not to recognise the essential ambiguity of *Ríagal Phátraic* and other contemporary sources that shed light on the pastoral ministry in early Ireland. It will scarcely suffice to argue selectively only from those passages of the texts that can be invoked in support of universal pastoral care, without attempting to account for the data that points to a different conclusion. An effort to evaluate all such data that seemed pertinent was made in detail in my book.

---

46 C. Mount, 'The promontory fort, inhumation cemetery and sub-rectangular enclosure at Knoxspark, Co. Sligo' in M. Timoney (ed.), *A celebration of Sligo: first essays for Sligo Field Club* (Sligo, 2002), 103–116.   47 Mount, 'Knoxspark', 114–15.   48 C. Swift, 'Early medieval Irish grave-slabs and their inscriptions' in *Durham Archaeological Journal,* 14/15 (1999), 111–18.

CONCLUSION

In drawing this paper to a conclusion, we may seek to explain the essential ambiguity of the evidence along something like the following lines. Members of the paramonastic Christian elite were closely bound to their churches, as recipients of more or less frequent pastoral care and, correspondingly, as payers of regular dues. Although this system involved directly only a minority in society, its maintenance was regarded as both a duty and a benefit for society in general, the *fir Érenn* 'men of Ireland' of *Ríagal Phátraic*. *Córus Bésgnai* may also bear witness to this, in a passage that I read differently from Ó Corráin. This declares *cóir ecalsa ó túaith: dechmada 7 prímite 7 prímgene dliged ecalsa dia memraib* 'the church's entitlement from the lay community: tithes and first fruits and firstlings are the right of the church from its members'.[49] For an appreciation of the significance of this, it is vital to realise that *memra* 'members' has the specific legal meaning of 'dependants'. It follows that we have to do, in this context, with the paramonastic elite that is sometimes designated *manaig*.[50]

In a significant passage of *Córus Bésgnai*, it is stated that the Church depends on lords (*flatha*) to levy dues on their clients, and on each great lord to levy his subject (lay) communities (*cach marflaith fora túatha*).[51] The basis of levying more widely than on a church's direct dependants was, therefore, comparatively precarious, in that it relied on the co-operation of the secular elite. Was this not likely often to be a counsel of perfection? To be sure, evidence of the reality of intervention by secular powers in support of ecclesiastical claims is to be found. One might instance Dub Dá Leithe of Armagh's visitation of Munster in 973, when Mathgamain mac Cennétig, king of Munster, endorsed Armagh's pretensions, as against those of Emly. By the same token, Mathgamain's younger brother and successor, Brian Bóruime, lent his support to Armagh and endorsed levies based on its apostolic, pastoral claims, as indicated by the famous inscription entered in the Book of Armagh in 1005.[52] Such favourable political accords may not always have been available, however. The basic network of pastoral care and dues was, in all likelihood, confined to the Church's particular dependants, the paramonastic *manaig*. The operation of this restricted network was itself seen as beneficial to society in general, however, rather as the professional intercession with the deity by the *oratores* 'those who pray' was undertaken on behalf of the rest of society in the classic model of the high middle ages.

This may be termed the benevolent clerical perception of the relationship between the more fully Christian elite, those I have dubbed 'paramonastics',

---

49 Binchy, *Corpus iuris*, ii, 530.32–3 (text; length-marks, punctuation and translation are mine).
50 Etchingham, *Church organisation*, 266–7, 285, 365, 372, 392, 424–5. **51** Binchy, *Corpus iuris*, ii, 526.20–21. **52** S. Mac Airt (ed.), *The Annals of Inisfallen* (Dublin, 1951), AD 973; A. Gwynn, 'Brian in Armagh, 1005' in *Seanchas Ard Mhacha*, 9 (1978–79), 35–50.

and the rest of society. From another perspective, however, ecclesiastical zealots viewed most of this nominally Christian society as leading a deeply sinful life of illicit violence and concupiscence, for which eternal damnation was the price to be paid, in the absence of a deliberate act of repentance. The present writer has argued that the centrality of repentance and penance to early Irish religious culture is to be explained in terms of this ideology of a truly Christian elite, contrasted with a majority steeped in sinfulness. The 'paramonastic' class included many who lived under a regime of perpetual, perfective penitence, having converted from the ways of the world.[53] For some, at least, among the lay aristocracy, whose doings are reported in the annals, it would seem that such conversion might be undertaken late in life. That, at any rate, is how one may interpret frequent reference to the adoption by such individuals of 'the clerical state' (*clericatus*), before their deaths in ecclesiastical retirement after repentance (*penitentia*).[54] One may suggest a parallel, perhaps, with the situation in late Antiquity, when baptism on the deathbed or upon retirement was replaced by early baptism. In consequence, repentance in old age became the safeguard against damnation for the nominal Christian who was regarded as living most of his life in sin.[55]

The Irish evidence, then, may bespeak the coexistence of benign and rigorous clerical perspectives on the mass of society. Both perspectives, however, presuppose a situation in reality that was far removed from the extensive and intensive system of pastoral care that some commentators envisage.

53 Etchingham, *Church organisation*, 290–318. 54 See e.g. S. MacAirt and G. Mac Niocaill (eds), *The Annals of Ulster (to 1131)* (Dublin, 1983) at AD 688, 689, 705, 723, 731, 740, 744, 765, 768, 782, 783, 784, 789, 826, 849, 861, 867, 869, 880, 885, 890, 903, 909, 912, 915, 917, 925, 933, 948, 949, 975, 980. 55 See A.H.M. Jones, *The later Roman empire, 284–602*, 3 vols (Oxford, 1964), ii, 979–85; iii, 329–30.

Church buildings and pastoral care in early medieval Ireland

TOMÁS Ó CARRAGÁIN

The issue of pastoral care in early medieval Ireland has only come to prominence quite recently as part of a major re-evaluation of early ecclesiastical organisation. The overwhelmingly monastic Church described by scholars like Binchy and Ryan[1] has been replaced with one characterised by a degree of functional diversity. Episcopal churches, *túath* churches associated with secular population groups, and minor proprietary churches now feature more prominently in the literature; and the interaction of monasteries with secular society is also better documented.[2] Nonetheless, the extent to which the population at large enjoyed pastoral care remains a controversial subject; and Etchingham in particular is adamant that it was usually restricted to monastic tenants.[3]

Confronted with a dense network of church sites on the ground, many archaeologists have readily taken to the idea that some were involved in pastoral care. Thus, while Henry had accepted the orthodoxy that they had to be eremitic monasteries, Thomas realised that many must have been 'subservient to popular needs'.[4] However, in contrast to the situation in England and on the

1 J. Ryan, *Irish monasticism: origins and early development* (London, 1931); D.A. Binchy, 'Patrick and his biographers, ancient and modern' in *Studia Hibernica*, 2 (1962), 7–173.   2 D. Ó Corráin, 'The early Irish churches: some aspects of organisation' in D. Ó Corráin (ed.), *Irish antiquity: essays and studies presented to Professor M.J. O'Kelly* (Cork, 1981), 327–41; R. Sharpe, 'Some problems concerning the organisation of the church in early medieval Ireland' in *Peritia*, 3 (1984), 230–70; R. Sharpe, 'Churches and communities in early medieval Ireland: towards a pastoral model' in J. Blair and R. Sharpe (eds), *Pastoral care before the parish* (Leicester, 1992), 81–109; T. Charles-Edwards, 'The pastoral role of the church in the early Irish laws' in Blair and Sharpe (eds) *Pastoral care*, 63–80; C. Etchingham, 'The early Irish Church: some observations on pastoral care and dues' in *Ériu*, 42 (1991), 99–118; C. Etchingham, *Church organisation in Ireland, AD 650 to 1000* (Maynooth, 1999).   3 Etchingham, this volume; Etchingham, 'The early Irish church', 106–9, 112–13; Etchingham, *Church organisation*, 289, 308, 311, 316; see also Ó Corráin, 'The early Irish churches', 334; D. Ó Cróinín, *Early medieval Ireland, 400–1200* (Dublin, 1995), 167. For a Scottish perspective see T. Clancy, 'Annat in Scotland and the origins of the parish' in *Innes Review*, 46 (1995), 91–115.   4 F. Henry, 'Early monasteries, beehive huts, and dry-stone houses in the neighbourhood of Caherciveen and Waterville (Co. Kerry)' in *PRIA*, 58C (1957), 45–166: 157; C. Thomas, *The early Christian archaeology of north Britain* (London, 1971), 80; C. Thomas, 'Recognising Christian origins: an archaeological and historical dilemma' in L.A.S. Butler and R.K. Morris (eds), *The Anglo-Saxon Church: papers on history, architecture and archae-*

Continent (see p. 94), the contribution of archaeology to our understanding of the issue has been quite limited. This paper is presented as a preliminary, and inevitably tentative, discussion of the pastoral functions of the surviving group of pre-Romanesque churches.[5] These can be divided into a number of different types[6], but for the purposes of this paper I will first consider the mortared churches as a group, and will then turn to the dry-stone churches which are largely confined to peninsular Kerry (fig. 1). An essential premise of the study is that general patterns discernable from the surviving group broadly reflect the situation in the early medieval period.[7]

CHANGES TO THE ECCLESIASTICAL NETWORK, *c.*900–1100

The dating of the mortared churches is a complex issue and not our principal concern here. Architectural simplicity and a lack of structural timbers mean that the annals provide the best available chronological framework, indicating that almost all mortared churches are tenth- to early twelfth-century.[8] Elsewhere, I have attempted to refine this chronology based on a combination

ology in honour of Dr H. Taylor. CBA Report 60 (London, 1986), 121–5: 124. **5** The information used derives from a country-wide survey which formed the basis for a PhD thesis which was not directly concerned with pastoral care: T. Ó Carragáin, 'Pre-Romanesque churches in Ireland: interpreting archaeological regionalisms', unpublished PhD (University College Cork, 2002). The term pre-Romanesque is not without its problems. As a number of writers have pointed out, some of the churches considered here are Romanesque in so far as they are contemporary with Romanesque buildings abroad and make use of 'Roman' forms, most notably the true arch. See, for example, M. Stokes, 'Introduction' in E. Dunraven, *Notes on Irish architecture* (London, 1875), xxv; H. Leask, *Irish churches and monastic buildings*, i (Dundalk, 1955), 79. Recently O'Keeffe has argued that such churches should be seen as belonging to an architectural phase of the late 1000s and early 1100s which he terms the 'First Irish Romanesque', T. O'Keeffe, 'Architectural traditions of the early medieval church in Munster' in M.A. Monk and J. Sheehan (eds), *Early medieval Munster: archaeology, history and society* (Cork, 1998), 112–24: 122; T. O'Keeffe, 'Romanesque as metaphor: architecture and reform in early twelfth-century Ireland' in A.P. Smyth (ed.), *Seanchas: studies in early and medieval Irish archaeology, history and literature in honour of Francis J. Byrne* (Dublin, 2000), 313–22: 315. This is a valid concept, both from a chronological and an architectural point of view. But, for the purposes of clarity, the term 'Romanesque' is used in its traditional sense here to denote buildings characterised by Hiberno-Romanesque sculpture. **6** P. Harbison, 'Early Irish churches' in H. Lowe (ed.), *Die Iren und Europa im früheren mittelalter* (Stuttgart, 1982), 618–29; Ó Carragáin, 'Pre-Romanesque churches', 24–5. **7** Ó Carragáin, 'Pre-Romanesque churches', 64–5. See, for example, I. Hodder, *Reading the past: current approaches to interpretation in archaeology*, 2nd edition (Cambridge, 1991), 132; M. Carver, 'Why that? Why there? Why then? The politics of early medieval monumentality' in A. MacGregor and H. Hamerow (eds), *Image and power in early medieval Britain: essays in honour of Rosemary Cramp* (Oxford, 2001), 1–22. **8** See especially C. Manning, 'References to church buildings in the Annals' in Smyth (ed.), *Seanchas*, 37–52: 51. See also A. MacDonald, 'Notes on monastic archaeology and the annals of Ulster, 650–1050' in Ó Corráin (ed.), *Irish antiquity*, 304–20: 305–9; Harbison, 'Early Irish churches'; A. Hamlin, 'The study of early Irish churches' in P. Ní Chatháin and M. Richter (eds), *Ireland and Europe: the early Church* (Stuttgart, 1984), 117–26.

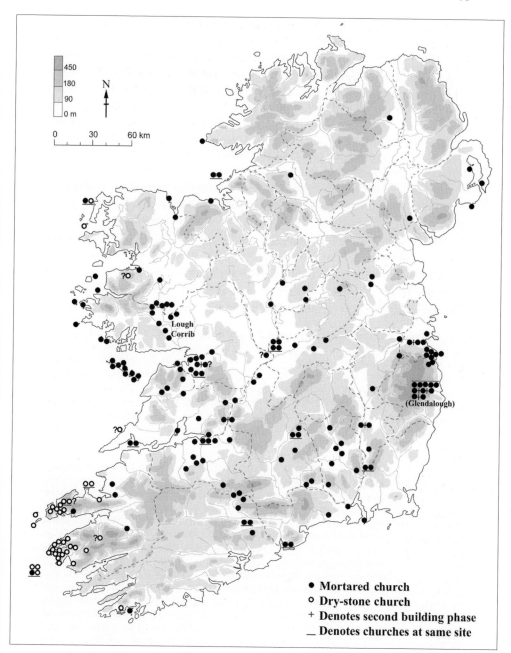

Fig. 1: Distribution of pre-Romanesque churches

of criteria including masonry analysis, formal variation and documentary evidence.[9] This study suggests that a large majority, especially those at sites of only minor or moderate importance, are eleventh- or early twelfth-century, with most probably dating from the mid-eleventh century onwards. On the Continent and in England, this period saw an unprecedented wave of local, non-monastic church building as part of the process of feudalisation.

Large aristocratic and ecclesiastical estates fragmented into the manors and villages of the emerging thegnly class who were anxious to invest in community churches.[10] On the Continent a good proportion of these new buildings were at long-established local church sites.[11] However, in the east and midlands of England a dense network of local churches had not developed prior to this; and excavations often reveal that 'first phase' churches and graveyards belong to the tenth and eleventh centuries.[12] Initially these churches were small and very simple but, especially from c.1050, there was a 'great rebuilding' during which they were replaced by more substantial structures and became 'fixed points in the landscape', forming the basis for the high medieval parish system.[13] In the words of Bishop Herman of Ramsbury, 'England [was] being filled everywhere with churches' through 'the most ample liberality of kings and rich men'.[14]

9 Ó Carragáin, 'Habitual masonry styles and the local organisation of church building in early medieval Ireland' in *PRIA*, 105C (2005); see also Ó Carragáin, 'Regional variation in Irish pre-Romanesque architecture' in *Antiquaries Journal*, 85 (2005). 10 S. Reynolds, *Kingdoms and communities in Western Europe, 900–1300* (Oxford, 1984), 89, 106; G. Tellenbach, *The Church in Western Europe from the tenth to the early twelfth century* (Cambridge, 1993), 135. 11 In southern Germany and Switzerland excavation of hundreds of parish churches in recent years has found that a considerable proportion were first built in the seventh century, the period of initial conversion: see S. Burnell and E. James, 'The archaeology of conversion on the continent in the sixth and seventh centuries: some observations and comparisons with Anglo-Saxon England' in R. Gameson (ed.), *St Augustine and the conversion of England* (Stroud, 1999), 83–106: 96. Burnell argues that they were initially proprietary churches reserved primarily for the local aristocracy, only gradually becoming community churches especially after the turn of the millennium: see S. Burnell, 'Merovingian to Early Carolingian churches and their founder-graves in southern Germany and Switzerland: the impact of Christianity on the Alamans and the Bavarians', unpublished DPhil (Oxford, 1988), 247, 534–5. For French examples of local churches founded in the Merovingian period that later became parish churches see C. Treffort, *L'Église Carolingienne et la Mort* (Lyon, 1996), 135–7. 12 J. Blair, 'Introduction: from minster to parish church' in J. Blair (ed.), *Minsters and parish churches: the local church in transition, 950–1200* (Oxford, 1988), 1–20: 7; A. Boddington, *Raunds Furnells: the Anglo-Saxon church and churchyard* (London 1996). See also S. Turner, 'Making a Christian landscape: early medieval Cornwall' in M. Carver (ed.), *The cross goes north: processes of conversion in Northern Europe, AD 300–1300* (Suffolk, 2003), 171–94: 185–9. Cambridge and Rollason have questioned the idea that developments in England essentially involved the disintegration of the pre-Viking *paruchiae*, preferring to see it as an organised royal imposition of a hierarchical system on the sub-diocesan church structure. E. Cambridge and D. Rollason, 'The pastoral organisation of the Anglo-Saxon church: a review of the "Minster Hypothesis"' in *Early Medieval Europe*, 4 (1994), 87–104: 101. 13 Blair 'Introduction', 6–10; J. Blair, 'Churches in the early English landscape: social and cultural contexts' in J. Blair and C. Pyrah (eds), *Church archaeology: research directions for the future* (York, 1996), 6–18: 12; R. Gem, 'The English parish church in the eleventh and early twelfth centuries: a great rebuilding' in Blair (ed.), *Minsters and parish churches*, 21–30. 14 Quoted in Gem, 'The English parish church', 21.

Irish society was also undergoing significant changes, though the jury is still out as to whether the term 'feudalisation' is helpful or apposite.[15] Certainly a more powerful form of dynastic, territorially based kingship developed, in which over-kings had the ability to maintain armies, re-grant land, pass judgement on their subjects and impose taxes on them.[16] Tax assessment was no longer based on social units but on new land units: the *trícha cét* and its subdivision, the *baile biatach*.[17] The same period saw a considerable fall-off in ringfort erection and occupation, at least in the east of the country where most radiocarbon-dated examples are situated.[18] Doherty and O'Keeffe see this as a corollary to the establishment of the *trícha cét* divisions, and suggest that the replacement settlements were unenclosed farmsteads, perhaps characterised by a greater emphasis on tillage.[19] It is likely that there was also some genuine nucleation of settlement around major ecclesiastical sites, which often doubled as royal residences,[20] and possibly also at new royal strongholds and settlement

A similar pattern emerges in many other parts of Europe, including for example the area around Florence. See I. Moretti and R. Stopani, *Chiese Romaniche in Val di Pesa e Val di Greve* (Florence, 1972). **15** H.B. Clarke, '1066, 1169, and all that: the tyranny of historical turning points' in J. Devlin and H.B. Clarke (eds), *European encounters: essays in memory of Albert Lovett* (Dublin, 2003), 11–36: 31. **16** Ó Corráin 'Nationality and kingship in pre-Norman Ireland' in T.W. Moody (ed.), *Nationality and the pursuit of national independence* (Belfast, 1978), 1–35: 16, 23–6; Ó Cróinín, *Early medieval Ireland*, 274. **17** C. Doherty, 'The Vikings in Ireland: a review' in H.B. Clarke, M. Ní Mhaonaigh and R. Ó Floinn (eds), *Ireland and Scandinavia in the early Viking age* (Dublin, 1998), 288–330; see also Ó Corráin, 'Nationality and kingship', 22–5; T. McErlean, 'The Irish townland system of landscape organisation' in T. Reeves-Smyth and F. Hammond (eds), *Landscape archaeology in Ireland*, BAR 116 (Oxford, 1983), 315–39; J. Hogan, 'The *trícha cét* and related land-measures' in *PRIA*, 28C (1929), 148–235; Ó Cróinín, *Early medieval Ireland*, 275, has equated these new land divisions with the introduction of shires, hundreds and the burghal hideage in Late Saxon England. The study of tenth- and eleventh-century Irish settlement patterns might also benefit from comparison with Middle Saxon England. This period saw the meteoric rise of certain powerful kingdoms at the expense of others, the imposition of a system of taxation based on land units (as evidenced by the tribal hideage) in order to finance, among other things, military operations, and a concomitant reorganisation of territorial units, many of which were preserved in the land divisions of the Late Saxon period and beyond. See S. Bassett, *The origins of Anglo-Saxon kingdoms* (Leicester, 1989); A. Reynolds, *Later Anglo-Saxon England: life and landscape* (Stroud, 1999), 85. Furthermore, this reorganisation was concurrent with a settlement shift dubbed the 'Middle Saxon shuffle'. See R. Hodges, *The Anglo-Saxon achievement: archaeology and the beginnings of English society* (London, 1989), 62–3. **18** C. Lynn, 'The medieval ringfort: an archaeological chimera?' in *Irish Archaeological Research Forum*, 2 (1975), 29–36: 33–5; M. Stout, *The Irish ringfort* (Dublin, 1997), fig. 2; M. Monk, 'Early medieval secular and ecclesiastical settlement in Munster' in M.A. Monk and J. Sheehan (eds), *Early medieval Munster*, 33–52: 48. See also K. D. O'Conor, *The archaeology of medieval rural settlement in Ireland*, Discovery Programme Monograph, 3 (Dublin, 1998), 90. **19** Doherty, 'The Vikings in Ireland', 323–4; O'Keeffe, *Medieval Ireland*, 26. **20** On churches doubling as political capitals see e.g. B.J. Graham, 'Early medieval Ireland: settlement as an indicator of economic and social transformation, *c*.500–1100 A.D.' in B.J. Graham and L.J. Proudfoot (eds), *An historical geography of Ireland* (London, 1993), 19–57: 26; C. Doherty, 'The monastic town in early medieval Ireland' in H.B. Clarke and A. Simms (eds), *The comparative history of urban origins in non-Roman Europe*, BAR International Series, 255 (Oxford, 1985), 63, 68; A. Mac Shamhráin, *Church and polity in pre-Norman Ireland: the case of Glendalough* (Maynooth, 1996); C. Manning 'Some notes of the early

mounds.[21] However, outside the Hiberno–Norse ports the nucleation was, at best, small in scale and confined to high-status sites; and to date, evidence is lacking for the network of lower status agricultural villages which was central to the development of feudalism in core regions of Europe.[22]

The interests of kings and major ecclesiastical sites became ever more closely entwined in this period. MacShamhráin's study shows how (at least in some areas) the territorialisation of kingship went hand in hand with a rationalisation and consolidation of ecclesiastical *paruchiae* that formed the basis for the twelfth-century dioceses. For example, Glendalough relinquished its claims over some churches outside the kingdom of north Leinster but gained authority over more sites within it. Other sites within the kingdom which had owed allegiance to churches like Kildare and Tech Mo Ling may even have been abandoned by the twelfth century.[23] But, in stark contrast to England, there is no evidence to suggest that a large number of new church sites were founded, either by major churches or secular lords. This writer has identified *c*.150 mortared churches at 130 different sites. They represent one of the most significant and at the same time relatively quantifiable, forms of ecclesiastical resource investment undertaken in Ireland during this period; but they clearly do not represent a new network of manorial church sites. Of the 130 sites 100 (77 per cent) have definite evidence, archaeological and/or historical, that they were established before the tenth century. Thirty (23 per cent) cases lack positive evidence for an early foundation date, but in the majority of these the place-name and/or traditional (as opposed to historically attested) dedication suggests they are early foundations. The only archaeologically attested exceptions are at Cashel, Co. Tipperary, and St Peter's, in Hiberno–Norse Waterford. A small amount of stone fabric visible under the chancel of Cashel cathedral may belong to the *c*.1101 cathedral,[24] while the roughly contemporary phase at

history and archaeology of Tullaherin' in *Shadow of the Steeple*, 6 (1998), 19–39: 24.   **21** Graham 'Early medieval Ireland': 29; T. O'Keeffe, 'Rural settlement and cultural identity in Gaelic Ireland, 1000–1500' in *Ruralia 1, Pamtky Archeologick Supplementum* 5 (Prague, 1996), 142–53: 145–7; O'Keeffe, *Medieval Ireland*, 84; see also Ó Corráin, 'Nationality and kingship', 30; P.F. Wallace, 'The origins of Dublin' in B.G. Scott (ed.), *Studies on early Ireland: essays in honour of M.V. Duignan* (Belfast, 1981), 129–43: 139.   **22** A. Simms, 'Rural settlement in medieval Ireland: the example of the royal manors of Newcastle Lyons and Esker in south county Dublin' in B.K. Roberts and R.E. Glasscock (eds), *Villages, fields and frontiers*, BAR International Series 185 (Oxford, 1983), 133–52; O'Keeffe, 'Rural settlement'. See, however, C. Doherty, 'Settlement in early Ireland: a review' in T. Barry (ed.), *A history of settlement in Ireland* (London, 2000), 50–80: 56–9. In this regard it should be noted that dispersed settlement also persisted in some areas of Britain, notwithstanding the social changes that were underway. See S. Turner, 'Christianity and the landscape of early medieval south-west Britain', unpublished PhD (University of York, 2003), 265; B. Yorke, *Wessex in the early Middle Ages* (London, 1995), 274; C. Lewis, P. Mitchel-Fox, and C. Dyer, *Village, hamlet and field* (Manchester, 1997), 82.   **23** MacShamhráin, *Church and polity*, 211–14, 231.   **24** This was exposed during Brian Hodkinson's excavations in and around Cormac's Chapel (pers. comm.). The wooden church and cemetery recently excavated just south of this structure appears to be earlier than it and must therefore be regarded as a royal chapel built before Cashel was give to the Church. The ancient seat of Cashel, with its strong ecclesiastical

St Peter's comprised a stone chancel and wooden nave.[25] The atypical character of both sites makes them exceptions that prove the rule.

This pattern supports Sharpe's assertion that a dense network of local churches was already well established in Ireland before the tenth century and possibly as early as the eighth.[26] Sharpe went on to suggest that, far from expanding, like it did in contemporary England, the Irish ecclesiastical network may have gone into decline by the end of the early medieval period. This was suggested to him by the substantial number of early ecclesiastical sites lacking evidence for twelfth-century activity.[27] This is an important observation, but two caveats need be added. First, it must be emphasised that not all 'early' sites are contemporary and so, at any given time, the network would not have been as dense as it now seems. The impression from many areas is that the early church network was more than adequate for the needs of the secular population as represented by ringfort distribution, but in the absence of a refined chronology we must be cautious about concluding that it was truly comprehensive. For example, excavations at the minor site of Caherlehillan, Co. Kerry, indicate that it was an early foundation that fell out of use in the eighth century (John Sheehan pers. comm.), while nearby Illaunloughan seems to have had an even shorter *floruit* centring on the eighth century.[28] Secondly, the degree of discrepancy between the 'early' network and the parish network seems to vary markedly. In peninsular Kerry, an area which Sharpe focused on in his 1992 paper, there is definite evidence of later ecclesiastical activity at only about 20 per cent of early ecclesiastical settlements.[29] While the actual level of continuity

associations is not typical of the new royal strongholds of the eleventh century. Nonetheless, it is possible that new churches were sometimes built in or near such sites. O'Keeffe apparently envisages this in his 1996 study, 'Rural settlement', 147, fig. 2. If so, they may have been primarily of organic materials at this stage. In general, however, kings involved in *incastellamento* continued to patronise long-established churches. On the Cashel chapel see B. Hodkinson, 'Excavations at Cormac's Chapel, Cashel, 1992, and 1993: a preliminary report' in *Tipperary Historical Journal*, 7 (1994), 167–74. On Cashel's ecclesiastical links see, for example, P. Harbison, 'A high cross base from the Rock of Cashel and a historical reconsideration of the 'Ahenny group' of crosses' in *PRIA*, 93C (1993), 1–20: 19.   **25** See M.F. Hurley and S.W.J. McCutcheon, 'St Peter's church and graveyard' in M.F. Hurley, O.M.B. Scully and W.J. McCutcheon (eds), *Late Viking Age and medieval Waterford: excavations, 1986–1992* (Dublin, 1997), 190–227; B. Murtagh, 'The architecture of St Peter's church' in Hurley, Scully and McCutcheon (eds), *Late Viking Age and medieval Waterford*, 228–43.   **26** Sharpe, 'Churches and communities', 109; See also Ó Corráin, 'The early Irish churches', 336.   **27** Sharpe, 'Churches and communities', 108–9. See also G.W.S. Barrow, 'Badenoch and Strathspey, 1130–1312' in *Northern Scotland*, 9 (1989), 1–16. This study would seem to suggest a similar situation in parts of Scotland where the number of ecclesiastical place-names is 'far in excess of the total of known parishes.'   **28** J. White Marshall and C. Walsh, *Illaunloughan Island: an early medieval monastery in County Kerry* (Dublin, 2005), 127.   **29** This estimate is based mainly on evidence in J. Cuppage, *Archaeological survey of the Dingle peninsula* (Ballyferriter, 1986) and A. O'Sullivan and J. Sheehan, *The Iveragh peninsula: an archaeological survey of south Kerry* (Cork, 1996). It only considers enclosed ecclesiastical settlements, omitting miscellaneous sites like isolated cross-slabs or altars. It does not include reuse for casual habitation as at Church Island and Illaunloughan, or clandestine burial as at Reask. Only *c.*30 per cent of late medieval church sites have positive evidence of an early origin, but the actual figure was probably substantially higher, there does seem to be a significant contrast here with areas such as Kilfenora, Co. Clare where many parishes appear to have had just one church site in both the early and later medieval periods.[30] Differences in archaeological visibility probably accentuate these contrasts. For example, minor sites that fell out of use at an early date may be relatively inconspicuous in Kilfenora due to the lack of an ogham stone or cross-slab tradition in the area and because in this area stone churches were generally confined to major sites.[31] But the contrast may also reflect real regional variations in how the church network developed.

At least four major stages can be identified in the development of the high medieval parish network: (a) the initial establishment of a network by *c*.800; (b) the affects of social change in the tenth and eleventh centuries; (c) the twelfth-century reform; and (d) the impetus provided by the Anglo-Norman colonisation. The impact of each of these developments must have varied substantially across the country.[32] Nonetheless, in many areas a significant number of early sites seem to have gone out of use by the time the parish system was formally established and, given that a substantial (though as yet unquantified) proportion of later medieval churches have early origins, some areas probably experienced an overall reduction in the number of functioning churches. At least in part, this must reflect the need to establish viable units for tithing and administering pastoral care, and it should therefore be seen as a process of rationalisation rather than decline.[33] A crucial question, to which we will

is probably much higher. See M.J. O'Kelly, 'Church Island near Valencia, Co. Kerry' in *PRIA*, 59C (1958), 57–136; J. White Marshall and C. Walsh, 'Illaunloughan, Co. Kerry: an island hermitage' in Monk and Sheehan (eds), *Early medieval Munster*, 102–11: 106; T. Fanning, 'Excavation of an early Christian cemetery and settlement at Reask, Co. Kerry' in *PRIA*, 81C (1981), 67–172. **30** S. Ní Ghabhláin, 'Church, parish and polity: the medieval diocese of Kilfenora, Ireland', unpublished PhD (University of California, Los Angeles, 1995), 133–4, 239; S. Ní Ghabhláin, 'The origin of medieval parishes in Gaelic Ireland: the evidence from Kilfenora' in *JRSAI*, 127 (1996), 37–61: 58. For a similar picture see E. O'Brien, 'Churches of south-east county Dublin, seventh to twelfth century' in G. Mac Niocaill and P.F. Wallace (eds), *Keimelia: studies in medieval archaeology and history in memory of Tom Delany* (Galway, 1988), 504–24. A recent study of Kerrycurrihy, Co. Cork, found that only about 40 per cent of potentially early sites remained in use. See C. Cronin, 'Continuity and change in ecclesiastical settlement: the barony of Kerrycurrihy to *c*.1830', unpublished MA (University College Cork, 2003). **31** Swan lists several sites in the area which were not discussed by Ní Ghabhláin. They are mainly children's burial grounds with no extant evidence for early medieval occupation, but it is possible that some are early church sites. See L. Swan, 'The churches, monasteries and burial grounds of the Burren' in J.W. O'Connell and A. Korff (eds), *The book of the Burren* (Kinvara, 1991), 95–118: 108, 115–16. **32** I am grateful to Dr Edel Bhreathnach for her insights on the development of the ecclesiastical network. See Ó Carragáin, 'Regional variation', on minor regional differences in the early Church network. On differences in the intensity of parochial formation see K.W. Nicholls, 'Rectory, vicarage and parish in the western Irish diocese' in *JRSAI*, 101 (1971), 53–84: 55; A.J. Otway-Ruthven, 'Parochial development in the rural deanery of Skreen' in *JRSAI*, 94 (1964), 112–32. **33** As well as the foundation of new churches, the provision of systematic pastoral care in England may sometimes have involved the abandonment of sites which were 'surplus to requirements'. See Cambridge and Rollason 'Minster hypothesis', 97.

return, is whether it had already begun before the formal establishment of parishes. First, however, we should briefly consider the character and function of ecclesiastical sites in the century or so leading up to the twelfth-century reform.

In the case of tenth- and eleventh-century western Britain, Blair has suggested that proto-parochial churches were developing through the 'privatisation' of long-established cult sites.[34] In Ireland a form of privatisation had taken place by the eighth century, insofar as the temporalities of many church sites were controlled by coarbs who were not usually celibate or in higher orders.[35] However, a clear distinction must be made between the administration of the resources of a church site and its ecclesiastical character or role within society. Coarbal control did not preclude a site from maintaining a vibrant monastic community nor did it prevent a bishop's involvement in the organisation of pastoral ministry;[36] and so functional variation appears to have persisted to a large extent. But Graham has argued that in the later tenth and eleventh centuries major sites in particular became more thoroughly secularised in their character as well as their administration; and certainly the role of some of them as, possibly nucleated, political capitals would suggest some degree of secularisation.[37] It should, however, be remembered that in this specific period major sites were also producing hagiography and investing in reliquaries that sought to glorify their ascetic, monastic origins.[38] Furthermore, the annalistic evidence has led Etchingham to conclude that there was not a radical decline in monasticism, at least not within the parameters of his study.[39] Graham's suggestion that these sites were becoming an 'essentially secular settlement form' is therefore open to question.[40] The situation at local church sites is even harder to gauge. The limited documentary sources for minor sites with extant mortared churches suggest that they varied in function, at least nominally. Some originated as minor family churches, while others, such as Donaghmore, Co. Limerick, and Killeenemer, Co. Cork, were secular *túath* churches. Many more claimed their own *érlam* or founding saint who was usually portrayed as an ascetic, but this cannot be taken as conclusive evidence that they supported a monastic community either in this period or previously.[41] The varied origins

---

34 Blair, 'Churches in the early English landscape', 12.   35 Ó Corráin, 'The early Irish churches', 338; Sharpe 'Some problems', 266–9.   36 See Etchingham, *Church organisation in Ireland*, 100.   37 Graham 'Early medieval Ireland', 32–6.   38 Graham argues that their enclosures were becoming analogous to urban defences, but the references to them in this hagiography suggest they retained their symbolic and legal functions to some extent. See, however, Doherty, 'The monastic town', 69–70 on the possibility that the law of sanctuary was slowly being superseded by royal authority.   39 Etchingham, *Church organisation in Ireland*, 356, 463. The parameters of this study are 650–1000, but Etchingham does note that references to anchorites remained quite common in the eleventh-century annals.   40 Graham 'Early medieval Ireland', 32–35.   41 T. Charles-Edwards, '*Érlam*: the patron-saint of an Irish church' in A. Thacker and R. Sharpe (eds), *Local saints and local churches in the early medieval west* (Oxford, 2002), 267–90: 289–90.

of these sites did not entirely determine their interactions with the secular population.[42] Documentary records relating to the sources and beneficiaries of their dues would be of greater use in assessing this interaction. Here, however, we are primarily concerned with what the architectural evidence can contribute to the debate.

I have suggested elsewhere that around 120 of the 150 mortared churches are mid-eleventh- to early twelfth-century in date.[43] Of the 120, forty-three are subsidiary churches at major complexes or situated on, often remote, islands, leaving under eighty that are the principal churches at mainland sites. This is quite a substantial number, but hardly comparable to the 'general, national activity' which left a substantial proportion of English parish churches with an eleventh- or twelfth-century core.[44] Nor are these plain, unicameral buildings, with their idiosyncratic masonry styles, aesthetically or technologically related to the Late Saxon and Early Romanesque buildings of contemporary England. Instead, they represent the more widespread adoption by modest establishments of a local building technology which had previously been largely confined to top-ranking sites. Furthermore, as the clustered distribution in figure 1 illustrates, this spread was usually confined to areas where building stone and lime for mortar was readily available, especially in the west of the country.[45] Clearly, quarrying and stone transportation was organised on a very *ad hoc* basis compared to contemporary England.[46] Elsewhere I have suggested that it may have taken some time for it to develop to the extent that most local sites could afford to commission a stone church. My impression is that the stock of local stone churches accumulated incrementally and unevenly, and the dearth of earlier fabric in some areas raises the possibility that wood was still seen as an acceptable alternative, possibly until the 'great rebuilding' of the fifteenth century.[47] Certainly, in our period, its continued use is a critical limiting factor in the ability of archaeology to map general developments in the church network. We cannot know, for example, whether the rise in the number of pre-Romanesque stone churches in some areas was complemented by rebuilding of timber churches elsewhere.

In my opinion, the simplicity of these buildings does not preclude a pastoral role. However, it is primarily for historians to decide whether establishing a more systematic pastoral network was already a major concern for eleventh-century clerics and secular lords.[48] Whatever about this, the various

---

42 See for example Sharpe, 'Some problems': 270.   43 Ó Carragáin, 'Habitual masonry styles'.
44 R. Morris, 'Churches in York and its hinterland: building patterns and stone sources in the 11th and 12th centuries' in J. Blair (ed.), *Minsters and parish churches*, 191–9: 191.   45 See further Ó Carragáin, 'Regional variation'.   46 For a fuller discussion see Ó Carragáin, 'Habitual masonry styles'.   47 Ó Carragáin, 'Pre-Romanesque churches', 251; Ó Carragáin, 'Regional variation'.   48 Empey, for one, would argue that the lack of legal disputes over tithing rights with the arrival of the Anglo-Normans indicates that it was not. See A. Empey, 'The layperson in the parish: the medieval inheritance, 1169–1536' in R. Gillespie and W.G. Neely (eds), *The laity and the Church of Ireland, 1000–2000: all sorts and conditions* (Dublin, 2002), 7–48.

developments mentioned above, including reorganisation of secular landholdings and ecclesiastical *paruchiae*, must have meant a rise in the fortunes of some early sites at the expense of others.[49] If English local churches were an expression of the growing wealth and ambition of the thegnly class and of independence from the fragmenting authority of the minsters,[50] perhaps the Irish ones were an affirmation on the part of these sites of their position within increasingly territorialised *paruchiae*, facilitated no doubt by the general economic prosperity of the period. Certainly the vast majority of the 130 sites with mortared churches remained successful. Only forty-one failed to achieve parochial status and twenty of these are on islands unsuitable for the purpose. Excluding these, 81 per cent (89/110) became parish churches, or in a few cases religious houses; and most of the others were also modified in the later medieval period, indicating that they served as chapels of ease or private chapels.[51] This might be taken as evidence that the network was indeed undergoing some rationalisation by the early twelfth century, for it shows that sites important enough to merit a stone church tended to remain important in the high medieval period. However, it must be emphasised that most of these churches occur at sites whose importance was never in doubt. Even in areas with moderate numbers of stone churches, wooden ones probably remained common at most minor sites, and so later medieval activity at an early site is a more widely applicable indicator of continued use. In most areas, therefore, the stone churches are of limited value in gauging changes to the network during this period.

REGIONAL VARIATION IN THE ELEVENTH-CENTURY ECCLESIASTICAL NETWORK

Stone churches are obviously more useful in this regard in high-density areas, most notably south Dublin/north Wicklow (pp. 102–4 below) and the area comprising southwest Galway and the vicinity of Lough Corrib (fig. 1). In the latter area the easy availability of limestone seems to have encouraged the erection of mortared churches at very minor sites which, elsewhere, usually made do with organic materials. These churches are important in that they suggest some discrepancies between the eleventh-century network and the

---

49 The lack of evidence for new church sites obviously reflects the density of the existing network and its ability to adapt to these changes. It also supports the conclusion (see above) that only a limited amount of nucleation took place outside of the ports and a few major church sites, for it has been argued that in areas of England where dispersed settlement continued to predominate, churches were more likely to be sited at pre-existing cult foci instead of virgin sites. See Blair, 'Churches in the early English landscape', 12; Turner, *Christianity and the landscape*, 269. 50 See for example Blair, 'Introduction', 10–11. 51 Examples of this are Churchfield, Co. Kerry, and Aughinish, Co. Clare. See Cuppage, *Archaeological survey*, 277; Ní Ghabhláin, 'Church, parish and polity'; Ó Carragáin, 'Pre-Romanesque churches'.

parish network: an indication that, in this area at least, the reorganisation of the system was not yet complete. Half of the mainland mortared churches at sites that did not achieve parochial status are in this area;[52] and more importantly five of these lack evidence for sustained ecclesiastical reuse. This group represents about three-quarters of the mortared churches at sites that may have fallen out of use in the high medieval period: namely Killeenamunterlane, Killagoola, and Portacarron, Co. Galway and Killursagh and Kilfraochaun, Co. Mayo. Some are on lands owned by the Church in the late medieval period, but none of the published documentary sources suggest that they were functioning churches.[53] While it is possible that some of them continued as chapels, there is no evidence for later alterations to them.[54] It may be that some of them fell out of use when the parish system was properly established. In the case of nearby north Clare, Ní Ghabhláin argues that parish formation took place in the late twelfth/early thirteenth century, based primarily on the ubiquity of Transitional churches there; but Nicholls believes that the process was still ongoing in parts of the west in the latter half of the thirteenth century.[55]

The south Dublin/north Wicklow area features the highest density of mortared churches in the country, but the context in which these were built appears to be slightly different. In this case environmental factors do not provide a ready explanation for the high density: the geology is quite complex and churches are variously built of shale, mica schist, poor calpy limestone and granite.[56] It is particularly remarkable when one considers the high destruction rate of churches in and around Dublin itself. Bradley argues that the Hiberno-Norse port featured twenty or more urban and suburban churches and that most of these were founded in the eleventh century, but virtually none of them have survived.[57] The surviving rural group is discussed at length elsewhere.[58] Here I want to briefly highlight the fact that, in contrast to the other high density area around Lough Corrib and southwest Galway, all of the mainland

---

52 This excludes the numerous examples off the coast of Galway, including those on Aran. 53 See especially H.T. Knox, *Notes on the early history of the dioceses of Tuam, Killala and Achonry* (Dublin, 1904). See also H.S. Sweetman and G.F. Handcock, *Calendar of documents relating to Ireland, 1302–7* (London, 1886). On references to chapels of ease in this source see Ní Ghabhláin, 'Church and community', 72. 54 The extension to Killagoola suggests it was reused as a domestic building some time after it had become ruined. There is a *cillín* nearby, and Kilfraochaun was also used as a burial ground in recent times. 55 Ní Ghabhláin this volume; Ní Ghabhláin, 'Church, parish and polity'; Ní Ghabhláin, 'The origin of medieval parishes', 47; Nicholls, 'Rectory, vicarage and parish'. 56 A good proportion are of granite, often derived from loose blocks and erratics, but this does not appear to have been particularly highly prized as a building stone, for two churches only slightly outside the granite area are built predominantly of other stone types. 57 See J. Bradley, 'The topographical development of Scandinavian Dublin', in F.H.A. Aalen and K. Whelan (eds), *Dublin city and county: from prehistory to present* (Dublin, 1992), 43–56: 48–52. Apart from Christ Church, the only one we know a substantial amount about is St Michael le Pole. See M. Gowan, 'Excavations at the site of the church and tower of St Michael le Pole, Dublin', in S. Duffy (ed.), *Medieval Dublin II* (Dublin, 2001), 13–52. 58 Ó Carragáin, 'Pre-Romanesque churches', 318–42.

churches in the south Dublin/north Wicklow area remained in use in the high medieval period, almost invariably as parish churches.[59] It may be that this high degree of continuity is partly because the process of parish formation was more thoroughgoing in south Dublin/north Wicklow, not least due to the Anglo-Norman influx. The parishes themselves were generally small, while those of the western area were quite variable in size and included some large examples, especially west of the Corrib. But this in itself does not explain why the proportion of parish churches with pre-Norman fabric is far higher in south Dublin/north Wicklow than anywhere else in the country.

There is some evidence to suggest that the origins of this contrast between the ecclesiastical network in south Dublin/north Wicklow on the one hand and that in parts of Galway on the other, lie in the period before the arrival of the Anglo-Normans. In particular, it must be significant that the south Dublin/north Wicklow group closely corresponds to the heartland of *Dyflinarskíri*, the Hiberno-Norse hinterland of Dublin.[60] Unlike most of the urban churches they all occur at pre-Viking foundations, and therefore, as elsewhere in the country, they represent continued use of a pre-extant network. This seems to contrast with Scandinavian-controlled areas of England where such a dense network does not appear to have existed previously.[61] But in other respects the eleventh- and early twelfth-century Church in *Dyflinarskíri* was slightly different from that elsewhere in Ireland, not least because of the influence that

---

59 The two sites not listed as parish churches in the Census of Ireland Index (1861) are Killegar and Kilcroney, Co. Wicklow. Archaeological and documentary evidence attests to the continued ecclesiastical use of both. See, for example, Sweetman and Handcock, *Calendar of documents*; L. Price, *The place-names of Co. Wicklow. V: the barony of Rathdown* (Dublin, 1957), 290, 312–13; Ó Carragáin, 'Pre-Romanesque churches'. **60** The extent of *Dyflinarskíri*, the lands controlled and/or settled by the Hiberno-Norse of Dublin, has been the subject of considerable debate. Smyth and Bradley argue that, as well as incorporating modern-day Co. Dublin, it extended south along the littoral as far as Arklow near the modern border between Wicklow and Wexford. But while they may have had some influence in this area, Etchingham found little evidence for Hiberno-Norse settlement in mid and south Co. Wicklow, except in the hinterlands of the ports at Arklow and Wicklow. Clarke notes that the kings of Brega remained a force to be reckoned with, and may have limited Hiberno-Norse settlement north of the Liffey. In this regard it is significant that the clearest historical, onomastic and archaeological evidence (especially in the form of the Rathdown slabs) is from south Dublin and north Wicklow where these churches are also concentrated. Obviously this discussion is not concerned with the seven early churches at Glendalough. See A.P. Smyth, *Celtic Leinster: towards a historical geography of early Irish civilisation, A.D. 500–1600* (Dublin, 1982), 44, 149 and J. Bradley, 'The interpretation of Scandinavian settlement in Ireland' in J. Bradley (ed.), *Settlement and society in medieval Ireland: studies presented to F.X. Martin* (Kilkenny, 1988), 49–78: 57–9; C. Etchingham, 'Evidence of Scandinavian settlement in Wicklow' in K. Hannigan and W. Nolan (eds), *Wicklow history and society: interdisciplinary studies on the history of an Irish county* (Dublin, 1994), 113–38: 132–3; H.B. Clarke, 'Conversion, church and cathedral: the diocese of Dublin to 1152' in J. Kelly and D. Keogh (eds), *History of the Catholic diocese of Dublin* (Dublin, 2000), 19–50: 37. **61** There the widespread occurrence of Viking Age sculpture at sites with no earlier insular sculpture suggests a process of secular church foundation similar to that more clearly documented in southern England. See R. Bailey, *England's earliest sculptors* (Toronto, 1996).

Canterbury exerted over it. The Dublin bishops did not yet control all the sites in the area; and Glendalough in particular remained a major force there.[62] But, from the latter half of the eleventh century, there were attempts to create a territorial diocese coterminous with *Dyflinarskíri*. Parish-formation was essential to the creation of a workable diocese;[63] and Doherty interprets a reference to the imposition of a reforming cleric on the monastery of Clondalkin by Bishop Patrick in 1076, as an instance of this determination to create a parochial system.[64] In light of this, one wonders whether some of the mortared churches in the area are a manifestation of this process at less important sites – a programme of renewal undertaken in tandem with church foundation in the port itself.[65] If so, it would appear that the Dublin bishops were not too prescriptive when it came to architectural form. While some churches, like those with chancels at Killiney and Palmerstown, represent new forms, probably transmitted from England through the port,[66] others are unicameral antae-less churches: the most common type in most areas of Ireland during the later eleventh century. Clearly, the more minor sites in *Dyflinarskíri* were happy to utilise local building expertise. Nonetheless, this regional contrast in the parochial status of sites at which mortared churches occur suggests that developments in the ecclesiastical network towards the end of the early medieval period did not affect all areas of the country equally.[67]

SIZE, FORM AND FUNCTION

The buildings themselves can contribute a great deal to the development of the debate about pastoral care before the parish. O'Keeffe has suggested that the absence of an eastern cell in the vast majority of eleventh-century churches makes them 'unlikely candidates for parish or proto-parish churches'.[68] Certainly, by this time most local churches abroad were bicameral, and some also had apses.[69] More importantly, the role of the eastern cell was changing in

62 See MacShamhráin, *Church and polity*, 212–13. 63 C. Doherty, 'Cluain Dolcáin: a brief note' in Smyth (ed.) *Seanchas*, 182–8: 187–8; S. Kinsella, 'From Hiberno-Norse to Anglo-Norman, *c.*1030–1300' in K. Milne (ed.), *Christ Church cathedral, Dublin: a history* (Dublin, 2000), 25–52: 37, 42. 64 Doherty, 'The Vikings in Ireland', 314; Doherty, 'Cluain Dolcáin'. Clondalkin had strong links with Glendalough, and it is interesting to note that these did not stop the bishop of Dublin from interfering in its affairs. 65 This suggestion echoes Ní Ghabhláin's argument for seeing the Transitional churches of Kilfenora as a reflex of parish formation in this part of Clare. See Ní Ghabhláin, 'Church, parish and polity'; Ní Ghabhláin, 'The origin of medieval parishes', 47. 66 Tadhg O'Keeffe, this volume; Ó Carragáin, 'Pre-Romanesque churches', 318–52. Another nave-and-chancel church at Clondalkin was excavated by Rynne. He suggested an eleventh-century date on architectural rather than stratigraphic grounds, but the lack of a west doorway makes this uncertain. See E. Rynne, 'Excavation of a church-site at Clondalkin, Co. Dublin' in *JRSAI*, 97 (1967), 29–37. 67 One wonders whether other evidence of this will emerge, for example in the rate and extent of ringfort abandonment. 68 O'Keeffe, this volume. 69 On early unicameral churches (*saalkirche*) on the continent, see for example Burnell,

the late eleventh and early twelfth centuries. Before this, the altar normally stood at the east end of the nave while the eastern cell essentially functioned as a presbytery where the clergy would sit. Increasingly, however, altars were being moved into the eastern cell.[70] This new arrangement was in tune with the emphasis among reformers on the differentiation of the clergy from the laity.[71] However, it was not solely a function of the pastoral role of these churches. Rather, it primarily reflected broader theological and liturgical developments, especially the ongoing debate about what would later be defined as transubstantiation.[72] Nonetheless, as O'Keeffe suggests, the absence of this layout in new churches in most parts of Ireland makes the idea of a sweeping systemisation of pastoral care, along the lines experienced in parts of England and the Continent, seem unlikely.

The unique mix of unicameral and bicameral churches in *Dyflinarskíri* is best understood as a reflex of the early stages of parish formation at a time when, even in England, there was still 'considerable uncertainty as to the best form of accommodation for parish worship'.[73] Elsewhere in Ireland virtually all churches were still plain unicameral structures; and there is no documentary evidence to suggest that parish formation had begun in earnest. However, it must be stressed that their unicameral plan in no way diminishes the possibility, indeed the likelihood, that some of these mortared churches had a pastoral role. The limited formal variation now discernible in this group primarily relates to chronological or regional differences rather than differences in function.[74] Thus, while on purely architectural grounds we should conclude that the barn-like *damliac* at Clonmacnoise is an unlikely candidate for a post-Carolingian episcopal-monastic church, we know this is what it was.[75] Formally identical buildings served variously as major episcopal and monastic churches, nunneries, mortuary churches, eremitic and reliquary chapels as well as *túath* churches with a pastoral role.[76] In the context of this remarkable

Merovingian to early Carolingian, 189.   **70** H. Taylor, 'The position of the altar in early Anglo-Saxon churches' in *Antiquaries Journal*, 53 (1973), 52–8; D. Parsons, '*Sacrarium*: ablution drains in early medieval churches' in Butler and Morris (eds), *The Anglo-Saxon Church*, 105–20; Boddington, *Raunds Furnells*, 66; C.F. Davidson, 'Change and change back: the development of English parish church chancels' in R.N. Swanson (ed.), *Continuity and change in Christian worship* (Woodbridge, 1999), 65–77: 75–6.   **71** P. Barnwell, 'The laity, the clergy and the divine presence: the use of space in smaller churches of the eleventh and twelfth centuries' in *Journal of the British Archaeological Association*, 157 (2004) 41–60: 55.   **72** I am grateful to Roger Stalley and Richard Gem for discussing their ideas on this subject with me. See especially H. de Lubac, *Corpus mysticum: Eucharistie et l'Église au moyen age* (Paris, 1944); F. Cross and E. Livingstone, *The Oxford dictionary of the Christian Church*, 3rd edition (Oxford, 1997); E. Mazza, *The celebration of the Eucharist: the origin of the rite and the development of its interpretation* (Collegeville, 1999); Barnwell, 'The laity', 55.   **73** Barnwell, 'The laity', 55.   **74** Ó Carragáin, 'Pre-Romanesque churches', 241.   **75** C. Manning, 'Clonmacnoise cathedral' in H. King (ed.), *Clonmacnoise Studies 1: seminar papers 1994* (Dublin, 1998), 56–86: 72–3.   **76** Even in areas with much greater architectural complexity and variety, there is rarely an exact relationship between form and function. Instances of form following function have been noted in Anglo-Saxon architecture. See R. Gem, 'Towards an iconography of Anglo-Saxon architecture' in *Journal of the Warburg and*

homogeneity,[77] in which even major churches show no *outward* sign of responding to developments like the transubstantiation debate, it would have been precocious for local pastoral churches to adopt the bicameral form. Nonetheless, these churches could have functioned much like any early medieval pastoral church in which the altar stood between the congregation to the west and a presbytery to the east (see above); and, sure enough, window position hints that altars were often sited some distance from the east wall.[78] Essentially the same arrangement was still current in bicameral churches like Raunds in Northamptonshire until its altar was moved into an eastern cell at the beginning of the twelfth century.[79] Even at this stage, Irish clerics who remained attached to the unicameral plan could, in theory, have responded to the need to increase the sense of mystery surrounding the Eucharist simply by moving the altar eastwards and by adding more substantial screens between the altar and the congregation like those proposed by Barnwell in the case of the mid-twelfth-century unicameral church at Upton, Northampton.[80] No evidence for such changes in layout is now evident in the standing fabric; indeed no trace survives of any of the internal partitions that we know characterised some Irish churches from at least the seventh century.[81] Because of this, overall area is the most useful variable when considering the possibility that some of them had a pastoral role.

In my opinion, too much has been made of the relatively small size of these churches. Macalister[82] went so far as to say that most were non-congregational, while Harbison[83] suggested that their size had, like the use of skeuomorphs, become symbolic of the hallowed ascetic origins of Irish sites. This is plausible in the case of the tiny shrine chapels that were erected to house relics at some major sites, and perhaps also the principal churches at certain island pilgrimage sites. However, viewed in its local context, it becomes clear that a building like Clonmacnoise cathedral would not have been perceived as small.[84] At

Courtauld Institutes, 46 (1983), 1–18: 9; Fernie remarks of the minsters, monasteries and cathedrals of pre-Viking Kent and Essex that there is a 'lack of any clear variation paralleling differences in function.' E. Fernie, *The architecture of the Anglo-Saxons* (London, 1983), 40, 94. For a similar observation about some pilgrimage churches on the continent see R. Ousterhout, '*Loca Sancta* and the architectural response to pilgrimage' in R. Ousterhout (ed.), *The blessings of pilgrimage*, Illinois Byzantine Studies, 1 (Chicago, 1990), 108–24: 108. 77 This homogeneity merits further consideration elsewhere. See Ó Carragáin, 'Pre-Romanesque churches'; see also T. O'Keeffe, *Romanesque Ireland*. 78 Ó Carragáin, 'Pre-Romanesque churches', 92. For a Scottish example of an altar in this position see P. Hill, *Whithorn and St Ninian: the excavation of a monastic town, 1984–91* (Stroud, 1997), fig. 4.13. 79 See Boddington, *Raunds Furnells*; On early unicameral churches (*saalkirche*) on the continent see for example Burnell, *Merovingian to early Carolingian*, 189. 80 Barnwell, 'The laity', 52. 81 See S. Connolly and J.M. Picard, 'Cogitosus: Life of Saint Brigit' in *JRSAI*, 117 (1987), 11–27. 82 R.A.S. Macalister, *Ancient Ireland: a study in the lessons of archaeology and history* (London, 1935), 247. 83 Harbison, 'Early Irish churches', 624. 84 Incidentally, *pace* Macalister and Lucas, there is no reason to believe that stone churches were any smaller than their wooden counterparts, especially given that they were erected at a time when many ecclesiastical sites were expanding significantly. Macalister, *Ancient Ireland*; A.T. Lucas, 'The plundering and burning of churches in Ireland, 7th

c.200m^2 this building is dwarfed by the great continental and, to a lesser extent, Anglo-Saxon churches of the day.[85] But this surely reflects the relatively modest resources available and the fact that its patron, king Flann Sinna of Clann Cholmáin (879–916), though styled king of Ireland, did not have the authority to mobilise these resources as effectively as some of his contemporaries overseas. It should be remembered that later Irish churches are also relatively small. Even the Dublin cathedrals are, in terms of scale, more akin to some out-sized parish churches on the continent than to their actual counterparts, though no one would suggest a symbolic motivation in this case.

Though none are very large in European terms, Irish pre-Romanesque churches vary considerably in size. Obviously, there is not a simple correlation between church area and the degree to which a site was involved in pastoral care. Area is influenced by a range of factors including the size of the resident community, the number of pilgrims it attracted and, perhaps more importantly, prestige and patronage.[86] For example, Clonmacnoise cathedral was not solely a new liturgical space but also a political statement marking the recent victory of Clann Cholmáin in battle and reinforcing their association with the site.[87] Generally speaking there seems to be a direct, though obviously not exact, relationship between the size of the principal church at a particular site and the status of that site. To illustrate the point, let us consider the areas of the six

to 16th century' in E. Rynne (ed.) *North Munster studies: essays in commemoration of Monsignor Michael Moloney* (Limerick, 1967), 172–229: 206. This is supported by the published archaeological record except in the case of Illaunloughan where, as discussed below, a sod-walled church was replaced by a smaller dry-stone one. See White Marshall and Walsh, 'Illaunloughan' and White Marshall and Walsh, *Illaunloughan Island*, 37–53. **85** See for example H.M. Taylor, 'Tenth-century church building in England and on the Continent' in D. Parsons (ed.), *Tenth-century studies* (Chichester, 1975), 141–168. It is comparable in size to some major pre-Carolingian churches including the nave of the seventh-century minster at Winchester. See B. Kjolbye-Biddle, 'The 7th century minster at Winchester interpreted' in Butler and Morris (eds), *The Anglo-Saxon Church*, 196–209. **86** Annalistic entries give us some indication of the capacity of certain churches, though usually at times of trouble when people were resorting to them for sanctuary. In 850 the *dairtech* at Trevet was burned with 260 people in it and Manning has concluded that it therefore 'must have been close to the size of Clonmacnoise cathedral to have held such numbers.' See Manning, 'References to church buildings'. This seems unlikely however, for Trevet was a middle-ranking site at best. If we accept Boddington's method of calculating *maximum* capacity (discussed below), Trevet could have been less than 100m^2, while conversely Clonmacnoise cathedral could have held over 500 people. In all likelihood, Trevet was somewhat larger than this and Clonmacnoise cathedral probably never held so many even when used as a sanctuary, but there are hints that Boddington's guide is not too far off the mark. No references indicating capacity pertain to surviving churches but in 1031 200 were burned in the *damliac* of Ardbraccan, a site situated near Kells and a subsidiary of it. Another nearby subsidiary of Kells is Dulane. The three sites are linked in the 967 obit of one Maelfinnen who was coarb of Ultan of Ardbraccan and Cairnech of Dulane as well as bishop of Kells. M. Herbert, *Iona, Kells and Derry: the history and hagiography of the monastic familia of Columba* (Dublin, 1988), 82, 89; A. Gwynn, and R.N. Hadcock, *Medieval religious houses, Ireland* (London, 1970), 35. It is therefore interesting to note that (using Boddington's guide) Dulane could just about have accommodated two hundred people. **87** See especially the definitive study of this building by Manning, 'Clonmacnoise cathedral'.

surviving principal churches that were mentioned in the annals before *c*.1050.[88] Of these Ardfert (61.2m²) Tuamgraney (67.7m²) and Dulane (probably 68.9m²) are at quite important sites. Significantly, though, they are on average less than half the size of the three at top-ranking sites, namely Glendalough (131.56m²), Lorrha (129.9m²) and Clonmacnoise (200.9m²).[89]

But the size of a church must also bear some relationship to its function. In this regard it is interesting to note that the size discrepancy between Ireland and England is not nearly as marked below the level of the major monastic church or cathedral. According to Morris, tenth-century English naves average just 20–30m², while naves of 60–80m² became typical from the later eleventh century.[90] In Ireland churches which later achieved parish status average 59m² and only 26 per cent are less than 40m². Thus they are, for example, the same size on average as the three multi-cameral churches at Killiney, Palmerstown and St Peters, Waterford which O'Keeffe[91] has quite rightly labelled 'Hiberno-Scandinavian parish churches' (average total area: 60m²). Significantly, mainland churches that later became chapels or fell out of use are substantially smaller: 29m² on average with only two greater than 40m².[92] Some of these could only accommodate a tiny congregation but others are not so small that a pastoral role can be dismissed out of hand. They are, after all, on average almost twice as large as mortared churches on island sites (16.6m²) which, given their isolation, are unlikely to have served substantial secular communities. My aim here is not to suggest that most pre-Romanesque churches were built with pastoral care in mind, but rather to point out that they cannot be used as evidence that pastoral provision was minimal or non-existent. However, these general observations tell us little about how it was administered in a particular area. In an attempt to address this issue, the rest of this paper focuses on the dry-stone churches of peninsular Kerry.

---

88 See Manning, 'References to church buildings', 48.   89 Such a relationship has been noted in other contexts including pre-Viking Durham. See E. Cambridge, 'The early Church in Co. Durham: a reassessment' in *Journal of the British Archaeological Association*, 87 (1984), 65–85: 75. 90 R. Morris, *Churches in the landscape* (London, 1989), 287.   91 O'Keeffe, this volume.   92 At *c*.55m², Longfordpass, Co. Tipperary, is the largest church not to have achieved parish status; and it is no coincidence that it is also the only such site for which a substantial amount of early history survives. Its decline is the result of an unusual set of circumstances, and it can therefore be seen as the exception which proves the rule. It was probably an early episcopal foundation and is mentioned in the 'Martyrology of Aengus' and three saints' lives, as well as a number of secular texts. See F.J. Byrne, 'Derrynaflan: the historical context' in *JRSAI*, 110 (1980), 116–26; C. Manning, 'Daire Mór identified' in *Peritia*, 11 (1997), 359–69. But it was eclipsed by nearby Liathmore possibly because the latter was favoured by the ascendant O'Briens. While it continued to function as an ecclesiastical site until at least the twelfth century, it was an outlying portion of Kilcooly parish in the high medieval period, and its monastic past was forgotten until recently. See K. Nicholls, 'A charter of John, Lord of Ireland, in favour of Mathew Ua Hénni, Archbishop of Cashel' in *Peritia*, 2 (1983), 273–4.

FUNCTIONAL VARIETY IN PENINSULAR KERRY

In 1970 Peter Harbison acted, in his own words, as devil's advocate and argued that dry-stone churches could be a twelfth-century phenomenon.[93] However, more recently he has moderated his views considerably, especially in the light of two excavations.[94] First, extensive use of radiocarbon dating on Illaunloughan leaves little doubt that its dry-stone church dates to the middle rather than the end of the early medieval period.[95] Second, a possible outlier of the main group on the summit of Croagh Patrick, Co. Mayo, produced a radiocarbon date of 'between 430 and 890'.[96] A number of factors are against the possibility that dry-stone churches developed earlier than, say, the eighth century, including the fact that they were usually preceded by churches of organic materials.[97] It seems likely that there was a significant 'overlap' in the erection, and especially the use, of dry-stone and mortared churches. Nonetheless, it may be that dry-stone churches were being built in peninsular Kerry a century or two before mortared churches became common elsewhere in the country.[98] Even more important in the present context is the fact that, in peninsular Kerry, the dry-stone church became the standard type even at minor sites, apparently to a greater extent than mortared churches in either south Dublin/north Wicklow or southwest Galway and the area around Lough Corrib. This, coupled with a generally high level of archaeological visibility, means that peninsular Kerry offers a unique opportunity to study the relationships between sites of different function and status.

It has recently been argued, on archaeological and historical grounds, that there were three sites of regional importance in the area of peninsular Kerry

---

93 P. Harbison, 'How old is Gallarus oratory?' in *Medieval Archaeology*, 14 (1970), 34–59. 94 P. Harbison, *Pilgrimage in Ireland: the monuments and the people* (London, 1991), 82; P. Harbison, *The golden age of Irish art* (London, 1999), 194. 95 White Marshall and Walsh, 'Illaunloughan', 106. 96 Quote from Harbison, *The golden* age, 194. See G. Walsh, 'Preliminary report on the archaeological excavations on the summit of Croagh Patrick' in *Cathair na Mart*, 14 (1994), 1–10. 97 See O'Kelly, 'Church Island'; Fanning, 'Excavation of an early Christian cemetery'; White Marshall and Walsh, 'Illaunloughan', and *Illaunloughan Island*. 98 Their recurring association with early cross-slabs, clochauns and stone shrines supports this idea. This point has been made by both Petrie and O'Keeffe and it is one which Harbison has always acknowledged. See G. Petrie, *The ecclesiastical architecture of Ireland*, 2nd edition (Dublin, 1845), 133; T. O'Keeffe, 'Architectural traditions of the early medieval church in Munster' in Monk and Sheehan (eds), *Early Medieval Munster*, 112–24; Harbison 'How old' 43–4, 46, 58. Dry-stone churches do share some features with the mortared types, including finials, stepped sills, inclining jambs, and plinths, though the latter are somewhat different in form. Features commonly found in mortared churches, but not in dry-stone churches, include gable-headed windows, and interior doorway rebates. Furthermore, only one dry-stone church, Gallarus, features a round-headed window, though this is by far the most common window type in mortared churches. Dry-stone churches also have markedly shorter proportions. These differences might also be taken as evidence that the types did not develop contemporaneously. In this regard, it should be noted that their distributions are not entirely discreet. Peninsular Kerry features two mortared churches, a density equal to or greater than most areas in the south-west.

west of the mountains: namely Kilmalkedar on Dingle and Inis Úasal and Skellig Michael on Iveragh.[99] The final identification may seem surprising but, viewed in its local context Skellig Michael emerges as a significant monastic centre that enjoyed greater resource investment and documentary coverage than any other site in the area. At all three sites, the main church was rebuilt in the twelfth or thirteenth centuries,[1] but there were at least three additional dry-stone churches on Skellig Michael, and probably two at Kilmalkedar.[2] Significantly, these constitute all of the definite supplementary churches in this western area.[3] A number of factors favoured the erection of multiple churches at important sites, but here I will briefly consider the main liturgical factor.[4] The eighth and ninth centuries in particular saw a dramatic increase in the number of masses celebrated at sites throughout Europe; and also in the number of monks who were ordained as priests.[5] Many of these masses were said in private and were specialised, with some marking saint's feast-days, others said for penitential purposes and still others for votive purposes especially for the newly baptised, the sick and the dead. Feast-day masses were celebrated in Ireland from an early date,[6] and some have argued that the Irish helped popularise votive masses on the Continent.[7] Although private, these masses were seen as apotropaeic actions that contributed to the spiritual well-being of the community as a whole and therefore remained notionally, though not physically, communal.[8] Therefore a multiplicity of altars became one of the defining traits of an important church site.[9] This often meant multiple churches,[10] but from the Carolingian period onwards, the favoured solution on

---

99 T. Ó Carragáin, 'A landscape converted: archaeology and early Church organisation on Iveragh and Dingle, Ireland' in Carver (ed.), *The cross goes north*, 127–52. **1** One wonders whether the principal churches at Kilmalkedar and Inis Úasal were relatively large structures of wood or mortared stone. The main church on Skellig Michael seems to incorporate some early mortared fabric. See R. Berger, '14C dating mortar in Ireland' in *Radiocarbon*, 34: 3 (1992), 880–89; R. Berger, 'Radiocarbon dating of early medieval Irish monuments' in *PRIA*, 95C (1995), 159–74. **2** See Cuppage, *Archaeological survey*. **3** Another occurs on Illauntannig off the north coast of Dingle. The subsidiary role of these churches at relatively important sites is confirmed by the fact that this small group includes the three smallest extant churches. At Killabuonia a subsidiary site, situated *c*.450m from the main terrace, also features a church, while another possible subsidiary church occurs at Killemlagh. The dry-stone church on Inishglora, Co. Mayo, also appears to be a subsidiary church. **4** For full discussion see Ó Carragáin, 'Pre-Romanesque churches', 233–44. **5** M. Dunn, *The emergence of monasticism: from the desert fathers to the early Middle Ages* (Oxford, 2000), 189–90. **6** J. Stevenson, 'Introduction' to the 2nd edition of F.E. Warren, *The liturgy and ritual of the Celtic Church* (Woodbridge, 1987), lxi. **7** See for example A. Angenendt, 'Missa Specialis: Zugleich ein Beitrag zur Entstehung der Privat-Messen' in *Frühmittelalterliche Studien*, 17 (1983), 153–221: 181–91, 212–21; F.S. Paxton, *Christianising death* (London, 1990), 98, 100, 204. **8** A. Haeussling, *Moenchskonvent und Eucharistiefeier: eine Studie ueber die Messe in der Abendländischen Klosterliturgie des fruehen Mittelalters und zur Geschichte der Messhäufigkeit* (Liturgiewissenschaftliche Quellen und Forschungen 58, Muenster Westfalen, 1973), 249, 252, 319. **9** A. Haeussling, 'Motives for the frequency of the Eucharist' in *Concilium*, 152 (1982), 25–30. **10** See for example E. James, 'Archaeology and the Merovingian monastery' in H.B. Clarke, and M. Brennan (eds), *Columbanus and Merovingian monasticism*, BAR International Series 113 (Oxford, 1981), 33–55: 41, 44.

the Continent was the elaboration of church plans to allow for the provision of several altars under one roof. In Ireland, however, single-altar churches remained the norm, and so at important sites several small churches were erected. The presence of four churches on Skellig Michael supports its identification as a significant cenobitic site rather than a minor hermitage. These indoor altars may have been supplemented by two or three outdoor dry-stone altars. In the case of one dry-stone altar, we can be confident of an early date because it is partly overlain by one of the churches,[11] while another was found to be coeval with the surrounding paving and apparently with another of the churches.[12] This multiplicity of altars provides a context for the legend, recorded by Giraldus Cambrensis about a hollowed-out stone which stood outside the (main?) church on the island in which 'there is found every morning through the merits of the saints of the place as much wine as is necessary for the celebration of as many masses as there are priests to say mass on that day.'[13] Therefore, the historical sources for the site complement the archaeological evidence for a liturgy based on the idea of multiple private masses, sometimes being celebrated concurrently.

Obviously Skellig Michael was not built with pastoral care in mind. A pastoral role seems likely in the case of Kilmalkedar and Inis Úasal, at least within their own *termon* lands,[14] but their main congregational churches do not survive. However, a case can be made that some of the churches at minor sites were congregational. In contrast to the mortared churches, only a small proportion of dry-stone churches occur at sites that survived into the high medieval period; and they must therefore predate the rationalisation of the network and the onset of parish formation. Nonetheless, Sharpe argues forcefully that this early network amounted to 'one of the most comprehensive pastoral organisations in northern Europe'.[15] No attempt is made here to evaluate the documentary evidence for or against this proposition; but it does seem to find some support in the archaeological record, notwithstanding the fact that these sites were not all contemporary. Indeed, such a dense distribution of sites would seem to support the model of a diverse Church in which some sites were more concerned with pastoral provision than others. There is a broad correlation between the distribution of secular and ecclesiastical sites. For example, on the Dingle peninsula the highest concentrations of both are south and west of the mountains. However, there are areas where their

11 T. Ó Carragáin, 'Leachta as indicators of ritual practice: the evidence of Iveragh and Dingle, Co. Kerry', unpublished MA (University of York, 1998), 31, 76–9. 12 A. Lynch, 'Sceilig Mhichíl, Sceilg Rock Great: early Christian monastic site' in I. Bennett (ed.), *Excavations 1987: summary accounts of archaeological excavations in Ireland* (Dublin, 1988), 17–18. 13 J.J. O'Meara (ed.), *The history and topography of Ireland by Giraldus Cambrensis* (Mountrath, 1982), 80. The phrase 'saints of the place' should be seen as a reference to the saints to whom the altars were dedicated. See Haeussling, *Moenchskonvent und Eucharistiefeier*, 220. 14 For the likely extent of their *termon* lands see Ó Carragáin, 'A landscape converted'. 15 Sharpe, 'Churches and communities', 90–1.

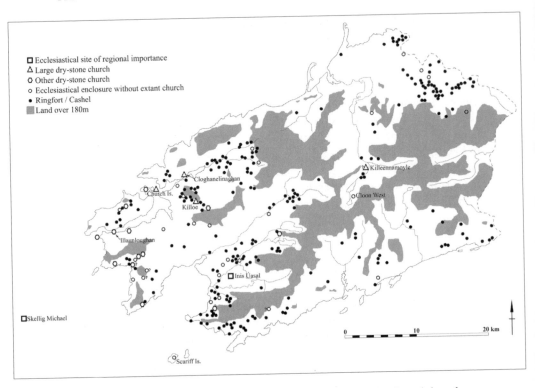

Fig. 2: Early medieval settlement on the Iveragh peninsula (based largely on information in A. O'Sullivan and J. Sheehan, *The Iveragh peninsula: an archae-ological survey of south Kerry*, Cork, 1996)

distributions appear to diverge. The most marked discrepancy is in southern Iveragh (fig. 2). Here, secular sites are common but there is only one definite early ecclesiastical site. The opposite is true at the west end of the Iveragh peninsula, especially west of a line from Church Island to Scariff where remarkably, even when Skellig Michael and isolated cross-slabs are excluded, ecclesiastical settlements are as common as ringforts with eighteen instances of each. The general consensus is that ringforts were a settlement type restricted to better-off farmers, and so they are not representative of the secular population as a whole. The number of secular households in the area is therefore likely to have been substantially higher than eighteen. Nevertheless, it is highly unlikely that all eighteen churches were primarily concerned with providing pastoral care to the secular population. Clearly these church sites varied considerably in function. The question is can archaeology help us to distinguish between them?

The small size of the dry-stone churches, averaging just 11.8m² in internal area, has led a number of scholars to suggest that masses and other sacraments were performed in the open air at an outdoor altar. In such a scenario the church would have been little more than a *secretarium*, the early medieval equivalent of a sacristy.[16] Another possibility is that the church acted as a *sanctuarium*, i.e. the equivalent of the sanctuary area at the east end of large churches where the mass was performed.[17] If either theory is accepted, it might further be argued that, unlike late medieval parish churches,[18] there should be no correlation between church area and congregation size. However, it seems likely that a site primarily concerned with pastoral provision would have articulated this identity by investing more in its church than in other ritual foci (see below for a possible example). Furthermore, the law tracts show that, as in the high medieval period, such a church could expect to be supported by its community;[19] and so a site's role in this regard must have affected the amount of resources and labour available to it. In any case, this writer is not convinced that these structures were conceived of as sacristies or sanctuaries. While it may often have been expedient for part of the congregation to stand outside, there is no reason to believe that these sites were actually laid out with this in mind.[20] It seems more likely that sites with unfeasibly small churches anticipated substantial congregations only on occasions such as the feastdays of their saints. In particular the 'oratory as sanctuary' idea falsely implies that it was normal practice in large churches for the mass to be hidden from the view of the congregation. As already mentioned, little evidence survives for the partitions within Irish churches, but elsewhere in Europe they were usually only waist-high and even the most substantial were designed to give the congregation a clear view of the celebrant and host,

---

16 F. Henry, *Irish art in the early Christian period* (London, 1940), 25–7; H. Leask, *Irish churches and monastic buildings*, i (Dundalk, 1955), 59; O'Kelly, 'Church Island', 127. On the *secretarium* see T. Sternberg, *Orientalium more secutus. Räeume und institutionen der caritas des 5. bis 7. Jahrhunderts in Gallien* (Muenster, 1991), 54–59. 17 See R.A.S. Macalister, *The archaeology of Ireland* (London, 1928); R.A.S. Macalister, *Ancient Ireland* (London), 247; J. Ryan, *Irish monasticism: origins and early development* (Dublin, 1931), 288; M.J. O'Kelly, *Archaeological survey and excavation of St Vogue's church, enclosure and other monuments at Carnsore, Co. Wexford* (Dublin, 1975), 21; L. Bitel, *Isle of the saints: monastic settlement and Christian community in early Ireland* (Cork, 1990), 71. J.W. Hunwicke, 'Kerry and Stowe revisited' in *PRIA*, 102C (2002), 1–19. This learned article attempts to use the commentary on the mass in the Stowe Missal to illuminate liturgical practice in and around the dry-stone churches of peninsular Kerry. It is somewhat ironic that the missal is associated with Lorrha, Co. Tipperary which features the third largest pre-Romanesque church in the country. 18 Ní Ghabhláin, 'Church, parish and polity', 187–236; C. Bond, 'Church and parish in Norman Worcestershire' in Blair (ed.), *Minster and parish churches*, 119–58: 119, 141–4. 19 Charles-Edwards, 'The pastoral role of the church', 70; Etchingham 'The early Irish Church', 101–2, 107, 110–13. 20 The state of grace necessary to take communion meant that most people did so infrequently. See for example D. Hurst (ed.), *Bedae Opera, Pars II* (Turnhout, 1960), 520; R.E. McLaughlin, 'The word eclipsed?: preaching in the early middle ages' in *Traditio*, 46 (1991), 77–122. It may be that only those communicating went into the church while others stayed outside. This distinction may help to explain the incident in the Life of Columba in which part of the mass, including the Gospel, took place outside, after which the saint and a select group entered the church to celebrate the Eucharist. This did not take place on Iona where the whole community normally heard mass inside the church, but on Hinba, a dependency of Iona which is known to have housed a group of penitents. See R. Sharpe (ed. and trans.), *Adomnán of Iona: Life of Columba* (London, 1995), 219, 368–9.

something which is taken for granted in the early Roman and Byzantine rites.[21] In the case of the dry-stone churches, the results of excavations to date argue against the possibility that they performed other key functions including, for example, a burial or reliquary function.[22] Most were clearly not congregational, but there is no reason to doubt that the largest ones were, and it is therefore possible that they were used for the provision of basic pastoral services.[23]

It must be emphasised again that there is no direct and universal relationship between the size of a building and the number of people it accommodated: this is something that is culturally determined.[24] However, in this case enough information is known about the cultural context of the buildings to make such estimates useful in formulating theories about them. It is suggested here that, to a greater or lesser extent, the size of a dry-stone church was a product of its function.[25] This is strongly supported by the huge variation within the group, with the largest ($24m^2$) being over five times the internal area of the smallest ($4.5m^2$). Obviously competitive emulation or disproportionate patronage by higher secular or ecclesiastical powers could result in larger-than-required churches at particular sites, but this is equally true of late medieval parish churches.[26] Andrew Boddington has suggested that a church of modest size could accommodate three people per square metre; and I have found this

---

21 T. Klauser, *A short history of the Western liturgy* (Oxford, 1979), 66, 98; T.F. Mathews, *The early churches of Constantinople: architecture and liturgy* (Philadelphia, 1971), 162–71; J. Dodds, *Architecture and ideology in early medieval Spain* (Philadelphia, 1990). For an excellent discussion of the arrangement at Kildare and its European analogues see C. Neuman de Vegvar, 'Romanitas and Realpolitik in Cogitosus's description of the church of St Brigit, Kildare' in Carver (ed.), *The cross goes north*, 153–70. 22 Thomas, 'Recognising Christian origins', 124, once suggested that some were martyrial buildings built over founders graves but the five examples excavated to date suggest that, unlike the mortared shrine chapels at major sites, they had no significant burial or reliquary function. See O'Kelly, 'Church Island', 62; Fanning, 'Excavation of an early Christian cemetery', 79–84; Marshall and Walsh, 'Illaunloughan', 104–6; Lynch, 'Sceilig Mhichíl', 18; John Sheehan (pers. comm.) on Caherlehillan. In this area, reliquary shrines are invariably outside in the cemetery. While the phase 2 churches at Church Island, Reask and Illaunloughan partially covered a number of burials, there is nothing to suggest they were special graves. Significantly the excavated churches are quite representative in that they span almost the full size range (e.g. Illaunloughan and Church Island) and occur at both minor (e.g. Reask) and important (Skellig Michael) sites. 23 The early medieval outdoor altars associated with pilgrimage routes in peninsular Kerry underscore the impression that there was no taboo in the area about lay participation in the Eucharist. See Ó Carragáin, 'A landscape converted', 131, note 7, 133, note 8, figs. 9.3 and 9.5a. 24 M. Shanks and C. Tilley, *Re-constructing archaeology: theory and practice*, 2nd edition (London, 1992). See also I. Hodder, *Symbols in action: ethnoarchaeological studies of material culture* (Cambridge, 1982), 193–4 on the relationship between settlement size and population. 25 It is important to avoid establishing a false dichotomy between the function of a building and its symbolic meaning. Hodder shows that, far from being contradictory, these are interdependent and equally vital. Hodder, *Reading the past*, 130, 188. See also S. Jones, *The archaeology of ethnicity: constructing identities in the past and present* (London, 1997), 119. 26 See Ní Ghabhláin, 'Church, parish and polity', 212–13. On competitive emulation see C. Renfrew, 'Introduction: peer polity interaction and socio-political change' in C. Renfrew and J.F. Cherry (eds), *Peer polity interaction and socio-political change* (Cambridge, 1986), 1–18: 7–9.

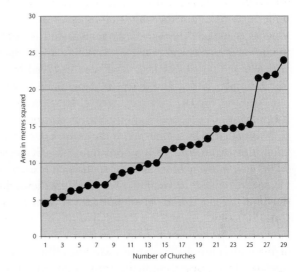

Skellig Michael 3	4.53
Skellig Michael 4	5.36
Illauntannig 2	5.39
?Reencaheragh	6.21
Feaghmann W	6.33
Kildreelig	6.92
Loher	7.03
Illaunloughan	7.04
Reask	8.16
Kilkeaveragh	8.64
Skellig Michael 2	8.94
Ballywiheen	9.36
Killabuonia 2	9.86
Inishtooskert	10
Kilfountan	11.81
Templecashel	12
Inishvickillane	12.2
Beginish	12.42
Illauntannig 1	12.54
Killabuonia 1	13.3
Gallarus	14.65
Cappanagroun	14.72
Temple Geal	14.74
Kilmalkedar	14.92
Lateevemore	15.24
Church Is.	21.56
Cloghanelinaghan	21.84
?Killeennamoyle	22.04
Killoe	24

Average: 11.78

Fig. 3: Interior areas of dry-stone churches in peninsular Kerry

appropriate for maximum estimates.[27] Taking the altar area into account, the smallest church could only have accommodated about five people.[28] As figure 3 illustrates, most of the others are evenly spread between 4.5m² and 15m², with almost every metre-squared interval being represented at least twice. But there is then a leap of over 6m² between Lateevemore and the largest four churches. Lateevemore could have accommodated up to thirty people and therefore might have been congregational; but the case is stronger for the largest four for they could have held a maximum of between 48 and 54 people and could quite comfortably have housed 30 or so. These are again quite similar in size, possibly an indication that anything much larger was deemed unstable.

We cannot know for certain the particular functions of these four churches but it is worth exploring the possibility that they had a pastoral role.[29] All four

27 Boddington, *Raunds Furnells*, 64, 66. See also Morris, *Churches in the landscape*, 288–9. **28** Boddington suggests that the easternmost two metres must be set aside for the priest and a freestanding altar but one-and-a-half metres would probably suffice if the altar was built against the east wall. That this was common in small Irish churches (though possibly not the larger ones) is supported both by archaeology and by the tract on the Mass in the eighth-century Stowe Missal which suggests that the priest normally faced east. For the archaeology see T. Ó Carragáin, 'Pre-Romanesque churches', 92–3. For the Stowe Missal evidence see É. Ó Carragáin, 'The meeting of Saint Paul and Saint Anthony: visual and literary uses of a Eucharistic motif' in Mac Niocaill and Wallace (eds), *Keimelia*, 1–58: 8–9. **29** It is impossible to determine whether this putative pastoral ministry was available to the laity at large or was restricted to tenants on their own, presumably modest, estates as Etchingham (this volume) would envisage. Their relationship to the three sites of regional importance (Inis Úasal, Kilmalkedar and Skellig Michael) is also difficult to establish. They are not on lands which belonged to the Church in the later medieval period and are on Iveragh, and significantly, Cloghanelinaghan and the likely example at Killeennamoyle, are the only dry-stone churches situated in modern grave-yards and among the few on this peninsula at sites with evidence for high or late medieval ecclesiastical reuse.[30] Arguably their distribution and siting also supports the possibility that they were involved in pastoral provision (fig. 2). For example, Killoe and Killeennamoyle are situated in significant ringfort clusters, and the latter in particular is strategically located at the junction of three valleys in the mountainous central portion of the peninsula. In contrast to Killeennamoyle, Cloon West, the only other church site in the vicinity, is sited high up in a sparsely populated valley. Killeennamoyle achieved parish status and, in the absence of later remains, it is even possible that the dry-stone church remained in use into the high medieval period. Sixteenth-century documents refer to the parish as *Túath Chlann Uí Shé*. These were the main Corco Dhuibhne family on Iveragh, and this name may refer to the area to which they were confined in the later medieval period.[31] Their hereditary rights to the church may explain why the O'Sullivans demoted it in favour of a new parish centre at Templenoe in the mid-fifteenth century.[32]

Church Island also appears to have had close links with a local secular power, and in this case the results of the excavation conducted there allow us to consider its development in greater depth (fig. 4, pl. 1). I want to conclude this essay by comparing Church Island with another excavated site, Illaunloughan (fig. 5). Neither of these two sites produced sixth- or seventh-century Continental pottery but it would appear that both were in existence by the end of the seventh century. The earliest dateable feature from Church Island is a slab inscribed with a cross-of-arcs design which may well be seventh-century, while radiocarbon dates suggest Illaunloughan was founded in the latter half of the seventh century.[33] At first glance they are very similar. Both are tiny islands in Valentia harbour, delimited by a stone enclosure and featuring a succession of organic to stone buildings and an outdoor reliquary shrine. There is also evidence that both benefited from interaction with secular society. But diver-gences in the way their resources were invested suggest significant differences in the nature of these interactions.

they may also have been outside the termon lands of these three major sites in the early medieval period. See P. McCotter, 'The see-lands of the diocese of Ardfert: an essay in reconstruction' in *Peritia*, 14 (2000), 161–204; Ó Carragáin, 'A landscape converted.' However, it remains possible that they were within the wider *paruchia* of one of these major sites which may therefore have been involved in sustaining their pastoral ministry in return for food renders. For an illuminating discussion of the relationship between Iona and minor churches on Islay see C. Swift, 'Sculptors and their customers: a study of Clonmacnoise grave-slabs' in H. King (ed.), *Clonmacnoise Studies*, 2 (Dublin, 2004), 105–124: 112–14. **30** See O'Sullivan and Sheehan, *The Iveragh peninsula*, 272. Skellig Michael probably continued to function in some capacity, and there is also a possible dry-stone church on the periphery of the parish centre of Killemlagh. **31** B. Ó Cíobháin, *Toponomia Hibernia*, 4 (Dublin, 1985), lxxi. **32** Ibid., lxii, lxx, lxxi. **33** White Marshall and Walsh, *Illaunloughan Island*, 11.

Pl. 1: Dry-stone church, Church Island, Iveragh – one of the largest extant examples

The usual characterisation of Illaunloughan as a remote hermitage is somewhat misleading.[34] In fact, even after twelve hundred years of erosion, it is still possible to walk to it at certain low tides. Furthermore, we can assume that the narrow sound in which is it located was an important route into Valentia harbour, as it still is today. Excavations revealed that its occupants received plentiful supplies of domesticated animals and processed grain, and that they produced high status metalwork such as ornamented penannular brooches.[35] Initially the ritual elements of the site comprised a sod-built church 12m² internally and a cemetery including the rock-cut special graves of the island's holy men. Changing requirements led to the church being replaced by a much smaller dry-stone one, just over 7m² internally; and, probably in the late

34 Henry 'Early monasteries'; Thomas, *The early Christian archaeology*; M. Herity, 'Les premiers ermitages at monasteres en Irlande, 400–700' in *Cahiers de Civilisation Mediéval*, 36 (1993), 219–61. **35** White Marshall and Walsh, *Illaunloughan Island*, 19–21, 67–80. While this is not an activity normally associated with hermits, it should be noted that Cuthbert, who was known for his asceticism, possessed a fine pectoral cross. Note also the following from Aldred's colophon in the Lindisfarne Gospels: '... and Billfrith, *the anchorite,* forged the ornaments which are on the outside, and adorned it with gold and gems and gilt-silver, pure metal ...' See G. Henderson, *From Durrow to Kells: the insular gospel books 650–800* (London, 1987), 112. Emphasis added.

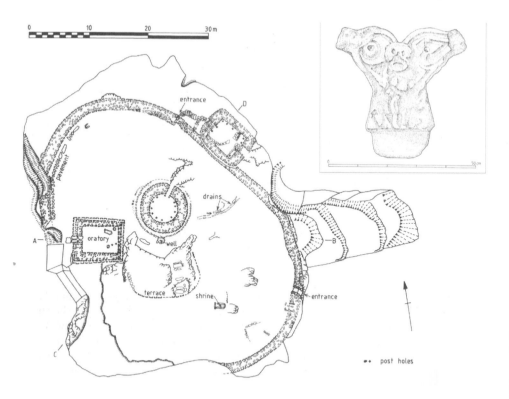

Fig. 4: Church Island, Iveragh, showing successive churches, peripheral corner-post shrine and finial from Phase II church (after O'Sullivan and Sheehan, *The Iveragh peninsula*: figs 151 and 152)

eighth century,[36] the bodies in the special graves were translated into an impressive gable shrine. This was built directly over the original graves on a stone-revetted platform, 9m x 7.6m and 1.5m high, complete with a western entrance-feature and carefully paved upper surface. Five privileged males were later buried *ad sanctos* at its east end. The shrine was by far the most prominent feature on the island, dwarfing the adjacent church and covered with a liberal scattering of conspicuous white quartz pebbles. It says a lot about the priorities of this community that one of the smallest extant churches stands next to this, the largest and most elaborate outdoor shrine known from any Irish site. The AD 1020–35 Hiberno-Norse coin found on the upper surface of the shrine[37] is emblematic of its role as the community's principal means of generating revenue.

Church Island was no more isolated than Illaunloughan. It produced remains of livestock and grain[38] and even today it can easily be reached on foot from

36 White Marshall and Walsh, *Illaunloughan Island*, 37.   37 White Marshall and Walsh, 'Illaunloughan', 108.   38 O'Kelly, 'Church Island', 130–1.

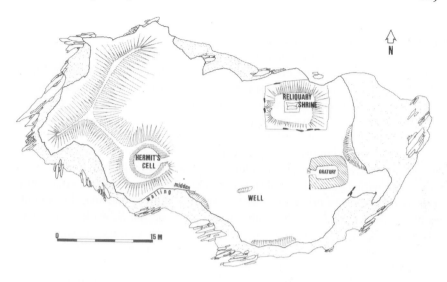

Fig. 5: Pre-excavation plan of Illaunloughan, Iveragh, showing dry-stone church, large gable shrine and severely eroded enclosure (after OPW). The layout shown here is essentially the same as that during the second main phase of occupation identified in the excavation. See White Marshall and Walsh, *Illaunloughan Island*, fig. 29. Except for the surviving section of the enclosure, which is seventh-century, the structures shown here were built in the eighth century, and occupation continued into the ninth century.

Pl. 2: Dry-stone church, Loher, Iveragh – one of the smallest extant examples

Beginish at low tide. At about 6m² the Phase I organic church on Church Island was only half the size of its Illaunloughan counterpart and Ó Corráin and Thomas may be correct in interpreting this phase as eremitical.[39] But here too requirements seem to have changed markedly, for the size and workmanship of the Phase II dry-stone church suggests it may have been congregational. It could comfortably have accommodated more than four times as many people as its phase two counterpart on Illaunloughan. Furthermore, unusual care was taken in its design and construction: it is the only dry-stone church built primarily of stone imported from an appreciable distance (*c.*1.5km) away,[40] one of only three with a second window, and one of two known to have been decorated with a butterfly finial (fig. 4).[41] The corner-post shrine to the south-east is on the same orientation as this second church, and may be roughly contemporary with it.[42] The sculpture on some of the Scottish corner-post shrines suggests they are mid-eighth to early ninth century in date.[43] This raises the possibility that on Iveragh corner-post shrines and gable shrines represent roughly contemporary, but alternative ways of enshrining corporeal relics.[44] But the contrast between these two examples is just as marked as between the churches, for the Church Island shrine is a modest, inconspicuous structure built into a hollow in a relatively peripheral part of the site.

39 O'Kelly, 'Church Island'; Ó Corráin, 'The early Irish churches', 339–40; C. Thomas, 'Cellular meanings, monastic beginnings' in *Emania*, 13 (1995), 51–67: 62.   40 O'Kelly, 'Church Island', 61, 118.   41 Ó Carragáin, 'Pre-Romanesque churches', 158. *Pace* Harbison, 'How old', 55–7, the finial does not support the possibility that this church is twelfth-century. It depicts a man flanked by animal heads of a type found in eighth-century metalwork. See Henry, 'Early monasteries', 152; O'Kelly, 'Church Island', 128. The down-turned mouth and large head of the man are like those of the Athlone plaque Christ, while his apparently sideways-pointing feet recall the St Matthew portrait in the Book of Durrow, folio 21v. The sharp upturn of the arms at the elbow suggests an *orans* position like that in the Arrest of Christ, Book of Kells, folio 114r, and in folio 2v, where Christ reaches out to touch an animal head to either side of him. As Ó Carragáin has shown, these images refer to the Canticle of Habakkuk which states that Christ will make himself known 'in the middle of two animals'. Patristic commentaries gave these animals a range of meanings including the Old and New Testaments and God the Father and the Holy Spirit. It has been argued that the visual representations also had a liturgical resonance for their audience, recalling the assistants who flanked the priest during mass. See É. Ó Carragáin, *'Traditio evange-liorum'* and *'susentatio':* the relevance of liturgical ceremonies to the Book of Kells' in F. O'Mahony (ed.), *The Book of Kells: proceedings of a conference at Trinity College Dublin, 6–9 September 1992* (Aldershot, 1994), 398–436: 422, 424, 435. We cannot know whether the Church Island sculptor envisaged this reading, but it does seem fitting given the *orans* position of the central figure, and the fact that the finial was positioned above the entrance to the main liturgical space on the island. The finial itself is clearly a skeuomorph of wooden examples that charac-terised some churches from at least *c.*AD 800 given their depiction in the Book of Kells (Folio 202v) and on high cross capstones. It may, therefore, have been conceived of as a way of signalling the sacredness of the building, for it creates a visual link between this distinctive local building method and the wider Irish architectural tradition.   42 It produced no human remains, due partly to acid soil conditions but mainly to disturbance. O'Kelly, 'Church Island', 89, 115.   43 C. Thomas, 'Sculptured stones and crosses from St Ninian's Isle and Papil' in A. Small, C. Thomas and D. Wilson (eds), *St Ninian's Isle and its treasures* (London, 1973), 8–44; C. Thomas, 'Form and function' in S. Foster (ed.), *The St Andrews sarcophagus: a Pictish masterpiece and its interna-tional connections* (Dublin, 1998), 84–96: 94–5.   44 Ó Carragáin, 'A landscape converted'.

It is suggested here that these contrasts are indicative of significant differences in the character of these sites. White Marshall and Walsh make a convincing case that Illaunloughan was monastic.[45] Certainly it appears to have been closer in character to a conventional monastery than most other minor sites in the vicinity including Church Island. Significantly, the Illaunloughan enclosure pre-dated most if not all of the domestic buildings and was therefore 'a primary feature',[46] while that at Church Island was the 'last work of improvement done during the [early medieval] occupation of the island'.[47] Clearly, signalling the sacredness of the site and its symbolic separation from the profane world was not as high a priority in the latter case. Furthermore, osteological analysis suggests that the cemetery on Illaunloughan was exclusively male and therefore, one might argue, monastic.[48] It appears that only one of the Church Island burials was properly examined but, significantly, this turned out to be female.[49] The Illaunloughan churches must have been designed for its resident community, and it is surely no coincidence that three organic circular houses were replaced by a single dry-stone example at the same time that indoor liturgical space on the island was almost halved with the erection of the tiny dry-stone church. In contrast, the contemporary gable shrine was clearly intended to broadcast the sanctity of the island's holy men to the wider world. The Church Island dry-stone church (pl. 1) was capable of accommodating more people than could ever have lived on the island; and other evidence also points to this site having strong secular associations. The slim documentary record suggests that, for a considerable part of the early medieval period, secular power in the region was centred immediately adjacent to Church Island at Ballycarbery.[50] The land here is the richest on the peninsula, and the area features impressive cashels at Leacanabuile, Cahergal and Caherna-Cath. Church Island itself occurs in Ballycarbery West townland. It must be seen as significant in this regard that the cross-slab from the site features an ogham inscription commemorating one BECCDIN MACI RITTECC of the *Uí Ráthach*, a prominent group whose name is preserved in the barony name, Iveragh.[51] It is clearly an addition to the monument, possibly dating to the

---

45 White Marshall and Walsh, 'Illaunloughan'; White Marshall and Walsh, *Illaunloughan Island*. 46 White Marshall and Walsh, 'Illaunloughan', 109. 47 O'Kelly, 'Church Island', 77. 48 White Marshall and Walsh, *Illaunloughan Island*, 84. The Irish laws stipulate that a monk must be buried at 'the church of which he is a *monachus*'. See Etchingham, *Church organisation*, 56, 438–9. A number of British monasteries, including Wearmouth and Ripon, have produced evidence of separate cemeteries for monks and lay people. See R. Cramp, 'Excavations at the Saxon monastic sites of Wearmouth and Jarrow, Co. Durham; an interim report' in *Medieval Archaeology*, 13 (1969), 21–66; R.A. Hall and M. Whyman, 'Settlement and monasticism at Ripon, North Yorkshire, from the seventh to eleventh centuries AD' in *Medieval Archaeology*, 40 (1996), 62–150. In the case of Illaunloughan it seems likely that some of the burials are of secular individuals wishing to be buried *ad sanctos*. 49 See O'Kelly, 'Church Island', 61, 91–3, 117, 132–3. 50 J. O'Donovan, *Leabhar na g-Ceart* (Dublin, 1847), 47; See also T.J. Barrington, *Discovering Kerry: its history, heritage and topography* (Dublin, 1976), 26. 51 M.J. O'Kelly and S. Kavanagh, 'A new ogham stone from County Kerry' in *Journal of the Cork Historical and*

eighth century,[52] and it is tempting to see it as marking the beginning of the second phase in the site's development during which its relationship with the local elite became ever more important.[53] As noted above, this is a development that was paralleled at sites throughout the country at about this time,[54] though only rarely can it be inferred from the material record. It would be overstretching the evidence to conclude that Church Island was run by an ecclesiastical lineage[55] of the *Uí Ráthach* and provided them and their dependants with pastoral care.[56] But it would be equally remiss not to seek reasons for the subtly different strategies pursued by these two ostensibly similar sites.

CONCLUSION

It would appear that differences like those identified in this comparison between Church Island and Illaunloughan are all we can usually expect when distinguishing between sites in terms of function, as distinct from status or regional variation. This is because churches generally followed the same basic 'grammar' when it came to site layout.[57] Even monuments that are often seen as quintessentially monastic may not always signal monasticism in its primary sense. An obvious example is the round tower that was erected at Cashel, probably at its transition from royal to archiepiscopal centre.[58] It might be concluded that there is a disconnect here between this broad morphological homogeneity and the new model of organisation that implies functional variety.

Archaeological Society, 59 (1954), 50–53; D. McManus, *A guide to ogham* (Maynooth, 1991), 70. **52** Henry 'Early monasteries', 159–60; McManus, *A guide*, 80, 172 note 29. **53** This is a relatively rare example of an ogham inscription added to a cross-slab. For a recent discussion of crosses added to ogham stones see G. Longden, 'Iconoclasm belief and memory in early medieval Wales' in H. Williams (ed.), *Archaeologies of remembrance: death and memory in past societies* (Cardiff, 2003), 171–92. **54** Ó Corráin, 'The early Irish churches', 338; Sharpe 'Some problems', 266–9. **55** See Charles-Edwards, '*Érlam*', 289. **56** It is even possible that the Church Island shrine, like its more illustrious Scottish cousin the St Andrews Sarcophagus, was intended for an important secular individual rather than the relics of a founding saint. See Foster (ed.), *The St Andrews sarcophagus*; see also R. Ó Floinn, 'Insignia Columbae I' in C. Bourke (ed.), *Studies in the cult of Saint Columba* (Dublin, 1997), 136–61: 160. One clear instance of this is the translation of King Ruaidrí Ua Conchobair in 1207 as part of a campaign to have him canonised. See Manning, 'Clonmacnoise Cathedral', 78. On secular benefactors being commemorated as saints in Anglo-Saxon England see J. Blair, 'A saint for every minster?' in Thacker and Sharpe (eds), *Local saints and local churches*, 455–94: 459–60. **57** Doherty, 'The monastic town', 45–75: 52–3; A. Hamlin, 'The early Irish Church: problems of identification' in N. Edwards and A. Lane (eds), *The early Church in Wales and the West* (Cardiff, 1992), 138–44: 142–4. This is one of the few primarily archaeological papers which takes full cognisance of the fact that, in most cases, site function cannot be determined simply on the basis of the presence or absence of particular monument types. For a similar observation on church sites in south-west England see Turner, *Christianity and the landscape*, 269, 245–50. **58** Indeed, seen in the European context, it would be peculiar if belfries in Ireland occurred only at strictly monastic sites. See Ó Carragáin, 'Pre-Romanesque churches', 257–64. On the possible secular functions of round towers see T. O'Keeffe, *Medieval Ireland*, 132.

But this depends on how we conceptualise this variety. In fact the documentary sources do complement the archaeology insofar as they are not usually concerned with making clear-cut functional distinctions between sites. To quote Etchingham, 'The extent to which ... [a monastic or specifically clerical element] predominates, even to the exclusion of others, may vary from church to church, but designations of churches are generally undifferentiated and terminology which is arguably of a distinctively 'monastic' kind is, in fact, most unusual.'[59] Clearly, sites that combined a range of functions were much more common than those that were purely monastic or purely pastoral. This is particularly true after the office of coarb became firmly established from *c*.700, the period to which much of our quantifiable archaeology belongs. We must therefore guard against placing these sites in excessively rigid, preconceived categories. The differences between them are usually differences in emphasis; and so the challenge for archaeologists is to distinguish between sites on the basis of nuances like those discussed above.

Acknowledgments
I would like to thank John Sheehan of UCC for supervising the thesis on which this paper is partly based; Prof. Martin Carver, Prof. Roger Stalley and Mick Monk for their input at the examination stage; the editors, and especially Dr Elizabeth FitzPatrick, for improvements to both the style and substance of the paper; Dr Edel Bhreathnach for invaluable comments on an early draft; Dr Tadhg O'Keeffe for stimulating discussion and pre-publication copies of a number of his articles; Con Manning for drawing my attention to several sites; Dr Jenny White Marshall and Claire Walsh for discussing their excavations on Illaunloughan with me; and the Irish Council for the Humanities and Social Sciences for funding the research. Finally, special thanks go to Maeve Sikora who surveyed most of these buildings with me. Any errors that remain are my own.

59 Etchingham, *Church organisation in Ireland*, 457.

The built environment of local community worship between the late eleventh and early thirteenth centuries

TADHG O'KEEFFE

The small ruined churches that dot the countryside constitute the most under-exploited archaeological resource for the study of community life in Ireland in the period between the twelfth-century reform and the Reformation. Although the publication of the Archaeological Survey of Ireland's county inventories is giving us a clear view at last of the scale and content of that resource, the inter-pretative literature on these buildings, and especially on those of post-1169 date and of general 'Gothic' style, is insubstantial. It certainly does not stand any comparison with the literature on contemporary cathedral and monastic churches. A quick perusal of the second volume of Leask's three-volume national survey[1] will reveal how, once we reach the thirteenth century, the dominant narrative of ecclesiastical architectural development connects only the larger buildings, the designs of which were appropriate to their regional roles (cathedrals) or to their attachment to national or international organisa-tions (abbeys, priories, friaries).

The relative neglect of 'local' churches, beyond their simple enumeration and description, reflects an under-appreciation of what these modestly engineered buildings have to offer us. As works of architecture permanently fixed to the landscape, they allow us to locate the presence, sometimes otherwise undocumented, of groups of laity in specific places during specific time-passages in the medieval period. They connect us experientially with those very communities at worship by allowing us to walk through the same doorways from the same directions and to occupy the same physical spaces. Phases of structural repair, alteration, whole or partial rebuilding, and abandonment – phases that are common to most of them – are choreographed with the biographies of their neighbouring and affiliated communities as well

1 H.G. Leask, *Irish churches and monastic buildings*, ii (Dundalk, 1960). The same can be said of A. Champneys' earlier survey, *Irish ecclesiastical architecture* (London, 1910) and of the relevant sections of B. de Breffny and G. Mott, *The churches and abbeys of Ireland* (London, 1976), which is an under-appreciated volume.

as with the fate of the Church in Ireland more broadly. Finally, their general lack of sophistication reflects practical, everyday constraints of resource and power within the worlds in which they operated, while their simple details hint at some essence, aesthetic and semiotic, of their 'Romanesque' or 'Gothic' architectural styles that is more difficult to locate in the hubris of larger churches.

This paper is about the built environment of local worship in Ireland in and around the 1100s, the century of indigenous church reform, and of the arrival first of reformed monasticism and then of Angevin lordship.[2] It is fundamentally a paper about the identification and characterisation of these environments. It must be noted that there are some conflicting views of the origins and early development of parishes. These cannot be refereed definitively from within archaeology, the discipline that informs this paper, because the type of evidence that is pertinent to the matter of parochial evolution – tithes and territories, advowsons, impropriations – lies outside the discipline's constituency. But, while I leave the adjudication on these issues to others (see Doherty and Etchingham in this volume), this paper is presented with cognisance of the wider issues of patronage and pastoral care that architecture might illuminate, especially for the later twelfth century.

TWELFTH-CENTURY REFORM AND PASTORAL CARE: THE EVIDENCE OF THE ARCHITECTURE

It is well established that there was an extensive system of pastoral care in Ireland in the 1200s. Organised geographically by parishes and dispensed from parish churches, its universality across Anglo-Norman and Gaelic Ireland[3] is well represented for us in the early fourteenth-century papal taxation. But problems arise once we shift the focus to the twelfth century. Until recently the

---

2 Critical works over the past forty years to which reference is made in this paper are, in chronological order: A.J. Otway-Ruthven, 'Parochial development in the rural deanery of Skreen' in *JRSAI*, 94 (1964), 11–22; K.W. Nicholls, 'Rectory, vicarage and parish in the western Irish dioceses' in *JRSAI*, 101 (1971), 53–84; M. Hennessy, 'Parochial organisation in medieval Tipperary' in W. Nolan and T.G. McGrath (eds), *Tipperary: history and society* (Dublin, 1985), 60–70; T. Charles-Edwards, 'The pastoral role of the church in the early Irish laws' in J. Blair and R. Sharpe (eds), *Pastoral care before the parish* (Leicester, 1992), 63–80; R. Sharpe, 'Churches and communities in early medieval Ireland' in Blair and Sharpe (eds), *Pastoral care*, 81–109; S. Ní Ghabhláin, 'The origin of medieval parishes in Gaelic Ireland: the evidence from Kilfenora' in *JRSAI*, 126 (1996), 37–61; A. Empey, 'The layperson in the parish: the medieval inheritance, 1169–1536' in R. Gillespie and W.G. Neely (eds), *The laity and the Church of Ireland, 1000–2000: all sorts and conditions* (Dublin, 2002), 7–48. 3 I use 'Anglo-Norman' to refer in temporal terms to the period 1169–*c*.1300 and in geographic terms to the area of *lordship*, or political control. The area of actual settlement – the *colony*, in the proper use of that term – was less extensive. The implications of these two concepts for the understanding of 'Anglo-Norman' culture, of which church design is a component, have yet to be thought through.

designation 'parish' would not have been used by scholars of ecclesiastical history in reference to any part of the territorial organisation or architecture of the pre-1170 Church in Ireland. It was understood that the arrival of the Anglo-Normans, followed by the decree of the Cashel synod of 1170–1 that tithes should be paid by every man to his parish church, marked the systematic institution for the very first time in Ireland of a territorial system of pastoral care.[4] This position was nourished in some quarters by the belief that the principal achievement of the reformers at the 1111 and 1152 synods was to break a monastic hegemony and so to create the requisite diocesan network for the development of parishes. In enfolding the matter of pastoral care into the parish, and then identifying the parish as a late phenomenon, it might be said that this model, at least in its crudest articulation, retrospectively disenfranchised generations of pre-1170 laity from their pastoral rights as Christians.[5]

Richard Sharpe launched a fresh and liberating debate more than a decade ago with his model of a territorial network of secular churches providing pastoral care for geographically contiguous family-group populations in pre-Norman Ireland.[6] His model brought into play the large number of 'early Christian' churches and church-sites known to us from landscape and place-name evidence. Continuity has now become the key concept. It has long been known that the territorial boundaries of pre-Norman Ireland are preserved in the secular-administrative structures of the twelfth century and later. But now these, combined with the occasional identification of *túatha* as constituting the population groups of the late twelfth- and early thirteenth-century parishes, are widely taken to indicate that the parochial organisation of the later medieval period has temporal roots deeper than *c.*1170.[7] Doherty has recently posited that the continuity of territoriality stretching back into the pre-millennium past had a system of 'primary' parishes superimposed on it during the century before the Anglo-Norman arrival.[8]

---

4 For Anglo-Norman Ireland see Otway-Ruthven, 'Deanery of Skreen', and Hennessy, 'Medieval Tipperary'. 5 See Sharpe, 'Churches and communities', 106, n79, quoting H.C. Mytum, 'The location of early churches in northern county Clare' in S.M. Pearce (ed.), *The early church in western Britain and Ireland* (Oxford, 1982), 351–61: 354. 6 Sharpe, 'Churches and communities'. The model acknowledged the *a priori* case for some pre-reform system of pastoral provision made by the sheer quantity of churches in first millennium Ireland, whether those are known to us from archaeological remains at hundreds of actual sites or from the thousands of *cill*- and related place-names. See also R. Sharpe, 'Some problems concerning the organization of the church in early medieval Ireland' in *Peritia*, 3 (1984), 230–70. 7 For case-studies see M.T. Flanagan, 'Henry II and the kingdom of Uí Fháeláin' in J. Bradley (ed.), *Settlement and society in medieval Ireland: studies presented to F.X. Martin* (Kilkenny, 1988), 229–39, and P.J. Duffy, 'Social and spatial order in the MacMahon lordship of Airghialla in the late sixteenth century' in P.J. Duffy, D. Edwards and E. FitzPatrick (eds), *Gaelic Ireland c.1250–c.1650: land, lordship and settlement* (Dublin, 2001), 115–37: 134–6. For *túatha* and the early Church see Charles-Edwards, 'Early Irish laws'. 8 C. Doherty, 'Cluain Dolcáin: a brief note', in A.P. Smyth (ed.), *Seanchas: studies in early and medieval Irish archaeology, history and literature in honour of Francis J. Byrne* (Dublin, 2000), 182–88, especially 188.

The pre-Norman (mid-eleventh to mid-twelfth-century) 'parish' in Ireland has clearly been moving from hypothesis to orthodoxy – some may regard it as having already moved – not least because it fits into a wider register of pre-invasion 'feudal' indicators.[9] Yet, the extent to which tithing was an operating element of this pre-Norman pastoral ministry is a critical matter – the definition of parish, at least as we understand it later in the medieval period, surely depends on it – that is still open to question. There is merit in Adrian Empey's recent argument that the absence of evidence in eastern Ireland of legal disputes over tithes and dues in the aftermath of the Anglo-Norman takeover actually supports Gerald of Wales' testimony of 1185 that the Irish 'do not *yet* pay tithes'.[10]

So, does the architectural record comply with or caution against this emergent orthodoxy? Church buildings are not, after all, incidental to the story of parish development. It is inconceivable that a comprehensive parochial network was conceptualised and its development undertaken early in the new millennium without some thought being given to the built environment for the participating clergy and – perhaps even more importantly, given that they were effectively paying for it – laity.

I think that Ireland's 'pre-Romanesque', or pre-1100, churches are – insofar as we can identify them[11] – unlikely candidates for parish or proto-parish churches. In the tithe-based conceptualisation of 'the parish' that is so familiar to us in the later medieval period, pastoral care was part-dispensed *within* the walls of the local church. Laity had access to the interior, or at least to part of the interior, of the church. In other words, the building had to accommodate

9 Flanagan, 'Henry II and Uí Fháeláin', 235; C. Doherty, 'The Vikings in Ireland: a review', in H.B. Clarke, M. Ní Mhaonaigh and R. Ó Floinn (eds), *Ireland and Scandinavia in the early Viking Age* (Dublin, 1998), 288–330: 313–14. For an interesting view of the historiography of feudal Ireland see H.B. Clarke, '1066, 1169, and all that: the tyranny of historical turning points', in J. Devlin and H.B. Clarke (eds), *European encounters: essays in memory of Albert Lovett* (Dublin, 2003), 11–36: 30–1. 10 Empey, 'The layperson in the parish', 13–14. It must be noted that Empey does not discount earlier systems of pastoral care involving tithes or otherwise: 'whatever systems of pastoral care may have emerged in the ninth and tenth centuries, it is extremely difficult to find evidence of their existence in the second half of the twelfth century'. For Gerald of Wales see J.J. O'Meara (trans.), *Gerald of Wales: the history and topography of Ireland* (Mountrath, 1982), 106. The italics are mine in the quotation in the main text. 11 Attributing dates, even usefully approximate ones, to churches that we confidently believe to be earlier than *c*.1100 is a very difficult task indeed, so the critical period of the eleventh century is rather fugitive for the architectural historian. It may well be that many of those stone churches that are usually described as 'pre-Romanesque' are in fact of eleventh-century date. References to the burning of churches in the 1000s are many (see C. Manning, 'References to church buildings in the annals', in Smyth (ed.), *Seanchas*, 37–52: 43–44), suggesting that, evidence for a stone-building industry notwithstanding, timber may even have been the preferred material in Ireland, just as it seems to have been in contemporary Anglo-Saxon England (see W.J. Rodwell, 'Anglo-Saxon church building: aspects of design and construction', in L.A.S. Butler and R.K. Morris (eds), *The Anglo-Saxon church: papers on history, architecture and archaeology in honour of Dr H.M. Taylor*, CBA Research Report 60 (London, 1986), 156–75: 171).

members of the local community. Although large churches capable of accommodating significant numbers of people are known to us from the documentary
record of pre-1100 Ireland, the extant stone churches of that date were single-
cell buildings that were poorly lit with, if one imagines an altar within,
relatively little interior room. By contrast, churches that were built to provide
local pastoral ministries in eleventh-century Anglo-Saxon England were almost
always two-celled, with separate spaces for the laity (the nave) and the clergy
(the chancel).[12]

While it is not inconceivable that the small, simple, Irish churches of pre-
1100 date were parochial in function, such an interpretation would require us
to conceive of a parish system quite unlike that of the later medieval period in
its general exclusion of the laity from the inside of church buildings. Indeed, I
suggest that the lintelled form of west doorway that was used in Irish church
buildings before the twelfth century may have been part of an architectural
language of *exclusion* of non-consecrated persons. Whereas round-arched
doorways of Roman-type framed points of entry into the sacred or privileged
interior spaces of churches, sometimes deliberately creating aedicule-type
affects,[13] the lintelled doorways of pre-Romanesque Ireland had no such
inherent iconography, and may have been favoured because they 'closed off' the
church interiors physically, visually and symbolically.

By contrast with the general pre-1100 period, the creation of the new
bishoprics and the appearance of new chevron-decorated Romanesque
churches with round-arched doorways certainly constitute a *prima facie* case for
the creation of a parochial system in Ireland after 1111 and before the Anglo-
Norman arrival. We will review that evidence and make a judgement on it
below (p. 132). First, however, it is important to turn to the urban Hiberno-
Scandinavians who were ahead of the posse with their episcopal appointments
of the later 1000s.

Hiberno-Scandinavian parish churches

Empey has argued that 'only in Dublin, and perhaps in the other Norse cities,
are there positive indications of pre-conquest non-monastic churches'
providing a pastoral ministry.[14] The one pre-conquest Hiberno-Scandinavian
church for which we have good architectural information is St Peter's in
Waterford city, discovered beneath later structural phases in excavations in the
1980s and now preserved as a foundation.[15] In its thirteenth-century incar-

---

12 C.F. Davidson, 'Change and change back: the development of English parish church chancels'
in R.N. Swanson (ed.), *Continuity and change in Christian worship* (Woodbridge, 1999), 65–77: 67.
13 See T. O'Keeffe, *Ireland's round towers* (Stroud, 2004) for a discussion of the symbolism of the
round-arched doorway.   14 Empey, 'The layperson in the parish', 11.   15 M.F. Hurley and
S.W.J. McCutcheon, 'St Peter's church and graveyard', in M.F. Hurley, O.M.B. Scully and S.W.J.
McCutcheon (eds), *Late Viking Age and medieval Waterford: excavations 1986–1992* (Waterford,
1997), 198–205, and B. Murtagh, 'The architecture of St Peter's Church', in ibid., 228–43.

nation this was a parish church, and it is likely that the earlier predecessor that interests us here was also parochial. The architectural parallels would suggest as much.

A small church of tripartite ground plan, with its nave, chancel and apse of more or less contemporary construction, St Peter's was almost certainly built in the early twelfth century.[16] It is not an 'Irish' building in the conventional sense.[17] Were it discovered in England and identified as a 'local' church (to use John Blair's preferred term[18]) of the early 1100s nobody would raise an eyebrow.[19] This is a critical point. St Peter's conforms to the type that was used for local community worship in the England of Henry I, and it served a community whose bishop from 1096, Malchus (Máel Ísu Ó hAinmere), had been trained in Winchester.[20]

We cannot say that St Peter's was a unique building back in the early 1100s, but given the number of churches of apparently similar status in the Hiberno-Scandinavian towns, one feels instinctively that it was not. It may therefore be significant that neither it nor any of the others presumed here to have existed exerted any obvious influence on native Irish church architecture of the period, even though they offered a tried-and-tested architectural template for a parochial church at precisely the time that the Irish Church was, so we are led to believe, developing its own parochial network. St Peter's chancel and apse were actually retained by the Waterford community right through the twelfth century – the Anglo-Normans pulled them down and replaced them with a single rectangular chancel in the thirteenth century – so it is not as if native Irish churchmen did not have ample chance to see them.

St Peter's is an early twelfth-century Norman-English model. The 'local' churches of the later Anglo-Saxons were usually a little simpler, being two-

---

16 T. O'Keeffe, *Romanesque Ireland*. This date fits with the likely chronology of a number of now-lost pre-conquest Dublin city churches that seem also to have been parochial (see Empey, 'The layperson in the parish', 11). 17 The apse is the oddity: it was not a feature used by builders in Ireland until the later seventeenth and eighteenth centuries. 18 'Churches in the early English landscapes: social and cultural contexts', in J. Blair and C. Pyrah (eds), *Church archaeology: research directions for the future*, CBA Research Report 104 (York, 1996), 6–18: 12. 19 Two examples of parallels: Barton Bendish (Phase I), a church that is mentioned in Domesday (see A. Rogerson, S.J. Ashley, P. Williams and A. Harris, 'Three Norman churches in Norfolk in *East Anglian Archaeology*, 32 (1987), 1–66, and Kilpeck in Herefordshire, extant by 1134 (M. Thurlby, *The Herefordshire school of Romanesque sculpture* (Logaston, 1999), 38) but no earlier than *c*.1120. Curiously, apses are also found in some rural twelfth-century Welsh churches, where they probably reflect influence from Norman architecture (W.J. Britnell, 'Excavation and recording at Pennant Melangell church' in *Montgomeryshire Collections*, 82 (1994), 41–102). St Peter's may have had a low tower over the chancel based on English parallels for the church's plan (see, for example, Asheldham, dated to the period 1100–35 (P.J. Drury and W.J. Rodwell, 'Investigations at Asheldham, Essex: an interim report on the church and the historic landscape' in *Antiquaries Journal*, 58 (1978), 133–51). 20 Malchus was consecrated by Anselm of Canterbury in 1096. He is named as archbishop of Cashel at Ráith Bresail in 1111 but within a decade is recorded as the bishop of a united diocese of Lismore and Waterford, and he dies octogenarian 'bishop of Port Láirge' in 1135 (O'Keeffe, *Romanesque Ireland*, 103).

celled, nave-and-chancel, buildings.[21] This particular plan-type is actually much older than the period under review.[22] Its appeal to the Anglo-Saxon thegns of the 1000s must have been its simple and efficient separation of clergy and laity. A number of churches of comparable type are known in the hinterland of Hiberno-Scandinavian Dublin, as at Clondalkin,[23] Killiney and Palmerstown, all in Co. Dublin, and I have dated these elsewhere (and without reference to the Anglo-Saxon parallels) to the period before *c*.1120 at the latest.[24] Given the possibility that Clondalkin at least was parochial in the late 1000s,[25] it is likely that parish churches of this very type stood alongside, and perhaps preceded, churches like St Peter's in the Hiberno-Scandinavian towns, and that these examples outside Dublin are products of a transmission of archi-tectural influence from late Anglo-Saxon England through that particular settlement. But the point made above about St Peter's and its apparent lack of influence on Irish church building holds true here as well. Churches of that coeval nave-and-chancel type that is represented at Clondalkin were simply not common in Ireland in the 1000s and early 1100s. The native Irish Church did not take up the architectural forms that seem to have been chosen for parochial churches of the Hiberno-Scandinavian communities before 1100.

Did reform generate a new parochial architecture?

Several related factors encourage the view of a complex parochial network emerging in the pre-Norman twelfth century. From the historical perspective we have, first, the creation of dioceses within the new ecclesiastical provinces of Armagh and Cashel (1111), and Dublin and Tuam (1152). Second, we have the earliest appearances of the two principal monastic organisations to which parochial tithes were diverted in the first fifty years after 1169. The Augustinians, generally native monastics who adopted the Rule of St Augustine, were around from the 1120s, and the Cistercians, the principal 'colonial' order, were around from 1140.[26] Moreover, from an archaeological

---

21 Few of these remained two-celled into the twelfth century, as did Raunds in Northamptonshire, for example. Most had apses added to them after 1100, and most of those apses were later replaced with rectangular chancels, as at Rivenhall in Essex, for example: W.J. Rodwell and K.A. Rodwell, *Rivenhall: investigation of a villa, church and village, 1950–1977*, CBA Research Report 55 (York, 1986).   **22** Escomb in Durham is dated to the seventh/eighth century (E. Fernie, *The architecture of the Anglo-Saxons* (London, 1983), fig. 26). See F. Oswald, L. Schaefer and H. Sennhauser, *Vorromanische Kirchenbauten*, 3 vols (Munich, 1966, 1994), passim, for parallels in the Continental German lands from about the same period onwards.   **23** The church no longer remains. See E. Rynne, 'Excavation of a church-site at Clondalkin, Co. Dublin' in *JRSAI*, 97 (1967), 29–37.   **24** O'Keeffe, *Romanesque Ireland*, 83–7. Of similar plan but with more elongated naves are Reefert and Trinity churches in Glendalough, two exceptional buildings that are made all the more puzzling by virtue of being a pair that straddle geographically the main monastic complex.   **25** Doherty, 'Cluain Dolcáin', 187.   **26** S. Preston, 'The canons regular of St Augustine: the twelfth-century reform in action', in S. Kinsella (ed.), *Augustinians at Christ Church: the canons regular of the cathedral priory of Holy Trinity, Dublin* (Dublin, 2000), 23–40; R. Stalley, *The Cistercian monasteries of Ireland* (New Haven, 1987). For an argument that no tithes

perspective we have new churches, or refurbishment of older churches, with sculptural details from the international, or more specifically English, Romanesque tradition.[27] Of some 160 buildings, or building fragments, known to me, 13 per cent were cathedrals, another 13 per cent were associated with reformed monastic orders other than the Cistercians, and virtually all (95 per cent) are on sites with histories of Christian use stretching back before the twelfth century.[28]

Churches built *ab initio* with Romanesque sculptural forms first appeared in Munster, where the early synods of the reforming Church convened. The architectural evidence suggests that St Flannan's oratory in Killaloe, Co. Clare, may be the earliest at *c.*1100, but the best known is Cormac's Chapel at Cashel, Co. Tipperary, built in the years around 1130.[29] By 1140 there was a small but significant group of buildings in Ireland's south-western region, including those at Cork, Ardfert and Kilmalkedar, Co. Kerry, Lismore, Co. Waterford, and Roscrea, Co. Tipperary. There was apparently very little elsewhere on the island of comparable style around that time. Romanesque sculptural forms appeared elsewhere in Ireland (especially in its southern half) around the middle of the century, and survived past 1170 in Connacht, as we will see later.

The association of St Flannan's oratory with Muirchertach Ua Briain, who presided over the 1101 synod at Cashel, and of Cormac's Chapel with Cormac Mac Carthaig, a king who had taken the tonsure at Lismore where he submitted to no less a person than Malachy of Armagh, suggests some relationship between the Romanesque tradition and the reform movement. The use of Romanesque in the cathedrals of Ardfert and Roscrea, both of which were built or refurbished to proclaim diocesan status after their sites were by-passed in 1111, suggests the nature of that relationship: Romanesque was the architectural correlative of reform.

The apparent absence of early twelfth-century fabric at so many of the sites chosen as diocesan centres in 1111 hampers our evaluation of that apparent relationship. It is difficult to know if that absence is a consequence of later refashioning of the buildings, especially in the thirteenth century, or if there was simply no building work carried out at many of the sites in the early 1100s. Leaving that problem aside, there are several reasons for us to doubt that Romanesque was specifically the architectural style of the reform movement.

issued to such monastic houses before the Anglo-Norman arrival see Empey, 'Layperson in the parish', 14.   27 Most of what follows is based on arguments presented in O'Keeffe, *Romanesque Ireland*. 28 Details of 120 sites are contained in T. O'Keeffe, 'Irish Romanesque architecture and architectural sculpture', unpublished PhD (University College Dublin, 1991), ch. 10; the increase is based on my fieldwork over the past decade and more.   29 See the following papers in D. Bracken and D. Ó Riain-Raedel (eds), *Ireland and Europe in the twelfth century: reform and renewal* (Dublin, forthcoming): R. Stalley, 'The construction and decoration of Cormac's Chapel at Cashel', R. Gem, 'Saint Flannán's oratory at Killaloe and the patronage of King Muirchertach Ua Briain', and T. O'Keeffe, 'Wheels of words, networks of knowledge: Romanesque scholarship and Cormac's Chapel'.

First of all, St Flannan's oratory and Cormac's Chapel, two key works in the early history of the style in Ireland, were fundamentally projects of secular kingship and its politics, and were connected with the reform movement only in the sense that their patrons were supporters of reform. Secondly, the chronology of surviving Romanesque works does not tie in especially well with the chronology of key events in the earlier phases of reform. Most of the churches post-date the 1111 synod by several decades. There was an increase in the number of new churches around the middle of the century, and this was conceivably related to the fine tuning of the diocesan system by the 1152 synodians.[30] However, as Romanesque forms were already in vogue in the early 1150s it stands to reason that they would be used for these new churches without their builders ever intending such forms to be a visual-cultural articulation of reform ideals. Finally, the low volume in north-east Ireland of Romanesque architecture of the type that we know elsewhere on the island is at odds with the importance of Armagh in the reform movement. If reform in that corner of Ireland did not require material expression through the use of Romanesque, why should we think that reform in the south-west did require it?

The upshot of this discussion is a reconfiguration of the relationship of Romanesque to reform. We need to see both of these as phenomena of twelfth-century political culture that, figuratively speaking, often shared the same spaces and contributed intelligibility to each other but were not actually dependent on each other. By distancing Romanesque from reform in this way, we are dissuaded from assuming that those new (non-cathedral, non-Augustinian) churches with Romanesque details were part of a trickledown of reformed ecclesiastical organisation from diocesan level to parochial level. This is not to say, of course, that none of those Romanesque churches operated as parochial churches. Some of them may well have done: a couple of dozen were either constructed as two-celled buildings, or were converted to two-celled churches by the addition of a nave or a chancel to a pre-existing church. However, the fact of their recurring location on long-established ecclesiastical sites, regardless of how central or peripheral those sites were geographically in the twelfth century, does suggest that most of the churches were generally more respectful of inherited tradition than of the pastoral needs of contemporary laity. If the reformers were envisaging ultimately a systematic provision of pastoral care issuing from non-monastic churches within a diocesan structure, the churches of the twelfth century do not look like the products of their ambition.

---

30 T. O'Keeffe, 'Romanesque as metaphor: architecture and reform in early twelfth-century Ireland', in Smyth (ed.), *Seanchas*, 313–22: 315.

PARISH CHURCHES OF THE ANGLO-NORMANS

The contribution of the Anglo-Normans to the parochial history of the eastern half of Ireland is acknowledged, and yet relatively few of the medieval parish churches that are still extant are identified explicitly in the literature as their work. There is a number of large medieval parish churches of indisputable Anglo-Norman attribution in urban contexts. For instance, there is New Ross, Co. Wexford, founded under the patronage of William Marshall (pl. 1), and Gowran, Co. Kilkenny, and Youghal, Co. Cork, which were collegiate churches patronised by the Butlers and FitzGeralds respectively. There is also the parish church at Carrickfergus, Co. Antrim, founded by John de Courcy, and that at Kinsale, Co. Cork, probably founded by the Cork branch of the de Courcys, and that at Fethard, Co. Tipperary, founded perhaps by the archbishop of Cashel. But these are few in number and were always exceptional buildings. There is a widespread perception that the medieval parish churches found in smaller settlements or in isolated rural locations in Ireland are largely of later medieval (fifteenth-century) date, and that they replaced older Anglo-Norman churches on the same sites. One need only peruse the appropriate chapters of the published county inventories of the Archaeological Survey of Ireland for evidence that this view is held. Lists of churches are introduced in a number of volumes with statements such as: 'while most parishes and most parish churches were established by the end of the 13th century, many of the structures would have been rebuilt at some time and most of the present remains probably date to the late 15th or 16th century'.[31] However, Anglo-Norman parish churches *do* survive outside of the principal towns, either as fairly complete buildings or as the cores of later medieval refashionings. It is not possible yet to suggest numbers of survivals, whole or partial, but it is important, as a first step, to dispel any impression that virtually nothing remains.[32]

Identifying Anglo-Norman parish churches

The key to identifying many of these churches is simple enough within the context of the long established Romanesque-to-Gothic architectural model. We

---

31 M. Moore (ed.), *Archaeological inventory of County Waterford* (Dublin, 1999), 162.   32 Empey's 'black hole' metaphor for our knowledge of Anglo-Norman parish churches (Empey, 'The layperson in the parish', 15) is much too strong but he can be forgiven it. Leask said very little about parish churches in the second, Anglo-Norman Gothic, volume of his trilogy (note 1 above). Stalley acknowledged that 'a great deal of energy was expended' on the construction of parish churches in the thirteenth and fifteenth centuries but described the survival rate as poor. He cited, somewhat perversely, two late fifteenth- to early sixteenth-century churches from Fermanagh as 'typical examples' of what was later built (R. Stalley, 'Irish Gothic and English fashion', in J. Lydon (ed.), *The English in medieval Ireland* (Dublin, 1984), 65–86: 68). The published volumes of the Archaeological Survey of Ireland's county inventory series often do not give dates for the churches that are described, even when thirteenth-century dates are fairly self-evident.

Pl. 1: St Mary's parish church in New Ross from the east, showing the chancel and south transept; this seems to have been the largest thirteenth-century parish church in Ireland.

are familiar with the lexicon and general chronology of Gothic stylistic forms in Ireland from the larger and generally well-documented cathedral and monastic churches. Such forms first appeared in Ireland in the 1190s in the church of Grey Cistercian abbey, Co. Down, and then appeared around different parts of the lordship from the start of the thirteenth century.[33] The first generation of Anglo-Norman builders in Ireland actually operated in the Romanesque idiom. The east end of Dublin's Christ Church cathedral, for example, was rebuilt to a typically late twelfth-century English Romanesque design in the 1180s or 1190s, and Gothic was only used in the cathedral when the nave was being constructed in the early 1200s,[34] while a number of Ireland's Anglo-Norman stone castles of the late 1100s (and indeed into the 1200s) also have Romanesque elements.[35] So, if the Anglo-Normans built new parish

33 Stalley, 'Irish Gothic and English fashion', is still a useful synthesis; the Gothic style itself is understood to have emerged in France in the 1130s and to have first appeared in England only about 1170 at Canterbury cathedral. 34 R. Stalley, 'The construction of the medieval cathedral, *c*.1030–1250', in K. Milne (ed.), *Christ Church cathedral, Dublin: a history* (Dublin, 2000), 53–74; T. O'Keeffe, 'Architecture and regular life in Holy Trinity cathedral, 1150–1350', in S. Kinsella (ed.), *Augustinians at Christ Church: the Canons Regular of the cathedral priory of Holy Trinity, Dublin* (Dublin 2000), 23–40. 35 There are roll-moulded window surrounds of *c*.1200 in the castle halls of Adare, Co. Limerick, and Ballyderown, Co. Cork, there is a chevron-decorated rear-

churches between *c*.1170 and *c*.1200 they would have built them in the Romanesque style. Indeed, given that Gothic forms were only appearing for the first time in Ireland around 1200 and were not that common at all before the 1220s, it is difficult to envisage their use before then in many parish churches outside of the main towns.

But identifying actual Romanesque parish churches built by the Anglo-Normans is very difficult. One definite example of a new urban Anglo-Norman parish church of the late 1100s is St Nicholas's in Carrickfergus.[36] A contemporary church is probably Bannow, Co. Wexford, its Romanesque elements suggesting that the foundation of that church had less to do with pastoral care and tithing than with the immediate memorialising of the successful Anglo-Norman landings in the bay beneath it. However, most of the local churches with Romanesque details in eastern and southern Ireland are located at sites of demonstrable antiquity and seem to have been built in the middle two quarters of the twelfth century. In other words, they generally pre-date 1170. Some of these churches acquired parochial roles within the Anglo-Norman system after 1170, but that is not the point: they were not new buildings.

It is an old mantra of archaeology that absence of evidence is quite different from evidence of absence. There may be many extant Anglo-Norman parish churches of that first fifty-year period that cannot now be identified because they have lost their original diagnostically-carved stonework. As we will see below, the two-celled plan with a long nave and/or a long chancel was frequently used for Anglo-Norman parish churches in the thirteenth century, so it is possible that some of the more ruined churches of this plan-type date from the late 1100s. However, the numbers of identifiable *pre*-1170 Romanesque and *post*-1200 Gothic churches suggests, I think, that the general absence of archaeological evidence for new Anglo-Norman parish churches in the late 1100s really does amount to evidence of absence, and that few parish churches were actually built at this time. One imagines that in the early stages of organising parishes the Anglo-Normans sometimes made use of existing churches, but the symbiosis between manor and parish suggests that, in its formative stages, the parochial system might more frequently have operated out of the castle complex, possibly out of its private chapel.

The building of a new church and the payment of tithes went hand-in-hand – they were interdependent. The architectural record is thus a very important part of the story, and it indicates that the new parish network did not really take off in earnest until the thirteenth century, by which time Gothic was its appropriate stylistic medium. Given the importance of the parishes to the financial

arch in the early thirteenth-century part of the *donjon* at Nenagh, Co. Tipperary, and shallow corner pilasters on the late twelfth-century *donjons* at Carrickfergus and Adare, as well as on the slightly later halls at Clonmacnoise, Co. Offaly, and Castle Kirke, Co. Galway. **36** For a description see T.E. McNeill, *Anglo-Norman Ulster* (Edinburgh, 1980), 47–50; McNeill dates it to *c*.1200 but it must be earlier (Stalley, 'Irish Gothic and English fashion', 69, n. 2).

Pl. 2: Knockgraffon parish church, Co. Tipperary, showing the chancel arch and the chancel behind it. The east window probably dates the church to the third quarter of the thirteenth century; this window was in-filled in the fifteenth century though its outline was preserved.

well-being of the monasteries, it is surely significant that there was also apparently very little building activity going on in the late 1100s and early 1200s in many of the monastic churches that were either founded by the Anglo-Normans or brought under their control. Indeed, parish formation in Anglo-Norman areas may actually have staggered over many decades of the thirteenth century, as witness those many instances where the Gothic details are probably no earlier than *c*.1250 (pl. 2).

Thirteenth-century Anglo-Norman parish churches
What do thirteenth-century Anglo-Norman parish churches look like? Two examples from opposite sides of Ireland are Wells, Co. Carlow (pl. 3) and St Finghin's at Quin, Co. Clare (pl. 4), probably dating from the 1240s and 1280s respectively. Wells has a separate nave and chancel; Quin is of undifferentiated nave-and-chancel design, but there would originally have been some demarcation of its chancel, probably by a screen. We do not yet know why some Anglo-Norman parish churches had their naves and chancels as separate structures while others did not.

Pl. 3: Wells church, Co. Carlow from the north-east; there was rebuilding in the later medieval period.

Pl. 4: St Finghin's church, Quin, from the north-west; the western tower (right-side of photograph) is the only significant post-1300 feature.

The length:breadth nave ratios in these buildings are in excess of 2:1, and the chancel of Wells is 2:1. Such proportions are commonly found in churches with thirteenth-century Gothic details.[37] How do we explain this elongation? Church width was fairly standard: the widest un-aisled churches were less than 10m in width as it was not possible to span a greater distance than this using timber beams and a pitched roof. Stretching the church lengthways, then, created more space. The questions then are why, and for whom, was more space needed?

Chancels

The long, flat-ended, chancel that one finds in many parish churches, such as Wells, and indeed in most cathedral and monastic churches in Anglo-Norman Ireland, reflects the pattern that emerged in England at the end of the twelfth century and remained dominant throughout the thirteenth century.[38] The chronology suggests that the experiences in England did not influence those in Ireland but that there were parallel processes of chancel development on both islands.

Given that the main or high altar was invariably at the east end of the chancel by the 1200s, either right against the back wall or standing very slightly in front of it,[39] the effect of a long chancel was to create more space between that altar and the chancel arch (or, in the case of a larger church, the crossing). The value of that additional space to a community of monks or canons in a monastic or cathedral church is self-evident. The eastern arm of such a church usually needed to be divided into the short sanctuary, where the sacramental celebration was centred on the altar according to some prescribed rite, and a longer choir to its west, where the Divine Office and parts of the Mass were sung. A screen or a wall usually kept the liturgical activities within the chancel out of sight of the laity or the *conversi* in the nave. That screen was sometimes treated as if a church façade in its own right (as at Athassel, Co. Tipperary, for example), thus emphasising the separate, self-contained, nature of the chancel and its rituals. Parish churches with their single priests did not require such long chancels, however. Where they exist, it is possible that they were built to

37 There has been far too little work done on proportional systems in medieval Irish church building. Anecdotally, proportions of less than 2: 1 are certainly a recurring feature of pre-Romanesque churches, but 2:1 is used (sometimes in imaginative ways) in Romanesque and later medieval churches, and possibly also in Anglo-Norman churches. Long naves (of 3:1 and more) and long chancels (between 2:1 and 3:1) are post-Romanesque and are often demonstrably of Anglo-Norman build, as in the case of the sadly neglected church of Ballyoughtera (the Anglo-Norman parish church of Castlemartyr), Co. Cork, for example.   38 R. Morris, *The church in British archaeology*, CBA Research Report 47 (York, 1983), 84.   39 Altars and their positions in medieval Irish churches need more research, but outside Ireland we know that prior to the early eleventh century the main altar of a church usually stood sufficiently forward of the back wall for the priest to face the congregation across it. Altars were increasingly fixed to the back walls of churches in England from the second quarter of that century (D. Parsons, '*Sacrarium*: ablution drains in early medieval churches', in Butler and Morris (eds), *The Anglo-Saxon church*, 105-20: 107).

accommodate some filtering down to local level of the liturgical rites practised in the larger churches, either the churches of monasteries to which the parish revenues in question issued or the local cathedrals. But it is more likely, I think, that long chancels, at least in Ireland, emulated architecturally the eastern arms of those larger churches, and, being funded by donation from local lords perhaps, they represent a design choice that may have had political motivation.

Naves

The elongation of naves is a more consistent feature of Anglo-Norman parish churches. Here too the elongation created more space. Spacious naves might reflect the sizes of lay populations, as big parishes presumably had big numbers of laity requiring accommodation.[40] It is also possible that in large parishes the church's nave, like that of the contemporary monastic and cathedral church, was effectively a self-contained liturgical space in its own right, created by a barrier or screen running across the span of the chancel arch. In this scenario, the elongation of the nave was not just to accommodate the laity but also an altar with a space around it.

Additional space could also be created in a parish church by building an aisle along one or both sides of the nave. This was done in the bigger thirteenth-century urban churches (pl. 5) but it was not done elsewhere. Aisles required arcades of timber or stone, and that extra structural sophistication required money, but the revenue coming into most parish churches was apparently not recycled into the architecture but simply flushed straight out again and into the monasteries. However, the fact that even the least prosperous of rural English parish churches often had aisles in the twelfth century, and that virtually all English parish churches had aisles in the thirteenth century, regardless of their resources, draws attention to this absence in Ireland and suggests that money is at best a small part of the explanation.

Lateral aisles were not the places of congregation that we know them to be in modern or contemporary churches, so they were not built in response to numbers of laity needing space to pray. This is a critical point. They were instead places of liturgy associated with, for example, baptism and matrimony, and even chantry.[41] They were presumably also spaces of lay circulation and clerical procession, just as they were in larger cathedral or monastic churches. The absence of aisles in the Irish parish churches, then, is clearly very significant. The day-to-day operations of the Irish parish community were

---

40 The sizes of churches have been matched with the sizes of the territories or (where there are Domesday records) populations served by them. The fit is not exact and it cannot be demonstrated that some size ratio was worked out in advance of any building, but there was clearly some general relationship. See C.J. Bond, 'Church and parish in Norman Worcestershire', in J. Blair (ed.), *Minsters and parish churches: the local church in transition, 950–1200* (Oxford, 1988), 119–58: 141–4; S. Ní Ghabhláin, 'Church and community in medieval Ireland: the diocese of Kilfenora' in *JRSAI*, 125 (1995), 61–84. **41** Morris, *The church in British archaeology*, 84–5.

Pl. 5: The aisled church at Thomastown, Co. Kilkenny, showing the top of one of the nave arcades and the clerestory windows

compromised by their architectural environment in a manner that was outside the experience of any contemporary English community. Baptismal rites, for example, had to compete for space with conventional worship, while the capacity of local lords to endow chantry priests within the existing architectural structures was virtually non-existent.

One likely explanation for the absence of aisles – and indeed of the continued if occasional use of west walls for church entrances – is that there was a major input from the Gaelic-Irish building tradition into the Anglo-Norman parish church template.[42] This explanation suggests a significant involvement of native builders in shaping the actual architectural spaces. Historical evidence does not rule out this possibility. Although the model of large-scale in-migration from England and Wales after 1169[43] would encourage a presumption that the new buildings of the Anglo-Norman lordship in Ireland were built by Anglo-Norman hands and represent a significant stylistic break

42 The corollary of this may be that the popularity of the aisled church in thirteenth-century England reflects continuity from Anglo-Saxon *porticus*. 43 See, for example, R.R. Davies, *Domination and conquest: the experience of Ireland, Scotland and Wales, 1100–1300* (Cambridge, 1990), 43.

with earlier tradition, the actual extent to which the lordship was populated with migrants is open to question. Witness, for instance, Mark Hennessy's demonstration that the manors of Tipperary had mainly Gaelic-Irish tenants prior to *c*.1250.[44]

I wish to suggest another possible explanation for elongated, un-aisled, naves in Ireland. The parish church was the focal building of an operation involving the passage of money from parishioner to monastery. It was thus a building of administration as well of salvation. It paralleled, then, the manorial hall, the focal building of the secular estate that was coterminous with the parish. We know little about the structures of manorial halls in Anglo-Norman Ireland, but it is conceivable that the experience of entering a parish church nave was not unlike entering one of these halls. The naves of churches like Wells are certainly hall-like in their elongation, in their high, side-wall, windows that allowed light in but prevented outward gazes, in their lower-end (west) entrances, and in their upper-end (east) altars/daises. Is it possible that the reason we know so little about manorial halls in thirteenth-century Ireland is because they were few in number to begin with? And is it possible, then, that the naves of newly-built churches were intended to be administrative spaces for the geopolitical entities that were simultaneously parishes and manors, and that their architecture, with its almost begrudging accommodation of liturgy, was conceptualised accordingly?

Anglo-Norman influence on the western dioceses after 1170

Parish formation is regarded as quite a late phenomenon in the western dioceses. Sinéad Ní Ghabhláin has attributed most of the principal churches in the diocese of Kilfenora to the late twelfth- or early thirteenth-century period (while identifying that there has also been some later medieval rebuilding at these sites). She argues on that basis for native Irish parish formation in Kilfenora about this time.[45] Kenneth Nicholls, who wisely warns against generalising on the basis of individual case studies, has suggested that some western parishes may have been formed in the early 1200s (Ballinacourty, Oranmore, Athenry, all Co. Galway). However, he describes as 'the usual Connacht system' the creation of large territorial rectories in the period between *c*.1200 and the arrival of the Anglo-Normans, followed then by parishes.[46]

Late parish formation in the west, whether its earnest beginning is dated to the late 1100s or to well into the 1200s, reduces considerably the possibility that the twelfth-century reform was directly responsible. It raises instead the probability of some Anglo-Norman responsibility, indirectly up to 1227 and thereafter directly. In the absence of more field data from the western dioceses it is difficult and dangerous to generalise, but I think that the architectural

---

44 M. Hennessy, 'Manorial organisation in early thirteenth-century Tipperary' in *Irish Geography*, 29 (1996), 116–25. **45** See Ní Ghabhláin, 'Church and community', and her essay in this volume. **46** Nicholls, 'Rectory, vicarage and parish'.

record for Cos. Clare, Galway and Mayo promotes the following working hypothesis. The parishes were taking shape before the Anglo-Normans arrived in the area but not before 1200, and it is the establishment of the parochial system in Anglo-Norman Ireland that provided the impetus and architectural expression.

The key to this hypothesis is the so-called 'School of the West' tradition of the 'Transitional' style of architecture.[47] These are two phrases that should really be abandoned, the first because it gives the wrong impression that there was a school of masons,[48] and the second because it implies an actual transitive phase between Romanesque to Gothic, a concept that has no validity anywhere, even in northern France where Gothic is supposed to have been invented.[49] The best description for those buildings that appear to be 'transitional' between Romanesque and Gothic is probably 'Late Romanesque' since this terminology acknowledges the directorial presence of that older tradition.

To support the working hypothesis offered above let us look briefly at Drumacoo, Co. Galway, a church that would be regarded as a classic example of this 'Transition'[50] and one that was parochial in the thirteenth century. The feature that most defines this as belonging to 'the transition' between Romanesque and Gothic is its magnificent south doorway (pl. 6). The decorative elements of Romanesque origin are the chevrons on two of its three orders of arch, and the small, snarling animal heads[51] that adorn one of the

---

47 'School of the West' was Harold Leask's term, used to describe a 'body of tradition' of church architecture and architectural sculpture of the early 1200s in Connacht and Thomond (*Irish churches and monastic buildings ii*, 53–76). For its most recent significant usage see B. Kalkreuter, *Boyle abbey and the school of the west* (Bray, 2001). The use of 'Transitional' has remained popular since Arthur Champneys used it in his *Irish ecclesiastical architecture* (London, 1910). 48 It is extraordinary that Leask himself recognised that there was no single 'guild' of masons and did not mean to give the impression that there was! The wider cultural-political implications of referring to a 'school' seem to have passed him by. 49 The concept of stylistic 'transition' as applied to our very period has been the subject of careful critique: see J. Bony, 'Introduction' in *Studies in Western art, i: acts of the twentieth international congress of the history of art* (Princeton 1963), 81–4, and W. Sauerlander, 'Style or transition?: the fallacies of classification discussed in the light of German architecture 1190–1260' in *Architectural History*, 30 (1987), 1–29. It is especially interesting to note that the Île de France in which Gothic first appeared was one of the few parts of France *not* to have a strong Romanesque tradition, even though it was wedged between Normandy and Burgundy! 50 The other classic examples are, alphabetically, the presbytery of Abbeyknockmoy church (Cistercian), Co. Galway, Ballintober priory church (Augustinian), Co. Mayo, the nave of Boyle abbey church (Cistercian), Co. Roscommon, the chancel of Clonfert cathedral, Co. Galway, Temple Rí at Clonmacnoise, Cong abbey church and claustral range (Augustinian), Co. Mayo, the presbytery of Corcomroe abbey church (Cistercian), Co. Clare, Inishmaine priory church (Augustinian), Co. Mayo, Killone nunnery church (Augustinian), Co. Clare, Killaloe cathedral, Co. Clare, O'Heyne's church (Augustinian) at Kilmacduagh, Co. Galway, Kilfenora cathedral, Co. Clare, and the east end of Temple Jarlath (Premonstratensian) in Tuam, Co. Galway. There are, of course, lesser churches that one could mention, such as Noughaval, Co. Clare, with its parallels at Corcomroe, or Kilronan, Co. Roscommon, with its parallels at Cong. 51 These are paralleled in the Shannon region at the Nuns' Church at Clonmacnoise (1166–7) and at Clonfert (*c*.1180).

Pl. 6: Drumacoo church doorway, Co. Galway

capitals (pl. 7). The relatively plain nature of the portal's inner order relative to the two outer orders can also be paralleled in Gaelic-Irish Romanesque work. The pointed arch is a feature that one routinely associates with Gothic, though it could also be a feature of Romanesque.[52] However, a number of the portal's

---

52 It can actually be a feature of Romanesque as well: see C.E. Armi, *Design and construction in Romanesque architecture* (Cambridge, 2004).

Pl. 7: The capitals on the east side of Drumacoo church doorway: small animal-heads decorate the capital in the centre and stylised plants and leaves decorate that on the right.

features – the slender three-quarter rolls flanked by chamfered edges that form part of the jambs; the 'bands' or rings halfway up those rolls; the pointed bowtell moulding underneath the chevron on the outer arch – have many parallels in Gothic work in eastern Ireland, particularly of the first half of the 1200s. Drumacoo's portal is a piece of architecture informed aesthetically by Anglo-Norman architecture elsewhere in Ireland. In fact, the stylised plants and leaves on this portal's capitals (pl. 7) may be adaptations of the so-called 'stiff-leaf' ornament that is characteristic of the Early English tradition of Gothic, found in Anglo-Norman parts of Ireland in the early 1200s.[53]

Many of the details of the Drumacoo portal can be paralleled in the other key works of this western, 'Transitional', architectural tradition. It is clear that these new churches were influenced aesthetically by Anglo-Norman Gothic in eastern Ireland, and that they are no earlier than the start of the thirteenth century. Although the architecture can provide no more than circumstantial support for parish formation in the west in the early 1200s, it is surely no co-incidence that tithes are alleged to have been levied in Connacht for the first time in the first quarter of the thirteenth century,[54] which is when most of these churches were built.

53 See its use in Christ Church cathedral, for example: R. Stalley, 'The medieval sculpture of Christ Church Cathedral, Dublin' in *Archaeologia*, 106 (1979), 107-22. 54 Nicholls, 'Rectory,

CODA: THE GREAT REBUILDING OF THE 1400S

The 'great rebuilding' of the later medieval period, a process that was clearly more marked in some areas or regions than in others, is not of direct concern to us here. Nonetheless, it is useful to consider three possible explanations for those instances in which older churches were replaced in their entirety or at least substantially modified.

The first explanation is that Anglo-Norman parish churches were deemed unsuitable for later needs, that late medieval parochialism required, in other words, a rather different architecture from that which it had inherited from the thirteenth century. However, this is not a convincing explanation. Despite significant changes in the devotional practices of clergy and laity in the second half of the fourteenth century,[55] fifteenth-century parish churches are not significantly different in terms of layout from those of the thirteenth century. Any features required for fifteenth-century devotion that were not already present in extant buildings – and most were present, it seems – could be integrated into such buildings without much demolition. Bell-ringing, for example, was more important in the later period, reflecting the increased interest in the Mass, but all that it required was the erection of a western bell-tower, if one did not already exist, or the addition of a bell-cote to an existing west gable. We need only look to the monastic orders to see how easily fifteenth-century needs could be accommodated in thirteenth-century churches: aisled transepts, for example, were often added to friary churches in the later medieval period. A further point is that later medieval parish churches tend to be slightly smaller in terms of interior area than those of the Anglo-Normans (pl. 8), suggesting that the accommodation of greater numbers of Mass-going laity was not a factor for rebuilding.

A second explanation is that the Anglo-Norman parish churches were in a poor state. This casts the 'great rebuilding' as a simple imperative. It is not an unreasonable explanation. We should be careful not to be sucked back into the narrow interpretation of the 1300s as a period of endemic warfare that left the countryside and its buildings in a state of dilapidation, but think instead of how population decline in the second half of the fourteenth century would have reduced the upkeep capacity of the churches. One wonders, though, how many thirteenth-century churches were so dilapidated that clearing them away entirely was easier than, say, simply re-roofing them and reinstating their interiors. In many cases there was no significant rebuilding at all: existing parish churches were simply modernised in the 1400s, just as were monastic churches.

The third possible explanation for rebuilding is perhaps the most convincing: it posits that the act of rebuilding itself, and obviously also any

vicarage and parish', 69, n. 50. **55** Empey, 'The layperson in the parish', 17.

Pl. 8: Garryvoe church, Co. Cork, a small parish church of the late medieval period

consequent similarities between the rebuilt church and the local tower-house, carried symbolic weight for those whose endowments financed the work. It was an act of social power. In some instances the intrinsic qualities or the conditions of the Anglo-Norman church did not particularly register, so that rebuilding constituted a kind of groundhog day on an older parish church site in that a new start was made, a new heritage created.

Late twelfth-century church construction: evidence of parish formation?

SINÉAD NÍ GHABHLÁIN

By the middle of the twelfth century the Irish Church had undergone a complete restructuring that resulted in the establishment of a hierarchical territorial institution. The reformed Church differed from the traditional Irish Church in two respects. In the reformed Church episcopal and monastic churches formed parallel, but separate hierarchies, with the bishop, and not the abbot, ruling over both. The reformed Church was also organised into fixed, territorial dioceses ruled by bishops.[1] The synod of Kells-Mellifont in 1152 established four provinces with metropolitan sees at Armagh, Dublin, Cashel and Tuam, and a total of thirty-four dioceses. The territorial framework established at Kells-Mellifont was to remain largely unchanged throughout the later medieval period. While the framework for the provincial and diocesan structures was established by the middle of the century, none of the reforming synods had issued guidelines for the establishment of parishes and it appears that parish formation took place within individual dioceses at varying rates. In Anglo-Norman Ireland manors provided a convenient framework for parish formation.[2] Where historical sources documenting the process of parish formation are available, they indicate that the pace of parish formation in Anglo-Norman areas was rapid. In Co. Tipperary, where knight's fees provided a framework for the establishment of parishes, a stable parochial network had been established by the early thirteenth century.[3]

The ecclesiastical reform movement inspired a renaissance in ecclesiastical art and architecture, as cathedral churches and reformed monasteries were built and furnished. The decades following the establishment of the dioceses witnessed the construction of cathedrals throughout the country. Romanesque cathedrals constructed from the middle of the twelfth century include Ardfert,

---

1 J.A. Watt, *The Church and the two nations in medieval Ireland* (Cambridge, 1970), 10–34; *The Church in medieval Ireland* (Dublin, 1971), 2–27; A. Gwynn, *The Irish Church in the eleventh and twelfth centuries* (Dublin, 1992), 234–70. 2 A.J. Otway-Ruthven, 'Parochial development in the rural deanery of Skreen' in *JRSAI*, 94 (1964), 112–22; M. Hennessey, 'Parochial organisation in medieval Tipperary' in W. Nolan and T.G. McGrath (eds), *Tipperary: history and society* (Dublin, 1985), 60–70. 3 Hennessey, 'Parochial organisation', 63.

Co. Kerry, Ardmore and Lismore, Co. Waterford, Clonfert, Co. Galway, St Flannan's, Killaloe, Co. Clare, St Mary's in Limerick, Roscrea, Co. Tipperary and Tuam, Co. Galway.[4] Construction of new cathedrals continued to the end of the twelfth century and into the early thirteenth century. The process of parish formation entailed the provision of clergy, a parish church and dependent chapels within the parish. Parish formation is reflected in a surge in the construction of parish churches and estate chapels in the late twelfth century and early thirteenth centuries, in Anglo-Norman areas where parish formation and the establishment of manors took place side by side.[5]

Kenneth Nicholls' theory for the development of parishes in Gaelic dioceses posits the formation of rural rectories consisting of between two and eight parishes 'in which the tribal state or territory was taken to constitute a parish'.[6] These rectories, which he views as an intermediate stage in parish formation, were later subdivided into parishes sometime after the middle of the thirteenth century, following the arrival of the Anglo-Normans in Connacht.

In Gaelic Ireland there is mounting evidence that parishes were formed from existing secular territorial units within the Gaelic lordships. In the lordship of Airghialla, Duffy found that parish boundaries corresponded closely with the boundaries of ballybetaghs, reflecting a strong connection with the secular landholding system.[7] An examination of parochial organisation in the diocese of Kilfenora also found a close correspondence between secular territorial units and the late medieval parishes.[8] Here, groups of parishes, so-called 'primary parishes', were identified on the basis of detached townlands, located within one parish but belonging to another, and it was argued that these primary parishes may have co-existed with the later medieval parishes, representing a hierarchical territorial subdivision within the lordship.[9] Nugent (this volume) has demonstrated that there existed a close correspondence between the parish and the *túath* in late medieval Clare, and he argues that this relationship was similar to that attributed by Otway-Ruthven to the manor and parish in Anglo-Norman Ireland. He also argues that the ecclesiastical hierarchical territorial

---

4 H.G. Leask, *Irish churches and monastic buildings, i: the first phases and the Romanesque* (Dundalk, 1955), 124–6, 164–5, 137–42, 151, 153–4; T. O'Keeffe, 'Lismore and Cashel: reflections on the beginnings of Romanesque architecture in Munster' in *JRSAI*, 124 (1994), 118–51: 121. 5 O'Keeffe (this volume) argues that parish formation may not have been achieved as rapidly in Anglo-Norman Ireland as previously thought. Based on his survey of Anglo-Norman parish churches in Co. Carlow, he concludes that few parishes churches were actually built in the late twelfth century, and that parish formation may have been staggered over many decades of the thirteenth century. 6 K.W. Nicholls 'Rectory, vicarage and parish in the western Irish dioceses' in *JRSAI*, 101 (1971), 53–84: 61. 7 P.J. Duffy, 'The territorial organization of Gaelic landownership and its transformation in Co. Monaghan, 1591–1640' in *Irish Geography*, 14 (1981), 1–26: 7; P.J. Duffy, 'Social and spatial order in the MacMahon lordship of Airghialla in the late sixteenth century' in P.J. Duffy, D. Edwards and E. FitzPatrick (eds), *Gaelic Ireland c.1250–c.1650: land, lordship and settlement* (Dublin, 2001), 115–37. 8 S. Ní Ghabhláin, 'The origin of medieval parishes in Gaelic Ireland: the evidence from Kilfenora' in *JRSAI*, 126 (1996), 37–61: 57–9. 9 Ibid., 46–9.

structure of diocese, rural deanery and parish was modeled on the existing Gaelic territorial hierarchy.[10]

The chronology of parish formation in Gaelic Ireland has not yet been established. While Nicholls argues that parish formation could not have taken place before the middle of the thirteenth century in the Gaelic dioceses, he does state that exceptions were possible, such as the parishes in the region of Athenry and Galway which appear to have been formed earlier than the majority of the parishes in the Connacht dioceses.[11] He also notes that tithes were reputed to have been first levied in Connacht during the reign of Cathal Crobhderg (1202–24).[12] The collection of tithes suggests that some form of parochial organisation was in place at that time.[13]

While documentary sources may yet provide solid evidence for the chronology of parish formation in Gaelic Ireland, it is suggested here that evidence for parish formation might be found in the construction history of the later medieval parish churches. Presented here are the results of a survey of later medieval churches within the diocese of Kilfenora. This survey documented a marked increase in church construction from the middle of the twelfth century, reaching a peak in the early decades of the thirteenth century. It is suggested that this increased rate of construction reflects the formation of parishes in the diocese, resulting in the construction, extension and rebuilding of existing churches to provide parish churches and chapels. The diocese of Kilfenora, situated in the north-west of Co. Clare, is the smallest diocese in Ireland (fig.1). It was formed out of the territory of Corcu Modruad, a sub-kingdom of Thomond.[14] The diocese of Kilfenora received episcopal status at the synod of Kells-Melifont in 1152.[15] There were nineteen parishes in the diocese in the later medieval period and a total of twenty-eight later medieval churches and chapels.[16]

METHODOLOGY

All the extant later medieval churches in the diocese were surveyed. Ground plans and elevations were drawn, and window and door styles were documented

---

10 S. Ní Ghabhláin, 'The origin of medieval parishes in Gaelic Ireland: the evidence from Kilfenora' in *JRSAI*, 126 (1996), 37–61: 57–9. 11 Nicholls, 'Rectory, vicarage and parish', 69. 12 Ibid., n. 50. 13 O'Keeffe (this volume) suggests that parish formation may have begun in the western dioceses after 1200, but that it was due to indirect influence from Anglo-Norman Ireland. 14 J. Hogan, 'The tricha cét and related land measures' in *PRIA*, 38C (1929), 148–235: 231–2; D. Ó Corráin, 'The families of Corcumroe' in *North Munster Antiquarian Journal*, 17 (1975), 21–30: 21. S. Ní Ghabhláin, 'Church, parish and polity: the medieval diocese of Kilfenora, Ireland', unpublished PhD (University of California, Los Angeles, 1995), 31–2. 15 A. Gwynn and D.F. Gleeson, *A history of the diocese of Killaloe* (Dublin, 1962), 130–1; Gwynn, *The Irish Church*, 233. 16 S. Ní Ghabhláin, 'Church and community in medieval Ireland: the diocese of Kilfenora' in *JRSAI*, 125 (1995), 61–84, for details of the churches and chapels of Kilfenora.

Fig. 1: Location of church sites in the diocese of Kilfenora, Co. Clare

in order to identify phases of construction for each church.[17] Documentation of constructional phases of individual churches was then used on a broader scale to observe regional trends in construction. This study of twelfth-century church construction was possible due to the generally good preservation of twelfth-century churches in the diocese of Kilfenora. In other parts of Ireland, fifteenth-century rebuilding of churches all but obliterated earlier church fabric,[18] but in Kilfenora older churches were rarely completely demolished (nor their sites deserted), they were in fact often extended or rebuilt in the fifteenth century.

Styles of masonry changed over the medieval period and different styles in masonry are one of the most obvious indications of phases of rebuilding. Masonry can vary in the size and shape of stones used, according to the type of

17 See W. Rodwell, *The archaeology of the English church* (London, 1981), 55–104 for methodology. 18 M. Ní Mharcaigh, 'The medieval parish churches of south-west County Dublin' in *PRIA*, 97C (1997), 245–96: 256–7.

stone, the frequency of small filling stones (spalls), and in the techniques of coursing and laying the stones. Traditionally these changes in masonry have been evaluated by eye. In the course of survey for this study, a number of masonry styles were identified in the churches. Most distinctive amongst these is the style found in the earliest stone churches of the diocese. This style, called 'cyclopean' by early writers, is distinguished by the use of massive facing stones with a rubble core.[19] In contrast to this early style, the masonry style used in the late medieval churches, those of the fifteenth and sixteenth centuries, is characterised by small stones (less than 50cm in width) and by the use of large numbers of spalls. A third style, consisting of squarish stones of medium size (50–100cm in width), was observed in buildings with features dating to the twelfth and thirteenth centuries.

As part of this analysis of regional trends in church construction, a statistical method was developed to identify masonry styles in order to provide an additional dating technique that could be used for all the churches in the study area. The presence of a number of simple parish churches and chapels with no dateable features, such as windows and doors, prompted this attempt to distinguish different styles of masonry dateable to broad periods. As the fabric of a church can pre-date even the earliest feature present, identifying distinct styles of masonry is essential to the interpretation of the architectural history of a structure.

Twenty-five wall sections from nineteen churches were chosen for analysis. Additional samples were taken from churches where more than one wall style was evident and where the original sample was felt not to be representative. A section of wall 2m by 2m was chosen, starting at ground level. In each case two measurements were taken of all of the stones within the 2-m grid, a horizontal (maximum length) and a vertical (maximum breadth). Around the edge of the grid, only those stones which lay more than fifty percent within the grid were measured.

Gibson's statistical analysis of masonry styles employed in the construction of cashels in the region,[20] served as a model for the analysis of masonry from the later medieval churches, but different variables were used in this analysis in response to the nature of the medieval masonry. Gibson used two variables in his analysis, the size of the stones and the number of spalls between blocks. The number of spalls turned out to be an unsuitable variable in this study due to the large number of small stones in the later churches, and the difficulty in distinguishing between construction stones and spalls. In calculating the mean

19 A.C. Champneys, *Irish ecclesiastical architecture with some notice of similar or related work in England, Scotland and elsewhere* (Shannon, 1970), 29–32; Leask, *Irish churches and monastic buildings*, i, 51–3. Champneys cautions that the use of so-called 'cyclopean' masonry does not guarantee an early date for a church, as had been assumed by earlier writers such as Petrie. **20** D.B. Gibson, 'Tulach Commáin: a view of an Irish chiefdom', unpublished PhD (University of California, Los Angeles, 1990), 235.

dimensions of the stones used, a cut-off point of 20cm in length was used to eliminate the smallest stones. This was necessary to avoid skewing the sample with large numbers of very small stones and because of the difficulty in measuring all of the smallest stones.

The walls sampled showed considerable variability in the mean dimensions of stones used. The mean width of stones ranged from 32.75cm (Killilagh 1) to 160.25cm (Kilmacreehy 1). In order to identify stylistic groups it was necessary to establish whether there was sufficient variability within the sample and that there were groups of walls which were not significantly different in the dimensions of their stones and therefore could be said to have come from the same population. Such a population might constitute a 'style'.

The mean and variance for each variable was calculated for each church wall sample and the data was subjected to a Student's t-test.[21] A number of variables were compared using the Student's t-test including the means of the width (horizontal dimensions) of the stones used, the mean of the heights (vertical dimension) of stones, and the mean of the product of both dimensions (surface area).[22] This last variable was also used as it would reflect the massiveness of the stones by taking both the horizontal and vertical dimensions into account. The results of these tests confirmed that there were significant differences between the means of the variables of certain churches, while the means of other churches were not significantly different. In order to identify different groups, the mean, standard deviation, and number of samples for the 'horizontal' variable and the 'surface area' variable for each church, was subjected to the Newman-Keuls multiple comparison test using the statistical program Kwikstat. Several groups of masonry samples were identified for each variable but there was considerable overlap between the groups. To refine the analysis, the data was submitted to a two-phase, Student's t-test, which compared first the horizontal and then the vertical dimensions and their standard deviations.[23] This procedure resulted in a grouping of walls which contained stones similar in both dimensions rather than just in size. In effect, this test eliminated much of the overlap evident in the results of the previous test. Three groups emerged and they are summarised in table 1.

The three stylistic groups appear to be assignable to distinct time periods. The 'cyclopean' masonry samples were all grouped together as Style 1. Within this group there is a range in size of stones used, but the samples are sufficiently different from Style 2 to be identified as a distinct group. The wall segments identified as belonging to Style 1 are all from the earliest phases of construction represented in their churches. The constructional phasing of

21 Student's t-test is a statistical method used to determine the probability that two populations are the same with respect to the variable tested. The hypothesis is nullified if the evidence is unfavorable to the hypothesis. 22 For a full description of methodology for this analysis see Ní Ghabhláin, 'Church, parish and polity', 91–105. 23 I would like to thank Gerard McAuliffe for his expert advice on statistics and for writing the programme to make this test possible.

TABLE 1: Masonry styles resulting from statistical analysis

Masonry style	Sample	Notes
Style 1	Killeany 1	Earliest phase of church
	Kilmoon	Early style masonry
	Drumcreehy	Earliest phase of church
	Noughaval 1	South wall of nave. Phase I of church, predates transitional door
	Oughtmama 1	North wall of nave, exterior. Phase 1 of church.
	Noughaval 2	Wall located to the west of the church, early style masonry
	Kilmacreehy 1	Earliest phase of church
Style 2	Kilmacreehy 2	Fifteenth-century construction, but reuse of stones from earlier phase of church
	Kilcorney	Twelfth to early thirteenth century
	Killonaghan	Twelfth century
	Carran	Fifteenth-century features but possibly twelfth-century fabric
	St Mac Duagh's 1	Phase 1 of church? Sample skewed by one large slab
	Crumlin 1	Twelfth-century features
	Templine	No dateable features, but large stones used around the doorway
	Oughtmama 2	Transitional. Late twelfth/early thirteenth century
	Temple Cronan 1 and 2	Twelfth century, reuse of stones from earlier church
	Corcomroe 1	North wall of chancel, Transitional – late twelfth/early thirteenth century
Style 3	Kilcarragh	Small chapel attached to a late medieval hospital. No dateable features
	Killeany 2	Phase two of this two-celled parish church, fifteenth century
	Killilagh	Phase two of this two-celled parish church, fifteenth century
	Corcomroe 2	Wall section from inserted tower, fifteenth century
	Oughtmama 3	Phase two of this single-celled chapel, fifteenth century?
	Gleninagh	Phase two, late fifteenth century
	St Mac Duagh's 2	Phase two. No dateable features – later medieval?

these churches is discussed below (pp. 156–60). The Style 2 samples are generally from churches with identifiable twelfth- or early thirteenth-century features. In two cases the sample came from a church with later medieval features, but it is possible that the fabric predates the later insertions. Where dateable features are present, the samples in Style 3 are associated with later medieval churches. This analysis played a part in identifying multiple phases of construction in the churches of Kilfenora, in addition to serving as a dating tool, and it is particularly useful in dating featureless churches where only masonry survives.

EARLY MEDIEVAL CHURCHES OF CORCU MODRUAD

The majority of the medieval church sites in the diocese of Kilfenora appear to have been founded in the early medieval period.[24] Of thirty medieval churches recorded in the diocese, twenty-two have physical features consistent with early medieval ecclesiastical foundations or are associated with an early saint (table 2). Large curvilinear earthen or stone enclosures have been identified at a number of the church sites in Kilfenora.[25] Other features indicative of an early medieval foundation include the presence of crosses, slab shrines, bullaun stones,[26] souterrains, dry-stone altars or pilgrimage stations (*leachtanna*), or fragments of early sculpture. Early style masonry, is also included in this list of features, with the caveat that such masonry may not date much before the eleventh or early twelfth century. The sites listed in table 2 include those at which no trace of a later medieval church remains.

While most of the church sites have traditions tracing their foundation to early saints, and many have archaeological evidence of early medieval foundations, there are few extant churches of the pre-twelfth century in the study area. At several sites in the study area, however, later churches were found to incorporate sections of masonry which can be identified as pre-twelfth century.

---

24 J. Sheehan, 'The early historic church-sites of north Clare' in *North Munster Antiquarian Journal*, 24 (1982), 29–45. Sheehan identified nineteen early historic foundations in north Clare, seventeen of which are located in the diocese of Kilfenora. My count of twenty-six sites includes some that he listed as probable sites, and which I have now identified as having definite early medieval origins based on additional information gathered in the course of fieldwork for this study. 25 J. Sheehan and F. Moore, 'An unrecorded ecclesiastical enclosure at Ballyallaban, County Clare' in *North Munster Antiquarian Journal*, 28 (1981), 5–8 ; J. Sheehan, 'Early historic church-sites of North Clare', 35–8; L. Swan, 'The churches, monasteries and burial grounds of the Burren' in J.W. O'Connell and A. Korff (eds), *The book of the Burren* (Kinvara, 1991), 95–118: 104–10; Ní Ghabhláin, 'Church, parish and polity': 417–18, 430–2, 435–7, 440–2, 443–5, 451–2, 453–5, 459–60, 465, 469–71, 474–7, 480–5, 486–7, 488–90, 491. 26 Bedrock grinding mortars or bowl-shaped mortars frequently found in association with churches.

TABLE 2: Early medieval church sites of Corcu Modruad

Site	Association with early saint	Enclosure	Early style masonry	Crosses	Slab shrines	Bullaun stone	Souterrain	Other
Ballyallaban		Yes				Yes		
Caherminnan West		Yes			Possible			
Clooney South	Yes	Yes						
Crumlin	Yes		Possible[27]				Yes	
Drumcreehy			Yes					
Ennistymon	Yes							
Formoyle								
Glencolumbkille	Yes	Yes				Yes		Sculpture[28]
Keelhilla (St Mac Duagh's)	Yes	Yes	Possible			Yes		Leachtanna
Kilcaimin	Yes	Yes						
Kilcolmanvara	Yes		Possible					
Kilcorney	Yes	Yes	Yes					
Kilfenora	Yes	Possible	Yes					
Killaspuglonane	Yes	Yes						Sculpture[29]
Killeany	Yes	Yes	Yes					Leacht
Killonaghan		Yes	Possible					
Kilmacreehy	Yes	Yes	Yes					
Kilmanaheen	Yes	Yes						
Kilmoon		Yes	Yes					
Kilshanny		Possible						
Noughaval		Yes	Yes	Yes				Leacht
Oughtdara	Yes	Yes	Yes					
Oughtmama	Yes	Yes	Yes				Yes	
Rathborney		Yes	Possible reused				Yes	
Temple Cronan		Yes		Yes		Yes		
Templeline		Yes			Two			

27 Churches with 'possible' early masonry were assigned a tenth-century date by Westropp, most likely on the basis of masonry style. Stylistic analysis of the masonry carried out for this study failed to distinguish the masonry of these churches from twelfth-century masonry. See T.J. Westropp, 'On the churches of County Clare and the origin of ecclesiastical divisions of that county' in *PRIA*, 6C (1900), 100–80: 130–8.   28 Carved stone head from Glencolumbkille, County Clare' in *JRSAI*, 118 (1988), 135–8.   29 D.I. Swan, 'A carved stone head from Killaspuglonane, Co. Clare' in E. Rynne (ed.), *Figures from the past: studies on figurative art in Christian Ireland* (Dublin, 1987), 159–67.

LATE TWELFTH-CENTURY BUILDING
IN THE DIOCESE OF KILFENORA

The final quarter of the twelfth century and the first decades of the thirteenth century witnessed intense rebuilding and expansion of existing churches in the diocese of Kilfenora. This building included the extension of the cathedral church, the construction of two abbeys, one Cistercian and one Augustinian, the expansion of the non-reformed monastic site of Oughtmama and the building or rebuilding of churches and chapels.

Cathedral of Kilfenora

Kilfenora (*Cill Fhionn Abhrach*), the principal monastery of Corcu Modruad, is said to have been founded by St Fachnan, probably St Fachtnan who allegedly founded the monastery of Ross Carbery in the second half of the sixth century.[30] Remnants of a large earthen enclosure, 300m in diameter, can be traced to the north-west and south-west of the cathedral.[31] The first mention of a church at Kilfenora is an entry in the Annals of Inisfallen for the year 1055 recording that the *damliac* (stone church) of *Cille Finnabrach* was burned.

During the first half of the twelfth century Kilfenora appears to have been the location of a sculptural workshop which produced a series of Romanesque high crosses distinguished by the use of high-relief carving, large-scale figurative sculpture and the use of Romanesque-style plant ornament and Urnes-derived animal ornament.[32] Six of the crosses are associated with Kilfenora, and their distribution is focused on North Munster and the Aran Islands. Cronin identifies two groups within the twelfth century crosses.[33] The earliest group of crosses, dating to the late eleventh to the early twelfth century, contains a large proportion of insular ornament and displays little Romanesque influence. The second group of crosses, including the crosses at Cashel, Monaincha, Roscrea, Dysert O'Dea and possibly also the Doorty cross in Kilfenora, features a large figure of Christ crucified on one face, and a prominent figure of an ecclesiastic on the other. Cronin argues that this group of crosses was produced in a Hiberno-Romanesque milieu and that the similarities in sculptural details of the crosses of this group and their associated Romanesque churches suggest that they were produced at the same workshops. The correlation between the location of high crosses of the twelfth century and diocesan sees – at Kilfenora, Cashel, Roscrea, Glendalough, Tuam, Cong and

---

30 A. Gwynn and R.N. Hadcock, *Medieval religious houses, Ireland* (London, 1970), 83. 31 Swan, 'Churches, monasteries and burial grounds', 110. 32 L. de Paor, 'The limestone crosses of Clare and Aran' in *Journal of the Galway Archaeological and Historical Society*, 26 (1957), no. 3–4, 53–71; 53–9, 60–1; F. Henry, *Irish art in the Romanesque period, 1020–1170 A.D.* (New York, 1970), 123–140; R. Cronin, 'Late high crosses in Munster: tradition and novelty in twelfth-century Irish art', in M.A. Monk and J. Sheehan (eds), *Early medieval Munster: archaeology, history and society* (Cork, 1998), 138–46: 145–6. 33 Cronin, 'Late high crosses', 140–5.

Down – and the prominence given to ecclesiastical figures on the Romanesque crosses, has been interpreted as confirmation that these crosses were produced in the context of the twelfth-century reform movement and the establishment of diocesan sees.[34] It would seem, on the evidence of the Romanesque high crosses, that Kilfenora was actively involved in the reform movement from the early twelfth century.

A section of the eleventh-century stone church may survive in the exterior north wall of the nave of the cathedral. The rendering of this section of wall has been weathered away, uncovering a 6-m length of Style I masonry. A chancel and north wing was added to the original stone church late in the twelfth century. The Transitional triple-light east window of the chancel is entirely framed by mouldings. The capitals of the triangular piers between the lights are carved, one with crockets and the other with figures of clergy. Westropp[35] dates this work to 1170 while Leask[36] favors a later date closer to 1200. The confirmation of episcopal status on Kilfenora in 1152 no doubt provided the impetus for the expansion witnessed in the late twelfth century. The resulting cathedral, although modest in size by comparison with other cathedral churches in Ireland, was the largest and most impressive church of the diocese at the time.

Monastic sites

The twelfth-century reform reinvigorated the monastic church through the introduction of reformed monastic orders. The Cistercian abbey of Corcomroe and the Augustinian abbey of Kilshanny represent two of these reformed orders in the diocese of Kilfenora. Kilshanny was founded *c*.1194, apparently from Clare Abbey, by Domnall Mór Ua Briain, King of Thomond.[37] There is little remaining of the twelfth-century church of Kilshanny, with the exception of some masonry of that period in the north and south walls, a doorway in the north wall and a lancet in the south wall. The church was almost entirely rebuilt in the fifteenth century.

Corcomroe Abbey, a Cistercian foundation, was founded from Inislounaght (Suir).[38] The date of foundation of Corcomroe is in dispute, with assigned dates ranging from 1175 to 1195.[39] Stalley argues for an early thirteenth-century date of construction based on architectural features.[40] Corcomroe was founded by either Domnall Mór Ua Briain or his son Donnachad Cairbreach, and the kings of Thomond continued to be benefactors.[41] The abbey church is a cruciform, aisled structure with one chapel in each transept. The finest

34 De Paor, 'The limestone crosses of Clare and Aran'; Cronin, 'Late high crosses in Munster', 62–3; Cronin, 'Late high crosses', 145.   35 Westropp, 'Churches of County Clare', 137.   36 H.G. Leask, *Irish churches and monastic buildings, ii: Gothic architecture to A.D. 1400* (Dundalk, 1977), 54.   37 Gwynn and Hadcock, *Medieval religious houses*, 184.   38 Ibid., 135.   39 Ibid., 130.   40 R. Stalley, 'Corcomroe Abbey' in *JRSAI*, 105 (1975), 24–46: 25–8.   41 Gwynn and Hadcock, *Medieval religious houses*, 184. After the battle of Suidaine in 1267, Conchobar Ua Briain was buried in the chancel of Corcomroe Abbey and an effigial tomb was erected. S.H. O'Grady (ed.), *Caithréim Thoirdhealbhaigh*, 2 vols, Irish Texts Society (London, 1929), ii, 5.

quality stonework is concentrated in the east end of the church, particularly in the presbytery and the north chapel. The presbytery has a ribbed herringbone vault and richly carved capitals. The north chapel has a decorated portal in two orders and capitals carved with fleur-de-lis. Stylistically, the carved stonework of Corcomroe Abbey belongs to the Transitional 'School of the West' as described by Leask,[42] and there are similarities between the stone carving at Corcomroe and other foundations west of the Shannon such as Boyle, Killaloe, Knockmoy, Kilfenora and Kilmacduagh (see also O'Keeffe, pp. 142–4, this volume). Of particular interest to this study is the fact that there are stylistic comparisons to be made between details of carved stonework at Corcomroe and the church at Noughaval and Kilfenora cathedral. The outcome of these comparisons is the suggestion that they were constructed within a short time of one another and possibly by the same group of masons.

Oughtmama,[43] located on the lower slopes of Turlough Hill in the Burren, is the best preserved of the early medieval sites in the diocese of Kilfenora. Oughtmama appears to have continued in use as a non-reformed monastic site after the twelfth century. It also served as the parish church of the parish of Oughtmama in the later medieval period. At Oughtmama three churches are located within a large, double oval enclosure. The inner enclosure contains two churches while a third church stands within the north-east quadrant of the outer enclosure. All three churches are aligned east–west to one another (fig. 2). The westernmost church (Church 1) is the earliest of the three, and it has many features of the pre-Romanesque churches of the west: a trabeate west doorway with large, finely dressed quoins and a massive lintel, and Style 1 masonry.[44] There may have been two phases of construction of Church 1 prior to the twelfth century. The earliest phase of construction here is represented by Style 1 masonry in the north and south walls of the nave. This early church may have had an architraved west doorway, as suggested by an architraved stone reused in a Transitional window in the south wall[45] and a monolithic east window. During the second phase of construction the architraved west doorway was replaced with the present lintelled doorway. This church was approximately 14m in length. The corbels projecting from the west wall of the church are of hollow-chamfer type, dateable to the second half of the eleventh century. They were most likely inserted in the second phase of building and therefore provide a *terminus ante quem* for the Style 1 masonry. In the late twelfth century Transitional round-headed lights were inserted in the south wall of the nave (pl. 1). A chancel was then added, as indicated by vertical fault lines and a change in masonry style around the chancel arch. The finely wrought chancel

---

42 Leask, *Irish churches and monastic buildings*, ii, 53–76.   43 T.J. Westropp, 'Corcomroe' in *JRSAI*, 25 (1895), 280–3; Gwynn and Hadcock, *Medieval religious houses*, 400.   44 Leask, *Irish churches and monastic buildings*, i, 82–3 and fig. 26.   45 T. O'Keeffe, 'Architectural traditions of the early medieval church in Munster', in J. Sheehan and M.A. Monk (eds), *Early medieval Munster* (Cork, 1998), 112–24.

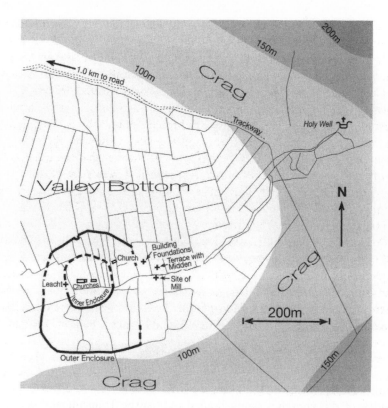

Fig. 2: Plan of Oughtmama (reproduced courtesy of Carleton Jones)

arch is rounded and has plain chamfered imposts and bases. Only the embrasures of the east and south chancel window remain, but it appears that the south window of the chancel differs from those in the nave, suggesting that the chancel was added in a separate building phase. This phase can be dated by the early thirteenth-century corbels with their bowtell mouldings, originally projecting from the east corners of the chancel.

In addition to extending the existing church by the addition of a chancel, two other stone churches were constructed at Oughtmama in the late twelfth century or the early thirteenth century. Church 2, a smaller single-celled church was built to the east of Church 1. The round-arched west door of this church has the same imposts and bases as the chancel arch of Oughtmama 1, and its east window is similar to the south windows of the chancel added to Church 1, indicating that it was built during the same phase of construction as the chancel of Church 1. Oughtmama 3, a small chapel, erected at some distance east of the first two churches, and within the outer enclosure, is poorly preserved. Its portal does not survive but it was formerly positioned in the

Pl. 1: South wall of the large church, Oughtmama 1

south wall, in contrast to the western portals of Oughtmama 2 and 3. The east window of this church is round-headed and may be Transitional.[46]

Parish churches
There are thirteen extant medieval parish churches (including the cathedral church of Kilfenora) and an additional twelve dependent churches and chapels in the diocese of Kilfenora.[47] Of the extant medieval parish churches, nine have features dateable to the late twelfth century and early thirteenth century (table 3). One additional parish church site, Killaspuglonane, contains a probable Romanesque stone voussoir suggesting that a Romanesque church was located there.[48] Of the other churches and chapels within the diocese, six have evidence of twelfth-century construction.

46 Analysis of the masonry of this church suggests two phases of construction here. The lower courses are of large squared blocks, similar in style to Church 2. The upper courses consist of much smaller stones and may represent rebuilding here in the later medieval period. **47** The three parish churches, for which there are no standing remains, are Kiltoraght, Kilmanaheen, and Killaspuglonane (see Ní Ghabhláin, 'Church and community'). **48** Swan, 'Carved stone head', 164–5. Swan identifies this carving as Romanesque on stylistic grounds, specifically the long pointed chin, presence of a hair-line, the pouting lips and high placement of the ears, features for which he finds parallels in the Temple Cronan, Kilvoydaune and Toomfinlough stone heads, in the voussoirs of the chancel arches of Dysert O'Dea and Cashel and in the crucifixion figure on the West Cross, Kilfenora.

TABLE 3: Construction trends in Kilfenora

	Masonry style	Early Christian foundations	Hiberno-Romanesque	Transitional	13thc	14thc	15–16thc
Aughinish							
Carran	2			Possible			X
Clooney		X		X			
Corcomroe	2 & 3			X	X		X
Crumlin	2	X		X			X
Drumcreehy	1	X		X			X
Glencolumbkille		X		X			X
Gleninagh	3			X			X
Keelhilla	2 & 3	X		?			X
Kilcarragh	3						X
Kilcorney	2	X	X				X
Kilfenora	1	X	X	X	X		X
Killeany	1 & 3	X		X	X	X	X
Killilagh	1	X		X			X
Killaspuglonane			X				
Killonaghan	2	X		X			
Kilmacreehy	1 & 2	X				X	X
Kilmoon 1	1	X					X
Kilmoon 2							X
Kilshanny		Possible		X			X
Noughaval 1	1	X		X			X
Oughtdara		X					X
Oughtmama 1	1	X		X	X		X
Oughtmama 2	2			X			X
Oughtmama 3	3				X		

Pl. 2: South door, Noughaval

Pl. 3: Example of Style 2
masonry, Kilcorney church

Four parish churches, Kilmoon, Kilmacreehy, Rathborney and Carran, constructed in the fifteenth or sixteenth centuries, may have been built on the sites of earlier churches. Sections of Style 1 masonry identified in the churches of Kilmoon and Kilmacreehy (table 2) indicate that these sites had stone churches prior to the twelfth century. They were subsequently modified and continued in use. The late medieval parish church of Rathborney was originally located within a circular earthen enclosure. The site also contains a souterrain (table 1). Westropp[49] noted Style 1 masonry in the lower courses of the east and north walls. The church is now so overgrown by ivy that it was not possible to confirm this. There is some evidence that the large late medieval parish church of Carran may have been built originally in the twelfth century. Diagonal tooling is visible on the splays of the south window suggesting that these stones were reused from an earlier church. In addition, a monolithic window head is built into the interior south wall, indicating an even earlier phase of building, if not for the present building, certainly for its predecessor. Given the evidence for earlier structures at these sites, it is highly likely that they were the locations of churches in use during the twelfth century, and it is possible that rebuilding in the later medieval period removed all trace of twelfth-century fabric from them.

Three types of construction are evident: the enlargement of an existing church by the addition of a chancel or transept; the construction of a new church *ab initio*; and the substantial rebuilding of an older church with the insertion of new, Transitional-style windows or doors.

REBUILDING AND NEW CONSTRUCTION

Twenty of the later medieval churches were constructed on sites founded in the early medieval period, indicating a high degree of continuity of site use in the diocese (tables 2 and 3). Although in some cases parish churches may have been built *ab initio* on virgin sites, the weight of evidence both from the diocese of Kilfenora[50] and other dioceses[51] suggests that there was a great deal of continuity in the use of pre-Reform church sites as parish church sites. Only seven of the church sites do not have any early medieval association. In the Dublin area, a recent survey of medieval church sites concluded that the vast majority was constructed in the fifteenth century, and that only one church out of a total of twenty-nine had pre-Norman fabric.[52] However, ten additional sites were early medieval foundations. It would appear in this case that there was some continuity in the use of ecclesiastical sites, but that later medieval building had

49 Westropp, 'Churches of County Clare', 131. **50** Ní Ghabhláin, 'Church, parish, and polity', 133–4; and 'Origin of medieval parishes', 57–9. **51** Gwynn and Gleeson, *Diocese of Killaloe* (Dublin, 1962), 323–4; E. FitzPatrick and C. O'Brien, *The medieval churches of County Offaly* (Dublin, 1998), 36, 161–4. **52** Ní Mharcaigh, 'Medieval parish churches', 245–96.

obliterated traces of earlier churches on the sites. In Co. Offaly, over half of the sixty medieval churches and chapels recorded were early medieval foundations, and of twenty-four later medieval parish churches, thirteen were constructed on the sites of early medieval monasteries or churches.[53]

Sections of Style 1 masonry were identified in eight of the twelfth-century churches indicating that these buildings incorporated portions of earlier stone churches. Masonry of Style 1 was identified in the lower courses at Kilmacreehy, in the nave of the west (large) church at Oughtmama, and at Noughaval, both in the south wall of the nave and in a wall lying to the west of the church. Style I was also recognised in the north wall exterior of Kilfenora cathedral and at Killeany, Kilmoon and Drumcreehy. Temple Cronan, a small oratory decorated with Romanesque heads, and the only extant Romanesque church in the diocese, appears to have been rebuilt in the twelfth century using masonry from an earlier church.[54] Statistical analysis of two sections of masonry from this church grouped the samples with other twelfth-century masonry samples in Style 2. The early appearance of the masonry is the result of the use of a number of very large construction blocks, probably re-used from an earlier church. The large blocks are intermixed with smaller blocks in a haphazard manner. At St Mac Duagh's church in Keelhilla,[55] a site reputed to have been the hermitage of St Colman Mac Duagh, who founded the nearby monastery of Kilmacduagh *c.*620, two styles of masonry were identified. Most of the fabric was consistent with the later medieval Style 3 masonry, while the masonry of the west gable is unusual in that large blocks are interspersed with smaller blocks in a haphazard fashion. This may indicate that masonry from an earlier church was re-used in the construction.

Radiocarbon dating of twenty-four mortar samples, from undated churches and associated structures throughout Ireland, placed the earliest construction of stone and mortar churches in Ireland in the seventh and eight centuries.[56] However, four churches from the Aran Islands with early 'cyclopean' style masonry and architectural features similar to the churches of Oughtmama were

53 FitzPatrick and O'Brien, *The medieval churches*, 160–4.   54 Harbison cites Temple Cronan as an example of an early-style church which is clearly dateable to the twelfth century, given the presence of Romanesque carved corbels and the Romanesque east window. O'Keeffe in contrast, has argued that the presence of a traditional west door with inclined jambs and lintel, in addition to the dimensions of the church and the style of the masonry, indicate that this is a pre-twelfth-century church that was re-modelled during the Romanesque period. See P. Harbison, 'Some Romanesque heads from County Clare' in *North Munster Antiquarian Journal*, 15 (1972), 3–7; T. O'Keeffe, 'The Irish Romanesque'. Unpublished PhD (UCD, 1991), 468; Leask, *Irish churches*, i, 74.   55 Westropp, 'Churches of County Clare', 134; J. Frost, *The history and topography of the county of Clare from the earliest times to the beginning of the eighteenth century* (Dublin, 1893), 29.   56 R. Berger, 'Early medieval Irish buildings; radiocarbon dating of mortar' in W.G Mook and H.T. Walterbolk (eds), *Proceedings of the second international symposium on ¹⁴C and Archaeology*. PACT (*Journal of the European Study Group on Physical, Chemical, and Mathematical Techniques Applied to Archaeology*) 29 (1990), 415–22; R. Berger, '¹⁴C Dating mortar in Ireland' in *Radiocarbon*, 34, no. 3 (1992), 880–9.

dated no earlier than the middle of the eleventh century. The construction sequence at Oughtmama I supports a mid eleventh-century date for the early masonry in that large church, while the historical reference to a stone church at Kilfenora confirms the existence of a stone church there by 1055. It is likely that the earliest stone churches in the diocese of Kilfenora were constructed from the middle of the eleventh century.

ADDITION OF CHANCELS

Although it has been argued that the introduction of the chancel dates back to the tenth or eleventh century,[57] there is no evidence for the construction of chancels in the study area before the middle of the twelfth century. It appears that all of the nave and chancel churches of the diocese, with one possible exception, were provided with chancels by the beginning of the thirteenth century.

The medieval parish church of Noughaval[58] appears to have been the site of a pre-twelfth-century stone church. The south wall of the nave is constructed in Style 1 masonry (pl. 2) and a second wall, to the west of the church, of unknown function, is also constructed in the same style. This early church was large, at least 15m long, similar in size to the early stone church at Oughtmama. This church was rebuilt in the late twelfth to early thirteenth century when a chancel was added and the south door in the nave was inserted. The imposts of the chancel arch have rounded mouldings, and the jambs of the arch, although clearly altered at a later period, also have shallow, rounded mouldings. There is an animal head at the north-east junction of the jamb and impost, the open mouth of which may have gripped the impost. These features of the arch indicate a late Romanesque/Transitional date for the construction of the chancel. The south doorway also belongs to this phase of construction. The pointed arch of the doorway has been blocked up, but tubular herringbone chevron is visible on the tympanum. Similar herringbone chevron is found in the north chapel of Corcomroe abbey and construction at that site has been dated by Stalley to the first decade of the thirteenth century.[59]

Another large parish church, Drumcreehy,[60] was expanded towards the end of the twelfth century by the addition of a chancel. Statistical analysis of masonry from this church identified some Style I masonry in the fabric of the

---

57 Leask, *Irish churches*, i, 76; F. Henry, *Irish art during the Viking invasions 800–1020 A.D.* (New York, 1967), 49; O'Keeffe, 'The Irish Romanesque', 142–7. Leask and Henry favour a tenth-century date for the introduction of the chancel, while O'Keeffe argues for an eleventh-century date for the earliest chancels. 58 Frost, *History and topography*, 29; Westropp, 'Churches of County Clare', 399–400; 'Notes on the antiquities around Kilfenora and Lahinch, Co. Clare' in *North Munster Antiquarian Journal*, 1 (1910), 24–7. 59 Stalley, 'Corcomroe Abbey', 25–8. 60 Frost, *History and topography*, 24; Westropp, 'Churches of County Clare', 130; 'Corcomroe', 280.

nave. The east window of the chancel is of Transitional type and the moulding outlining the window arch can be compared to the moulding around the east window at Kilfenora. The chancel arch has fallen and its form is unknown. The chancel at this church is unusually large, larger than the nave to which it was added.

Kilcorney[61] is a small two-celled church located within a double earthen-banked enclosure. Westropp described the east window, which is no longer extant, as a 'remarkable east window of the eleventh century, with boldly projecting human head and curious foliage'.[62] The accompanying illustration suggests Romanesque work dating to the middle of the twelfth century. There are indications that the chancel arch in this church was flush with the walls – an unusual feature.[63] The south doorway is described by Westropp as 'early decorated', indicating a thirteenth-century date. The sequence of construction is difficult to discern here due to the poor condition of the church. The masonry style in both nave and chancel is consistent, and it seems likely that the church was constructed *ab initio* as a two-celled structure (pl. 3).

The nave and chancel church of Killeany[64] was constructed in at least two phases, late twelfth to thirteenth century, and fifteenth to sixteenth century. The east window is a round-headed light of Transitional type. The chancel arch, which is tall, pointed and faced with thin slabs, dates to the second phase of the church and is clearly an insertion. Two samples of masonry from this church were analysed, one of which was consistent with Style I masonry, and the second of which was assigned to the later medieval style. There is a possibility that some of the fabric of an early church was incorporated into the twelfth-century church. The sole exception to the twelfth- and early thirteenth-century chancels is the large nave and chancel parish church of Kilmacreehy,[65] near Liscannor. The chancel in this church is large, almost as long as the nave, and it appears to have been constructed in the later medieval period.

The pattern that emerges from an examination of the construction history of the churches of Kilfenora is that in the late twelfth century, chancels were added to existing single-celled churches. Doorways in the south wall were also inserted at the same time. At Oughtmama the chancel was added, but the west doorway was retained.

---

61 Frost, *History and topography*, 33; Westropp, 'Churches of County Clare', 133.   62 Westropp, 'Churches of County Clare', 133.   63 O'Keeffe notes the presence of chancel arch responds that are flush with the side walls of the chancels at two early nave-and-chancel churches: T. O'Keeffe, *Romanesque Ireland: architecture and ideology in the twelfth century* (Dublin, 2003), 83, 307, n. 65. 64 Frost, *History and topography*, 31–2; Westropp, 'Churches of County Clare', 132.   65 Frost, *History and topography*, 107; Westropp, 'Churches of County Clare', 135; T.J. Westropp, 'Ancient remains near Lisdoonvarna' in *The Limerick Field Club*, 3 (1905–1908), 205.

CONCLUSIONS

The surge in church building in the late twelfth and early thirteenth centuries cannot be adequately explained as simply the result of the introduction of new architectural styles to Ireland. The reform of the church was central to the changes taking place at this time. The intensive building documented in the diocese of Kilfenora at the end of the twelfth century and during the early thirteenth century may reflect the establishment of parishes and the construction and renovation of churches to serve them. The similarities in architectural details found at Corcomroe, Kilfenora, and Noughaval, and the similarity in window mouldings at those churches and Drumcreehy, Killonaghan and Killeany suggests that they were constructed within a short time of one another, and possibly by the same school of masons. Given the evidence of the churches themselves, it would appear that the process of parish formation in this diocese was quite rapid.

While Kenneth Nicholls argues that formal parish formation did not begin in the west until the middle of the thirteenth century at the earliest, there are some indications that some parishes were being established in Connacht in the early decades of the thirteenth century.[66] If the construction and renovation of churches observed in the diocese of Kilfenora was indeed the result of parish formation, it would appear that the process was underway by the late twelfth century and that it reached its peak by the end of the first quarter of the thirteenth century.

66 Nicholls 'Rectory, vicarage and parish', 69, n. 50.

Priests' residences in later medieval Ireland

HELEN BERMINGHAM

Priestly residences are integral to the study of late medieval parish church archaeology and architecture. In Britain a number of fine examples of priest's houses, such as that at Muchelney in Somerset, have been the subject of scholarly enquiry since as early as the 1950s.[1] In Ireland parish church studies have tended to concentrate on the architecture of the churches themselves rather than the quarters occupied by the priests. Moreover, there has been, with the exception of Leask who was among the earliest scholars to identify priestly accommodation,[2] a lack of acknowledgment of the fact that priests' quarters ought to be expected at parish churches. In recent years, research based in counties Offaly, Dublin and Leitrim has sought to rectify the situation.[3] The published inventories of the Archaeological Survey of Ireland continue to make important contributions, providing architectural descriptions of churches throughout the country. Occasionally however, some architectural features, pointing directly to priests' residences, have been overlooked or have not been recognised as such.

This paper explores the kinds of quarters that constituted priestly accommodation in parishes in later medieval Ireland. It also asks whether there are differences in the types of priestly residences found in colonial and Gaelic Ireland, and the extent to which patronage, or the lack of, dictated the style and quality of the building. It should be borne in mind that one of the main sources of information for this paper are studies of parish churches completed to date in various areas of Ireland. There is as yet no complete record of the number of priests' residences that survive countrywide. Therefore, it must be appreciated that the interpretations presented here are based upon a limited corpus of information.

The basis of the parochial system was the provision of a resident parish priest, financially supported by the payment of tithes, who served the spiritual

---

1 W.A. Pantin, 'Medieval priests' houses in south-west England' in *Medieval Archaeology*, 1 (1957), 118–46: 121–4; S. Friar, *A companion to the English parish church* (Stroud, 1996), 361–2. 2 H.G. Leask, *Irish churches and monastic buildings*, 3 vols (Dundalk, 1960), iii. 3 E. FitzPatrick and C. O'Brien, *The medieval churches of County Offaly* (Dublin, 1998), 134–9; M. Ní Mharcaigh, 'The medieval parish churches of south-west County Dublin' in *PRIA*, 97C (1997), 245–96: 249, 266–77; S. Scully, 'Medieval parish churches and parochial organisation in Muintir Eolais', unpublished MA (NUI, Galway, 1999), 149.

needs of the local community. Proportions of the tithes were allocated for the maintenance and upkeep of the church, while the remainder was divided between the bishop, clergy and the poor.[4] As the parish system developed it was realised that accommodation for the incumbent priests, situated close to their churches, was a basic requirement, and one of the prerequisites of an efficiently run parish. The priest was also apportioned glebeland within the vicinity of the church. This meant that the priest could cultivate his own crops and provide most of his own food, depending on the quantity and quality of the glebeland. While only the masonry structures such as the church and priest's house tend to survive, it must be noted that there may have been additional buildings, constructed of wood, in the vicinity of the churchyard. A tithe barn, for instance, was probably necessary in order to store the agricultural produce received from the tithe collection.

A working classification for priests' residences in Ireland is proposed here, based upon both published and unpublished surveys, and studies of parish church architecture in a number of Irish counties. The sources consulted include the published Archaeological Survey of Ireland county inventories and regional studies conducted in Dublin, Leitrim and Offaly by individual scholars, in addition to a case study undertaken by the author in the baronies of Clare and Dunmore, Co. Galway. The evidence provided by these collective works enables the identification of at least four types of priestly accommodation:

- accommodation incorporated into the body of the church, at the west gable end. In order to counteract any shortening of the church, as a result of inserting priest's quarters, the nave or chancel was occasionally lengthened. Accommodation is also very occasionally incorporated into the east end of the church, over the chancel.
- accommodation attached to one side or gable end of the church.
- residential tower attached to the parish church (usually west end).
- the free-standing priest's house, which is less common.

The poor survival of the fabric of parish churches makes it difficult to determine how common each of these types were and indeed whether still others existed. Heavy growth of vegetation on upstanding church buildings also often precludes the identification of the diagnostic architectural features of priests' quarters. In addition, the data acquired for this classification is to a certain extent compromised by the lack of recognition of priest's quarters during some of the respective surveys of the churches. Accommodation incorporated into the west end of the church is often mistakenly recorded in a number of the county inventories as a 'loft' or 'gallery', one of the functions of

4 S. Ní Ghabhláin, 'Church and community in medieval Ireland: the diocese of Kilfenora' in *JRSAI*, 125 (1995), 61–84: 75.

which was to provide additional space for the congregation. At Glebe, Co. Galway, for example, the architectural evidence, which would indicate the presence of priests' quarters, is incorrectly interpreted as a former loft.[5]

In cases where there is no archaeological evidence for priestly accommodation, medieval records such as the *Calendar of Papal Registers* may refer to the maintenance of quarters or to the presence of a concubine, thereby indicating the existence of a former priestly residence. For example, in a papal letter from 1469, there is a complaint that the vicar of Killanummery, Co. Leitrim, had neglected the parish church and its residence.[6] At Kiltubrid in the same county, the vicar had not been residing at the church for some time when a petition was made for his removal in 1488.[7] Surviving priestly residences tend to be masonry buildings, but it must also be considered that some could have been constructed from wood where timber supplies were near at hand. A case in point is the timber-built priest's house revealed during the Linlithgow friary excavations in Scotland.[8]

ACCOMMODATION INCORPORATED INTO THE WEST GABLE END OF THE CHURCH

This type of accommodation is the most common and is widespread throughout Ireland. The division of this particular type of priest's quarters into ground and first floor is by two means (a) timber floor (b) stone vault. There were a number of methods of constructing the upper floor. The first method was the placing of corbels and/or beam-holes on the interior of the north and south walls at the west end of the church (and occasionally also on the west gable) to support the timber beams of the first floor. This method of construction was quite commonplace and is not regionally biased. Another, but less common method of constructing the upper floor was the placing of beam-holes/corbels along the inner face of the west gable, as can be seen at Kilbennan church, Co. Galway (pl. 1). The beams were supported on the near side by a masonry or timber partition which separated the priest's quarters from the nave of the church. It is also possible that the beams were held in a beam slot, such as seems to be the case at Moycarky, Co. Tipperary, where there are corbels located along the inner face of the west gable and beam slots at the west end of the north and south walls.[9] A beam slot, possibly similar to that used at

5 O. Alcock, K. de hÓra and P. Gosling, *Archaeological inventory of county Galway (north Galway)* (Dublin, 1999), 309. 6 A. Fuller (ed.), *Calendar of entries in the papal registers relating to Great Britain and Ireland* (Dublin, 1994), xvii, 750. 7 W.H. Bliss and J.A. Twemlow (eds), *Calendar of entries in the papal registers relating to Great Britain and Ireland* (London, 1960), xiv, 119–20. 8 W.J. Lindsay, 'Linlithgow: the excavations' in J. Stones (ed.), *Three Scottish Carmelite friaries: excavations at Aberdeen, Linlithgow and Perth 1980–86*, Society of Antiquaries of Scotland, monograph series no. 6 (Edinburgh, 1989), 57–93: 69–70. 9 J. Farrelly and C.

Pl. 1: View of west gable of Kilbennan church, Co. Galway, showing beam holes for first floor of priest's quarters

Moycarky was found during the excavations at St Mark's, in Lincoln, England.[10] This method is found in Cos. Louth at Glebe East and Shanlis,[11] in Galway at Killower and Kilbennan for instance, and at Glebe in Co. Kerry,[12] with possible examples in south-west Co. Dublin.[13] No particular number of beam-holes was required apparently, with the number varying from four to eight, probably depending on the width of the particular church.

An example of this type of accommodation was found at Dysart church, Cummeen, Co. Roscommon, where excavations were undertaken in the area of the priest's quarters in advance of conservation work at the site.[14] The church has evidence for a number of phases of building. Two windows in the north and south walls and a south doorway (uncovered during excavations), are dated to the twelfth century, while the eastern gable is a late fifteenth-/early sixteenth-century phase of building, as is the eastern corner of the north wall. The

O'Brien, *Archaeological inventory of County Tipperary (North Tipperary)* (Dublin, 2002), 260–1. **10** M.J. Jones, 'Excavations at Lincoln: 3rd interim report, sites outside the walled city 1972–1977' in *Antiquaries Journal*, 61 (1981), 83–114: 99–100. **11** V.M. Buckley, *Archaeological inventory of County Louth* (Dublin, 1986), 231–2, 257. **12** A. O'Sullivan and J. Sheehan, *The Iveragh peninsula: an archaeological survey of south Kerry* (Cork, 1996), 355–6. **13** Ní Mharcaigh, 'The medieval parish churches', 254. **14** Personal communication, J. Higgins.

western gable retains a sixteenth-/seventeenth-century doorway and a window that may be slightly earlier. When this door was inserted, the western end of the church was separated by a cross wall that reached the full height of the interior of the church. Joist holes on the interior of the west gable, for the insertion of a floor, were in evidence until 1992 when a portion of the wall collapsed. The footings of the cross wall were uncovered during excavations. A garderobe tower was also constructed on the exterior of the north wall during this phase of refurbishment. It was two storeys in height and was reached from the first floor of the priest's quarters. Two cuttings were made outside and within the turret-like structure. Finds from the interior comprised organic deposits, with quantities of animal bone. Outside, a group of late burials, possibly dating to the famine period was encountered. The only artefacts recovered were a few sherds of seventeenth-century pottery (North Devonshire sgraffito ware) found in the vicinity of the garderobe.

A third method of constructing the upper room flooring is similar to the previous method, but instead of creating individual beam-holes, a supporting ledge is placed on the interior of the west gable. This method was found in Co. Waterford at Ballynagigla/Ballyristeen and Kilmacomb.[15] At Kilmacomb, the west gable is the only wall to survive. It has an internal ledge to support the timbers for the priest's quarters, and a window. The church at Ballynagigla/ Ballyristeen is now badly ruined consisting of a grass-covered cairn of rubble. O'Donovan *c.*1840 described the church as comprising only the north wall and the west gable. Power, at the end of the nineteenth century, noted a supporting ledge for the timber floor, a doorway at the south end of the west gable with a window immediately above and a second window in the centre of the wall, and a belfry overhead. It is not specified whether the ledge is actually located on the west gable. It may be the case that it was part of the north wall, with a corre-spondent on the south wall.

A fourth and more elaborate method of providing first-floor accommodation was the use of stone barrel vaults. In Co. Offaly there are a number of good examples of churches with intact barrel vaults. At Kilbride for instance, the barrel-vaulted ground floor is aligned north–south at the west end of the church. It has been identified as a later insertion, probably when the church was elevated to parish church status. The first-floor room is lit from the west gable by a single-light, cusped ogee-headed window, which is set into a wide embrasure and provided with a stone seat.[16] In 1948, at Gallon and Raffony, Co.

---

15 M. Moore, *Archaeological inventory of County Waterford* (Dublin, 1999), 167, 180. J. O'Donovan, 'Letters containing information relative to the antiquities of the county of Waterford collected during the progress of the Ordnance Survey in 1841', compiled by M. O'Flanagan (Bray, 1929), 23–4; P. Power, 'The ancient ruined churches of Co. Waterford' in *Waterford Archaeological Journal*, 2 (1896) 2–15, 195–208. 16 C. O'Brien and P.D. Sweetman, *Archaeological inventory of County Offaly* (Dublin, 1997), 99; FitzPatrick and O'Brien, *The medieval churches*, 114, 134.

Cavan, Davies noted barrel vaulting. He claimed that the west gable of Gallon church formerly adjoined a barrel vault 'nine feet wide running across the church, which may have supported a gallery'. He also suggested that a separate chamber at the west end of Raffony church may have been 'part of a vault which supported a gallery'.[17]

In south-west Co. Dublin, Ní Mharcaigh has found evidence to indicate the former existence of 'galleries' at a number of the churches she surveyed. Some of these 'galleries' could represent former priests' quarters. For instance, joist holes and ledges at the west end of the churches, with small windows placed at first-floor level are found at Drimnagh, Esker, Kilmahuddrick and Lucan.[18] At Drimnagh only the western half of the church and a section of the east gable remain upstanding. No diagnostic architectural features remain to indicate a date for the church. Over the doorway in the west gable is a plain narrow window set into an embrasure in the interior. A single corbel on the north wall, in association with two (or three) joist holes in the west gable, supported the timbers for an upper floor.[19] However, the church is quite small (7.4m by 3.5m internally) and may be early medieval in date. At Esker a ledge above a ground floor window in the west gable is indicative of a former 'gallery'.[20]

In accommodation that was incorporated into the west end of the church, the priest's quarters were screened off from the nave by a cross-wall or a wooden partition containing a doorway to allow access to the priest's quarters. Windows in the north, south or west walls lit the apartment. Occasionally, the priest may have had direct access into his private quarters through a doorway in the west gable. In many cases the doorway was broken through an earlier gable or an original early medieval entrance preserved in the fabric of the later medieval church was used. The re-use of an early medieval trabeate doorway as the entrance to a priest's quarters can be seen, for instance, in the church at Ower on the eastern shores of Lough Corrib, Co. Galway. Access between the ground and first floor was by means of a stairway or ladder. The stairway, which is also found in the other types of priestly accommodation, may be of either stone or wooden construction, straight or spiral. In cases where there is no evidence for a stone stairway it is likely that a wooden stairway was used. Windows sometimes lit the stairway. In the absence of a window, a niche for a lamp was provided, as can be seen at St Barrind's church, Co. Offaly.[21] The second method of reaching the first floor was by means of a ladder and a drop-hole. While no wooden drop-hole entrances are known to have survived, a masonry example is found at Cross East, Co. Mayo, where a well-formed square opening survives in the vault between the ground and first floor.

While accommodation in the interior of the church is usually found at the

17 P.F. O'Donovan, *Archaeological inventory of County Cavan* (Dublin, 1995), 199, 207; O. Davies, 'The churches of County Cavan' in *JRSAI*, 78 (1948), 73–118. 18 Ní Mharcaigh, 'The medieval parish churches', 254. 19 Ibid., 266–7. 20 Ibid., 267–8. 21 FitzPatrick and O'Brien, *The medieval churches*, 134–5.

west end there are occasional examples incorporated into the east end such as at Leighmore, Co. Tipperary. The large multi-period nave and chancel church has a room over the vaulted chancel. A garderobe tower was built against the east end of the north wall with access to the first floor via a mural stairs in the south wall of the chancel.[22]

Of the four types of priestly accommodation found throughout Ireland, accommodation incorporated into the west end of the church is the least elaborate. The standard of priestly accommodation varies greatly throughout Ireland, as it does in Britain. For instance, in Britain, some priests lived in a room over the porch or sacristy, while others enjoyed the luxury of a house. Pantin points to the fact that in the south-west of England at least, the more elaborate houses belonged to appropriated benefices, with Muchelney for instance, being appropriated to Muchelney Abbey.[23] Pantin's method of studying priest's houses can be applied to the study of Irish priests' houses. His basic premise is that clergy with richer benefices had better accommodation, while those with the poorer benefices had a lower standard of residence, and this is borne out to a certain extent by the Irish evidence. The priests who resided in these apartments at the end of the church had a very rudimentary and basic standard of living. Conditions were quite cramped for the incumbent, and heating was not usually provided. As the ground floor of the quarters were often unlit, with quite dark and damp conditions, it is possible that the ground floor area was only used for storage, with the better-lit upper floor comprising the actual living quarters. It must also be considered that the resident priest may have had additional domestic quarters of timber in the vicinity of the church. The provision of such poor quality accommodation for the parish priest, who would have been considered as one of the elite in the community, seems to be indicative of the poverty of the benefices in which they were situated. This is indicated in a case study conducted in the diocese of Tuam in the baronies of Clare and Dunmore, north Co. Galway, where no church exceeded a value of £2 in the Ecclesiastical Taxation of 1306. The churches with evidence for priestly accommodation generally had apartments incorporated into the interior of the church at the west end. The priests of the area were not however overly content with their living arrangements. A letter to the archbishop of Tuam in 1401 mentions a complaint from William Ranny, dean of Tuam, in relation to the fact that many of the priests were 'refusing to reside in their churches' and 'openly and publicly keep concubines'.[24] This was despite the fact that the priests were bound by the statutes of the Church in Tuam to reside in the churches, celebrate Mass in person, and exercise the cure of souls.[25] If the priests were refusing to reside at their churches, then the

22 Farrelly and O'Brien, *Archaeological inventory of County Tipperary vol. 1*, 253. 23 Pantin, 'Medieval priests' houses', 120. 24 W.H. Bliss and J.A. Twemlow (eds), *Calendar of entries in the papal registers relating to Great Britain and Ireland* (London, 1904), v, 399. 25 J.A. Twemlow (ed.), *Calendar of entries in the papal registers relating to Great Britain and Ireland* (London,

quality of pastoral care being provided to the parishioners was probably relatively poor too.

ACCOMMODATION ATTACHED TO ONE SIDE OF THE CHURCH

This type of accommodation is relatively widespread throughout Ireland. In many cases the building is attached to the west gable end of the church, but this is not necessarily the situation at all of the churches. Accommodation attached to one side of the church or to a gable end provides more commodious quarters for the priest than does the accommodation incorporated into the west end of the church. A stairs, instead of a ladder and drop-hole, is usually provided in order to reach the first floor and there is better lighting, and storage facilities. More importantly for the incumbent there are improved heating conditions with, in the case of Doorus, Co. Galway, a fireplace being provided.

The church at Doorus is a differentiated nave and chancel building, with accommodation for the priest attached to the west end of the church. The church displays evidence for three phases of building, dating from the early medieval period, with the nave and priest's quarters seeming to date to the late medieval period. The priest's accommodation, which was built as a complete unit, is two storeys in height. A lobby is entered through a semi-pointed doorway from the west end of the nave. Opposite this is a second doorway, which led into the ground floor of the priest's quarters. This chamber was unusually commodious, provided with light and storage areas in the form of numerous wall cupboards. The ground floor is lit by windows in the north and south walls. A spiral stairway, lit by a small lancet window gives access to the first floor. The first-floor chamber was lit by windows in the north (ogee-headed) and south (lancet) walls. There are the remains of a fireplace in the west wall and wall cupboards in the north and south walls and in the south-west corner. The garderobe is situated in a small chamber at first-floor level, with three steps leading up to the opening of a rectangular chute, which discharges at ground floor level. A single-light window, now minus its head, lights this chamber.

An example of this type of accommodation is also found at Lynally Glebe in Co. Offaly, where a two-storey transept with a barrel-vaulted ground floor was, in this instance, added to the south wall of the church, probably when it was elevated to parish status in the fifteenth century. It was entered through a narrow pointed doorway at the east end of the south wall.[26] The ground floor of the transept was divided into two rooms, one of which may have served as a sacristy, while the other in conjunction with the room overhead comprised the parish priest's quarters.[27]

1904–60), xii, 749. **26** O'Brien and Sweetman, *Archaeological inventory of County Offaly*, 106–7; FitzPatrick and O'Brien, *The medieval churches*, 133–5. **27** Ibid., 134.

One of the few excavations carried out on priest's quarters in Ireland was at St Peter's church in Waterford city where the remains of a church and priest's house were discovered. The two-roomed stone building (8.5m by 5m) was constructed to the south of the chancel.[28] The building appears to have had two or more storeys, with two mural garderobe chutes and associated cesspits. The absence of a hearth or a chimney breast has been noted and may suggest a non-residential function for the building. However, the excavators have proposed that the upper floor, which was furnished with garderobes, contained the main living area and that there may have been a chimney breast on the first floor. It is likely that, similar to the previous examples, the ground floor was used as a sacristy, while the upper floors constituted the priest's quarters. The building continued to be used and modified for some time and was eventually abandoned in the late seventeenth century.

THE FREE-STANDING HOUSE

The free-standing priest's house is quite rare in Ireland. Often the only indication of the existence of a possible house may be foundations located in the vicinity of the church and/or graveyard. At Kilbrickan, Co. Galway, for instance, there are the rectangular foundations of a second building in the graveyard,[29] and at Lemanaghan, Co. Offaly, the lower masonry courses of a rectangular building to the north-west of St Manchan's church could yet prove to be a priest's house.

There are a small number of extant free-standing priest's houses scattered throughout the country. At Howth, Co. Dublin, a free-standing priest's house is located close to the parish church of the Blessed Virgin Mary.[30] The house which has been dated to the sixteenth century, has undergone renovations in recent years with both the west and east ends currently occupied. The house has a T-shaped plan and is two storeys in height. It is constructed from roughly coursed blocks, with dressed limestone used in the quoins, windows and doorways.[31]

At Graffan in Co. Offaly there is a two-storey house associated with the nearby late medieval parish church of Ballintemple.[32] The house, which was built in the early seventeenth century, has two storeys and a T-plan, similar to Howth. Originally the ground floor was divided by means of a wooden

28 M.F. Hurley, S.W.J. McCutcheon and B. Murtagh, 'St Peter's church and graveyard' in M.F. Hurley, O.M.B. Scully and S.W.J. McCutcheon (eds), *Late Viking age and medieval Waterford: excavations 1986–1992* (Waterford, 1997), 190–244: 212–13; Moore, *Archaeological inventory of County Waterford*, 190–1. 29 P. Gosling, *Archaeological inventory of County Galway, i* (Dublin, 1993), 98–9. 30 Leask, *Irish churches*, iii, 29–30; M. McMahon, *Medieval church sites of north Dublin* (Dublin, 1991), 23. 31 G. Stout, 'Priest's house at Howth', Co. Dublin. Unpublished OPW file (Department of the Environment, Heritage and Local Government). 32 FitzPatrick and O'Brien, *The medieval churches*, 117.

partition and lit by windows in the west, east and north walls. Rooms in the west and east sides of the house were heated by large fireplaces, both of which have protruding stacks. Access between floors was by means of a stairway, located in a small tower centrally placed in the north wall.[33]

A building beside Banagher church, Dungiven, Co. Derry, and close to the north entrance of the graveyard, has also been identified as a priest's residence.[34] The church was founded by Muiredach O'Heney in the thirteenth century and was used up to the seventeenth century.[35] The residence is a rectangular structure and originally there was no entrance at ground floor level. In the early nineteenth century it was described by Sampson as being 'entire', except for the roof and the door which was mentioned as being several feet from the ground. G.V. du Noyer visited the site in the nineteenth century, and in his drawings he calls the building a 'sacristy' or 'monk house'. The view from the north shows the church and a tall building with three floors and narrow windows.[36] When the Royal Society of Antiquaries visited the site in 1915, only the base of the structure remained upstanding.[37] During excavations at the site, sherds of everted-rim ware were found in and around the suspected priest's residence at Banagher, suggesting that it was occupied up to and possibly including the sixteenth century. Waterman and Hamlin maintain that the residence with the first-floor entrance appears to have been some form of strong-house.[38] Fortified priests' houses were built in the north of England between the fourteenth century and the seventeenth century as a result of the troubled conditions of the time. In Ireland unsettled conditions and warfare meant similar precautions were necessary.

Another and probably the finest example of an upstanding priest's house in Ireland is found at Kilmalkedar in Co. Kerry (pl. 2). To the north of the Romanesque nave and chancel church there is a two-storey building called St Brendan's House.[39] The house is a rectangular gabled structure (11.7m by 7.15m externally), three storeys high, with a battered base. The entrance to the house is situated in the south wall and leads into the west chamber. There is also a doorway at first-floor level in the south wall, which may indicate the former presence of a fore-building. The ground floor was lit by narrow loops on both the north and south walls. Access to the first floor was by means of a wooden stairs, located either in the interior of the house or in the fore-building. The floor was carried by a combination of corbels and beam-holes. The garderobe was situated in the north-east corner of the east room.[40]

33 O'Brien and Sweetman, *Archaeological inventory of County Offaly*, 175. 34 D.M. Waterman and A. Hamlin, 'Banagher church, Co. Derry' in *Ulster Journal of Archaeology*, 3rd series, 39 (1975), 25–41: 36. 35 T. Barry, *The archaeology of medieval Ireland* (London, 1987), 142. 36 Waterman and Hamlin, 'Banagher church', 36. 37 Anon, 'Banagher' in *JRSAI*, 45 (1915), 233–8: 237. 38 Waterman and Hamlin, 'Banagher church', 37. 39 J. Cuppage, *Archaeological survey of the Dingle peninsula* (Ballyferriter, 1986), 318–321; A. Hill, *Ancient Irish architecture: Kilmalkedar, Co. Kerry* (Cork, 1870); Anon., 'Kilmalkedar and Gallarus' in *JRSAI*, 27 (1897), 291–6: 296. 40 Cuppage, *Archaeological survey*, 318–21.

Pl. 2: St Brendan's House, Kilmalkedar, Co. Kerry (photo courtesy of the
Department of Environment, Heritage and Local Government)

TOWER ACCOMMODATION

This type of priestly residence was usually either built onto the west end of the
church or attached to the church and resting on its own foundations. While
between two-to-four examples of this type are found in most counties covered
by the Archaeological Survey of Ireland, there is a significant density in Co.
Meath where there are approximately twenty sites. The tower is usually
situated at the west end of the church, but this is not necessarily the case at all
of the church sites. The towers usually range in height from two-to-four
storeys. At Townparks North, Co. Meath, there is a west tower of five floors,
with a projection which contained the stairs.[41] Many of the towers are provided
with barrel vaulting, garderobes and fireplaces. At a few of the sites in Co.
Meath there are two towers attached to the church. At Killeen there is a
fifteenth-century nave and chancel church, with two towers at the west end of
the nave, that on the south-west having a spiral stairs.[42] At Glebe in Co.
Wexford a tower survives at the west end of the church. The entrance to the
tower was from the church (which was fortified) and was protected by a
murder-hole. The ground floor was vaulted and a stairs led up to a first-floor
doorway, while the second floor was constructed with timber joists set into the

41 M.J. Moore, *Archaeological inventory of County Meath* (Dublin, 1987), 147.   42 Ibid., 137–8.

walls. There is a gun loop in the east wall and a possible wall-walk as indicated by the stairs continuing on the north wall.[43]

In south-west county Dublin, Ní Mharcaigh noted that the parish churches at Crumlin, Kilbride, Newcastle and Tallaght had residential towers attached. The tower at Kilbride was constructed over the west end of the church, whereas those at Crumlin, Newcastle and Tallaght rested on their own foundations at the west end.[44] At Newcastle the tower functioned as both a priest's residence and a belfry. Access to the church was through the vaulted ground floor of the tower. A stone stairway in the north-west corner led to the priest's quarters. The first-floor apartment was provided with a fireplace in the north wall, with the chimney continuing to the second floor. It was lit by windows in the west and south walls. The second floor was lit by a window in the south wall.[45]

McMahon's survey of churches in north county Dublin has yielded numerous examples of attached western towers, which she acknowledges must have functioned as both belfries and priests' residences.[46] The churches at Balrothery, Lusk, Portrane, Swords and Baldongan all exhibit fine examples of medieval western towers. The church at Baldongan was probably a manorial church, being situated close to the site of Baldongan Castle.[47] The church is a nave and chancel building, with a three-storey tower at the west end. A doorway in the west face of the tower led to the nave of the church. Near the top of the tower on the west side there is a projection to accommodate the stairway. Windows along the faces of the tower lit the interior.

The number of priests' residences recorded throughout Ireland continues to increase, with two new residences recently identified, at Cashelboy, Co. Sligo, and Kilmurry, Co. Kilkenny. A two-storey, free-standing tower, adjacent to the parish church at Cashleboy, was noted during the archaeological survey of Co. Sligo (P. O'Donovan pers. comm.). Its proximity to, and architectural contemporaneity with, the church suggests that it was a priest's residence. The castle at Kilmurry, Co. Kilkenny was long believed to be a fifteenth- or sixteenth-century tower house, with an attached modern dwelling. It was not until the structure was archaeologically investigated by Murtagh in 1998 that the 'castle' was discovered to be a fortified church with an attached residential tower at the west end.[48] Kilmurry was a chapel of ease, under the patronage of the Fitzgerald O'Deas of Gorteens.[49] The church, which went out of use after the Cromwellian settlement in the seventeenth century, was renovated and incorporated into the two-storey dwelling house, which was vacated in 1955. The tower had been abandoned in the late nineteenth or early twentieth century. The archaeological investigation concentrated on the dwelling house which

43 Ibid., 127. **44** Ní Mharcaigh, 'The medieval parish churches', 249. **45** Ibid., 272–4. **46** McMahon, 'Medieval church sites', 32. **47** Ibid., 17. **48** B. Murtagh, 'Kilmurry Castle and other related sites in Slieverue parish, in the light of recent investigations' in *Old Kilkenny Review*, 52 (2000), 26–107: 26. **49** Ibid., 53.

adjoined the tower. The plaster was removed from both the interior and the exterior of the building, revealing the walls of the church. The internal features of the church such as the stoup and piscina had been blocked up and the altar was replaced with a fireplace.[50] The church is an undifferentiated nave and chancel building (9.15m by 4.62m internally), which according to documentary evidence may have been constructed in the 1430s. The church was entered through a doorway in the south wall and was lit by windows in the north, south and east walls, of both round- and ogee-headed form.[51] At the west end of the church a doorway leads into the ground floor of the tower (7.4m by 6.52m externally). Towards the south end of the ground floor, another doorway leads into a lobby at the base of a mural stairway to the upper floors. The tower was reached from the exterior through a doorway (now blocked) at the south side of the lobby. The first floor of the tower was supported by corbels and was roofed with a pointed barrel-vault. At either side of the chamber, doorways through the soffit of the vault led into two long mural chambers. Murtagh notes that this situation is similar to the tower house at nearby Ballinlaw. The chamber on the second floor is reached from the top of the mural stairway. The roof of the chamber and the battlements were renovated in the late eighteenth/early nineteenth century. The defensive features of the building include the bartizans at the north-west and south-east corners, at wall-walk level. The south-east bartizan provided protection for the doorways to both the church and the tower.

A fine example of a residential tower in the west of Ireland is that at Cross East in Co. Mayo, where there are the remains of a church with a residential tower situated at the west end (pl. 3). The tower consists of ground and first-floor chambers. A window in the dividing wall between the tower and the church allowed a view of the nave. Access between the floors was by means of a ladder, for which the opening in the vault remains. The first floor is lit by round-headed lancet windows, which have smooth finished stone, chamfered sides and moulded spandrels. The possible remains of a stone roof are present at this level. It was suggested by Neary that the tower at Cross East was a secular tower, constructed, so it would seem, to take advantage of the stone in the church.[52] However, it is doubtful that the tower was a purposefully built secular residence, as the architecture suggests that the church and tower were contemporary. Moreover, the tower would not have been large enough to facilitate the requirements of a lord.

A number of residential towers have been identified as fortified structures, for instance that at Taghmon, Co. Westmeath (pl. 4). The church is an undifferentiated nave and chancel building, with an attached western tower, four storeys in height. The church is lit by ogee-headed windows, in the north and south walls, and has a stone vault.[53] Battlements are not only situated on the

---

50 Ibid., 57.   **51** Ibid., 62.   **52** J. Neary, *Notes on Cong and the Neale* (Dundalk, 1938), 51–2.   **53** Leask, *Irish churches*, iii, 20–1; S. Rothery, *A field guide to the buildings of Ireland* (Dublin, 1997), 16.

Pl. 3: View of church and tower at Cross East, Co. Mayo, from the north-west, with tower in foreground

tower, but also on the long walls of the church (east–west). The ground floor of the residence, which was entered from the church, was vaulted and lit by two small loops. This chamber was probably only used for storage. Above this on the first floor was the main living area, provided with a fireplace and lit by two windows with stone seats. Just off the main living area, there was a small room/chamber with a doorway leading to the stairway. The second floor, according to Leask, contained the bedroom with a garderobe. Two more rooms were located on the third floor, which had a timber roof.[54]

The residential tower for the parish priest may have had its origins in the crossing towers that provided accommodation for abbots and priors in religious houses of the fourteenth and fifteenth centuries. It is interesting to speculate that these in turn may have originated in the secular tower house, which itself became the most common fortified residence for Gaelic and Anglo-Irish gentry in fifteenth-century Ireland. Clyne has noted that the Prior's tower at Kells, Co. Kilkenny, which was the private accommodation for the prior, was built in the style of a tower house.[55] Some features which Prior's Tower has in common with tower houses include a base batter, a murder-hole inside the entrance, small windows at ground floor level, with larger openings on the upper floors and a walkway at roof level which was enclosed by parapet walls. Murtagh has also noted architectural similarities between the residential tower at Kilmurry

---

54 Leask, *Irish churches*, iii, 20–1. **55** M. Clyne (forthcoming), *Excavations at Kells Priory, Co. Kilkenny*.

Pl. 4: Church and tower at Taghmon, Co. Westmeath (photo: S. Rothery, 1997)

and the tower house at nearby Ballinlaw.[56] So it would seem that the parochial residential tower may be viewed as a diminutive version of the tower house.

CONCLUSIONS

Priestly accommodation in Ireland largely falls into three of the categories mentioned above, that is, accommodation incorporated into the west end of the church, accommodation attached to one side of the church and the residential tower (fig. 1). The free-standing priest's house appears on present evidence to be quite scarce in this country. While this opinion is as yet compromised by the lack of fieldwork carried out or published for some counties, such as Mayo and Sligo for instance, it seems the situation in Ireland is similar to Britain where Pantin notes that relatively few free-standing priests' houses survive.[57]

While the types of priestly accommodation have quite a widespread distribution throughout the country, a number of patterns emerge. As regards the accommodation incorporated into the west end of the church, there are minor variations in respect of flooring. Beam-holes in the west gable have a pocket distribution, found in counties Galway, Kerry and Louth. The ledge method is noted in Waterford, while in Co. Offaly and North Tipperary there is a preference for barrel vaulting. Meanwhile, the paucity of free-standing houses may be explained by the fact that they were possibly constructed from non-

56 Murtagh, 'Kilmurry Castle', 46, 74.   57 Pantin, 'Medieval priests' houses', 145.

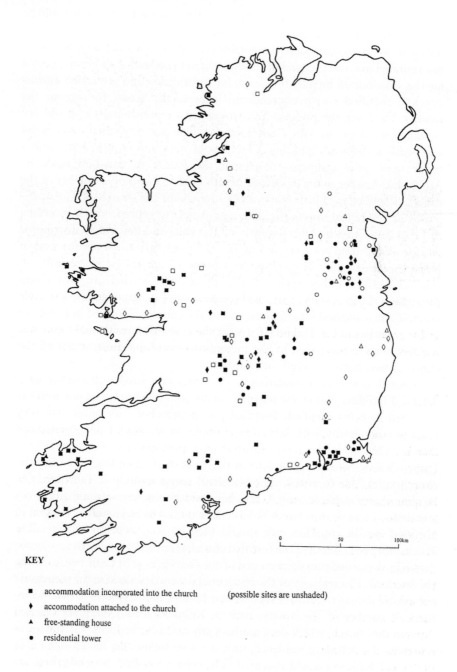

KEY

	accommodation incorporated into the church	(possible sites are unshaded)
■	accommodation incorporated into the church	
♦	accommodation attached to the church	
▲	free-standing house	
●	residential tower	

Fig. 1: Distribution map of the types of priests' residences in Ireland

durable materials, such as wood. In this case archaeological excavation would be the only method of increasing our knowledge of them. The dense concentration of tower accommodation is notable (as is the absence of accommodation incorporated into the west end of the church) in Co. Meath. Reasons suggested for this distribution include the desire for fortification and protection against attack.[58] Fortified parish churches are occasionally found throughout the country. However, the presence of a tower with a parish church should not automatically imply that the church was fortified, as a residential tower is not necessarily a defensive building. Churches of nave and chancel form with a tower were quite common throughout the Pale.[59] A visitation made by Archbishop Ussher to the diocese of Meath in 1622 mentions a number of the towers, described as 'a little castle at the west end of the church'.[60] The distribution of residential towers (fig. 1) is comparable to belfries, which according to Leask are somewhat characteristic of the Pale, and not widely distributed outside of it.[61] The presence of a number of residential towers in the west of Ireland indicates that they are not just found in the east of the country in colonial Ireland. Other types of priestly accommodation are also found throughout the Pale, such as attached residences in Co. Meath and the probable examples incorporated into the west end of the church, identified in a number of the churches in Co. Dublin. If it were the case that a residential tower was required for the protection of the incumbent would not most, if not all the churches have been provided with one?

As noted, tower accommodation is sometimes associated with a desire for a defended building, but of the possible twenty sites in Meath, just one tower is described as being fortified. Fortified parish churches with towers are very much in the minority, with only a few examples to be found. Leask pointed out that churches with 'defensive features' were probably not truly defensive.[62] Large windows situated quite low on the walls of the building, often left the church vulnerable to attack. The 'fortified' parish church at Taghmon, Co. Westmeath, for example, with its attached residential tower, retained quite low-set windows that lit the church.[63] Towers ought not to be viewed as integral to 'fortified' parish churches, nor should they be seen as necessarily lending defensibility to a church. True fortified churches are also found with accommodation incorporated into the west end of the church, as at St Catherine's, Nook, Co. Wexford. The majority of the residential towers described in the sources do not exhibit defensive features such as base batters, murder-holes or machicolations. A number of the towers, such as Killiney in Co. Kerry are reached through the church, which does not have any defensive features.[64] If the tower represented a defensive residence, then it would follow that the church (as in the case of Killiney) would also need to have been fortified. So while there are

---

58 Waterman and Hamlin, 'Banagher church', 37.   59 Ní Mharcaigh, 'The medieval parish churches', 257–8.   60 Cited in Leask, *Irish churches*, iii, 19–20.   61 Leask, *Irish churches*, iii, 21.
62 Ibid., 12.   63 Rothery, *A field guide*, 16.   64 Cuppage, *Archaeological survey*, 305–7.

recognisable fortified residential towers, it ought not to be assumed that every residential tower is necessarily a defended building.

The residential tower is probably the result of better lay patronage and financial resources and the outcome of the influence of the tower house tradition in secular building. Better patronage of a parish would also have allowed for more commodious priestly residences. In Scotland, Fawcett noted that the church and tower at Dysart are located in one of the more affluent areas of medieval Scotland.[65] It would appear that Ireland may be comparable to Scotland in this regard, with residential towers being found in the wealthier parishes of the country. Leask suggested that the families of English descent were not susceptible to Irish influences and practices; instead the buildings of the area reflected the architectural influences from England.[66] In fifteenth-century documents, Kilmurry, Co. Kilkenny was described as one of the wealthiest townlands in the area.[67] It is surely no coincidence that in such an affluent area an elaborate residence was provided for the priest.

Acknowledgment

This essay is based on research for a Masters degree completed at the Department of Archaeology, NUI, Galway. My thanks to Liz FitzPatrick.

65 R. Fawcett, *Scottish architecture from the accession of the Stuarts to the Reformation, 1371–1560* (Edinburgh, 1994), 232.   **66** Leask, *Irish churches*, iii, 11.   **67** Murtagh, 'Kilmurry Castle', 42.

The dynamics of parish formation in high medieval and late medieval Clare

PATRICK NUGENT

The archaeological record of early monastic enclosures, church sites, anchorite cells, *cillíns*, and place-name evidence, would suggest that the Church had a significant presence in Irish society from the sixth century onwards. However, the Church and secular society were mutually interdependent and this informed the practice of Christianity, placing it at variance with canon law. Such a scenario was not unique to Ireland. In AD 1070 Pope Gregory VII issued twenty-seven propositions known as *Dictatus Papae* that sought to disengage the Church from secular control throughout Christendom.[1] Ironically the Gregorian reforms had little chance of success without the aid of secular rulers. Muirchertach Ua Brian was one such ruler. While he did convene the first two reforming synods at Cashel and Ráithbreasil in 1101 and 1111, which saw the extension of these Gregorian reforms to Ireland, separation of church and state was unlikely to have been his primary motive. A reorganised island-wide Church under his patronage would have greatly strengthened his position as high-king of Ireland and would have conveniently undermined the existing powerful monastic communities and their patrons. Little was achieved at these synods apart from the proposal that the many abuses, which had arisen from the preceding centuries of interdependency, be rectified. It was not until the synod at Kells in 1152 that the territorial organisation necessary to establish the Church on a more independent footing took form. This territorial structure of diocese, rural deanery and parish was largely in place by the early fourteenth century. However, the Church never managed to develop a separate sphere of influence. What did emerge was a more stable relationship between church and state in that they together formed the twin pillars that underpinned Clare society until the sixteenth-century Reformation and after.

The reforming synods utilised the existing Gaelic territorial structure in delineating their diocesan and rural deanery boundaries. Gaelic territorial units were again used in demarcating medieval parishes. A hypothetico-deductive model of the territorial organisation of high and late medieval Gaelic regions

---

1 N. Davies, *Europe: a history* (London, 1997), 39–42.

Table 1: The territorial hierarchies evident within the territorial organisation of Co. Clare in the high and late medieval periods[2]

	Gaelic	Anglo–Norman	Ecclesiastical	New-English
A	*Mór-thúath*	County	Diocese	County
B	*Tríocha-Céad*	Cantred	Rural Deanery	Barony
C	*Túath*	Manor	Parish	Civil Parish
D. Large Land Assessment	Ballybetagh *Baile*	Colp Vil		
E. Intermediate Land Assesment Terms	Carrow (1/4) Seisreach (1/6) Ballyboe	Martland Plowland		Townland
F. Small Land Assessment Terms	Gnive	Town Colp Fraction Martland Fraction		
G. Minor Land Assessment	Gort Gragan	Gallon Pottle		Plantation Acre (Irish Acre)

has been constructed to illustrate the high degree of correspondence between Gaelic and ecclesiastical boundary processes. Table 1 attempts to capture this symbiotic interrelationship between the two territorial hierarchies.

The continental-style monastic orders, such as the Cistercians and the Augustinians, had begun to delineate parishes immediately prior to the Anglo-Norman colonisation. The ethnic origins of the patrons appear to have influenced whether they utilised existing *túatha*, ballybetaghs or *bailte*. The *baile* and ballybetaghs were favoured by the Anglo–Norman colonisers, while the larger territorial unit the *túath* was favoured by the Gaelic Irish. The delineation of parochial divisions would appear to signify the condensing stage of the diffusion of the Gregorian reforms. It possibly meant that the reforms had permeated to the lower tiers of society.

2 By combining the research of P.J. Duffy, 'The territorial organisation of Gaelic landownership and its transformation in Co. Monaghan, 1591–1640' in *Irish Geography*, 14 (1981), 1–26; P.S. Robinson, 'The plantation of Co. Tyrone in the seventeenth century', unpublished PhD (QUB, 1974); and T. McErlean, 'The Irish townland system of landscape organisation' in T. Reeves Smith and F. Hammond (eds), *Landscape archaeology in Ireland*, BAR 116 (Oxford, 1983) 315–39, a seven-tiered hypothetico-deductive model of the pre-existing Gaelic territorial hierarchy has been created from the lordship/county level downwards. These are listed below in descending order in accordance with their established average size; Lordship, *tríocha céad, túath*, large, intermediate, small and minor land units. The equivalent territorial units of the territorial hierarchies of the Church and the New-English administration have been added to reveal their relationship with the pre-existing Gaelic territorial hierarchy.

When Nicholls' island-wide mosaic of parish typologies are combined with Empey's and Hennessey's regional studies,[3] the establishment and diffusion of Ireland's medieval parish matrix can be described as follows. Prior to the twelfth century, parish formation was confined to Viking towns. The initial impetus for extensive parish formation came with the introduction of continental monastic orders. These orders were the primary facilitators of the Gregorian reforms, until the colonising Anglo-Normans at the end of the century. The continental-style orders were given extensive additional lands along with the compact territory in which their monastic establishments were to be situated by their patrons. Ecclesiastical historians generally believe that these additional lands were administered as parishes.[4] However, these dispersed territories may only have been embryonic parishes since many are not listed in the early fourteenth-century ecclesiastical lists. Parish formation and manor delineation were central to the Anglo-Norman colonisation strategy and consequently the diffusion of a parochial network mirrored the expansion of the Anglo-Norman colony. The nearby presence of the Anglo-Norman colonisers appears to have encouraged the local Gaelic chieftains to accelerate the process within their own territories. Even so, the diffusion of a parish network throughout the entire island was not complete even by the beginning of the fourteenth century. Marchland and remote Gaelic regions were still without a parish network.

THE EVOLUTION OF THE PARISH IN HIGH MEDIEVAL CLARE

If one accepts Nicholls' theory on the formation of parishes in Connacht, then parish formation did not occur in Clare until 1248 when Robert de Muscegros got a grant in fee-farm from Henry III, of Tradry (cantred) for £30 per annum.[5] This hypothesis will be tested here through an examination of the role of the following three agents, the continental-style monastic orders, the Anglo-Normans and local Gaelic chieftains, in the evolution of the parish in high medieval Clare.

In the late twelfth century, two continental-style monastic orders were introduced to Clare. The Augustinians established Clare Abbey under the patronage of Donal Mór O'Brien in 1189, while the Cistercians founded Corcomroe Abbey under the patronage of his son Donogh Cairbreac in 1195. The debate as to whether these two orders were responsible for the county's first parishes

---

3 K.W. Nicholls, 'Rectory, vicarage and parish in the western Irish dioceses' in *JRSAI*, 101 (1971), 53–84; C.A. Empey, 'The Norman period: 1185–1500', 83–6 in W. Nolan and T.G. McGrath (eds), *Tipperary: history and society* (Dublin, 1985) and M. Hennessey, 'Parochial organisation in medieval Tipperary' in ibid., 60–70. 4 A. Gwynn and D.F. Gleeson, *A history of the diocese of Killaloe* (Dublin, 1962), 199–200, 203. 5 Chart. 32 Henry. III., cited in G.U. MacNamara, 'Bunratty, Co. Clare' in *North Munster Antiquarian Journal*, 13:4 (1915), 220–313: 28.

is hampered by ambiguous transcripts of the original royal charter of the earlier abbey and the lack of extant documentation for the second. Gleeson states that the Augustinians not only reformed communal monastic life in accordance with the Gregorian reforms, but that they also undertook parochial work.[6] He continues by surmising that in time so many parishes were administered by these orders that they became just as powerful as the older monastic houses. The following analysis of the two Clare Abbey transcripts will explore Gleeson's supposition.

The 1461 transcript of the founding charter made by Thateus, bishop of Killaloe,[7] reveals that Donal Mór's grant is similar in style to contemporary Norman charters, in that the Augustinians were presented with lands, possessions and rectories as a complete and perpetual gift for future time.[8] The transcript then lists the lands taken with the abbey. The abbey and these lands are depicted in figure 1. It was only by cross-referencing with the second transcript that their location was determined (cf. fig. 1).[9] Differentiated circles have been deployed to show the approximate amount of rent and tithes payable to Clare Abbey from each of these lands. These range from five shillings to eight marks. Accepting McErlean's principle that the primary determinant of territorial extent within Gaelic territorial organisation was economic potential,[10] and that similar economic potential meant a similar position in the territorial hierarchy, then these fifteen lands represented a range of territorial units ranging from *túatha* and *bailte*, to small land units. Therefore the paying of rents and tithes alone cannot be taken as proof of the existence of parishes. While it is tempting to surmise that territories paying larger amounts of rent may have been parochial units, an examination of the seven tithe-paying land denominations which bore the same names as parishes on the ecclesiastical taxation list of 1302–6 reveals no clear correlation between larger rents and parochial status. However, these seven territories did possess ecclesiastical structures in contrast to only two of the remaining eight. While the presence of ecclesiastical structures combined with the paying of rent suggests the possible existence of embryonic parishes, nevertheless, it is impossible to sustain the argument that these ecclesiastical territories were similar in size, layout and function to the Anglo-Norman parishes.

Recognisable parish formation should coincide with the establishment of Bunratty by the Anglo-Norman knight, Richard de Clare, in the mid-thirteenth century. Contemporary documents relating to this manor do not focus on the ecclesiastical territorial units. They are primarily concerned with the internal cadastral territorial units within the manor itself. However, ecclesiastical buildings are mentioned. An inquisition post mortem *c.*1287 suggests a definite link between church and manor by the inclusion of the following

6 Gwynn and Gleeson, *Diocese of Killaloe* (Dublin, 1962), 199. 7 TCD, MS, 579. 8 Gwynn and Gleeson, *Diocese of Killaloe*, 201. 9 BL, Royal MS, 13 A xiv, f. 117. 10 McErlean, 'The Irish townland system', 316.

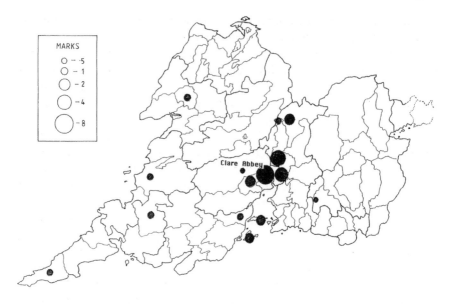

Fig. 1: Clare abbey lands, *c*.1189

statement 'the church in Bunratty, with ten adjacent chapels, were in advowson
to the manor'.[11] Since the ecclesiastical taxation list of 1302–6 returns eleven
parochial units within the limits of Bunratty manor, which bore the same name
as eleven contemporary ecclesiastical structures, Otway-Ruthven's assertion
that 'nothing is clearer than the identification of manor and parish'[12] may have
some relevance in a Clare context.

    An analysis of the mid seventeenth-century Books of Survey and
Distribution (BSD), the first source to record the boundaries of the Clare
parishes and provide their areal extent, shows that they generally conform to
the accepted hypothesis on the form and size of Anglo-Norman parishes. With
an average acreage of 3000 statute acres, these relatively compact territorial
units are also revealed to be coextensive with either a ballybetagh or a territorial
unit that consisted of a multiple of *bailte*. The writings of Empey, Hennessey,
Nicholls and Otway-Ruthven[13] would suggest that sociopolitically Anglo-
Norman parishes were defined by a rigid hierarchical society, which
restructured the territory's resources in accordance with its own perception of
society and its needs. Internal land units were measured in ploughlands or
fractions of a ploughland. This land assessment unit was far closer to
standardised measurement than the Gaelic quarter and consequently reveals a

11 McNamara, 'Bunratty, Co. Clare', 236.   12 A.J. Otway-Ruthven, *A history of medieval
Ireland* (New York, 1968), 119.   13 Empey, 'The Norman period', 71–91; Hennessey, 'Parochial
organisation in medieval Tipperary', 60–70; Nicholls, 'Rectory, vicarage and parish', 53–6;
Otway-Ruthven, *A history*, 118–21, 126–43.

qualitatively different societal ideology, one defined by an elite to which the general population within the territory had no kinship ties. In terms of settlement, each parish had one central place that evolved about the manor. The parish coincided with the territory controlled by this centre. These nucleated settlements invariably included a church, which functioned as the parish centre. This spatial contiguousness of the principal secular and ecclesiastical structures possibly mirrored a shared social and political ideology.

This idealised model of an Anglo-Norman parish was rarely completely realised in Ireland, and particularly in south-east Clare, which lay on the periphery of the Anglo-Norman colony. Empey's research on neighbouring Tipperary provides a more appropriate template by recognising that Anglo-Norman settlement was 'essentially of the do it yourself variety'.[14] In the identification of five different types of lesser manors, he offers a radical perspective on continuity that stresses evolutionary rather than revolutionary change and demonstrates how the Anglo-Normans built upon or were constrained by existing political, social and settlement structures.[15] Simms recognises the primary constraint that another variable placed upon this evolution. She holds that the existing territorial hierarchy was ultimately to prevent the evolution of the large nucleated villages found elsewhere in medieval Europe.[16] While this may be an overly enthusiastic interpretation of the role of continuity in the core area of Anglo-Norman colonisation in the south and east of Ireland, an analysis of the internal territorial organisation of Bunratty manor shows that it is certainly the case in south-east Clare. Consequently the particularity of place coupled with the scale of colonisation also tempered the cultural interface between Anglo-Normans and Gaelic Irish.

In 1287, Bunratty would appear to be closest in form to a colonial type manor, one of the five typologies identified by Empey. His analysis of the rental of Lisronagh manor, 1333, reveals, what he terms, a colonial settlement with free tenants, cottiers, a significant burgess community and a large number of Irish betaghs.[17] While Bunratty did not possess a cottier class it did have a proportionately smaller number of free tenants at twenty-one, a burgess community of 226 and an unknown number of Irish betaghs.[18] This initial similarity unravels somewhat when the domain of both manors is compared. Bunratty controlled a vast territory of at least 30,000 acres that corresponded approximately to *Tríocha Céad Tradraighe* while Lisronagh was a modest lesser manor of about 5,000 acres. In fact, Bunratty being the only manor in Clare, it functioned more as a *caput* manor since it controlled almost all Anglo-Norman settlement within the county.

14 Empey, 'The Norman period', 81.   15 C.A. Empey, 'The Anglo-Norman settlement in the cantred of Eliogarty' cited in B.J. Graham, 'The High Middle Ages: *c*.1100–1350 AD' in B.J. Graham and L. Proudfoot (eds), *An historical geography of Ireland* (London, 1993), 58–98: 66. 16 A. Simms, 'Core and periphery in medieval Europe: the Irish experience in a wider context' in W.J. Smyth and K. Whelan (eds), *Common ground* (Dublin, 1988), 22–40: 33–8.   17 Empey, 'The Norman period', 81.   18 McNamara, 'Bunratty, Co. Clare', 234–6.

Table 2: Bunratty manor parishes

Parish Name	14th century Taxation Levy (sterling)	1622 Tithe Levy	1641 Quarter totals	Rounded to nearest *Baile*
Tomfinlough	2 marks (£1–6s.)	£15	13.5	3
Kilnasoolagh	3 marks (£2)	£18	22.25	6
Kilmaleery	3 marks (£2)	£14	13.25	3
Kilconry	3 marks (£2)	£12	16	4
Clonloghan	1 mark (13s.–4d.)	£16	12.125	3
Drumline	3 marks (£2)	£20	13	3
Feenagh	10 shillings (10s.)	£12	9	2
Inisdadrum	10 shillings (10s.)	—	1	0.25
Killoo	3 marks (£2)	£15	13	3
Kilfinaghta	4.5 marks (£3)	£24	21.5	5
Bunratty	6 marks (£4)	£20	11.25	3

The 1302–6 taxation list facilitates the identification of the ten chapels stated as being in advowson to Bunratty church in the inquisition. These were the principal churches of the following parishes; Tomfinlough, Kilnasoolagh, Kilmaleary, Kilconry, Clonloghan, Drumline, Feenagh, Inisdadrum, Killoo, Kilfinaghta and Bunratty. However, the precise boundaries of the eleven parishes cannot be determined until 1641. While it would be foolish to think that these boundaries would have remained unchanged since the late thirteenth century, a comparison of their seventeenth-century quarter-totals and fourteenth-century taxations levels, depicted in Table 2, shows that the relative economic potential of most of these parishes had remained relatively constant, possibly suggesting a reasonable stability in their boundaries.

This table also facilitates the exploration of the widely held view that Anglo-Norman parishes were delineated in accordance with the existing Gaelic territorial structure. Hypothetically these parishes should be equivalent to the sixteen quarter ballybetagh, the four quarter *baile* or a multiple of either territorial unit. Column five shows that when their quarter totals are rounded to the nearest multiple of four, Feenagh was equivalent to two *bailte*. Tomfinlough, Kilmaleary, Clonloghan, Drumline, Bunratty and Killoo were equivalent to three *bailte*, Kilconry was exactly equivalent to a ballybetagh and Kilfinaghta and Kilnasoolagh were equivalent to five and six *bailte*, respectively. Such a pattern supports Simms' hypothesis that the Anglo-Normans were possibly constrained by the existing territorial superstructure in their delineation of the parochial network. However, when the constituent *vills* of the manor are superimposed on the parish matrix (cf. fig. 2), the degree of correspondence is so poor as to question whether the Anglo-Normans were even responsible for parish delineation. The following three factors would appear to support this hypothesis. The inquisition records just one major nucleated settlement, the

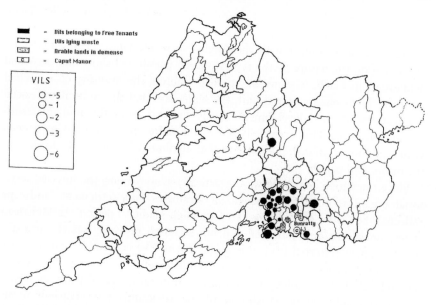

Fig. 2: Bunratty manor, *c*.1287

town that had evolved about the *caput* manor of Bunratty, and the most likely abode of the 226 predominantly agriculturalist burgesses. Secondly, the Anglo-Norman colonisation had no impact on the parish names since all are entirely Gaelic. Thirdly, two of the chapels, Killoo and Inisdadrum, were the ecclesiastical centres of territories granted to the Augustinian abbey at Clare in the previous century. Collectively these factors illustrate how the Anglo-Normans had not radically altered the existing territorial structure thus further emphasising the degree to which Bunratty was a colonial manor. Apart from the parish of Bunratty, the evidence of a significant influx of newcomers in the rest of the manor is limited. Consequently the more numerous Irish betaghs, were loosely controlled by a comparatively small free tenant 'elite'. In conclusion, the Anglo-Normans were not the first agents of the Gregorian reforms in this area. They would appear to have been responsible for the delineation or stabilisation of only some of the parishes. They were profoundly constrained by the existing territorial structure. Consequently, they failed to create a network of stereotypical Norman parishes, with the exception of Bunratty and possibly Drumline, Clonloghan and Feenagh.

Nicholls has stated that parish formation west of the Shannon dates from the mid-thirteenth century.[19] This implies that the Gaelic chieftains of Clare were establishing parishes at the same time as the Anglo-Norman lord, Richard de Clare. The ecclesiastical taxation list records a near countywide parochial

---

19 Nicholls, 'Rectory, vicarage and parish', 62; however, see Ní Ghabhláin, above, for her argument in favour of earlier parish formation in the diocese of Kilfenora.

network by 1302–6. This rapid adoption of territorial innovation in Gaelic regions would appear to suggest that the Gaelic Irish were 'irrevocably' changed by their contact with the Anglo-Normans. However, the following discussion on the nature of the typical Gaelic parish will show that parochial delineation in Gaelic regions was perhaps merely the granting of parochial status to the Gaelic territorial unit, the *túath*, and that the cultural and social implications of this development slowly evolved from the mid-thirteenth century onwards. This eventually led to the *túath* and parish having a deep symbiotic interrelationship similar to that attributed by Otway-Ruthven,[20] to the manor and parish.

Since the parish and *túath* were practically synonymous, the internal territorial organisation, land management strategies and settlement landscape reflected the Gaelic clan ideology[21] of the high medieval period. As McErlean states, since economic potential and not standard measure was the primary determinant of internal land unit size,[22] it could be concluded that territory still defined society to some degree. While Gaelic society was profoundly hierarchical, a clan ideology based on, actual or fake, shared pedigree meant that theoretically a *túath*/parish was still the patrimonial inheritance of all the clan regardless of existing fortunes at a particular time. Consequently, there was a degree of fluidity in the societal hierarchy, unknown in a feudal society. The clan system was by no means an unregulated system, but the brehon law code differed fundamentally from common law, in that adjudication was by arbitration and not by decree. The spatial order of settlement landscape was also symbolic of this ideological context.[23] Therefore the dispersion of the secular dwellings of the elite throughout the *túath*/parish, coupled with the trend that the parish centre was rarely contiguous to any of these secular centres, reveals a more fluid and dispersed societal hierarchy.

As the medieval period progressed, the parish centres invariably remained in their original position if the local patron retained control of the *túath*, although changes in the spatial geography and nature of the dwellings of the elite, reveals an evolution and change in the ideology of the clan. The adoption of the tower house alone reveals a Gaelic society embracing outside influence. In certain parishes particularly those geographically closest to areas of contemporary or

---

20 Otway-Ruthven, *A history*, 119. **21** R.A. Dodgshon's definition of a clan as an evolving institution continually adjusting to historically specific circumstances differs from the contemporary Irish historiographical interpretation of a clan as anachronistic institution within a high and late medieval context. He stresses that clans need to be defined as a complex, interlocking system of activity that had vital economic and cultural inputs, as well as the socio-political inputs normally attributed to them. He also acknowledges the role of a belief in a particular order, an ideology of relationships, in binding the system together. 'Pretense of blude and place of thair dwelling: the nature of highland clans 1500–1745' in R.A. Houston and I.D. Whyte, (eds) *Scottish society, 1500–1800* (Cambridge, 1989), 169–98. **22** McErlean, 'The Irish townland system', 334. **23** R.A. Dodgshon, 'The changing evaluation of space 1500–1914' in R.A. Dodgshon and R.A. Butlin (eds), *An historical geography of England and Wales* (London,1991), 255–83: 255.

former Anglo-Norman control, there was a marked tendency to locate the principal tower house of the parish/*túath* adjacent to the parish centre. This geographical shift from dispersed elite secular settlements and parish centres to the evolution of a principal secular and ecclesiastical centre and other secondary secular settlement nucleations suggest that the Gaelic clans in these areas were becoming increasing feudalist in mentality. It also demonstrates that as the medieval period progressed, the parish appears to have supplanted the *túath* as the fundamental territorial unit of both secular and ecclesiastical order. A possible explanation for this is that the 'awarding' of parish status to a *túath* in the late thirteenth century appears to have stabilised the *túath* matrix, which hitherto had an inherent tendency to continuously fracture, subdivide and re-amalgamate in accordance with the geopolitical fortunes of its patrimonial clan. As a clan embraced certain aspects of feudalism, namely the production of marketable surpluses and the increasing prevalence of primogeniture succession, the patronage of the church by the clan chieftain greatly augmented his position within the clan and allowed him to influence succession in his immediate family's favour. Nevertheless the Irish clan system, which was similar to its Scottish counterpart, was just as capable of engaging with outside influences, while still retaining 'a belief in a particular order of things, an ideology of relationships',[24] which allowed the system to survive through the late medieval period.

RECREATING THE LATE SIXTEENTH-CENTURY PARISH MATRIX:
THE EVOLUTION FROM *TÚATH*/PARISH TO PARISH/*TÚATH*

In order to explore this evolution from *túath*/parish in the late thirteenth century to parish/*túath* in the late sixteenth century, the following sources have been examined. The only extensive record of the parish matrix before the sixteenth century is the ecclesiastical taxation list of 1302–6. A curious manuscript in TCD (Ms E.2.14) called the Description of Thomond in 1574,[25] gives a list of seventy-six vicarages. The vast majority of these vicarages can be easily equated with parishes on the fourteenth- century list. Given the time lapse between both documents, some of the earlier parishes had ceased to exist, while others had emerged by the later sixteenth century. However, the inclusion of some parishes and the absence of others pose particular problems. Most of these can be addressed by comparing both sources with the three early seven-teenth-century reports of the established Church – the Visitation of 1615, the Royal Answer of 1622 and the Visitation of 1633. Since the definite boundaries of any of these parishes cannot be determined until the returns of the BSD of

24 Dodgshon, 'Pretense of blude', 170.   25 R.W. Twigge, 'Edward White's description of Thomond in 1574' in *Journal of the North Munster Antiquarian Society*, 1:2 (1910), 55–84.

1641, all of these six sources have been included in table 3, along with one other source. The first column records the standard spelling of these parishes as returned in mid nineteenth- century censuses and Ordnance Survey maps.[26] The surveys of the late nineteenth-century antiquarian T.J. Westropp, which record late medieval renovations to parish churches or the building of new parish churches,[27] together with entries in the relevant annals,[28] have also been used to provide complementary indicators of parish vitality.

Table 3 reveals that a total of ninety-one parishes feature in one or more of these sources. The definitive or probable location and boundaries of these ninety-one parochial units are delineated in figure 3. Of these, one can only confidently state that sixty-eight of the 1574 list were operational. The consistent inclusion of a further seven in all other sources would strongly suggest that they were operational also. Inconsistent appearances in the late sixteenth- and early seventeenth-century sources combined with non-civil parish status in 1641 suggests that thirteen of the sixteen remaining parishes had ceased to function independently of a neighbouring 'sister' parish by the early seventeenth century, while three had definitely ceased to function at all.

The extinction of Danganbrack, Inisdadrum and Killargenayn will be discussed initially since they add to our understanding of the dynamics of parish formation in the high medieval and late medieval period. While Danganbrack is returned as a parish in the early fourteenth-century taxation list, its parochial status would appear to have been short-lived, since it never appears in other extant documentation. The following sets out what is an entirely speculative reason for its late thirteenth- and early fourteenth-century existence. Today, Danganbrack is a 187-acre townland to the north of Quin, the present parish centre. In 1302–6 both Danganbrack and Quin were required to contribute four marks to the diocesan economy. This would suggest two parishes of equal economic potential. A brief history of Quin might shed light on the demise of Danganbrack parish. In 1280–1 Thomas de Clare built a castle at Quin on the southern bank of the Ardsollus River.[29] This river divides the modern parish of Quin equably, and it appears also to have been the northern limit of Anglo-Norman colonisation in late thirteenth-century Clare. Due to political tensions resulting in considerable strife between the Anglo-Norman colonisers and the ruling McNamara clan, whose area of control was now

26 Throughout the chapter it is the standardised spelling in the first column which will be used and not the plethora of phonetic renditions of the earlier sources.   **27** T.J. Westropp, 'The churches of Co. Clare and the origins of the ecclesiastical divisions in that County' in *PRIA*, 20C (1900), 100–80.   **28** In J. O'Donovan, *Ordnance Survey letters for County Clare*, ed. M. Comber (Ennis, 1997), 1–266, the Annals of the Kingdom of Ireland by the Four Masters are regularly referenced in his account of each of the nineteenth-century civil parishes. He also describes and attempts to date most of the ecclesiastical sites in the respective parishes; S. Ó hÓgáin, *Conntae an Chláir* (Dublin,1936) also references these annals and cites the Book of Lecan (RIA, MS 23.f.14) for the years 1297 and 1298, p. 135.   **29** T.J. Westropp, 'Notes on the lesser castles or "peel towers" of County Clare' in *PRIA*, 19C (1899), 348–414: 349.

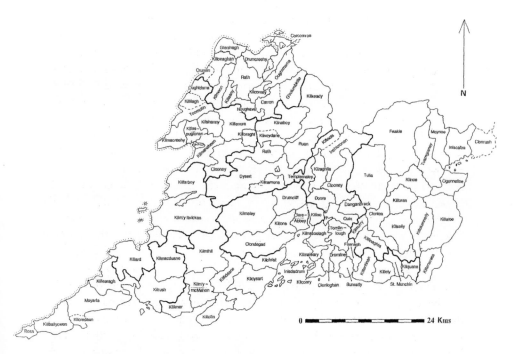

Fig. 3: The late sixteenth-century parish matrix

confined to the northern half of the parish, two parishes may have been created to facilitate an easier coexistence. This hypothetical coexistence was short-lived. By 1305, the castle was destroyed by the McNamaras. Subsequently they reasserted their authority over the 'Anglo-Norman' parish of Quin.[30] This geopolitical territorial reunion may have coincided with parochial amalgamation resulting in an end to Danganbrack's parish status.

The other two extinct parishes raise the contentious issue of abbey charter parishes. Inisdadrum is a *c.*300-acre island in the Fergus estuary. Its association with monastic life dates to an early Christian community reputedly founded by St Brendan in AD 550. In the tenth century the powerful local Viking chief Imar and his two sons were slain there in AD 977.[31] By 1189 it is included in the abbey charter of Clare Abbey. It appeared to have parish status in 1302–6, when it was required to contribute a paltry ten shillings. This may signify the beginning of its decline as a parish entity. However, it still had official parish status in 1615, even though it was described as having no church or inhabitants. A similar entry appears in both 1622 and 1633. It is not given civil parish status in 1641, being returned as an island denomination of the parish of Clondegad

30 N.C. MacNamara, *The story of an Irish sept: the origins and history of the MacNamaras* (1896; reprint Ruane, 1999), 110–1. 31 From the 'Wars of the Gaedhil with the Gaill', cited in Westropp, 'The churches of Co. Clare', 163.

Table 3: The changing parish matrix from 1302 to 1641

Parish Name	1302–6	1574	1615	1622	1633	1641
Category A						
(Danganbrack)	Danganbrack	<	<	<	<	<
(Inisdadrum)	Inisdadrum	<	Inisdadrum	Inishdadrom	Inishdadrum	<
(Templeharraghan)	Killargenayn	<	<	<	<	<
Category B						
(Cappafean)	<	Kilvilly	<	<	<	<
(Kilcredaun)	<	Kylcoridan	<	<	<	<
(Ross)	<	Rosse	<	<	<	<
(Glencolumbkille)	<	Glanecolmekill	<	<	<	<
(Kilvoydane)	<	Kilvedayn	<	<	<	<
(Oughtdarra)	<	Owghtory	<	*	<	<
(Killoo)	Killoo	<	Killughe	Killuh	Killagh	<
(Kiltoola)	Kiltoola	<	Killtoolaghe	Kiltoolah	Kiltoolagh	<
(Toomullin)	Thuomlynny	<	Tomalyn	*	<	<
(Crumlin)	Cromglaon	<	<	*	Cromlynn	<
Oughtmama	<	<	Uchtmawm	*	<	Oughtmama
Killaspuglonan	Killesconolan	Killaspule	Killaspoclanan	*	<	<
Killtoraght	Kiltocowragh	Kyltoraght	Kiltoraghe	*	Kiltowragh	<
Category C						
Tuamgraney	Tuamgraney	<	Tomgreny	Tomgreeny	Tomegreeny	Tomgraney
Kilmacreehy	Kilmaccrick	<	Killmakrie	*	Killmacree	Kilmacree
Clonlea	Clonolea	<	Clonilea	Clonlea	Clonlea	Clonley
Kilnasoolagh	Kilnasoolagh	<	K'nafinlaghe	Killinasoolah	Killensalagh	Killanasulogh
St Munchin	Kilrussce	<	*	*	*	St Munctions
Killofin	Killofin	<	Killofin	Killofin	Killafin	Killofin
Kilcorney	Kilcorney	<	Kill(k/t)orney	*	Kilkooney	Kilkorney

Category D							
Ruan	<	Ruan	<	<	<	<	<
Kilmaley	Kilmayley	Kilvale	Kilmaly	Kilmaly	Killmealy	Killmealy	<
Iniscaltra	Iniscaltra	Inishkealtragh	Inisgealtra	Inishgaltrah	Innisgaltra	Innisgaltra	Iniskalto
Moynoe	Moyne	Muyno	Moynoe	Moinoe	Moyno	Moyno	Moinoe
Feakle	Feakle	Ffiekle	Feikle	Ffeacle	Feakell	Feakell	Feakle
Tulla	Tulla	Tullaghe	Tulloghe	Tulloh	Tullagh	Tullagh	Tulla
Kilnoe	<	Kilnow	Killnoa	Kilnoa	Killno	Killnoe	Killnoe
Ogonmelloe	<	Aglissonill	Oginola	Ogonilla	Ogonilla	Ogonilla	Toogenela
Killaloe	<	Killalowe	Killalow	Killaloe	Killaloe	Killaloe	Killalow
Kiltenanlea	Enagh	Kiltenayn	Killtinanlea	Kiltinanleh	Kiltanley	Kiltanley	Kiltanlea
Killokennedy	Killokennedy	Kilogenedy	Killokennedy	Killokenedy	Killikeneda	Killikeneda	Kilikeneda
Killuran	Killuran	Killurayne	Killvran	Killurain	Killuran	Killuran	Killurane
Kilseily	Kilseily	Kyltede	Kilteely	Kilteely	Kilseily	Kilseily	Killseyly
Kilmurry	<	Kilvorry	Killmoringall	K'mormagall	K'm'ynegall	K'm'ynegall	Killmurry
Kilfinaghta	Kilfinaghta	Kilmaghty	Killfinaghta	Kilfinaghta	Kilfinaghta	Kilfinaghta	Kilfenaughta
Inchicronan	Inchicronan	Inishcronan	Inchicronan	Inscronan	Ensycronan	Inscronan	Inchicronan
Clooney (b)	Clooney	Cluny	Clonee	Clonee	Cloney	Cloney	Cloney
Quin	Quin	Quinhy	Quyn	Quin	Quin	Quin	Quin
Kilraghtis	<	Kilraghtis	Killraghtas	Kilraghtas	Killraghtas	Killraghtas	Kilraghtis
Templemaley	Imalli	Templelmale	Templemaley	Templemaly	Templemaly	Templemaly	Templemally
Doora	Doora	Dury	Dury	Dury	Doury	Doury	Dowrey
Tomfinlough	Tuaimfinlough	Toymenlagh	Tomfinloh	Tomfinloh	Tomenlough	Tomfinloh	Tominlagh
Kilmaleary	Kilmaleary	Kilmalyre	Killmaleery	Killmallery	Kilmalery	Killmalery	Killmallyry
Clonloghan	Clonloghan	Clonloghan	Clonloghan	Clonluhein	Clonloghane	Clonloghane	Clonloghan
Bunratty	Bunratty	Bonraty	Bonratty	Bonralty	Bunrattie	Bonrattie	Bunratty
Dromline	Dromline	Dromlyn	Drumlein	Dromline	Dromline	Dromline	Drumline

Parish Name	1302–6	1574	1615	1622	1633	1641
Feenagh	Feenagh	Ffynnagh	Finnoh	Ffinnah	Fynnagh	Fynagh
Kilfentinan	Kilhyntena	Kylantynan	*	*	*	Kilfintenan
Killely	Kilheil	Kiliele	*	*	*	Kilely
Kilquane	Kilcohan	Kilchwayn	*	*	*	Kilquane
Kilfenora	^	Kylvurg	Killfenoraghe	*	<	Kilfenora
Clooney (c)	Clonurpis	Cluny	Cloen	*	Cloney	Cloney
Kilmanaheen	Kilmankyn	Lonayne	Killmanahyn	*	K'anyheene	Kilmanaheen
Kilshanny	Kilsanyg	Kiltean	^	*	Kilshonnuy	Kilshany
Killilagh	Killadlagh	Killaleagh	Killeylaghe	*	Killydea	Killelagh
Drumcliff	Dromcliffe	Dromcliew	Drumkleiffe	Dromcliffe	Drumcliff	Drumkleeuve
Killone	Ab of St John	St Johns	Killone	^	Killone	Killone
Clondegad	Clondagad	Cloyndaghad	Clonidagad	Cloundagad	Clondigad	Cloundegad
Clare Abbey	Ab. of Forgio	Clare	^	^	^	Clare Abbey
Kilchrist	Eribanub	Kilchriste	Kilchrist	Kilchrist	Killchrist	Kilchrist
Kildysart	D. Murthile	Dmorehely	Killedisert	Killidysert	Killidisart	Kildisart
Kilfiddane	Kilfiddane	Kyllydayne	Killfeddan	Kilfeddain	Killfeadan	Kilfaddan
Kilmihil	^	Kilvihite	Killmichell	Kilmihill	Kilmihill	Kilmighill
K'm'y McMahon	Knock	Kilmury	Kilmurry	Kilmurry	Killmurrie	Kilmurry
Killimer	Killimer	Kileymury	Killamure	Killoemuir	Killemure	Killeimer
Kilmacduane	Kilmacduane	Kylmyedwayn	Killmcaduan	K'macdowan	Killmcduan	Kilmacduan
Kilrush	Kilrush	Kilruish	Killrush	Kilrush	Killrush	Kilrush
Kilfearagh	Killforagh	Kylioragh	Killfieraghe	Kilfierah	Killfeiragh	Kilferagh
Moyarta	Moyarta	Moyartha	Moefartah	Moeffartah	Moyfarta	Moyferta
Killballyowen	Kilballyhone	Kilbalehuen	Kilballihone	Kilballihon	Kilballihone	Kilballyhone
Kilfarboy	Kilfarboy	Kilfearwaye	Killfarboy	Kilfarboy	Killfarboy	Killfarboy
K'm'y Ibrickan	Collenboynm	Kilmorinbrikan	Kilmurry Ib.	Kilmurry Ib.	Killmurrie	Killmurry
Killard	Killard	Killairde	Killarda	Kilardah	Killard	Killard
Corcomroe	C. of Monks	Templeglan	^	*	Corcomroe	Abbey

Carron	Carne	Carne	^	*	Carne	Karne
	New Church	Mouglevaell	Nochvall		Noghaval	Nohavall
Noughaval	Kilconry	Kilconry	Kilconry	*	Kilconrie	Kilconry
Kilconry	Rath	Rasboernagh	Rathbornie	Kilconry	Rathborny	Ragh
Rath	Drumcruth	Templecrigh	Drum–Krye In.	*	Dromcree	Drumcrehy
Drumcreehy	Glaniedragh	Glaneynagh	Glaninaghe	*	Glaninagh	Glaniny
Gleninagh	Killonean	Killonagh	Killenoghan	*	Killonoghane	Killonehan
Killonaghan	Kilmugoun	Kyluouy	Kilmuney	*	Killmoonye	Killmouney
Kilmoon	Killeeny	Kileyne	Killeny	*	Killeeny	Killany
Killeany	Kilkeedy	Kilkidea	Kilkeady		Kilkerdie	Kilkedy
Kilkeady	Kilnaboy	Kyllyneboy	Killeneboy	Kilkeedy	Killineboy	Killinaboy
Kilnaboy	Rath	Rahe	Rath	Killinaboy	Rath	Ragh
Rath	Disert	Desert	Disert	Rath	Disert	Disert
Dysert	Kilnamona	Kylnemone	Killnamona	Disert	Kilnemona	Killnamona
Kilnamona				Kilnamona		

Key: * = source not available; ^ = not returned in source; ( ) = townland status in the nineteenth century; (c) = Corcomroe; (b) = Bunratty; M'y = murry; Ib. = Ibrickan; K' = Kill; C. = Church; Ab.= Abbey; D. = Disert.

which was located on the western side of the estuary. Its inclusion with Clondegad is a little puzzling since it was part of the rural deanery of Tradry on the eastern side of the estuary from 1302 to 1633. Given its diminutive area, lack of a church and inhabitants in 1615, it is unlikely that it existed as a parish in any real sense in 1585. Inisdadrum's depopulation possibly coincided with the dissolution of the monastery in the post-Reformation era. Another possible Clare Abbey charter territory, Templeharraghan, may have been the fourteenth-century parish of Killargenayn. The precise location of this parish has baffled many historians, but Westropp suggests a probable location in eastern Kilmaley or Drumcliff.[32] These three parishes reveal the intimate inter-relationship between the fortunes of the church patrons and parish longevity and vitality. These fortunes were determined by internal processes such as the organic tendency of a clan-based society to wax and wane and disruptive external forces such as the Reformation.

The second category that will be examined are the thirteen parishes that ceased to exist independently of a neighbouring parish. These parishes can be subdivided into three sub-categories in accordance with the frequency with which they appear on table 3. The six questionable vicarages on the 1574 list, Kilvilly, Kilcredaun, Ross, Glencolumbkille, Kilvoydane and Oughtdarra all lend their name to early Christian churches, some with late medieval modifications.

The case for Kilvilly and Ross being centres of parishes is slim indeed, since both appear to have been solely early Christian sites with no evidence of modifi-cations to the original church structures. The only indicator of possible religious activity is the presence of a nearby holy well or graveyard. However, the case for Kilcredaun, Glencolumbkille, Kilvoydane and Oughtdarra is much stronger. The church at Kilvoydane has fifteenth-century architectural features, which confirm that it was modified at this time.[33] This church is located in the southern region of the parish of Kilnaboy. In 1585 the *Compossicion Booke of Conought* (CBC) records the existence of a secular territory, *Tuath Innse Uí Chuinn* in this region. Kilvoydane may have been the ecclesiastical centre of this territory. The twin churches at Kilcredaun occupy a similar geographical position in the extensive parish of Moyarta. The larger of these churches Tempall an Aird also possesses late medieval modifications that implies continued use since their joint early Christian beginnings.[34] The CBC does not record a secular territory, of which Kilcredaun would have been the only ecclesiastical focus. However, the BSD does reveal that it was the only ecclesiastical site in the *c*.2000-acre *baile* of Rahoone, a Gaelic territorial subdi-vision of Moyarta in 1641. The parochial status of Glencolumbkille and Oughtdarra is not solely reliant on late medieval architectural evidence. The

---

32 Ibid., 174. The third edition OS map, sheet 33, records an early Christian site located in a ringfort called Temple Varaghan in the townland of Drumcliff.   33 Westropp, 'The churches of Co. Clare', 140–1.   34 Ibid., 167.

latter parish was possibly the 1302 parish of Wafferrig. This co-relation has been derived from the frequent use of 'W' or 'V' for the letter 'U' and the 'ff' for the letter 'd' in late medieval documentation. Oughtdarra was one of three possible late medieval parishes within the civil parish of Killilagh which coincides with *Túath Ghlae* the bailiwick of the MacClancy legal family. Glencolumbkille's parochial status is confirmed by a 1599 entry in the Annals of the Four Masters.[35] Glencolumbkille appears to have been the ecclesiastical centre of the 1585 territory of *Sliocht Donogh Uí Lochlainn*. When three entries in the Annals of the Four Masters dating from the late fourteenth century are cross-referenced with the genealogy of the Uí Lochlainn clan, the particular historical circumstance underlying the creation of this parish emerges. It would appear that the chieftainship of this clan was hotly contested between the three sons of the deceased chief, Donnchadha, after 1361. The killing of Maol Seachlainn by his brother Iriail in 1389 and his usurpation of the chieftainship left a lingering bitterness between rival septs that culminated in Iriail's revenge killing in 1396.[36] Subsequently the territory of the Uí Lochlainn clan appears to have been split between the descendants of Iriail, Sliocht Iriail, and the descendants of his father, the 'proper' line of descent, Sliocht Donogh Uí Lochlainn.[37] A division of the fourteenth-century parish of Carron[38] occurred with the building of two fifteenth-century parish churches at Carron and Glencolumbkille.[39] This again reveals the interdependent relationship between parish vitality and the fortunes of the secular patron.

The vicarage status of these six churches would appear to have ceased sometime between 1574 and 1615, since they are not returned in any of the early seventeenth-century ecclesiastical documentation. Neither does the mid seventeenth- and nineteenth-century official documentation record their existence as civil parishes. These combined factors would call into question what the 1574 list was actually recording, since at least twelve other parishes with stronger cases for vicarage status were not returned. What the list does highlight is that the transition from early Christian church to parochial church was not axiomatic. While the reasons for this are complex and numerous, the primary reason would appear to be once again the sociopolitical fortunes of a church's patron.

The parochial status of the next four parochial units dates at least from the fourteenth century. However, they would all appear to have undergone a major diminution in status by the late sixteenth century. While none of them feature

---

35 'The Annals of the Kingdom of Ireland by the Four Masters' (AD 1599) cited in Westropp, 'The churches of Co. Clare', 134–5.   36 'The Annals of the Kingdom of Ireland by the Four Masters' (AD 1361, AD 1398, AD 1396) cited in Ó hÓgáin, *Conntae and Chláir*, 134–5.   37 The genealogy of the Uí Lochlainn (O'Loghlin) (AD 1594) according to Mhaoilín Óig Mhic Bruaideadha is cited in Ó hÓgáin, *Conntae an Chláir*, 135. The phrase *'nitráchtar a shliocht'* (his descendants will not be spoken about) which appears after Iriail (Ithrail) suggests that his sept were out of favour with the rest of the clan.   38 Carne (Carron) is returned in the 1302–6 ecclesiastical taxation list (cf. table 3).   39 Westropp, 'The churches of Co. Clare', 133–5.

on the 1574 list, they do feature in the ecclesiastical reports of the established Church of the early seventeenth century. Killoo and Kiltoola feature in all three early seventeenth-century ecclesiastical documents with Toomullin and Crumlin featuring only once. Their absence from the 1574 list may be either attributable to the unreliability of this source or it may be a real indication of their declining status. The seventeenth-century material leaves us in no doubt that these four parishes were dependent on a neighbouring 'sister' parish. In fact these documents record their demise. The 1615 Visitation notes that Toomullin was then being serviced by a Murtogh O'Daveryn who administered and resided within Noughaval – a non-contiguous parish five miles to the east. There is no subsequent reference to it in later ecclesiastical records. Crumlin's status is even bleaker. Missing from the 1615 Visitation, the 1633 Visitation possibly provides the reason, since its vicarage was recorded as vacant and without a tithe value. Killoo and Kiltoola feature in all three ecclesiastical reports, where they are consistently recorded as being without a vicar, and with their churches and chancels remaining 'down'. However, tithes were levied on Killoo possibly due to its location within the more populated core of the county.[40] The BSD reveals that all four parishes formed distinct regions within four civil parishes with which they had historic links. Killoo, one of the land parcels recorded in the founding charter of Clare Abbey, lay immediately to the east of this abbey. The adjoining parishes of Kiltoola and Inchicronan formed the secular territory *Cinéal Dunghaile*. Similarly Crumlin and Killonaghan formed the territory known as *Túath Flaithniad*. Toomullin, Oughtdara and Killilagh were the three ecclesiastical subdivisions of *Túath Ghlae*. The fact that none of these four parishes ever became nineteenth-century civil parishes means that they were quickly subsumed within the territories of their dominant neighbours.

The final three parishes in this section appear also to have been dominated by a neighbouring parish. However, nineteenth-century civil parish status separates them from the previous ten parishes. Oughtmama is similar to the aforementioned parish of Killoo. Its proximity to the Abbey parish of Corcomroe and the fact that together they were known as *Gleann na Manach* would appear to suggest a close relationship with this parish. This parish may have been the parish called 'Dissert' on the 1302–6 taxation list, given the presence of the early Christian hermitage site at Oughtmama, which was perched half way up the steep rock face that formed the eastern boundary of this ecclesiastical *túath*. It is only returned in one of the early seventeenth-century reports.[41] While Oughtmama is returned as a civil parish in both the BSD and the so-called 1659 census, a comparison of these two sources reveals a degree of confusion as to its precise boundary with its more dominant neighbour, the abbey parish of Corcomroe. The definitive boundary can only be determined by examining the nineteenth-century censuses and maps.

Killaspuglonan's growing dependence on neighbouring Kilmacreehy can be traced through the successive early seventeenth-century reports. While both parishes were returned in the early fourteenth-century taxation list, only Killaspuglonan figures on the 1574 list. Both again appear in the 1615 Visitation, but the 1633 Visitation, the BSD and the so-called '1659 census' only return Kilmacreehy. The following extract from the 1615 Visitation supports the hypothesis that Killaspuglonan had become effectively subsumed into Kilmacreehy – 'Mr. Evan Jones minister and preacher ... hath united ... the vicarages of Killmakrie and Killaspoclanan'.[42] The BSD reveals that the constituent land denominations of Killaspuglonan occupied the eastern third of Kilmacreehy. Killaspuglonan and Kilmacreehy were collectively known as *Túath Reanna*. Killaspuglonan only achieved cadastral independence again in nineteenth-century official documentation.

Kiltoraght is the final parish that was linked to a larger parish. The dominant parish in this case was the cathedral parish of Kilfenora. By cross-referencing the '1659 census' with nineteenth-century official documents and maps, Kiltoraght occupied the south-eastern sixth of the seventeenth-century civil parish of Kilfenora. While it does not appear in the BSD as a civil parish, it does consistently feature in all preceding extant ecclesiastical documentation. However, these early seventeenth-century reports provide evidence of its progressively feeble state. Kiltoraght was clearly one of the parishes whose 'livinges belongeth to the Deanrye of Killfenoraghe' in 1615. But the Dean at the time had 'revolted to popery', and the church was ruined. In 1633 it was still without a dean and a tithe valuation.[43]

In conclusion, of the thirteen parishes within this category, eleven have a reasonable claim to vicarage status in the late sixteenth century. However, none existed independently of a contiguous more dominant 'sister' parish. Given the archaeological field evidence and the total lack of ecclesiastical documentation, the vicarage status of Kilvilly and Ross is questionable. Glencolumbkille and Kilvoydane appear to have been the only ecclesiastical sites of note within two contemporary minor *túatha*. Kilcredaun, Oughtdarra, Toomullin and Crumlin were the ecclesiastical focus of a lesser Gaelic territorial unit, the *baile*. Collectively these six vicarages suggest an intrinsic and inseparable links between the secular and ecclesiastical wings of society. Parish fission and *túath* fission were part of the same process, as *túatha* and large Gaelic land units tended to subdivide and re-amalgamate in accordance with the fluctuating fortunes of their secular patrons. Documentary evidence for the remaining five, demonstrate how Killoo, Kiltoola, Oughtmama, Killaspuglonan and Kiltoraght progressively lost their 'independence' in the early seventeenth century. The

42 Ibid.   43 Ibid., 178.

overpowering presence of two continental-style core abbey parishes and a cathedral parish clearly overwhelmed Killoo, Oughtmama and Kiltoraght. This process appears to have happened organically. The lack of established church clergy necessitated multiple amalgamations of parishes, as evidenced by the experiences of Kiltoola and Killaspuglonan. A common characteristic to all eleven is that they were less extensive than their dominant 'sister' parishes.

The next group of parishes requiring examination is those that do not feature on the 1574 list even though they appear in all subsequent official and ecclesiastical documentation. Tuamgraney's association with the O'Grady clan dates from the late-fourteenth century when they were emplaced on its extensive termon lands of seventh-century monastic origin. This fortuitous emplacement by their overlords, the MacNamaras, arose from the policy of the MacNamaras of placing kinsmen or close allies in newly acquired territories – in this case the half-cantred of *Uí mBloid* that had been controlled by the Anglo-Normans prior to 1318.[44] Kilmacreehy has just been alluded to in the previous paragraph, where its ascendancy over its 'sister' parish has been charted. The other five parishes, Clonlea, Kilnasoolagh, St Munchin, Killofin and Kilcorney require a brief general examination. The following argument for their absence relates to the *túath* listings in the CBC. All five are located in *túatha* that contained at least two medieval parishes within their boundaries. This may suggest a degree of dependence on the other parishes within their respective *túatha*. With the decreed demise of the *túath* as a cadastral unit in all official documentation after 1585,[45] the near equivalent New-English territorial unit, the civil parish, would appear to have been used in its place. A curious addendum to this discussion hints at the possible longevity of shared *túath* identity. When the Catholic Church reorganised the Catholic parishes during the nineteenth century, none of these parishes survived as independent entities. Significantly their late sixteenth century constituent *túatha* appear to form the basis for the nineteenth-century parochial amalgamations.[46]

The final category consists of the sixty-eight parishes that can be considered operational in 1574. Two parishes in particular, Kilmaley and Ruan, need to be addressed here. Table 3 shows that Kilmaley consistently appears on all ecclesiastical records between 1302 and 1633. However, it was not given civil parish status in either the BSD where its land denominations are listed within Drumcliff. The prioritising of Drumcliff over Kilmaley reflects the contemporary geopolitical environment. The principal manor of the palatinate-style Earl of Thomond was situated at Clonroad in Drumcliff parish, as was the emerging county town Ennis, consequently the Drumcliff side of the civil

44 T. Coffey, *The parish of Inchicronan* (Whitegate, 1993), 77; G. Madden, 'Shameful neglect of a historic place, Tuamgraney', in *Sliabh Aughty*, 5 (1994), 5–8: 7. **45** A.M. Freeman (ed.), *The Compossicion Booke of Conought* (Dublin, 1936), 17. **46** P. Nugent, 'A historical geography of the territorial organisation of Gaelic society in Co. Clare during the early modern period', unpublished PhD (NUI Cork, 2002), 293–301.

parish greatly eclipsed the peripheral Kilmaley side. The historical basis for the amalgamation of these two parishes is the fact that both were part of the *tríocha céad* of Uí Chormaic. The inconsistent appearance of Ruan is more problematic. Ruan only appears on the 1574 list. However, it is difficult to argue against vicarage status in 1574 given that its parish church was a late fifteenth-century edifice.[47] Ruan's nineteenth-century civil parish boundary possibly approximates to the areal extent of its ministry in the late sixteenth century. If so, Ruan accounted for one-third of the county's largest civil parish, the *c.*35,000-acre Dysert, as returned in the BSD. An analysis of the parish churches of the remaining sixty-six parishes, based primarily on the research of O'Donovan[48] and Westropp,[49] reveals that sixty were either renovated or built after the late twelfth century. The six exceptions, Clondegad, Clooney (Corcomroe), Doora, Templemaley, Killseily and Killonaghan shared the experience of either being overshadowed by a neighbouring parish centre or a continental-style abbey.

CONCLUSION

This exploration of parish formation in the high medieval period and the recreation of the late-sixteenth century parish matrix reveals that parish formation in Gaelic regions tended to progress through the following stages. Prior to the twelfth century reforms, *túatha* possessed many dispersed ecclesiastical sites of varying degrees of importance. These sites served as the ecclesiastical centres of the constituent *bailte* of a *túath*. In Co. Clare as a whole, 218 definite early Christian sites can be identified, with a possible 44 others.[50] Initially parish formation merely involved the granting of parochial status to the existing *túatha*. With the granting of parish status to a *túath*, the prioritising of one of the constituent ecclesiastical sites over the others began. Ecclesiastical sites located within the *baile* of the contemporary clan chieftain became parish centres while ecclesiastical sites in the remaining *bailte* were ignored. The granting of parish status appears to have encouraged the building of new churches also. However, the thirty-four churches that can be dated to the high medieval period represent but *c.*40 per cent of parish centres on the 1302–6 taxation list. While this signifies a considerable deliberate break with the pre-twelfth century situation, the majority of the parish centres are still of early Christian origin. With the elevation of one site to parochial status, the other sites declined.

47 Westropp, 'The churches of Co. Clare', 142.   48 J. O'Donovan, 'Letters containing information relative to the antiquities of the County Clare collected during the progress of the Ordnance Survey in 1839–41', compiled by M. O'Flanagan, typescript in 3 vols (Bray, 1928).   49 Westropp, 'The churches of Co. Clare', 122–71.   50 This statistic is based on Westropp, 'The churches of Co. Clare', 100–80 and on an analysis of all six-inch first edition Ordnance Survey maps for Co. Clare (Dublin, 1842–3).

Analysis of churches built or renovated in the late medieval period points towards a general consolidation of these parish centres. This more dynamic period of church construction, 1450–1550, coincided with the tower house building era which, in Clare, represents somewhat of a 'Golden Era'. Of these sixty-four churches, thirty-four were built in the late medieval period, and a further eleven were renovated high medieval structures. Significantly, a number of early Christian churches were also renovated. These twenty-one churches were either early Christian sites that had gained parochial status in the twelfth and thirteenth century, or sites that had reasserted themselves.

The reassertion of secondary sites would appear to be linked to the vacillating fortunes of their secular patrons. Rival septs of the patrimonial clan or formerly subjugated clans, through the patronage of former downgraded early Christian sites or virginal sites, began to threaten the primacy of the parish centre of the declining clan chief. This led to three probable outcomes. The *túath* fissioned into smaller *túatha*, each with its own parish centre. The parish centre under the patronage of the faltering clan chief declined, and one of the ecclesiastical sites of the upcoming septs assumed dominance and parish centre status. Thirdly, the *túath* splintered into many parishes reflecting an inability of any single sept to assume total control of the *túath*. The recreated late sixteenth-century parish matrix reveals examples of parishes in all three situations. A final feature of parochial evolution is that the ten abbey parishes, the twenty-four former monastic termon parishes, and the nine Anglo-Norman parishes were far more stable than the forty-three Gaelic 'secular' parishes.

PART III

Perspectives on the Reformed Parish

Parishes and pastoral care
in the early Tudor era

HENRY A. JEFFERIES

Churches have been features of the Irish landscape for more than fifteen hundred years. They have been important as centres of pastoral care, and as focal points for local communities. Yet they, and the clergy who served them, have not received their due attention from historians. In this essay I wish to outline something of our knowledge and understanding of the provision of pastoral care in the parishes of Ireland in the first half of the sixteenth century, and offer indications of where further research is needed.

PARADIGMS

Historians of the pre-Reformation Irish Church have tended to neglect the subject of parishes and pastoral care, partly because of the scarcity of relevant source materials, and partly because some of the documents which have chanced to survive among the state papers gave the illusion of conveying more insight into the provision of pastoral care in the pre-Reformation Church than was actually the case. One source, more than any other, has been particularly influential: the 'Description of Ireland, 1515', which stated that 'there is no archbishop nor bishop, abbot nor prior, parson nor vicar, nor any other member of the Church, high or low, English or Irish, accustomed to preach the word of God, except the poor mendicant friars ...'[1] This became the key-stone of the conventional paradigm for the study of the pre-Reformation Church in Ireland in which evidence drawn primarily from the Tudor state papers was 'seen by historians as indicating an overall degree of disorder in the late medieval Irish Church not far short of the total breakdown in the organised religion in that war-torn country'.[2]

I regard the conventional paradigm of late medieval Irish Church history as

---

1 'Description of Ireland, 1515', National Archives, London, SP 60/1, no. 9. 2 The quotation is taken from J. Watt, *The Church in medieval Ireland* (Dublin, 1972), 182–3. However, see H. Jefferies, 'The Armagh registers and the re-interpretation of Irish Church history on the eve of the reformations' in *Seanchas Ard Mhacha*, 18 (1999–2000), 81–99: 81–4.

flawed because it is too reliant on superficial surveys of state papers that are inherently political and often hyperbolic in their descriptions of the pre-Reformation Church in Ireland.[3] Instead, there is a great need for systematic studies of the Church in Ireland before and during the Tudor Reformations, based primarily on close analyses of the Church's own records, rather than on quotations drawn from haphazard references to the Church and/or religion among the state papers, or cryptic references in the annals. Of course, ecclesiastical sources have to be subjected to critical assessment and used with realism. They have their own inherent biases and limitations, as all sources have, and the relative paucity of such evidence for Ireland poses tremendous challenges for the church historian. Nonetheless, an investigation based upon the complete range of evidence available (including the physical remains of ecclesiastical buildings and monuments, as well as documentary records), offers a realistic possibility of examining how the Church actually endeavoured to provide pastoral care in the parishes, and of forming some assessment of its endeavours, in place of the very generalised and politics-centred interpretations that predominate in conventional studies of the Irish Church in the late medieval and early Reformation eras. Furthermore, diocesan and even more local studies where possible, are clearly needed to reveal the range of the Church's experiences in Ireland's diverse regions.

CHURCHES AND PARISHES

Any consideration of pastoral care in late medieval and early-Reformation Ireland should start with the churches and chapels – the foci of the Church's pastoral ministry. The existence of churches are, fortunately, reasonably well documented through the various financial records pertaining to the Church, from both ecclesiastical and state sources. These financial records can be used to establish the numbers, and to map the distribution of churches and chapels. They can often offer indications of parochial revenues and clerical incomes – key components of any consideration of the provision of pastoral care in any period.

Irish historians of the later middle ages and Reformation periods have largely resisted the temptation to map out the great many churches and chapels which can be identified from contemporary sources, though the results would certainly reward the effort. In the case of Armagh diocese there are visitation lists of the churches and chapels from *c*.1544 which allow one to identify more than sixty churches and chapels in Armagh *inter Anglicos* (most of Co. Louth) which were served by priests (with another ten being identifiable from diocesan records dating from a few years earlier), and another forty-four parish churches

3 Jefferies, 'Armagh registers', 84–8.

in Armagh *inter Hibernicos* (most of the later county of Armagh, east Tyrone and the south of the later county of Derry).[4] The number of church buildings that can be identified in Armagh *inter Anglicos* alone reveals a remarkable density of churches and chapels – of one for every 2,000–2,500 acres within the Pale ditch.[5] That indicates that not only were pastoral centres very numerous in Co. Louth, but they were readily accessible. It would seem reasonable to infer that the Church throughout the inner Pale provided as dense a network of pastoral care centres as that found in Co. Louth in the first half of the sixteenth century. That may be readily established once the churches across the Pale are comprehensively identified and mapped.

Identifying all of the churches and chapels served by priests at any particular point in time is difficult, but Archbishop Alen compiled a list of churches in Dublin diocese in 1533,[6] and there are procuration lists available for Meath diocese from the late fifteenth and early sixteenth centuries.[7] For dioceses with little, if any, surviving ecclesiastical records one may turn to the *Valor in Hibernia*, a record of the value of clerical benefices in 1538–9, and to the monastic extents which offer indications about many non-beneficed parish cures in 1540–1.[8] Together, these two sources can be used to trace the pastoral network of the Irish diocesan Church over most of the east, and much of the south of Ireland *c.*1538–41. This must be an imperative for the study of the Church in the English lordship in Ireland in the future.

I wish to emphasise that the use of the *Valor in Hibernia* in isolation to study the provision of pastoral care in the early Tudor Church is very misleading because it only records the values of benefices held by clergymen, and does not include information on unbeneficed clergymen. Hundreds of parishes in early Tudor Ireland were not served by beneficed clergymen. In theory there ought to have been a beneficed clergyman responsible for the pastoral ministry in each parish. However, in late medieval Ireland there were many impropriated parishes without a vicar, with the cure of souls served by a stipendiary priest.[9] For example, the Hospitallers of Kilmainham held many rectories in Co. Louth

---

4 PRONI, DIO 4/2/12, 'Dowdall's register', pp 234–6 (119, E). The calendar number is drawn from L.P. Murray (ed.), 'A calendar of the register of Primate George Dowdall' in *Louth Archaeological Society Journal*, 5–6 (1926–30); 252 (128 B); H. Jefferies, *Priests and prelates of Armagh in the age of reformations* (Dublin, 1997), 19–20, 62–5.   5 Jefferies, *Priests and prelates*, 20.
6 N.B. White (ed.), 'The reportorium viride of John Alen archbishop of Dublin, 1533', in *Anal. Hib.*, 10 (1944) 171–222, and also C. MacNeill (ed.), *Calendar of Archbishop Alen's register, c.1172–1534* (Dublin, 1950).   7 Procurations and synodals of Meath diocese, TCD, MS 1060 (5), as well as Dowdall's register, pp 253–68 (129).   8 The pioneering work on the *Valor in Hibernia* was, of course, S. Ellis, 'Economic problems of the Church: why the reformation failed in Ireland' in *Journal of Ecclesiastical History*, 41 (1990), 239–65. The *Valor in Hibernia* was published as *Valor beneficiorum ecclesiasticorum in Hiberniae: or the first fruits of all of the ecclesiastical benefices in the kingdom of Ireland, as taxed in the king's book* (Dublin, 1741). The monastic extents, which are a relatively neglected source for Irish ecclesiastical and economic and social history, were published in N.B. White (ed.), *Extents of Irish monastic possessions, 1540–1* (Dublin, 1943). See also C. McNeill (ed.), 'Accounts of monastic chattels', in *JRSAI*, 52 (1922), 11–37.   9 H. Jefferies, 'The

impropriate; half of them were served by a beneficed vicar but the rest had 'no vicar, but a stipendiary priest', and that was part of a general pattern, not only in Armagh but across those parishes in Ireland which were impropriated.[10] Therefore, while the *Valor in Hibernia* has records for only twenty-four churches in Armagh *inter Anglicos* entrusted to a beneficed rector or vicar in 1538/9, there were many more parishes where the cure of souls was entrusted to unbeneficed curates.

The distinction between parish churches and chapels cannot, in any case, be drawn too rigidly before the Reformation. For example, there is a degree of ambiguity about the status of the churches in Co. Louth that were impropriated to the Cistercian monastery at Mellifont and to the Hospital of the Crutched Friars at Ardee. These churches were located in areas contiguous with the monastery and hospital respectively and were officially designated as chapels within the parishes of Mellifont and Ardee respectively, while the cure of souls attached to the churches was entrusted to stipendiary curates.[11] Yet these churches were little different from those parish churches impropriated to the Hospitallers of Kilmainham that were entrusted to stipendiary priests. Whatever their status *de jure*, for the parishioners who were served by the unbeneficed curate responsible for the cure of souls in their area, the local church was in most respects their parish church *de facto*. The jurors who outlined the extents of the possessions of the Hospital at Ardee referred to 'the parishes or chapels' of Moorestown and Knock Louth.[12] They also referred to the 'parish of Richardstown', though the church there was served by a stipendiary curate. Significantly too, one finds church procurators or churchwardens acting on behalf of the parishioners of Tullyallen, a church impropriated to Mellifont and served by an unbeneficed curate.[13] One might observe that in the registers attributed to Archbishops Cromer and Dowdall '*ecclesia*' was the term normally, though not always, used to describe churches, whether they were served by a beneficed clergyman or an unbeneficed curate. Hence, it serves no purpose to attempt to draw rigid distinctions between parish churches entrusted to a beneficed clergyman, parish churches entrusted to unbeneficed curates and churches which were technically termed chapels but whose priest was responsible for the cure of souls within a well-defined area and drew his income from the parishioners of that area.[14] These areas commonly formed the

---

role of the laity in the parishes of Armagh *inter Anglicos*, 1518–1553' in *Archivium Hibernicum*, 52 (1998), 72–84: 73–4. **10** White (ed.), *Monastic extents*, 108–10, 213, 220, 238–9. A cursory examination of the Monastic extents shows how widespread the practice was. **11** Ibid., 219, 226. **12** Ibid., 225. **13** PRONI, DIO 4/2/11. Cromer's register, i, f. 1 (1). The calendar number is drawn from L.P. Murray (ed.), 'A calendar of the register of Primate George Cromer' in *Louth Archaeological Society Journal*, 8–10 (1938–43). **14** The curates who served the churches impropriated to the Hospital at Ardee were assigned the altarages of the area of their cure of souls as their stipends: White (ed.), *Monastic extents*, 226. See also Cromer's register, i, f. 70 (91) where the curates of Kilclogher and Termonfeckin sued the parishioners of Callystown for the payment of thrice yearly offerings.

basis of the later 'civil parishes' in the same way as the late medieval parishes served by beneficed clergymen. The Irish parliament of 1541 was presented with a bill ' ... to establish certain vicars or parsons in the parsonages lately appropriated unto houses of religion, endowing them with certain livings of the profits thereof ...'[15] This bill was not enacted, but it serves to confirm the argument that there were many parishes in Armagh *inter Anglicos*, and elsewhere in Ireland, where the cure of souls was served by an unbeneficed priest.

The number and density of parish churches in the Ulster rural deaneries of Armagh diocese were lower than those *inter Anglicos* – averaging one parish church for every 14,000–15,000 acres - indicating that churches there were far less accessible.[16] There were some chapels in Armagh *inter Hibernicos*, but they would appear to have been very few indeed. By mapping the distribution of the churches known from the 1544 list one can see graphically the fairly even distribution of the parish churches and chapels across that part of Co. Louth within the Pale ditch. Beyond the ditch there were fewer churches, even before the conflict of the late 1530s caused a collapse of the Church's ministry in the marches.[17] The distribution of parish churches in Armagh *inter Hibernicos* was greatly affected by the physical geography of the district. There were very few churches in the Sperrin Mountains or in the Fews, but there were clusters of churches along the lowlands to the south and west of Lough Neagh.[18] One may assume that the uneven distribution of churches reflected, to no small degree, uneven economic productivity across the district, which further suggests that the churches were more numerous and accessible where the population densities were greatest. I have mapped churches and chapels for Derry diocese and Dromore, which conform with the pattern observed for Armagh *inter Hibernicos* of much lower densities of churches than in the Pale, with particularly scant provision of churches in upland areas.[19] This is work that needs to be done for other dioceses, but already we have some insights into the Church's provision of pastoral care across the north of the Pale and a broad swathe of Ulster.

TERRITORIAL BOUNDARIES

The question as to the extent to which the provision of pastoral care was provided within clear territorial boundaries cannot be answered with great

---

15 National Archives, London, SP 60/10/6.   16 Jefferies, *Priests and prelates*, 64–5. Inclusion of known chapels improves the figure moderately to something over 10,000 acres.   17 Jefferies, *Priests and prelates*, 21.   18 Ibid., 63.   19 H. Jefferies, 'The diocese of Dromore on the eve of the Tudor reformations' in L. Proudfoot (ed.), *Down: history and society* (Dublin, 1997), 123–40: 126; ibid., 'Derry diocese on the eve of the plantation' in G. O'Brien (ed.), *Derry/Londonderry: history and society* (Dublin, 1999), 175–204: 200.

precision. Certainly there were parochial boundaries that were well-defined for financial purposes, not just for the levying of tithes on agricultural produce (though they were clearly important) but also for personal tithes. The later civil parishes in areas colonised in the middle ages offer useful indications as to where many late medieval parish boundaries lay. K.W. Nicholls has used the considerable degree of continuity between late medieval and civil parish boundaries to striking effect in his analysis of the emergence of the parochial system in the west of Ireland.[20] Yet civil parish boundaries are not always identical to medieval parish boundaries because the civil parish boundaries reflect something of the changes in the Church of Ireland's parochial system in the seventeenth and eighteenth centuries, with the emergence of some new parishes where the Anglican population became substantial and the disappearance of others from official records. The civil parish boundaries in the plantation counties of Ulster are especially problematical as a guide to late medieval parish boundaries because of the tremendous changes across the plantation watershed.[21] The organisation of the Church in plantation districts was rationalised to a significant, if now indeterminable, degree.

The extent to which pastoral care was ever strictly circumscribed by parochial boundaries must be open to question. Given the great difficulties of travelling for the *cois mhuintir* in medieval times, it seems certain that people would generally have looked to the nearest church/chapel and its priest(s) for pastoral care, so that the outer limits of a parish's territorial boundaries might not coincide precisely with its effective pastoral reach. Indeed, given the difficulties of travel, with distance being compounded by the poor quality of the roads and the lack of bridges, it is probable that a considerable portion of the population – especially in the more extensive parishes beyond the Pale and the towns – infrequently visited a church/chapel, except for rites of passage such as baptisms and funerals. In urban areas the territorial boundaries of parishes did not always coincide with those of the provision of pastoral care because the accessibility of a choice of pastoral care centres, be they neighbouring churches/chapels, or friaries or monasteries, facilitated the indulgences of personal preferences when it came to attending celebrations of the liturgy or seeking some sacraments.

On the other hand, it is probable that most parishioners looked to their local parish church or chapel, and priest, for pastoral care – however often they may have availed of the Church's ministry in practice. Convenience, and also an attachment grown from long association, would have drawn parishioners to their local churches. The interment of family members would have cemented people's attachment to their church, as one can see most clearly in the wills that have chanced to survive and also in the foundation of chantries, mainly, one

---

20 K.W. Nicholls, 'Rectory, vicarage and parish in the western Irish dioceses' in *JRSAI*, 101 (1971), 53–84. 21 Jefferies, *Priests and prelates*, 65.

must observe, from urban milieu.[22] The surviving wills processed by the church court in Armagh *inter Anglicos* in the early years of the sixteenth century reveal that strong lay piety was fairly general, at least among the middling sort of people who made wills.[23] The number of surviving wills is small, yet they seem to confirm that the primary loyalties of the laity (perhaps especially those who were not poor) were directed towards their local parish church or chapel. The mendicants occupied a subordinate place, yet still a significant one, in their affections.

The scale of the church building and extension in Co. Louth on the eve of the Tudor Reformations has been revealed in striking detail by Victor Buckley, and may be interpreted as another reflection of lay people's attachment to their local church or chapel.[24] In the case of St Peter's church, Drogheda, it can be demonstrated that the great extensions made to the parish church before the Tudor Reformations were financed by a small number of wealthy citizens.[25] The massive investment of the laity in building new churches and chapels, and in extending and embellishing older buildings, together with the surviving wills, point towards a generally positive relationship between the Catholic church in Armagh *inter Anglicos* and the wider population in the decades prior to the Tudor Reformations. One may venture further and suggest that the widespread church building and embellishment shows that the diocesan church of Armagh enjoyed considerable commitment and support from the laity up to the eve of the Reformations. The last Catholic confraternity to be established in the archdiocese before the Henrician Reformation was licensed at Ardee as late as 1534.[26] Against such positive evidence of commitment, there is no evidence at all of disenchantment with the Catholic Church, or of a desire for Reformation.

---

22 See especially H.F. Berry (ed.), *Register of wills and inventories of the diocese of Dublin, 1457–83* (Dublin, 1898) passim; M. Murphy, 'The high cost of dying: an analysis of pro anima bequests in medieval Dublin', in W.J. Shiels and D. Wood (eds), *The Church and wealth: studies in Church History*, xxiv (Oxford 1987), 111–22. Wills from elsewhere in Ireland are few indeed, but for Co. Louth cf. Jefferies, 'Laity', 80, which clearly show the testators' stronger attachment to their local churches as against the local friaries. For people's attachment to family graves cf. H. Jefferies, *Cork: historical perspectives* (Dublin, 2004), 102–4.   23 PRONI, DIO 4/4/9. Octavian's register of wills.   24 V.M. Buckley and P.D. Sweetman, *Archaeological survey of County Louth* (Dublin, 1991), 218–66; Jefferies, *Priests and prelates*, 21–6.   25 Dudley Loftus' collection of annals, civil and ecclesiastical, relating to Ireland, sub annos 1506, 1525, 1527 (Marsh's Library, Dublin, MS Z4.2.7); see also D. Mac Iomhair (ed.), 'Two old Drogheda chronicles' in *Louth Archaeological Society Journal*, 15 (1961), 58–75: 72–5; J. Bradley, 'The topography and layout of Drogheda' in *Louth Archaeological Society Journal*, 19 (1978), 98–127: 114.   26 L.P. Murray, 'The ancient chantries of County Louth' in *Louth Archaeological Society Journal*, 9 (1940), 181–208: 206–7.

ROLE OF THE LAITY

The role of the laity in the parishes is difficult to define for want of evidence, but work by Adrian Empey suggests that it was a significant feature in the pre-Reformation Church, at least in the Pale and the towns (if not elsewhere).[27] Laymen enjoyed the right to present men to be the incumbent of a quarter of the benefices in Armagh *inter Anglicos* on the eve of the Tudor Reformations.[28] It was unusual for lay patrons to present men of their own surname to the benefice in their gift, presumably because most of the benefices were too poorly remunerated to appeal to men of gentry backgrounds.[29] In any case, a co-incidence of surnames merely suggests, but does not of itself prove, a family relationship. This is a pattern one could safely assume for most of Ireland.

While laymen enjoyed the right of patronage to a quarter of the benefices in Armagh *inter Anglicos* they were still able to exert influence over the appointment of priests to benefices where they did not have the right of presentation. Leading laymen were consulted before a priest could be instituted into any of the parish benefices in Armagh *inter Anglicos*. The consultations with the laity were formally organised. Whenever a benefice fell vacant, the archbishop commissioned an inquisition to be held to discover how the benefice came to be vacant, who had the right of presentation, and whether the candidate presented to the benefice was suitable. The juries were made up of local priests and laymen (usually members of the gentry), and the laity almost always made up a sizeable number of the jurors in such inquisitions.[30] The inclusion of laymen on the inquisition juries was important as it gave the laity the opportunity of expressing their judgement of the proposed candidates. There is no sixteenth-century record of an inquisition rejecting a candidate for a benefice, but it seems safe to presume that a priest would not have been promoted to a benefice in the face of strong lay opposition.

One has the impression that the church authorities were relatively careless about the appointment of unbeneficed priests who were responsible for a cure of souls.[31] The monasteries which had the right to appoint them sometimes delegated the right to lay tithe farmers.[32] The diocesan authorities did not conduct inquisitions before such priests were appointed to a cure of souls. Again and again one encounters complaints in Armagh's synodal records that

---

27 A. Empey, 'The layperson in the parish: the medieval inheritance, 1169–1536' in R. Gillespie and W.G. Neely (eds), *The laity and the Church of Ireland, 1000–2000: all sorts and conditions* (Dublin, 2001), 7–48. Jefferies, 'Laity', 73–84.   **28** Cromer's register, i, f. 1 (1), f. 13v (30), f. 15 (35), f. 30 (50), f. 37v (86), f. 39v (93), f. 52 (125), f. 58v (139), f. 65v (160); Dowdall's register, p. 7 (6), p. 46 (42), p. 129 (95).   **29** Cromer's register, ii, f. 1 (1). The calendar numbers for Book ii of Cromer's register are drawn from J. McCafferty, 'The act book of the Armagh diocese, 1518–1522', unpublished MA (University College Dublin, 1991).   **30** Cromer's register, ii, f. 1 (1); f. 13v (30); II, f. 15 (35); ff 72v–73 (172).   **31** Jefferies, *Priests and prelates*, 47–8.   **32** White (ed.), *Monastic extents*, 108–10.   **33** Cromer's register, ii, f. 47 (121), f. 59 (140), f. 68 (167); Dowdall's register, pp 88–90 (76), Decree 6.

these curates were serving the parish cures before they were admitted by the archbishop's administration.[33] This may indicate that the church authorities, and the leading laymen, were more interested in appointments made to benefices because of their financial rather than their spiritual significance.

Lay interest in the routine operation of their local parish, whether it was served by a beneficed clergyman or an unbeneficed curate, was institutionalised by the office of church procurator or churchwarden.[34] Churchwardens were the representatives through whom the parishioners fulfilled certain 'collective' responsibilities; such as holding and administering any form of parish property; raising funds as required for parish needs; keeping custody of the ornaments and utensils provided by the parishioners for the services of the church; and they were the acknowledged representatives of the parishioners in any collective action which they might wish or be compelled to undertake.[35] They also represented their parish communities at diocesan or archdiaconal visitations.

The primary responsibility of the procurators or churchwardens was for the maintenance of the nave of the local church. The Armagh court book contains records of procurators suing parishioners for failing to pay their share of the maintenance levy, or for failing to pay other monies due to the church.[36] As custodians of church ornaments and other utensils needed for services in the church, the procurators of Drumcar, Co. Louth, sued the holy water clerk, and some other individuals there, for breaking a bell and detaining other property belonging to the parish church.[37] In another dispute processed by Armagh's consistory court it was claimed that a surplice belonged to the parish church of Drumcar and not to the vicar.[38] Church procurators could also represent the parishioners in collective legal actions.[39] Interestingly, in a case brought by the parishioners of Tullyallen, Co. Louth, against the monks of Mellifont to increase the stipend of their curate one of the procurators or churchwardens who brought the suit was an Irishman and the other was English, a reflection of the mixed population in the Pale.[40] Procurators or churchwardens can be identified in Dublin.[41] The most interesting reference to churchwardens in the first half of the sixteenth century is for St Nicholas' Collegiate church, Galway, where they mortgaged the church's plate before the English crown could confiscate it in 1546.[42]

The role of the laity in Gaelic and gaelicised Ireland has yet to receive scholarly attention, except for the erenaghs who were such a feature of the Church in the north of Ireland.[43] Erenaghs were, essentially, tenants on

---

34 Jefferies, 'Laity', 77–8. 35 C. Drew, *Early parochial organisation in England: the origins of the office of church warden* (London, 1954), 5–6. 36 Cromer's register, i, f. 65 (84), f. 6v (19). See also f. 67 (87). 37 Ibid., i, f. 36v (55). 38 Ibid., i, f. 55 (73). 39 Ibid., i, ff 49–50, 50v, 51v (67). 40 Ibid., i, f. 1, a loose sheet (1). 41 E. Curtis (ed.), *Calendar of Ormond deeds*, iv, *1509–47* (Dublin, 1937), no. 232; White (ed.), *Monastic extents*, 87. 42 R. O Flaherty, *A chorographical description of west or h-Iar Connaught, written A.D. 1684*, ed. J. Hardiman (Dublin, 1846), 230. 43 Jefferies, *Priests and prelates*, 125–8. Information about the erenaghs can be gleaned from the appendix to the Ulster inquisitions: *Inquisitionum in officio rotulorum cancellariae Hiberniae … Ultoniae* (Dublin, 1829); 'Sir John Davies' letter to Robert, earl of Salisbury, 1607' in H. Morley

episcopal land who enjoyed some residual prestige (and carried some residual responsibilities) from the men who held their title before the twelfth-century reforms. Their importance for episcopal finances has been highlighted, and especially their role in the parish churches. Most of the clergy of Derry diocese, for instance, and many of those for Armagh *inter Hibernicos*, Clogher and Dromore, came from the erenagh clans.[44] Erenaghs were responsible for maintaining the nave of the local parish church, or two thirds of a unicellular building – effectively the equivalent of the laity's portion of churches *inter Anglicos*. It is probable that the erenagh was among the lay representatives questioned during episcopal visitations of their parish church (and also archdi-aconal or ruri-decanal visitations where such were conducted).[45] Certainly erenaghs play a significant role in the life of the Church over much of the north of Ireland. For most of Ireland, however, the role of the laity has yet to be investigated. However, Adrian Empey's pioneering work on the layperson in the parish is a major contribution to this field.[46]

FINANCE

I have already indicated that the distribution of churches and chapels reflected the distribution of economic production to no small degree, while economics underlay the settlement patterns across Ireland. The decisions to locate any particular ecclesiastical foundation at any particular site was subject to the vagaries of history – the result of personal or collective choices made for reasons and in circumstances which are now usually unfathomable for want of documentation. Nonetheless, it is becoming clear that there was a myriad of ecclesiastical sites from early Christian times that were available for use as the sites of churches or chapels into the later middle ages and beyond. It was primarily economic considerations which determined which of the very many early Christian sites continued to host a church or chapel with a priest in late medieval times. The dense distribution of churches and chapels in Armagh *inter Anglicos* shows that the Church there was able to garner sufficient income to finance the provision of many churches, and priests to staff them. Gaps in the network of early Christian church sites could be filled by new foundations in the later middle ages, as at Beaulieu, Co. Louth. The total number of staffed

(ed.), *Ireland under Elizabeth and James the first* (London, 1890), 367; H. Jefferies (ed.), 'Erenaghs in pre-plantation Ulster: an early seventeenth century account' in *Archivium Hibernicum*, 53 (1999), 16–19; H. Jefferies (ed.), 'Erenaghs and termonlands: another early seventeenth century account' in *Seanchas Ard Mhacha*, 19 (2002), 55–8.   **44** Jefferies, *Priests and prelates*, 73–5; ibid., 'Derry diocese', 175–204; H. Jefferies, 'Papal letters and Irish clergy' in H. Jefferies (ed.), *History of the diocese of Clogher* (Dublin, 2005), 81–107; ibid., 'Dromore', 127–8.   **45** H. Jefferies, 'The visitation of the Church in Armagh *inter Hibernicos* in 1546', in C. Dillon and H.A. Jefferies (eds), *Tyrone: history and society* (Dublin, 2001), 163–80.   **46** A. Empey, 'The layperson in the parish'.

churches sustained in Armagh *inter Anglicos* was determined by the availability of economic resources, and a local economic collapse brought about by a war or disorder could cause individual parishes, or clusters of parishes, to collapse also. This is documented in the case of the north of Co. Louth in the late 1530s as a result of conflict between the Geraldine League and the English crown.[47] Archbishop Bodkin's visitation of 1565/7 reveals that about 10 per cent of the parishes of Clonfert, Tuam and Kilmacduagh lay waste at that time, and were unable to support priests.[48]

Parish revenues also reflected economic conditions in that both the great tithes and small tithes were levied on the wealth generated within parishes – though the Church's ability to levy tithes fell far short of the nominal 10 per cent of agricultural production and non-agricultural incomes it claimed.[49] I have suggested elsewhere that parochial revenues were relatively fixed by custom.[50] There were local variations in the customs for collecting tithes – which encouraged sporadic challenges to the Church's claims to individual tithe levies in different parishes as, for example, at Carlingford in 1521 when the local people claimed exemption from a tithe on butter.[51] Personal tithes were a particular problem for the Church, despite repeated Church legislation insisting that they be paid.[52]

The *Valor in Hibernia* gives simply a gross monetary value for the benefices they record. It gives no indication as to the constituent sources which went to make up the income of the benefice. Fortunately the monastic extents are a little more informative in this regard, giving at least some idea of the values of the great tithes and altarages for several parishes. The monastic extents for Co. Louth were compiled in 1540 and 1541 through sworn juries from a number of locations across the county, presumably with access to monastic estate records. The jurors who conducted the inquisition into the properties of the priory of Louth referred explicitly to 'the ancient evidences of the priory' as one of their sources.[53] The juries, doubtless following the accounting practices of the religious houses whose extents they reported, provided information on impropriated benefices in different forms.[54] These variations in accounting practices mean that the monastic extents are more useful for the study of some parishes' revenues than others. A further problem is that the price at which the tithes were leased by a religious community might not bear a very close relationship to their true value. For example, the rectory of Drumcar, Co. Louth, was leased

47 Jefferies, *Priests and prelates*, 20. **48** K.W. Nicholls, 'The visitation of the diocese of Clonfert, Tuam and Kilmacduagh *c.*1565–7' in *Anal. Hib.*, 26 (1970), 144–57. **49** J. Murray, 'The sources of clerical incomes' in *Archivium Hibernicum*, 46 (1991–2), 146–57; Jefferies, *Priests and prelates*, 26–37, 68–73. **50** Jefferies, *Priests and prelates*, 28–9, 30. See also Murray, 'Clerical incomes', 153. **51** Cromer's register, i, ff 96–96v (121). **52** Jefferies, *Priests and prelates*, 30; Murray, 'Clerical incomes', 150–2; Swayne's register, no. 250, p. 12; TCD, MS 808 (5), 'Statutes of the provincial synod of Cashel, 1453', no. 34. **53** White (ed.), *Monastic extents*, 229; Jefferies, *Priests and prelates*, 28. **54** White (ed.), *Monastic extents*, 108–10, 214–20.

by the monks for £9 6s 8d per annum, but was sub-leased for £20 by the farmer.[55]

A major limitation on the revenue base of the late medieval Irish Church was the general exemption of pasturelands from tithes – at a time when a very high proportion of the country was given over to pasture. This meant that in disturbed borderlands, where tillage farming could be suspended for some time, the Church could not depend on tithes to sustain its ministry. Hence, parishes could be classified as 'wasted' in ecclesiastical sources, though they continued to be inhabited by a presumably reduced population. The monastic extents show that extensive areas of Ireland were 'wasted' in 1540–1, with clear implications for the Church's ability to provide pastoral care in such circumstances.

Evidence about parochial income in Gaelic Ireland is scarce. The 1609 Ulster inquisitions are useful in that context in recording many pre-plantation practices in ecclesiastical finances. The jurors at Dungannon reported that in Armagh *inter Hibernicos* tithes were levied in kind on corn, wool, fish and flax, and that 4d was taken for every milch cow, a pig from every swine herd, and that no other tithes were paid in the archdiocese *inter Hibernicos*, either in kind or otherwise.[56] The exemption of dry cattle and sheep meat from liability to tithes in an economy where pastoral farming was very important would inevitably mean that the tithes did not reflect the full extent of agricultural output. Research on this subject is needed for the Church across Ireland, but one may confidently assume that the Irish Church failed to garner anything like the nominal 10 per cent of wealth it claimed as its due.

For England it has been calculated that £10 sterling was a 'reasonable and adequate sum' for an incumbent without a curate, or £15 sterling for an incumbent with a curate, yet in Armagh *inter Anglicos* only nine of its twenty-four parochial benefices were worth more than £5 sterling per annum while five benefices were worth less than £2 10s. sterling.[57] The average values of the rectories and vicarages were only £4 7s. and £4 1s. 11½d. sterling respectively in Armagh *inter Anglicos*, only £4 19s. 8d. and £4 12s. 6d. sterling in Dublin, only £7 11s. 10d. and £4 11s. 6d. sterling in Meath diocese, and only £4 0s. 1d. and £3 14s. 2d. sterling in Kildare.[58] The records of the twentieth tax on benefices in Tullyhogue in Primate Dowdall's register suggests that the average income of fourteen rectors there was only £2 2s. 9d. (Stg£1 8s. 6d.) while the average income of eight vicars was a mere £1 7s. 1½d. (Stg 18s. 1d.).[59] It may be argued that the values of the parochial livings recorded for Tullyhogue are incredibly low, and that the clergy may have been able to understate their incomes to an ordinary who was an infrequent visitor to their parishes. That is indeed conceiveable, but the consistency of the values across the rural deanery

55 Ibid., 17. **56** *Inquisitionum in officio rotulorum cancellariae Hiberniae … Ultoniae*, appendix, Co. Tyrone, sixth page. **57** P. Heath, *The English parish clergy on the eve of the reformation* (London, 1969), 173, Jefferies, *Priests and prelates*, 32–3. **58** *Valor in Hibernia*, 2, 3–5, 9–10; Jefferies, *Priests and prelates*, 32–3. **59** Jefferies, *Priests and prelates*, 70–1.

suggests otherwise, as does the fact that the Tullyhogue values are very comparable to the low values recorded for benefices in Cashel and Leighlin according to the *Valor in Hibernia*.[60] Furthermore, many of the unbeneficed curates to whom the cure of souls was delegated were obliged to subsist upon the altarages alone.[61] An important consequence of clerical poverty, even assuming that the *Valor* understated clerical incomes, was the small number of graduates among the Irish parish clergy. It also made the clergy in Ireland more dependent upon the goodwill of their parishioners than may have been the case in England.

PASTORAL CARE

The priest charged with a cure of souls had to celebrate Mass on Sundays and holydays, and on a number of other days during the week.[62] The priest had also to recite the Office publicly in his church on Sundays and holydays, and on some other days during the week.[63] The priest had to celebrate the key rites of passage, at baptisms, marriages, the churching of women after childbirth, and at funerals. Visitation of the sick and anointing the dying were other regular responsibilities of the parish priests. The priest was obliged to hear his parishioners' confessions, at least once a year, usually prior to the reception of the eucharist at Easter. Finally, a priest was obliged to instruct the parishioners in the Catholic faith.

A reductionist historian would be justified in arguing that very little can be known about the quality of pastoral care provided by the late medieval Church in Ireland. The scant records that survive, particularly if one excepts the Armagh registers which have significant limitations, are mainly made up of financial records. To do more than despair about the lack of source materials one must scrutinise the materials we have to hand in order to make informed inferences about what they may tell us about the provision of pastoral care in the parishes.

Once one can establish which churches or chapels were served by a priest (with a reasonable degree of confidence) one can begin to make at least some basic inferences about the provision of pastoral care in an area – without making assumptions about the quality of the care actually afforded. The distribution of churches in Armagh *inter Anglicos*, and the numbers of churches and chapels which can identified for Dublin and Meath diocese strongly suggests that throughout the Pale churches or chapels and priests were accessible for people to avail of if they so wished. In Armagh dioceses priests were directed in 1526 to acquire a copy of *Ignorantia sacerdotum*.[64] This was a schema of

---

60 *Valor in Hibernia*, 13, 14–15.   61 Jefferies, 'Laity', 73–4.   62 TCD, MS 808, (5), The provincial synod of Cashel, 1453, no. 2.   63 Ibid., no. 1.   64 Cromer's register, ii, f. 20v (48).

Catholic instruction for the laity that was to be expounded to congregations in the vernacular four times a year. Extended sermons were not generally expected of the parochial clergy before the Reformations. The general requirement was for parish priests to provide their congregations with, at least, four sermons a year, by a priest commissioned for the purpose if need be.[65] The comparative neglect of preaching by the parochial clergy was compensated for to no small extent by the vigorous pastoral activities of the mendicant friars.

I inferred from the volume of church building and ornamentation which Victor Buckley identified in the *Archaeological Survey for County Louth* for the late fifteenth and early sixteenth centuries, together with documentary evidence of further ornamentation in the churches at Drogheda and Dundalk and records of the foundations of chantries and the establishment of a confraternity at Ardee, that the Church in Armagh *inter Anglicos* enjoyed much support from the laity who financed the buildings, ornamentation and foundations, and that the Church was probably in relatively good order on the eve of the Tudor Reformations.[66] The wills that have chanced to survive among the Armagh registers seemed to confirm the impression of lay support reflected in the archaeological and documentary records. An examination of the annual synodal legislation for the parishes of Armagh *inter Anglicos* offered even stronger confirmation of the assessment that the Church's pastoral ministry was reasonably effective.[67] A survey of the church court records for Armagh diocese from the years 1518 to 1522 offered definite indications of how the church authorities were able to impose their stated requirements upon the clergy and the laity in the parishes of Armagh *inter Anglicos*,[68] while offering impressionistic evidence to reinforce the overall judgement that the Church in the parishes in that part of Ireland provided a level of pastoral care which matched the expectations set for it by the archbishops of Armagh. For that small corner of Ireland, at least, organised religion was certainly not on the verge of total breakdown.

Evidence for the Church in Gaelic Ireland is hard to come by, but the visitation of Tullyhogue in 1546 offers a unique insight into the Church in parishes in the heart of Ulster.[69] It shows that in every parish, with one possible exception, there was a priest who celebrated the Mass and prayed. It showed that every church visited had the necessary ecclesiastical ornaments and utensils. It also showed, though, that most of the church buildings were either defective or ruinous due, doubtless, to the disturbed conditions in which the

65 R.E. Rodes, *Ecclesiastical administration in medieval England: the Anglo-Saxons to the Reformation* (Notre Dame and London, 1977), 168 shows that the quarterly sermon became a requirement in the fourteenth century. See also Dowdall's register, pp 99–106 (85), Article 17. 66 Jefferies, *Priests and prelates*, 55–6; ibid., 'Laity', 80–3. 67 H. Jefferies, 'Diocesan synods and convocations in Armagh on the eve of the Tudor reformations' in *Seanchas Ard Mhacha*, 16 (1995) 120–33; ibid., *Priests and prelates*, 96–102. 68 H. Jefferies, 'The church courts of Armagh on the eve of the reformation' in *Seanchas Ard Mhacha*, 15 (1993), 1–38; ibid., *Priests and prelates*, 103–17. 69 Jefferies, 'Visitation', passim.

Church operated. The visitation report tells against assumptions that the Irish Church in the late medieval/early Reformation periods was on the verge of 'total breakdown' – as indeed does the work done on the adjoining dioceses of Clogher, Derry and Dromore. Nonetheless, the impression made by the visitors' peremptory questions as to whether the priests celebrated the Mass or prayed, and the peremptory answers recorded, is of a very basic provision of pastoral care. The report about Clogher cathedral in 1517 – 'Mass is celebrated only on Sunday; one set of vestments; a wooden cross; a chalice; one bell' – seems to confirm that impression.[70] So do the better-known reports on Clonmacnoise and Ardagh cathedrals in 1515 and 1517 respectively.[71] I have qualified such stark reports elsewhere by pointing to more positive evidence.[72] Nonetheless, I retain an impression that the provision of pastoral care across most of Ireland was of a spartan nature.

I am not going to rehearse my views on clerical concubinage, which has received a disproportionate amount of historians' attention in the past. Suffice it to say that I do not regard priests who had intimate relations with women as moral reprobates! Aubrey Gwynn once remarked that the impression left by the entries relating to Ireland in the papal registers is that 'the late medieval Church was in a state of lamentable disorder'.[73] However, a review of the papal entries for Ireland before the Reformation reveals that the annual number of delations brought against Irish clergymen was small, and only a small fraction of them involved allegations of serious misconduct or negligence which may or may not have been substantiated.[74] That should serve as a warning against exaggerating the failings of the parish clergy of Gaelic Ireland. Indeed, whatever their failings, one cannot but be impressed by the resilience of the parish clergy of late medieval/Tudor Ireland in view of the very difficult political, social and economic circumstances in which they ministered.

REVIVAL?

From *c.*1450 onwards there was considerable investment in the extension and ornamentation of parish churches and chapels in Arnagh *inter Anglicos*, and many were completely re-built. While similar research is needed for other dioceses, apart from Brendan Scott's work on Meath diocese, there is some evidence that this pattern of increased spending on the fabric of the Church was replicated across the Pale and in the outlying English urban settlements in

70 M.J. Haren, 'A description of Clogher diocese in the early sixteenth century' in *Clogher Record*, 12 (1985), 52–4. 71 A. Theiner, *Vetera monumenta Hibernorum et Scotorum* (Rome, 1864), 518, 521. 72 Jefferies, 'Armagh registers', 85–6. 73 A. Gwynn, 'Anglo-Irish Church life: fourteenth and fifteenth centuries', in *A history of Irish Catholicism*, ii (Dublin and Sidney, 1968), 73. 74 Jefferies, 'Papal letters', 81–90.

Ireland.[75] It seems that a general economic recovery in the English lordship in Ireland allowed the devotion of greater resources to the Church. It is likely that the greater spending on religion also reflected some increase in piety.

Colm Lennon has revealed the existence of a very rich religious culture in late medieval Dublin with many religious and craft guilds that employed priests to celebrate Mass for the souls of their members and relatives.[76] Mary Ann Lyons has highlighted the intense lay piety among the gentry of Kildare, another part of the Pale, who invested in chantries, elaborate funerary monuments and various benefactions to the Church.[77] Brendan Scott has pointed to 'significant investment in the pre-Reformation Church' by the laity in Meath as a strong indication of popular support for religion.[78] Generally, late medieval wills (although these survive in relatively small numbers and chiefly for middling to wealthy townspeople) reflect a strong concern for the welfare of their souls after death.[79] The wills invariably include bequests for the celebration of intercessory Masses, as well as gifts of cash or clothing to the local parish clergy, some money for the fabric of the local church or for the purchase of sacred ornaments, offerings for the maintenance of perpetual lights before hallowed statues, together with a bequest to one or more of the local mendicant communities. Interestingly, a small sample of wills from Cork in the mid-sixteenth century seems to show a diminution of such piety (even after allowance has been made for the dissolution of the religious houses and the abolition of the Mass) under the impact of the Tudor Reformations.[80]

In general, the evidence suggests that in the most anglicised parts of Ireland the diocesan Church in the reign of Henry VIII was in relatively good order by English standards and the laity engaged in forms of piety which would have been readily recognisable to their fellows in England. Brendan Bradshaw found evidence of significant contemporaneous investment in monasteries across much of colonial Ireland, though he has queried whether it was matched by any upsurge in monastic spirituality.[81]

Studying the Church *inter Hibernicos* is difficult because of the relative dearth of documentation, and progress has been piecemeal and slow since Canice Mooney's pioneering survey.[82] Nonetheless, between 1400 and 1508 no

75 H.G. Leask, *Irish churches and monastic buildings*, 3 vols (Dundalk, 1960), iii, 1–40; B. Scott, 'Religion and reform in the Tudor diocese of Meath', unpublished PhD (NUI, Galway, 2004), 32–3; B. Bradshaw, 'The reformation in the cities: Cork, Limerick and Galway, 1534–1603', in J. Bradley (ed.), *Settlement and society in medieval Ireland: studies presented to F.X. Martin, O.S.A.* (Kilkenny, 1988), 445–76: 446; W. Neely, *Kilkenny: an urban history, 1391–1843* (Belfast, 1989), 35–7. 76 C. Lennon, *The lords of Dublin in the age of reformation* (Dublin, 1989), 122–50. 77 M.A. Lyons, *Church and society in County Kildare, c.1470–1547* (Dublin, 2000), 82–96. 78 Scott, 'Meath', 32–3. 79 Murphy, 'High cost', 111–22; C. Lennon, *Sixteenth century Ireland: the incomplete conquest* (Dublin, 1994), 122–4; Jefferies, 'Laity', 80–1. 80 Jefferies, *Cork*, 112–14. 81 B. Bradshaw, *The dissolution of the religious orders in Ireland under Henry VIII* (Cambridge, 1974), 25–6, 35–6. 82 C. Mooney, *The Church in Gaelic Ireland: thirteenth to fifteenth centuries* in *A history of Irish Catholicism* (Dublin and Sidney, 1969), passim.

fewer than ninety new friaries were founded in Ireland, chiefly in Gaelic and gaelicised districts.[83] Half of those were Franciscan Third Order foundations with small communities who supported the ministry of the local diocesan clergy and offered education to children. This remarkable expansion may safely be taken as a reflection of a contemporary religious revival. Nor was this simply a matter of numbers; many of the new communities of friars were 'Observant', committed to a stricter observance of their rules.[84] Observantism won over most of the existing communities, and thoroughly penetrated friaries in the Pale and in outlying towns. William Neely and Brendan Bradshaw have posited a late medieval religious revival inspired by the friars in Kilkenny and in the cities of the south and west respectively. The work of the friars has long been seen as a factor in the survival of Catholicism across Ireland in the face of the Tudor Reformations.

The recent work on the dioceses of Armagh, Clogher, Derry and Dromore suggests that the greatest problem for the institution was not clerical concubinage and the tendency of the sons of churchmen to seek preferment in the Church, but the poverty of the institution. The prevalence of subsistence agriculture among the Irish and the frequency of petty wars depressed clerical incomes from land and tithes. The beneficed clergy and erenaghs had considerable difficulty in maintaining the parish churches from their own resources alone. Yet, though church buildings were often in a poor state, there were resident clergy in place to meet the pastoral needs of the laity, except in those districts wasted by war. Indeed, it is the resilience of the diocesan Church in conditions of widespread lawlessness and sporadic warfare that was its most striking feature.

Beside the evidence of widespread breaches of the strictures of canon law by the clergy and laity, most notably in the realm of sexual relationships, there is a growing realisation that the institutional Church continued to provide a level of pastoral care which was comparable with that elsewhere in Latin Christendom, and there is also an increasing appreciation of the strength of late medieval piety in Ireland. Nonetheless, historians are conscious now, as never before, of the tremendous amount of research still required into the provision of pastoral care in the Irish Church, before and during the Reformations.

---

83 Watt, *Medieval Ireland*, 113. 84 Ibid., 193–202.

Urban parishes in early seventeenth-century Ireland: the case of Dublin

RAYMOND GILLESPIE

In early modern Ireland the parish, as both pastoral and administrative unit, has very considerable claims on the historian's attention. Perhaps nowhere is this clearer than in the case of towns where the urban sprawl of sixteenth- and early seventeenth-century Limerick, Dublin or Cork, with their high densities of population, were broken into more manageable, local communities by the parish. Such parishes acted as a way of articulating senses of the local that bound people together regardless of their confessional divisions and provided a forum for organising social life in a rapidly changing world. One obvious example of this was the parochial graveyard. All residents of the parish, regardless of their confessional allegiance, had the right to be buried there and in time the graveyard became a very tangible representation of the parish.[1] While outsiders may sometimes have been buried in the parochial graveyard simply because they died in the parish or had some connection with it they were clearly demarcated from parochial residents. The vestry of St John's parish in Dublin made the point in 1595 when they decreed that 'strangers' buried in the parish were to pay double the fee charged to parishioners.[2] A second symbol of parochial loyalties was the parish bells. Parish bells, it was repeatedly made clear, belonged not to the incumbent or to any impropriator of the living, but to the parish. When the Irish monastic houses were being dissolved in the 1530s those appointed to account for their assets declared in the case of some religious houses 'for that those churches are and were in the time of the dissolution of the late monasteries, priories and houses aforesaid parish churches and to the parishioners of those churches the bells belong of right and not to the monasteries, priories or houses aforesaid and they remain at present in the custody of those parishioners for their use'.[3] Bells fulfilled a wide range of roles across the local community. They announced deaths and funerals to the community and

---

1 For the suggestion that such burial arrangements may have served to diffuse confessional tensions see V. Harding, *The dead and the living in Paris and London* (Cambridge, 2002). 2 R. Gillespie (ed.), *The vestry records of the parish of St John the Evangelist, Dublin, 1595–1658* (Dublin, 2002), 21. 3 C. McNeill (ed.), 'Accounts of sums realised by sales of chattels of some suppressed Irish monasteries' in *JRSAI*, 53 (1922), 11–37: 20.

in the world of traditional religion month's and year's minds were rung and knells continued to be rung in Dublin into the 1560s.[4] Thereafter bells might also be rung to announce funerals but they had none of the religious overtones of the later Middle Ages. Bells called others to prayer and Dublin corporation decided in 1577 that a bell was to be tolled 'in time of great tempest and storms to the end that every well disposed citizen may be remembered to pray for their neighbours which be in danger upon the seas'.[5] In the 1630s the canons of the Church of Ireland stipulated, in a way that the English canons did not, that on the afternoon before the celebration of holy communion the minister should warn his parishioners 'by the tolling of a bell' so that they might prepare themselves for the sacrament.[6] In more secular ways too bells mattered. Bell ringing was an important way of marking important moments in the political calendar and ringing bells on royal events, which Protestants and Catholics shared, the king's birthday, 5 November, the date of his succession to the throne and occasional royal events such as the return of the future Charles I after the failed negotiations for the Spanish match in 1624.[7] More mundane time was also regulated by the sound of bells. The parish of St Audoen, for instance, ordered in 1638 that the parish bell was to toll at six every morning, at eleven 'according to ancient custom' and at eight at night to mark the passing of time.[8] Bells might also summon the parish to meeting or action as in Clondalkin, near the city, in the late sixteenth century where the church bells were rung to warn people that intruders were enclosing the common land.[9] Indeed the theft of parish bells around Dublin in the early weeks of the rising of 1641 may have been as much to prevent them sounding an alarm as for the value of the metal.[10]

The parish therefore was an important sign of the localism of early modern society. It represented a strong sense of place with its own history within which a community could develop. In the 1640s when the government took depositions from those affected by the insurrection almost all described themselves by referring to the parish where they lived. However, the parish was as much a state of mind as a geographically bounded place. In the absence of maps, boundaries were remembered by the oldest residents and hence were mutable. This was particularly the case in a period of considerable urban development, such as occurred in early seventeenth-century Dublin. In the case of the parish of St John, in the core of the medieval city, the boundary with the parish of St

---

4 B. Mac Cuarta, 'A planter's funeral, legacies and inventory: Sir Matthew De Renzi (1577–1634)' in *JRSAI*, 127 (1997), 18–33: 27; R. Refaussé (ed.), *The registers of Christ Church cathedral, Dublin* (Dublin, 1998), 89; R. Gillespie (ed.), *The proctor's accounts of Peter Lewis, 1564–1565* (Dublin, 1996), 28, 109. 5 J.T. and Lady Gilbert (eds), *Calendar of the ancient records of Dublin*, 19 vols (Dublin, 1889–1944), ii, 115–16. 6 G. Bray (ed.), *The Anglican canons, 1529–1947* (Woodbridge, 1998), 496. 7 For example, Gillespie (ed.), *Vestry records of the parish of St John*, 38; RCB, P326/27/2/21. 8 Marsh's Library, Dublin, MS Z2.2.24, vol ii, ff 32–3 printed in C.T, McCready, 'St Audoen's church, Cornmarket' in *Irish Builder*, 28 (1886), 202. 9 NAI, Chancery bills, N25. 10 For example TCD, MS 810, f. 126v.

Werburgh was ill-remembered and contested in the 1630s which give rise to
legal actions. The building of Copper Alley in a previously undeveloped part of
the city, for instance, procedeed along the parochial boundary with the
northern side of the street lying in St John's parish while the sourthern side
was in St Weburgh's parish with different pastoral and taxation arrangements.[11]
However, the parish was not a purely local institution. It was rather a meeting
point of a series of different tensions that served to shape local societies. At one
level the hierarchical world of the church decreed how the parish should
operate and how its church should be furnished. Late medieval synodal legislation tried to regulate how churches should look and there is some evidence
from the late medieval churchwardens' accounts of the Dublin parish of St
Werburgh that they did try to meet these standards.[12] That parish certainly had
silver chalices, as required by the legislation, as well as the prescribed statues of
saints and it maintained its priest.[13] Provincial legislation, however, said
nothing about another range of religious activities in which the laity engaged.
They set up religious guilds, established and maintained side chapels,
frequented religious sites outside their parish, such as the holy wells at
Kilmainham or at St Stephen's, and in some cases maintained the poor of the
parish although not legally required to do so. St Auoden's maintained an annual
patronal feast at which alms were given for the poor and on the feast of St
Werburgh the people of that parish met to 'keep the same [day] holy by giving
of alms to the poor house belong[ing] to this church'.[14] By the late fifteenth
century at least six religious guilds can be identified either in the city or close
to it.[15] Within the parish churches a number of chapels served by stipendiary
priests can also be identified. In St John's there was the chapel of the Blessed
Virgin Mary, which was associated with the guild of tailors in the city. In St
Werburgh's there was an altar dedicated to Our Lady and a chapel dedicated to
St Martin and in St Michan's another chapel of the Blessed Virgin. St
Auoden's parish church also had an altar dedicated to St Clare.[16] Such chapels
and guilds were funded by local bequests and from parish funds and as such
they represented the parish community making choices about how the parish at
worship would operate.

11 Gillespie (ed.), *Vestry records of the parish of St John*, 76, 97, RCB, P326/27/3, 26–8.   12 For
the synodal legislation, M. Burrows, 'Fifteenth-century Irish provincial legislation and pastoral
care' in W.J. Shiels and D. Wood (eds), *The churches, Ireland and the Irish: studies in church history
xxv* (Oxford, 1989), 55–68.   13 RCB, P326/27/1–9.   14 BL, Add. MS 4813, ff 31v, 33v–4.
15 M. Clark and R. Refaussé (eds), *Directory of historic Dublin guilds* (Dublin, 1993), 33–40.
16 J. Robinson, 'On the ancient deeds of the parish of St John, Dublin' in *PRIA*, 33 C (1916–17),
190–215: 198, 201, 204, 205; H.F. Twiss, 'Some ancient deeds of the parish of St Werburgh,
Dublin, 1234–1676' in *PRIA*, 35 C (1918–20), 282–315: 292; H.F. Berry (ed.), *Register of wills and
inventories of the diocese of Dublin ... 1457–1483* (Dublin, 1898), 70, 80–1; C. Lennon and J.
Murray (eds), *The Dublin city franchise roll, 1468–1512* (Dublin, 1998), 56, 60; [Aquilla Smith],
'Ancient testaments' in *Miscellany of the Irish Archaeological Society*, i (Dublin, 1846), 106–12:
111–12, translated in Gilbert (ed.), *Anc. recs Dub*, i, 131.

What gave the parish its local identity was the interplay between local communitarian initiatives and the need to obey or evade the hierarchical rules of the Church. The same interplay was characteristic of the reformed parish. As the world of hierarchy insisted that the inhabitants of Dublin's parishes adopt the religion of the secular ruler the local world accepted this with varying degrees of reluctance. The result was a patchwork of responses. By 1618 St John's, St Nicholas Within and St Werburgh's parishes in Dublin had the lowest number of Catholic recusants fined, suggesting that these were the most strongly Protestant parishes.[17] This position would seem to be confirmed by Archbishop Bulkeley's visitation in 1630, which noted that only 10 per cent of householders in St Werburgh's parish were recusant while in St John's 'most of the parishioners are Protestants, and duly frequent their parish church'. In St Nicholas Within while there were 'many Protestants' the majority of the people in the parish were Catholics.[18] The other city parishes were dominated by Catholics. The dominance of Catholics in St Audoen's parish may well account for the fact that by the 1630s they had failed to reshape the church's layout in line with Protestant principles. By 1639 the medieval rood loft was still in place, albeit in a ruinous state, so that, as the archbishop of Dublin observed, people could not see the east window or the communion table. He instructed that the screen was to be removed and replaced with a partition 'such as may not in any wise debar or hinder the congregation of or from beholding the minister officiating at the altar'.[19]

However, the picture is more nuanced than this. Within the predominantly Protestant parishes, St John's had a strong sacramental tradition. In the 1620s, when churchwarden's accounts first become available, the parish of St John celebrated communion on five occasions a year rising to ten by 1633, considerably more than was canonically required. The Laudian reforms of the late 1630s resulted in the chancel being paved and panelled and the communion table being railed in and raised up, and the area around the church improved, all without local opposition. A font was acquired in 1637.[20] Again the St John's clergy before the 1640s all tended, especially in the 1630s, to be of a Laudian persuasion, particularly so since it was a prebendal church of Christ Church cathedral which was the power house of Laudian reform in Dublin. Such men argued for the importance of a symbolic distance between themselves and their parishioners. St Werburgh's, by contrast, was a more godly church where word took precedence over sacrament. In the 1590s communion services were held only in Easter week with three services and a fourth on Whit Sunday. Attendance at communion services to judge from the amounts spent on bread and wine fluctuated a good deal from 2s. 6d., in 1594 to 4s. in 1597. From the

17 J. Meagher (ed.), 'Presentments of recusants in Dublin, 1617–18' in *Reportorium Novum*, 2:2 (1959–60), 269–73: 272–3.   18 M. Ronan (ed.), 'Archbishop Bulkeley's visitation of Dublin, 1630' in *Archivium Hibernicum*, 8 (1941), 56–98: 58, 60–1.   19 Marsh's Library, Dublin, MS Z2.2.24, vol ii, ff.34–5 printed in McCready, 'St Audoen's church, Cornmarket', 202.   20 Gillespie (ed.), *Vestry records of the parish of St John*, 53, 88, 100, 110–11.

amounts mentioned in 1590 it seems that most parishioners received the communion bread and wine on Easter day and that may represent the continuity of the practice of traditional religion whereby one received communion only at Easter.[21] Their minister for most of the early seventeenth century, Joshua Hoyle, was of a strong godly persuasion and was one of those who testified against Archbishop Laud at his trial, accusing him of popish innovations. Clearly local parochial traditions as much as central ecclesiatical control dictated how parochial arrangements would work in the seventeenth century.

By the time the Henrician reforms of Irish Church had begun to bite, in the 1530s, the network of parishes that had to accommodate those reforms in Dublin was already old. Archbishop Alen's description of his diocese in the 1530s described twenty churches in or near the city.[22] Three of these were prebends of Christ Church cathedral and a further six churches were attached to St Patrick's cathedral. One result of the intensification of reform of the Irish Church in the late 1530s and 1540s was that this parochial structure came under scrutiny mainly as a result of the inability of the parishes to support their clergy.[23] The problem, it is fair to note, was not a peculiarly Irish one but rather an urban one and was shared by many English cities that contained a number of small parishes in a small area, reflecting high urban population densities. Early sixteenth-century Bristol, for instance, with which Dublin had strong links, saw significant periods in which some city parishes had no incumbents due to lack of funds.[24] In Dublin George Browne, the archbishop of Dublin, united the extra-mural parishes of St Mary le Dam and St Andrew's with that of St Werburgh.[25] St John's Kilmainham and St Catherine's were united with St James's in 1546.[26] By the middle of the 1550s the old parish of St Olav (or St Tullock) had been united with St John's.[27] The structure thus established changed little until 1660.

For Catholics parochial reform was much more radical. Shortage of clergy together with the difficulties in establishing new churches to replace those now in Protestant use made it impossible to maintain the cumbersome network of medieval parishes. At the 1614 synod of Kilkenny the process of parochial reform for the diocese of Dublin began. Provision was made for the amalgamation of parishes in the case of vacancies, although those who acquired parishes in this way were not deemed to have any title to them.[28] The outcome

21 RCB, P326/27/2/19–20. 22 N.B. White (ed.), 'The *Reportorium Viride* of John Alen, archbishop of Dublin' in *Anal. Hib.*, 10 (1941), 171–222: 180–3. 23 For this question J. Murray, 'The sources of clerical income in the Tudor diocese of Dublin, *c.*1530–1600' in *Archivium Hibernicum*, 46 (1991–2), 139–60. 24 M. Skeeters, *Community and clergy: Bristol and the Reformation, 1530–1570* (Oxford, 1993), 93–4, 98. 25 N.B. White (ed.), *Registrum diocesis Dublinensis* (Dublin, 1959), 5–6. Robert Ware wrongly noted that this was in the time of Queen Elizabeth, BL, Add. MS 4813, f. 39v. 26 J. Morrin (ed.), *Calendar of the patent and close rolls of chancery in Ireland, Henry VIII to 18 Elizabeth*, (Dublin, 1861), 122. 27 *The Irish fiants of the Tudor sovereigns*, 4 vols (Dublin, 1994) Edward VI, no. 1108; Philip & Mary, no. 6. 28 *Constitutiones provinciales et synodales ecclesiae metropolitane et primatialis Dubliniensis* (n.p., 1770), 9–10.

of this can only be guessed at since record keeping was not a major preoccupation of early seventeenth-century Catholicism. On the basis of the 1630 report by the Church of Ireland primate, Archbishop Bulkeley, on the location of Mass houses, it seems that St John's and St Michael's were united and an entry in the 'per obitum' volumes implies that St Werburgh's was also united to St John's. Such an arrangement may have been one of convenience as much as anything else. The 'per obitum' volumes mention separate parishes of St Audoen's and St Michan's. The fate of the extra mural parishes seems to be revealed by another entry in the 'per obitum' volumes, which states that by 1663 the Catholic parish of St Nicholas Without included the older extramural parishes of SS Brigid, Kevin and Peter and Paul. It seems highly likely that most of the extramural parishes were united into that of St Nicholas with St Catherine and St James as a second parish.[29] Certainly by 1633 one Catholic priest in the city believed that the ten medieval parishes had now been reduced to five, two of which were inside the walls.[30]

A second implication of the coming of reform in the 1530s was that the administrative structure that had developed in the late medieval parishes now lay under the control of the established Church. The Catholic parish was recognised in the 1614 decrees of the synod of Kilkenny as essentially a pastoral unit in which the sacraments were administered and the faithful taught the catechism, especially the Creed and the Lord's Prayer, on holy days and as the priest moved around his parish.[31] From at least the middle of the fifteenth century, and probably earlier, the Dublin parochial system utilised the idea of proctors or churchwardens to manage parochial assets. Proctors first appear in the St Werburgh parish deeds by 1454 and in the St John's parish deeds by 1467 while St Mary le Dam had proctors by 1474. St Michael's had proctors by the 1490s.[32] These men had the function of managing the parochial property and acted as trustees for the parish goods.[33] By the early seventeenth century this was an important role although the size of parish estates, and hence the workload in managing them, might vary considerably. In the case of the parish of St John the income of the parish estate more than covered normal parochial expenses, the salary of the minister being raised by parish cess. The churchwardens were, in a real sense, the embodiment of the parish and it was they who spoke on its behalf at episcopal visitations. If the parish became involved in legal action over debt or other matters the process was carried on in the name of the churchwardens.[34] The Church of Ireland parish as an administrative

29 N. Donnelly (ed.), 'The "per obitum" volumes in the Vatican *archivo*' in *Archivium Hibernicum*, I (1912), 28–38: 31, 32, 33–4, 35.   **30** P. Harris, *The excommunication published by the lord archbishop of Dublin, Thomas Fleming* (Dublin, 1633), 47.   **31** *Constitutiones*, 10–12.   **32** Twiss, 'Ancient deeds of the parish of St Werburgh', 288–9; Robinson, 'Ancient deeds of the parish of St John', 200; Berry (ed.), *Wills and inventories*, 88; Lennon and Murray (eds), *Dublin city franchise roll*, 66.   **33** A. Empey, 'The layperson in the parish: the medieval inheritance' in R. Gillespie and W.G. Neely (eds), *The laity and the Church of Ireland, 1000–2000: all sorts and conditions* (Dublin, 2002), 7–48: 25–31.   **34** For example NAI, RC6/1, p. 104, 106 for cases in chancery.

unit linked to a pastoral one, and underpinned by the sense of a local community, was clearly of considerable importance in the development of a local government structure in sixteenth- and seventeenth-century Dublin.

From the 1570s the corporation of Dublin began to make use of this structure. In 1573, for instance, the corporation declared that chains, ropes and ladders were to be kept in each parish church in case of fire, the cess for this 'to be made by the oversight of the chief in every parish'.[35] Similar regulations were enacted in 1593 requiring each parish to keep six buckets and two ladders in the parish church in case of fire.[36] Whether or not this was judged to be a failure is not clear but certainly by the late 1590s the organising unit for fire prevention had become the ward.[37] In the early seventeenth century the parish re-emerged as an organisational unit. Parliament required it to look after roads that ran through it and Dublin corporation assigned the role of scavanging to the parishes.[38] Further fire-fighting duties were also assigned to the parishes in 1620 and by the 1630s buckets and ladders were normal parochial property.[39] Perhaps more significantly in 1631 the parish became responsible for its own poor.[40] By 1636 St Audoen's parish was maintaining twelve poor and in 1644 St John's marked out its own poor by issuing badges.[41] This meant not only raising a poor cess but also appointing a beadle to administer poor relief. It also meant contributing at parish level to the house of correction maintained by the corporation.[42] This practice of using the parish as a unit of local government had important repercussions for its inhabitants. It was hardly a new idea. In the late sixteenth century on the manor of Crumlin, close to the city, the manor court rather than the parishioners had elected the churchwardens for the parish, suggesting that the office was seen as more than simply an ecclesiastical one.[43] Within early seventeenth-century Dublin the churchwardens, as brokers between the world of government and the parish, inevitably learnt a good deal about the priorities of Dublin castle or the city corporation. Inevitably this translated into a greater understanding of the art of managing power within their own communities through defining the rights and obligations of those living the parish. In this way a political and social elite was formed and, since the officials were elected each year, reformed on a regular basis.

The trend of using the parish as a local government unit after the Reformation has been seen by some historians as part of a process of turning the parish from a religious community into a branch of government. However, in the Irish context, at least, this is something of an exaggeration. Parishes were reluctant to become involved in functions that they did not see as part of their

---

35 Gilbert (ed.), *Anc. recs Dub*, ii, 79.   36 Ibid., ii, 253–4.   37 Ibid., ii, 297, 301, 364.   38 11, 12 & 13 Jas I c. 7; Gilbert (ed.), *Anc, recs Dub*, iii, 312.   39 Gilbert (ed.), *Anc. recs Dub*, iii, 128–9, 160–1; Marsh's Library, Dublin, MS Z2.2.24, vol i, f. 4.   40 Gilbert (ed.), *Anc. recs Dub*, iii , 250–1.   41 Marsh's Library, Dublin, MS Z2.2.24, vol ii, f. 4; Gillespie (ed.), *Vestry records of the parish of St John*, 167.   42 Gilbert (ed.), *Anc. recs Dub*, iii, 293–4.   43 E. Curtis (ed.), 'The court book of Esker and Crumlin' in *JRSAI*, 55 (1930), 137–49: 148.

core activity. In the case of poor relief the absence of central legislation in Ireland throughout the sixteenth and early seventeenth centuries meant that parishes involved themselves little in what might have been seen as Christian charity. Even in the mid-1630s when Dublin corporation began to seize the initiative in this area the parishes moved only slowly in the appointment of parish beadles and overseers of the poor. Even when, as in the case of the parish of St John, they did appoint parochial officers to deal with the problem, the churchwardens' accounts do not record any expenditure relating to the poor, which suggests that the initiatives were probably realised only on paper. The Dublin churchwardens' accounts suggest that the parish continued to be primarily a unit of pastoral care with much larger sums being spent on the maintenance of the church fabric than on these additional duties.

What this process of attempting to use ecclesiastical units for civil adminis-tration may suggest is that even church business was becoming increasingly bureaucratic. The move from personal tithes to parochial rates after 1616, as a way of funding the clergy, required the making and keeping of cess lists and the collection of money not by clergy but by church officials. At a more formal ecclesiastical level the canons of 1634 required that parishes keep registers of baptisms, marriages and burials. These were to be kept by the minister and churchwardens and churchwardens were required to prepare formal accounts of their expenditures.[44] All this seems to have had some effect. The earliest parish register for Dublin, that of St John's, begins in 1619 but in the late 1620s and early 1630s many parishes acquired registers for the first time. St Werburgh's purchased a register in 1627 and by the early 1630s St Michan's, St Audoen's, St Nicholas Without and St Bride's all had registers. By the late 1630s St Catherine's also kept a register.[45] Churchwarden's accounts appear more sporadically. While St Werburgh's has a number of accounts for the late sixteenth century and St John's a fairly complete set from 1619, others were less diligent.[46] St Audoen's, for instance, complained in 1640 that the parish could find no set of churchwarden's accounts at all and asked for a special commission to investigate the situation.[47] In the case of parish of St John's it is possible to see administrative improvements taking place over the seventeenth century. In the 1620s two wardens were elected each year and it was rare for the same person to hold the office twice. In the 1630s, however, a custom developed of each warden serving two terms and retiring in rotation so as to maintain conti-nuity of office over a number of years.[48] All this may explain why the Dublin

44 Bray (ed.), *Anglican canons*, 508–9, 525. **45** RCB, P326/1/21 for the purchase of a register 'to write christenings and burials in'; J. Mills (ed.), *Registers of the parish of St John the Evangelist, Dublin, 1619–99* (Dublin, 1906, rpt Dublin, 2000), iv. **46** RCB, P326/27/1; Gillespie (ed.), *Vestry records of the parish of St John*. **47** C.T. McCready, 'St Audoen's church, Cornmarket' in *Irish Builder*, 28 (1886), 203. **48** For a list of the wardens see Catherine Anderson, 'The evolution of the parish of St John the Evangelist, Dublin, 1600–1700', unpublished MA (NUI Maynooth, 1997), appendix 1.

parishes not only survived the disestablishment of the state church in 1647 but, in fact, thrived on it, with a number of vestry books, such as that for St Catherine's commencing for the first time in the 1650s. Whatever about religious practice the parish had become an important social and administrative unit which helped ensure stability.

Unfortunately a great deal of the documentation, which this increasing bureaucratization of the parish in the late sixteenth and early seventeenth centuries produced, has disappeared, or in some cases was possibly never kept. Some evidence has survived from St Werburgh's but it is only in the case of St John's that the evidence is good enough to begin to reconstruct not only the parish at prayer but also the churchwardens balancing the parish accounts. St John's was a well-established parish in the core of the medieval city. On the basis of the poll tax returns of 1660 it had the third highest population total of the city, notwithstanding its small size, being outstripped only by the larger suburban parishes of St Catherine and St Michan.[49] The population structure of the parish was relatively stable. On the basis of the entries in the parish register there were 280 baptisms in the 1620s with 248 burials. In the 1630s the balance was 391 baptisms against 462 burials. As a result the population of the parish was largely reproducing itself and did not had to rely, as many larger English towns did, on significant immigration for growth in population. Considerable stability in the population is also suggested by a comparison of names on the cess lists with the previous list. Of the 159 names on the cess list of 1626 some 98, or 61 per cent, had been on the previous list of 1622. Again of the 255 names on the 1640 cess list 210, or 83 per cent, had been on the list of 1638. Such limited migration fields, many only within the city, created personal networks based on kinship, neighbourliness and mutual interest which helped to create and perpetuate attachments to the parish community. As a parish St John's was not particularly rich and in the 1647 cess list for the Cromwellian army it was one of the poorest of the Dublin parishes on the basis of cess paid per head of population.[50] However, it did have a number of high status residents and a considerable group of merchants and those in the middle of the social order. In the 1620s about a quarter of those paying the parish cess were described as gentlemen or had titles but about half the parish were engaged in the provision of food or drink. Within the parish the cess lists do not suggest any clustering of wealth with a rough equation between the percentage of population resident in the street and the percentage of cess paid.

The evidence of the St John's vestry records allows some reconstruction of the world of those who operated the parochial administrative system. At an initial glance a relatively small number of individuals within a parish with a large Protestant population took an active interest in parish affairs. On the

---

49 S. Pender (ed.), *A census of Ireland, c. 1659* (Dublin, 1939), 373.   **50** Dublin City Archives, Pearse Street, MR/16, pp 11–14.

evidence of the signatures at the twenty-one Easter vestry meetings for which records survive from 1606 to 1641 the attendance never rose above twelve people, the mean being just over nine. This may point to the emergence of a closed vestry. However, these figures are derived from signatures appended to the resolution for the appointment of churchwardens and therefore may under-state considerably the participation rates. Those who were illiterate, for instance, may have been omitted although there are some examples of marks rather than signatures on the lists. Again signatures may not be a complete attendance list but simply a random selection of persons willing to witness the appointment. This suggestion finds some support in the fact that few signa-tures appear more than once testifying to the appointments. Of almost ninety individuals who witnessed the churchwardens' appointments before 1641 only twenty appear more than twice the most active being William Plunkett, who also wrote most of the resolutions in the vestry book suggesting that he acted as clerk to the vestry, and Jeremy Bowden.

Given these reservations a better measure of how the parish elite was composed may be the collective biographies of those who served as parochial officials, churchwardens, auditors of the parish accounts, compilers of the parish cess lists and from the 1630s sidesmen and overseers of the poor. In the case of St John's parish 82 individuals can be identified as holding these offices in the early seventeenth century. In the main these represented neither the very rich nor the very poor. In the sixteenth century the office of churchwarden had been dominated by merchants. Of the 22 pre-1600 churchwardens whose occupations can be recovered, 14 were merchants. The remainder included two fishermen, a pewterer, a lawyer and a master gunner. Only one described himself as a gentleman.[51] In the early seventeenth century, and using the wider measure of parish officers, in 50 cases the occupation of the office holders can be determined either from references in the vestry records or in the freemen's rolls. About half of these were divided equally between gentlemen and merchants. The remainder were divided between bakers (6), tailors (4), victuallers (4), administrators (4), shoemakers (3), smiths (2) and one brewer, chandler and goldsmith. Most of these were literate, although a few such as Thomas Dongan, churchwarden from 1635 to 1637, or the baker and cesser of the parish in 1626 Thomas Jacob, were not. These were a small minority and the high level of literacy among parochial officials points to their origins among the 'middling sort' of the inhabitants of the parish.

It is difficult to understand the attitudes of those who accepted parochial offices towards their positions. On the one hand William Plunkett, prothonotary of the court of common pleas since 1627, was very active in parochial administration notwithstanding that his father was Catholic.[52] From

51 Anderson, 'The evolution of the parish of St John', appendix 1. 52 TCD, MS 809, ff 318–8v; C. Lennon, *The lords of Dublin in the age of reformation* (Dublin, 1989), 263. He was admitted member of Kings Inns in 1636: E. Keane, P.B. Eustace, T.U. Sadlier (eds), *Kings Inns*

serving as churchwarden in 1621–2 in St John's parish he occupied a parochial position as cessor every year to 1641. In addition the records of most of the vestry proceedings are recorded in his hand.[53] It may be that given the family's long association with the parish that such a level of activity was expected. By contrast William Stoughton who served as churchwarden in 1631–2 had no previous parochial involvement, despite living in the parish since at least 1626, and took no further interest in parish affairs until he was buried in the parish churchyard in 1642.[54] There were many grades of involvement between these two positions. For some, parochial office was the first stage to involvement in wider civic affairs. Thomas Evans, for example, began his political career as churchwarden of St John's in 1618–19. He served as auditor of the parish accounts almost every year until his death. Building on this parochial experience he became an alderman and finally mayor in 1626–7 and again in 1630–1 and in 1632 he was treasurer of the city. By 1634 he was dead but his mantle had fallen on his nephew the merchant William Smith who used the same parochial base for political advancement. He was admitted free of the city in 1628 and in 1633–5 served as churchwarden of St John's and auditor of the parish accounts each year thereafter. In 1636 he became deputy alderman and sheriff of the city and in 1638 became alderman and finally mayor in 1642–7.

For such people parochial office was a pathway to others things. For others civic office seems to have been a spur to accept parochial duty. The tailor Alderman Richard Wiggins, for instance, was admitted free of the city in 1600 and was certainly living in Fishamble Street in the first surviving cess roll of St John's parish, yet he took little interest in parochial affairs. Rather he became involved in the affairs of the city being sheriff in 1611, alderman in 1617, mayor in 1622–3 and treasurer in 1624.[55] After discharging his civic responsibilities he turned his attention to his parish, acting as auditor of the parish accounts in 1627, 1628 and 1631 and cesser in 1634. In this case the exercise of civic office seems to have been a spur to accept local office. From another perspective holding parochial office may have been seen as a way into local society for the recently arrived. The goldsmith William Cook was churchwarden of St John's in 1639–41 yet he had only become free of the city in 1638 and Oates Crowder who became free in 1638 was sidesman in St John's in 1639–40. Again the innkeeper John March was churchwarden in St John's in 1637–8 in the same year that he was admitted free in the city. This may have been a particularly important way of making contacts in the 1630s as migration into the city speeded up since the gap between admission to freedom and parochial office seems to have shortened significantly in that decade.

One problem which this parochial elite, motivated to office by many diverse concerns, had to grapple with was how it would administer a parish which was

---

admission papers (Dublin, 1982), 404.   **53** Gillespie (ed.), *Vestry records of the parish of St John*, 17. **54** Mills (ed.), *Registers*, 48.   **55** Gilbert (ed.), *Anc. recs Dub*, iii, 15, 83, 146, 149.

often religiously divided. To maintain credibility it was necessary to support that elite on as inclusive a basis as possible. Words such as 'consent' and 'assent' are characteristic of the language of the vestry minutes in the early seventeenth century. This does not mean that all were equal before the vestry for it is clear that some of the more senior offices were reserved for worshiping members of the Church of Ireland and those with enough substance to support the office. Given the need for a broad support base it is hardly surprising, therefore, that Catholics should appear among the officers of the parish from time to time. Catholics within the city did not reject parish churches at the Reformation. They still had powerful local and familial associations with them and the process by which they removed themselves from the parish is better thought of as one of progressive disengagement from the later sixteenth century until the 1660s. This was possible because before the canons of 1634 there were no requirements that churchwardens or sidesmen should take any religious oaths marking them out as Protestants and while such requirements were introduced in 1634 they seem to have been ineffective before 1660. James Bellew, one of the auditors of the St John's parish accounts for 1603 was strongly Catholic in his outlook and was fined in the mandates controversy of 1605.[56] Similarly the baker Patrick English who was also fined during the mandates controversy and discharged from his office as sheriff paying £40 in 1613, presumably for his Catholicism, appears as a cessor in St John's parish in 1622, a year before his death.[57] In some cases the Catholicism of the officeholders may have been less marked. One example may be Alderman Richard Browne, churchwarden of St John's in 1638–40, who in 1642 was deprived of his position on the aldermanic bench because of his sympathies with the Catholic rebels.[58] While others may not have been practising Catholics they certainly had strong contacts in that world. William Plunkett, St John's churchwarden in 1621–2 and one of the most active members in the parish, was a son of Thomas Plunkett, the well-known recusant who lived in Fishamble Street.[59] Similarly in 1642 Richard Duff, the son of a former cessor in St John's parish and later churchwarden of St Audoen's, and his mother moved with considerable ease among the houses of the Catholic gentry of Dublin and Louth who were then in rebellion suggesting a well established set of contacts.[60]

It seems clear that at parish level religious boundaries were often more fluid than they may at first appear. While parish churches may have now been in the hands of the Church of Ireland that did not mean that they could no longer articulate a sense of local identity. The parish graveyard, after all, still continued to be the final resting place of all. A case in point may the

56 Lennon, *Lords of Dublin*, 231. **57** Historical Manuscripts Commission, *Report on the manuscripts of the earl of Egmont* 2 vols (London, 1905–9), i, 30–1; Gilbert (ed.), *Anc. recs Dub*, iii, 43. In 1622 he also reappears as auditor to the city, Gilbert (ed.), *Anc. recs Dub*, iii, 150, 162. **58** Gilbert (ed.), *Anc. recs Dub*, iii, 393. **59** Lennon, *Lords of Dublin*, 263. **60** TCD, MS 834, f. 24.

relationship between the parish church of St Audoen and the guild of St Anne, which maintained its guild chapel in the parish church. In the sixteenth century such guilds had not been dissolved, as they were in England and St Anne's guild continued as an overtly Catholic body until its dissolution in 1630s.[61] Despite this it continued to contribute to the maintenance of the fabric of the now Church of Ireland church. The payment of £13. 6s. 8d. a year to the Church of Ireland clergyman may have been the result of pressure on the guild by the Dublin Castle administration but much more difficult to explain are the annual payments to the organist and choristers for singing in the church and for mending the organs.[62] These are unlikely to have been covert payments to Catholics since when the singing men and organist are identified they were from Christ Church cathedral. Moreover the guild also contributed to repair works in the church in 1605 and again during a major building campaign in the early 1630s it was noted that St Anne's guild 'have before contributed largely to the reparacion of that church'.[63] All this suggests a more complex relationship between the urban parish church and those living in the parish than simply a confessional one, issues of local identity and common societal bonds being at least as important as the issues of confessional division before the outbreak of rebellion in 1641.

To dismiss the reformed parish in Dublin as simply a vehicle for Protestant pastoral care or as an agency for the workings of central government would be a mistake. Not only did it fulfil administrative roles for the local community but it also helped to articulate a sense of local identity that led to recusants, and later dissenters, serving in minor parochial offices. Equally it would be a mistake to assume that the parish lay at the heart of the lives of all its members. Those who lived in the Dublin parishes had interests beyond their parishes that required their attention. William Cook, the churchwarden of St John's, 1639–41, began life as a goldsmith but by 1641 had acquired lands on lease at Powerscourt.[64] Again Anthony Gayton, a sidesman in St John's parish in 1640–1 and churchwarden the following year, had property in Kilmainham from which he drew his income in 1641 and William Stoughton, churchwarden in 1631–2 had land in the same area.[65] Most spectacularly William Plunkett held lands in Cos. Dublin, Meath, Louth, Wexford and Longford which he reckoned brought in rents of £500 a year in 1641.[66] Moreover one did not necessarily spend one's life in the same parish. Tady Duff, for instance, who

61 C. Lennon, 'Chantries in the Irish Reformation: the case of St Anne's guild, Dublin, 1550–1630' in R.V. Comerford, M. Cullen, J.R. Hill and C. Lennon (eds), *Religion, conflict and coexistence in Ireland* (Dublin, 1990), 6–25. 62 RIA, MS 12 D 1, pp 46, 51, 58, 64. 63 RIA, MS 12 D 1, p. 45; Marsh's Library, MS Z2.2.24, ii, ff 16–17. Again the Catholic corporation of Dublin contributed significantly to the repair of the Protestant Christ Church cathedral in the late sixteenth century, R. Gillespie, 'The shaping of reform, 1558–1625' in K. Milne (ed.), *Christ Church cathedral, Dublin: a history* (Dublin, 2000), 174–94: 178–9. 64 TCD, MS 809, f. 263. 65 TCD, MS 810, f. 146; PRONI, D 430/135. 66 TCD, MS 809, ff 318–8v; R.C. Simington (ed.), *The Civil Survey: vii, Co. Dublin* (Dublin, 1945), 112, 114–15.

appears as a cesser in St John's parish in 1622 was in living in St Audoen's by 1636.[67] On a wider scale Derrick Hubberts, the St John's churchwarden in 1618–19 later acquired land at Holmpatrick where he was murdered in 1641.[68] However, the parish did have a part to play in constructing local social relationships. When Jeremy Bowden, the churchwarden of St John's from 1632 to 1634 and a frequent auditor of parish accounts and cesser of the parish, died childless in 1650 he left most of his property to his godson but found a legacy for the daughters of William Smith who had been churchwarden from 1633 to 1635.[69] Again when William Billey, churchwarden in 1624–5 died it was Elizabeth Leadbetter, wife of Edmund the churchwarden in 1631–2, who witnessed his will.[70] Again marriage patterns were influenced by parochial geographies and some of those who held office in St John's married local girls. Thomas Ellis, cesser in 1629, for instance, married Susan Proudfoot, daughter of Richard who had been churchwarden in 1606–7, and the cessor for 1634, William Samon, in 1630 had married the widow of Richard Tenbridge who was living in the parish in 1622.[71] Parochial widows may have been seen as a good catch since Jeremy Simpson, churchwarden in 1634–5, married the widow of Thomas Neale, a victualler in the parish, in 1631.[72] It is difficult to be sure how widespread this practice was because of the late date of the surviving marriage registers.

The early modern Dublin parish was a multifunctional institution, at once spatial and administrative but also providing one social horizon within which the lives of Dubliners of a number of confessional positions could be lived out in the early modern world. Not only did it provide a framework for the organisation of a social world that was constantly in motion but it also provided a way in which contemporaries could learn the process of shaping the rights and obligations that were necessary for the working of that world. The community of the parish was one of the most central institutions in the lives of early modern Dubliners.

67 Marsh's Library, Dublin, MS Z2.2.24, vol ii, ff 3,6. **68** I am grateful to Maighréad Ní Mhurchadha for this information. **69** NLI, GO MS 290, p. 33. **70** Ibid., p. 25. **71** Mills (ed.), *Registers*, 8, 18. Susan seems to have predeceased him and he married again. His second wife survived him, TCD, MS 810, f. 138. **72** Mills (ed.), *Registers*, 19. Thomas in 1620 cess list.

Kildare Hall, the countess of Kildare's patronage of the Jesuits, and the liturgical setting of Catholic worship in early seventeenth-century Dublin

ROLF LOEBER AND MAGDA STOUTHAMER-LOEBER

The liturgical setting of Catholic worship in chapels and parish churches in early seventeenth- century Dublin is a neglected study. Among Dublin's lost ecclesiastical architecture is Kildare Hall, with its chapel, novitiate and college built for the Jesuits, which opened in 1628. The interior of its main chapel provided a novel liturgical setting for Catholic worship, albeit in an extra-parochial context, which even in England had few parallels. This essay details the role of the countess of Kildare in the founding of the Jesuit house in Dublin, in the context of the increasingly successful Counter-Reformation missions of continental Catholic religious orders in Dublin, which were concentrated in the parish of St Audoen's in Dublin. The essay identifies the location of Kildare Hall, and uses several contemporary descriptions to recon-struct the chapel's interior. The novel liturgical setting of Catholic worship in Kildare Hall is compared with that of Dublin parish churches and the Counter-Reformation chapels founded by other orders which established themselves in Dublin during the first decades of the seventeenth century.

THE COUNTESS OF KILDARE AS THE MOTHER OF THE SOCIETY OF JESUS IN IRELAND

In 1645, the Superior of the Jesuit Irish Mission, the Jesuit, Robert Nugent, honoured Elizabeth, countess of Kildare, as 'truly the mother of our society in this realm [of Ireland]' (*Hoec vere erate mater Societatis nostrae in hoc Regno*),[1] a title which she well deserved, having been a protector of the Jesuits in Ireland

---

1 F.M. O'Donoghue, 'The Jesuit mission in Ireland, 1598–1651', unpublished PhD (Catholic University of America, 1982), 273.

for several decades in an age of frequent persecutions. The countess was the daughter of Christopher Nugent, 14th Baron Delvin, and presumably spent her childhood at Cloneen in Co. Westmeath, the principal seat of the Nugents. The Nugents were of Anglo-Norman stock and owned large tracts of land between the Pale and the territories of the Gaelic lords in the west of Ireland.[2] Loyalty to the crown, a firm adherence to Catholicism, and an ability to speak and read Gaelic were characteristic of most of the generations of Nugents in the sixteenth and early seventeenth centuries.[3] The countess's brother, Richard, 10th Baron Delvin, was created 1st earl of Westmeath in 1621 and became an important spokesman for Catholic interests in Ireland.[4]

Sometime after 1600, Elizabeth Nugent, by dispensation of the pope, married her cousin Gerald Fitzgerald, 14th earl of Kildare.[5] They shared the same grandfather, Gerald Fitzgerald, the 'wizard' 11th earl of Kildare, whose daughter had married the 14th Baron Delvin.[6] The countess's patronage of the Jesuits can best be understood in the context of a tradition on the Kildare side of her family, of endowing religious establishments, such as the now lost chantry chapel (St Mary's, popularly known as 'the earl of Kildare's chapel') in Christ Church cathedral, Dublin, and the 'College of the Blessed Virgin Mary of Maynooth' with its chapel, 'built in a most beautiful form' in the sixteenth century.[7] Because of the death of three earls in rapid succession, the Kildare estate was burdened for over thirty years with three jointures, leaving little income for the male heir.[8] When Elizabeth Nugent married the 14th earl of Kildare, he was too poor to provide his bride with a dower. He died in 1612, leaving her with an infant son.[9]

The rearing of this son in the Catholic faith was not only an issue for the countess, but for the Jesuits as well. The missionary activities of the Jesuits aimed to prevent the conversion of Catholics heirs to the Protestant faith, and to dissuade individuals from going to Protestant services as a first step towards

---

2 A. Gwynn and R.N. Hadcock, *Medieval religious houses, Ireland* (London, 1988), 106; H.G. Leask, *Fore, Co. Westmeath* (Dublin, [1959]). 3 F.X. Martin, *Friar Nugent: a study of Frances Lavallin Nugent, 1569–1635, agent of the Counter-Reformation* (Rome-London, 1962), 4; V. Gibbs and H.A. Doubleday (eds), *The complete peerage* (London, 1916), iv, 4, 17 n.c., 6 Sept. 1591, Christopher Nugent to Lord Burghley; M. Caball, *Poets and politic: reaction and continuity in Irish poetry, 1558–1625* (Cork, 1998), 66–7. 4 A. Clarke, *The Graces, 1625–41* (Dundalk, 1968), 9ff. 5 She is not to be confused with her contemporary, Frances, countess of Kildare (d. 1628), wife of Henry Fitzgerald, 12th earl of Kildare. 6 The 11th earl of Kildare left in his will to his daughter, Lady Delvin, 'the fourth best suit of hangings of tapestry or arras'. See B. FitzGerald, *The Geraldines: an experiment in Irish government, 1169–1601* (London, 1951), 299. 7 R. Loeber, 'Sculptured memorials to the dead in early seventeenth-century Ireland: a survey from *Monumenta Eblanae* and other sources' in *PRIA*, 81C (1981), 267–93: 282–3; Duke of Leinster, 'Maynooth Castle' in *Journal of the Kildare Archaeological Society*, 1 (1891–5), 223–39: 224; M.A. Lyons, *Church and society in County Kildare, c.1470–1547* (Dublin, 2000), 88–95. 8 V. Treadwell, *Buckingham and Ireland, 1616–1628* (Dublin, 1998), 117–18. 9 Marquis of Kildare, *The earls of Kildare, and their ancestors: from 1057 to 1773* (Dublin, 1858), 231–2; Marquis of Kildare, *The earls of Kildare, and their ancestors: from 1057 to 1773. Addenda* (Dublin, 1862), 332, 354–5, 359.

encouraging them to convert from Protestantism to the Catholic faith.[10] After the demise of the houses of Desmond in Munster and Tyrone in Ulster at the end of the sixteenth century, the key nobility to be secured were the earls of Ormond, Clanricarde and Kildare, and their heirs. Among the early prose-lytising successes of the Jesuits was the conversion of Ulick Burke, third earl of Clanricarde in 1605, Thomas, 10th earl of Ormond (d. 1614), Theobald Butler, Lord Ormond's heir, and Walter Butler of Kilcash, 11th earl of Ormond (d. 1633).[11]

When the 14th earl of Kildare married Elizabeth Nugent, he had found a strong Catholic woman ready to educate her son in the Catholic faith. In 1612 she was granted her son's wardship for five years and one-third of the revenue of the Kildare estates.[12] David Rothe, Catholic bishop of Ossory, dedicated his book on St Brigid (*Brigida thaumaturga,siue dissertation*), published in Paris in 1620, to the countess's son, which indicates that he was seen as a Catholic patron. However, he died in that year, depriving the countess of part of the income of the Kildare estate. Charles I arbitrated the legal proceedings about the Kildare lands in 1621, and assigned one-third of the newly-delimited Kildare estate as a jointure for the dowager countess during the minority of her nephew, the 16th earl. The most valuable of these properties was the manor of Kilkea in south Kildare, which she eventually would lease to the Jesuits.[13] Thus, from 1621 onwards the countess's finances were more firmly established. She soon freed funds to support the activities of the Jesuits in Dublin.[14]

THE RE-ESTABLISHMENT OF RELIGIOUS ORDERS IN DUBLIN

The re-establishment of religious orders in Ireland (and the introduction of the new order of the Jesuits) was greatly aided by changes in religious toleration resulting from English political relations with Spain and France during the first quarter of the seventeenth century. This has been well-documented in recent historical writings.[15] As a result of these international political changes,

---

10 O'Donoghue, 'Jesuit mission', 87.   **11** Ibid., 36; D. Edwards, *The Ormond lordship in County Kilkenny, 1515–1642* (Dublin, 2003), 242, 273.   **12** *Acts of the Privy Council*, 1613–14, 65–6, 100; *Calendar of Patent Rolls, Ireland, James I* (Dublin, 1830, rept Dublin, 1966) 239, 249; see also K.W. Nicholls, 'Irishwomen and property in the sixteenth century' in M. MacCurtain and M. O'Dowd (eds), *Women in early modern Ireland* (Dublin, 1991), 17–31; M.A. Lyons, 'Lay female piety and church patronage in late medieval Ireland' in B. Bradshaw and D. Keogh (eds), *Christianity in Ireland: revisiting the story* (Dublin, 2002), 57–75.   **13** Marquis of Kildare, *Earls of Kildare*, 232–3; *Cal. pat. rolls Ire., Jas. I*, 501, 507.   **14** Evidence for this can be found in *Acts of the Privy Council*, 1613–14, 65–6, 100; ibid., 1617–19, 265; Marquis of Kildare, *Earls of Kildare*, 241. For the countess lending money to others in 1628, 1635, and 1639, see J. Ohlmeyer and É. Ó Ciardha, *The Irish statute staple books, 1596–1687* (Dublin, 1998), under nos. 1496, 2023, and 2761.   **15** C. Lennon, *The lords of Dublin in the age of reformation* (Blackrock, 1989), 166–205; A. Ford, *The Protestant Reformation in Ireland, 1590–1641* (Dublin, 1997), passim; K.S. Bottigheimer and U. Lotz-Heumann, 'The Irish Reformation in European perspective' in *Archive for Reformation*

religious orders were able to establish Catholic chapels in Dublin independent of the Catholic parish system. The orders also promoted, following the Tridentine reforms, strict religious practices, and introduced confessions and regular sermons. Since returning orders were unable to occupy their old abbeys and priories in the city, which as a result of the suppression of the monasteries under Henry VIII and Elizabeth I had been transferred into private hands, the religious orders had to find new locations for their missionary establishments.

Seven religious orders are known to have established themselves in Dublin in the 1620s. In addition, parochial chapels were open for Catholic worship. Protestants expressed concerns about the increased presence of the religious orders in Dublin and the establishment of parochial and other chapels, with Sir John Bingley reporting fourteen Mass houses in Dublin in 1629.[16] The earliest order to return to Dublin was the Franciscans, who built a chapel in 1615 in Cook Street, close to Merchant's Quay, where the present friary stands. According to a contemporary description, its interior contained a pulpit and religious paintings.[17] The Dominicans were re-established in Dublin in 1622. Four years later, they included a prior, three priests and three students (novices) and one lay brother, at their residence in Cook Street.[18] In 1624 a Capuchin house was founded in Thomas Street, outside of Newgate, by Fr Francis Nugent, a relative of the countess of Kildare.[19] However, this order probably moved to Bridge Street where their building later became known as St Stephen's Hall. A description of 1635, when it had been taken over by Trinity College, indicates that it had space for eighteen scholars in its college and that there was a hall annexed, which was referred to as a 'pretty little chapel or chamber'.[20] A nunnery of encloistered Poor Clares, which included a niece of the countess of Kildare, was established in 1625 (one source states 1629), and was in all likelihood situated near the Newgate.[21] The residence of the Augustinan friars was probably founded on the north bank of the Liffey at the

History (1998), 313–53; H.F. Kearney, 'Ecclesiastical politics and the Counter-Reformation in Ireland, 1618–1648' in *Journal of Ecclesiastical History*, 11 (1960), 202–12. **16** *Cal. S.P. Ire.*, *1625–32*, 401, 442; Historical Manuscripts Commission, *12th Report* (London, 1890), *App. I*, 361. **17** Historical Manuscripts Commission, *Report on the Franciscan manuscripts* (London, 1906), 17; Gwynn and Hadcock, *Medieval religious houses*, 248–9. **18** T.S. Flynn, *The Irish Dominicans, 1536–1641* (Dublin, 1993), 160. The residence of the Dominicans may have been in the vicinity of Bridge Street (Flynn, *Irish Dominicans*, 264 n. 6), but another source places the Dominicans in Cooke Street; this chapel apparently became the Catholic parish church of St Audoen's in the late seventeenth century. See A. Coleman, *The ancient Dominican foundations in Ireland* (Dundalk, 1902), 24–5. **19** Martin, *Friar Nugent*, 217 and ff. **20** E. Hawkins (ed.), *Sir William Brereton: travels in Holland, the United Provinces, England, Scotland, and Ireland, 1634–5* (London, 1844), 143. **21** Ware MS (Dublin Public Library, Pearse St, Gilbert MS 169), f. 198; P. Guilday, *The English Catholic refugees on the continent, 1558–1795* (London, 1914, reprint 1969), 298; P. Kilroy 'Women and the Reformation in seventeenth-century Ireland' in M. MacCurtain and M. O'Dowd (eds), *Women in early modern Ireland* (Dublin, 1991), 170–97: 190; T. Concannon, *The Poor Clares in Ireland (AD 1629–AD 1929)* (Dublin, 1929), 10–11.

current Arran Quay.[22] The Discalced Carmelites came to Dublin in 1625, where they founded a novitiate between Cooke Street and Merchant Quay.[23] The superior of this order reported in 1629 that Catholic ecclesiastics had been publicly performing their sacred duties since 1628, and had places with open doors where they preached and celebrated Mass without being molested. The Carmelites lived in a rented house, and included twenty students and novices. Their church was sufficiently large to allow processions including that of the Blessed Sacrament.[24] Most of the religious orders had their residences in the parish of St Audoen's.

Before describing the Jesuits' Kildare Hall, it is useful to review what is known about the appearance of chapels in Dublin. None of the Catholic churches of the seventeenth century in the city has survived. The Capuchin house in Bridge Street consisted of two houses 'knocked into one house of residence'.[25] The appearance of the other establishments is less clear, other than that they were often set back from the street, or were hidden by domestic facades. In that sense, there were remarkable similarities between Catholic churches in the cities of Dublin and Amsterdam, where one example survives practically unchanged. In order to create space for a Catholic congregation in Amsterdam the central part of a house's upper floors were cut through to make a very tall galleried hall for religious service. One of these churches, called in translation 'Our Lord in the attic' (Onze Lieve Heer op Zolder), still survives and is open to the public.[26] In Dublin, where many houses were made of timber, similar arrangements must have made it possible to create chapels during the 1610s and 1620s.

Irish Catholic patronage of the Jesuit order is an important touchstone in this essay. The order, founded in Italy in 1540, was successful in establishing seminaries and churches in many Catholic countries on the continent. Unlike other orders, however, it did not have a permanent residence in Ireland before the 1620s. The Jesuits tended to work in small networks in Britain and Ireland without establishing new buildings for their work. Only in 1625 were the Jesuits able to open a novitiate in London.[27] In Ireland, the majority of the Jesuits was members of the Old English rather than the Gaelic Irish families and had received their education at colleges on the continent. Initially, the Jesuits in Ireland resided as chaplains in the private residences of Catholic nobility, gentry, or merchants, for whom they celebrated Mass and heard confessions.[28]

22 T.C. Butler, *John's Lane: history of the Augustinian friars in Dublin, 1280–1980* (Dublin, 1983), cited in Flynn, *Irish Dominicans*, 264 n. 6.   23 O'Donoghue, 'Jesuit mission', 134; A. Clarke, *The Old English in Ireland, 1625–42* ([London], 1966), 117 n. 5.   24 Flynn, *Irish Dominicans*, 264; R. Steele (ed.), *Bibliography of royal proclamations of the Tudor and Stuart sovereigns* (Oxford, 1910), v, 34.   25 C. Maxwell, *A history of Trinity College, Dublin, 1591–1892* (Dublin, 1946), 37.   26 W. Kuyper, *Dutch classicist architecture* (Delft, 1980), 8, 41–2.   27 L. Stone, *The crisis of the aristocracy, 1558–1641* (Oxford, 1965), 730.   28 Lennon, *Lords*, 143–5; J. Bossy, 'The social history of confession in the age of Reformation' in *Transactions of the Royal Historical Society*, 5th series, 25 (1975), 21–38.

In 1628, the general of the order, Vitelleschi, wrote about his reluctance to approve the building of a Jesuit residence in Dublin, preferring that members of the order should maintain low profiles by continuing to live in private houses. The political situation was indeed far from secure, with Lord Deputy Falkland requesting permission in March 1628 to expel the titular bishops, the Jesuits, and other regulars.[29] However, approval for the building of the college, novitiate and chapel at Kildare Hall must have been obtained at an earlier date, because the complex had already been built by 1627, and was opened in the next year.[30]

WHERE WAS KILDARE HALL?

The countess of Kildare could have built the Jesuits' chapel and auxiliary buildings on her family's lands in Co. Westmeath (for example, at the large Benedictine monastery at Fore, granted to the countess's father in 1588), or on the Kildare lands in Leinster.[31] Instead, she chose the city of Dublin, where she did not own property, but where she leased land at Back Lane from the chapter of Christ Church Cathedral for forty years at a rent of £12 per annum.[32] The central location in the parish of St Audoen's was within a three-minute walk from Dublin Castle. Aside from financing the construction of buildings on the site, she supported the yearly operating budget of the establishment. By 1628, the income of the college was 280 'scuta', with the promise of more funds in Lady Kildare's will (apparently she had set aside 12,000 scudi for the Jesuits in her will). The novitiate had an annual income of 252 'scuta'.[33]

Historians believed that Kildare Hall formerly stood where Tailors' Hall now is, that is on the northern side of Back Lane (figure 1 shows this street on Speed's map of 1610).[34] There are several reasons why this is incorrect. The earl of Cork, writing in 1630, stated that the residents of Kildare Hall had direct access to the town walls.[35] This places the building on the south side of Back Lane, where properties adjoined the town wall between Newgate and St Nicholas's Gate, and where there were two mural towers, Fagan's Tower and

29 Historical Manuscripts Commission, *12th report, app. I*, 341, 21 March 1627[-8], Lord Falkland to secretary John Coke; B. Jennings (ed.), 'Acta sancrae congregationis de Propaganda Fide' in *Archivium Hibernicum*, 22 (1959), 28–129: 45.   **30** O'Donoghue, 'Jesuit mission', 201–2.   **31** Carbury, the former house of the earl of Kildare, at Christ Church Place S., built in the early sixteenth century, at this time was no longer in the possession of the family. See H.B. Clarke, *Dublin, part I, to 1610, Irish historic town atlas, No. 11* (Dublin, 2002), 30.   **32** Marsh's Library, Dublin, MS Z2.2.24.   **33** O'Donoghue, 'Jesuit mission', 203, 212. One scudo d'oro was the equivalent of 500 quattrini. However, it proved impossible for us to translate this into a contemporary equivalent.   **34** For example, J.P. Mahaffy, *Epoch* (London, 1903), 215; O'Donoghue, 'Jesuit mission', 248; G.A. Little, 'The Jesuit university of Dublin (c)1627' in *Dublin Historical Record*, 13 (1952), 36–7. Back Lane was formerly called Roche Street, also Rochelle Lane or Street.   **35** *Cal. S.P. Ire., 1625–32*, 509.

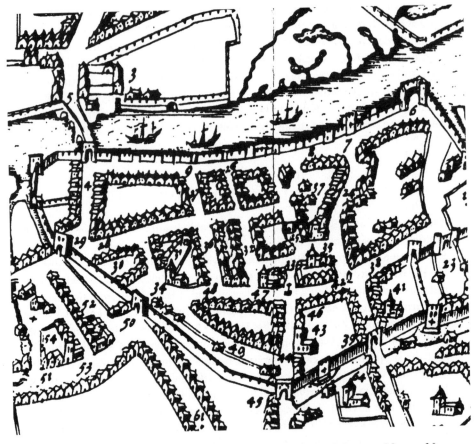

Fig. 1: Part of Dublin in 1610 (Speed's map), showing Back Lane at No. 49, New Gate at No. 50, St Audoen's Church at No. 34, Christ Church at No. 35, and Dublin Castle at No. 23

Sedgrave's Tower. This supposition is confirmed by firm evidence from seventeenth-century deeds in the archives of Christ Church cathedral,[36] showing that the Jesuits' buildings, including their later adaptations such as 'Kildare Chapel now hospital' (1662), 'Kildare House' for the use of a school in 1672, and the 'hospital' (1697),[37] were bordered by the Back Lane on the north and the town wall on the south.

36 For example, the first surviving deed referring to the property is dated 1645, and mentions 'the College' West of half a plot of the 'common garden' assigned to John Bryce and a piece of waste land in possession of John Walsh. Both of these properties are bounded on the North side by Back Lane and on the South by the city wall (M.J. McEnery and R. Refaussé (eds), *Christ Church deeds* (Dublin, 2001), no. 1551). 37 McEnery and Refaussé, *Christ Church deeds*, nos. 1636, 1646, 1762, 1937.

A nineteenth-century surveyor's map of the area (figure 2), together with earlier leases and maps, makes it possible to identify the lands owned by Christ Church cathedral in Back Lane.[38] Using the property numbers on figure 2 as a guide, the Christ Church property started at No. 45 Back Lane (north-west of Fagan's tower) and ended at No. 50 Back Lane (south-east of the former Newgate). Another map, dated 1793,[39] shows that lot No. 49 was next to 'Mr James Nowlans hold[ing]s formerly the Kings Hospital' (the later use of the site, prior to the building of the Royal Hospital at Kilmainham), as indicated by lot 48 on figure 2. That map also shows a passage at No. 48, which may have coincided with the entry passage into Kildare Hall, leading in the nineteenth century to 'Mr Hylands leather store', a building 73 by 18 feet, which approximates to the size of Kildare chapel as reported by the earl of Cork in 1630.[40] Buildings on either side of this structure and close to the town wall (lot No. 47, the 'currying loft' and lot No. 49, the 'stable') may have been the site of the residences for the clergy, the scholars, and the countess of Kildare. It is possible that the residential buildings were situated at the back of lots No. 45 and 46, which was reached by a separate passage from Back Lane (later known as Fagan's Court).[41]

The evidence of the map shown in figure 2 and the current street profile along Back Lane, makes it possible to further specify the location of Kildare Hall. Numbers 45–46 on Fig. 2 now constitute Mother Redcap's Tavern. The distinct projection of this building in the street, as shown on figure 2, is still recognisable. Immediately east of Mother Recap's Tavern there is a three-storey building, four windows wide, which may represent No. 47 on figure 2. The site immediate next to that (currently a building of three storeys and six windows) is likely to be the site of Kildare Hall (opposite the entrance to Tailors Hall). On the south side, the area is bounded by parts of the old town wall, along which now runs Dillon Street.

THE BUILDING COMPLEX AT KILDARE HALL

The complex of buildings consisted of five components, each with a separate function. These included a 'college', a novitiate, a sodality, the main chapel

---

38 NLI, MS 21F87, f. 77. 39 NLI, MS 2789, f. 39, Christ Church cathedral maps. 40 *Cal. S.P. Ire., 1625–32*, 509, Jan. 1630, the earl of Cork to Lord Dorchester. The map shown in Fig. 2 of this article has also been published by P. Pearson in *The heart of Dublin: resurgence of an historic city* (Dublin, 2000), 254, but the site of Kildare Hall is not identified in this source. Two other maps of 1697 and 1699 showing the location of Kildare Hall are mentioned among the Christ Church cathedral deeds (McEnery and Refaussé, *Christ Church deeds*, nos. 1937 and 1951), but do not appear to have survived (personal communication by Raymond Refaussé). 41 If these two (or more) storey buildings had been situated elsewhere, they probably would have taken light away from the main chapel.

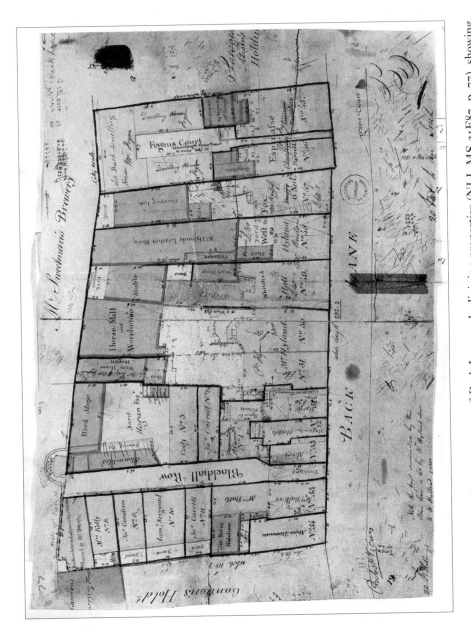

Fig. 2: Late nineteenth-century map of Back Lane and adjoining properties (NLI, MS 21F87, p. 77), showing the town wall on top (including the turret). Lots 45 to 48 were part of the Kildare Hall property. North for this map is at the bottom.

(called Kildare Hall), and the countess of Kildare's private residence. Only four contemporary descriptions and a few short notes are known of the complex of buildings, each of which reveals unique information. The descriptions include an annual report by the Jesuits for the year 1629 that was sent to Rome; a description (January 1630) by the earl of Cork who as lord justice was instrumental in the suppression of the Jesuits' establishment; a description by a traveller, Sir William Brereton, who reported on the chapel in 1635, after it had been handed over to Trinity College; and a letter by the dowager countess of Kildare.[42] Before describing the features of the main chapel, the other buildings and their functions will be reviewed.

The college
The college served as a school of higher learning for lay students. In 1629 it had seven priests, with four teaching grammar and one teaching humanities. Even though the college was later called a university, it is unlikely that its program of studies was broad enough to compete with Trinity College.

The novitiate
The novitiate served to train students for priesthood in the Jesuit order. In a modest way, the novitiate was a competitor to Trinity College, because each focused on the training of clergy of strongly opposed religions.[43] The novitiates had their own chapel, distinct from the main chapel. Judging from James Ware's diary, the novitiate consisted of 'very many chambers for priests' and it was situated next to the main chapel'.[44] It is probable that this novitiate was the largest of any of the religious orders that had established themselves in Dublin in the 1620s.

The sodality
The complex of building also housed a sodality for Dublin citizens, which was dedicated to the Blessed Virgin Mary, and was restricted to 'selected people of tried virtue'. Its members received monthly communion and, in an extension of the work of the Jesuits, tried to reform their families where necessary. The Jesuits used the sodality model from 1565 onward in Limerick to spread the Tridentine reforms in Ireland.[45]

42 J. MacErlean, Transcript of Status Missionis in Iberia, 1629, Jesuit Archive, Leeson St, Dublin, Cat. MISS Hib. S.J.; O'Donoghue, 'Jesuit mission', 203–4; *Cal. S.P. Ire.*, 1625–32, 509, Jan. 1630, the earl of Cork to Lord Dorchester; BL, Sloane MS 3827, f. 177; Hawkins, *Brereton*, 141–2.   **43** H. Robinson-Hammerstein, 'Archbishop Adam Loftus: The first provost of Trinity College, Dublin' in H. Robinson-Hammerstein (ed.), *European universities in the age of Reformation and Counter Reformation* (Dublin, 1998), 43, 51–2.   **44** Ware MS, f. 198, under date 7 Jan. 1629[–30].   **45** P. O'Dwyer, *Highlights in devotion to Mary in Ireland from 1600* (Dublin, 1981), 20; R. Gillespie, *The sacred in the secular: religious change in Catholic Ireland, 1500–1700* (Colchester, VT, 1993), 16; R. Gillespie, 'Catholic religious cultures in the diocese of Dublin, 1614–97' in J. Kelly and D. Keogh (eds), *History of the Catholic diocese of Dublin* (Dublin, 2000),

The countess of Kildare's private quarters

The buildings on the site included housing for the countess of Kildare, who after the seizure of the complex in 1630, claimed losses of her 'household stuffe'. It is possible to somewhat reconstruct these quarters thanks to the survival of an inventory, made in 1656 upon the death of Joan Boyle, the earl of Cork's daughter and wife of the 16th earl of Kildare. The title of the inventory states 'earl of Kildare's goods, Dublin', but does not mention the location of the building.[46] However, the only dwelling that the earl, a notorious spendthrift, legitimately could claim was Kildare Hall (as his son, the 17th earl, later did after the Restoration). The inventory lists the dining room, parlour, study, six bedrooms, and a dressing room. In addition, the document mentions the kitchens, buttery, laundry, and a hall. It is unclear, however, whether the latter refers to the Jesuit chapel or to a smaller space. The size of three bedrooms can be deduced from the fact that each had two window curtains, referring to either a single window with two curtains or two windows with a curtain each. The same arrangement applied to the dining room. Four of the bedrooms and the dining room had tapestry 'hangings'. Except a single piece of furniture belonging to the earl of Cork, the inventory does not reveal which, if any, of the furnishing had belonged to Elizabeth, dowager countess of Kildare. It is likely that the inventory did not cover the whole building, because it did not list spaces reserved for administrative officers and servants.

The main advantage of the arrangement of the countess's private quarters with the Jesuits college, novitiate, sodality, and main chapel was that when religious intolerance increased, as it regularly did under the shifting doctrines of the Dublin government and the changing pressures from the government in London in response to the international situation, the public chapel could be closed while the private chapel of the novitiate would allow religious practices to continue for the religious community only.

The size of the complex was substantial. A note dated 1643–4 mentions the '5 howses belonging to the Hospitall' (the later use of Kildare Hall) in Back Lane.[47] The Protestant Sir John Bingley noted in 1629 that the buildings housed 80 people,[48] but it is unlikely that he actually counted the individuals. The more reliable Jesuit annual report of 1629 mentions that the priests and their students were housed in 26 rooms with a hall; 12 were reserved for novices. The house had domestic furnishing for 24 individuals, including 17 sets of Mass vestments, 11 silver chalices, and 'a reasonably equipped library'.

127–43. **46** Published in J. Fenlon, *Goods and chattels: a survey of early household inventories in Ireland* (Kilkenny, 2003), 39–40. The following summary is based two versions of the inventory, which differ in details (NLI, MS 18, 996). **47** Historical Manuscripts Commission, *14th report* (London, 1896), app. VII, 152. It is unclear whether the five houses include any structure built on the site between 1627 and 1643. The buildings are much more difficult to recognise from the hearth tax list of houses in Back Lane in 1664 (*57th report of the Deputy Keeper of the Public Records in Ireland* (Dublin, 1936), 559, 561). **48** *Cal. S.P. Ire., 1625–32*, 442, 2 March 1629, description by Sir John Bingley.

A few books from this library survive, one on sundials and the measurement of time, the other on the movements of the sun and the moon.[49] The earl of Cork mentioned 'a cloister above with many other chambers'. When the building had been handed over to Trinity College in 1630, James Ware's diary noted that 50 'collegians' had been sent over from the college to live at the site. Another source from 1633 describes how the buildings were able to accommodate 10 fellows and 22 scholars.[50]

THE MAIN CHAPEL AT KILDARE HALL

The function of the main chapel at Kildare Hall was the celebration of the Mass, the preaching of sermons, and the hearing of confessions. Compared to the chapels of the other orders in Dublin in this period, the main chapel at Kildare Hall appears to have been the largest and probably the most ornate. A computer-generated, approximate reconstruction, based on the contemporary descriptions, is shown in figures 3–5. The chapel measured 75 by 27 feet and was comparable in size to several of the Protestant parish churches in Dublin, such as St John's and St Michan's, but because the chapel at Kildare Hall had galleries, a larger congregation could attend service there than in most Dublin Protestant parish churches.[51] Although we do not know the height of the chapel, the prevailing renaissance rules of architecture suggests a height of 25 to 27 feet, which would have made the whole structure the shape of a triple cube, each cube measuring about 25 feet square.[52]

The earl of Cork, in a letter of 1630, mentioned Kildare Hall as 'one of the houses erected by the countess dowager of Kildare and by her richly adorned and furnished for the Jesuits'.[53] This is perplexing because it is the only reference to more than one building, but it may refer to the complex of buildings at Kildare Hall. In another letter of the same year, he commented that the countess of Kildare called the structure her 'hall', even though it did not

---

49 Sebast. Munsterum, *Horologiographia* ... (Basle, [1531]), and Tychonis Brahe Dani, *Astronomiae instavaratae progymnasianata* ... (Prague, 1610), now both in Marsh's Library, Dublin. We are indebted to Muriel MacCarthy for this information. Few books of the other Dublin missions appear to have survived. An exception is a Dominican copy of Pedro de Covarrubias, *Pars estiualis* (Paris, 1520), annotated 'Est fratris Marci Rochifort pro Conventu Dubkinensi Sacri Ordinis Predicatorum' which was listed in cat. 71/48 by de Búrca Rare Books. **50** Ware MS, f. 203; J.W. Stubbs, *The history of the university of Dublin* (Dublin, 1889), 63 n. **51** St John's Church measured internally 70 by 35 feet, St Michael: 60 by 25 feet; and St Nicholas Within: 80 by 35 feet; see H.A. Wheeler and M.J. Craig, *The Dublin city churches of the Church of Ireland: an illustrated handbook* (Dublin, 1948), 22, 27, 32. **52** Note that Inigo Jones's chapel at Somerset House measured 104 by 36 feet, and therefore may have been a triple cube as well. **53** Historical Manuscripts Commission, *12th Rep.*, app. I, 398–99, 9 Jan. 1629[–30], earl of Cork to Viscount Dorchester. The use of the plural 'houses' is puzzling, because it is not known that the countess has established other buildings. It could be that the earl referred here to the complex of houses at Kildare Hall.

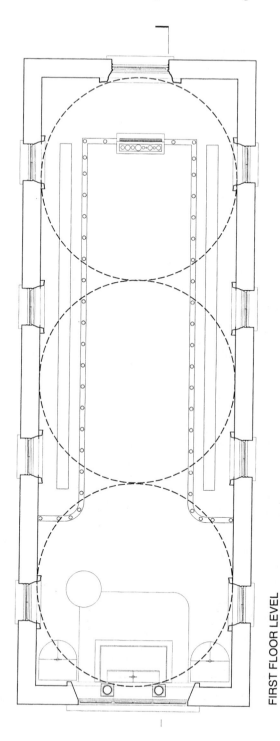

FIRST FLOOR LEVEL

Fig. 3: Reconstruction of the plan of the main Jesuit chapel at Kildare Hall, Back Lane, Dublin (circles indicate the triple cube proportion of the structure)

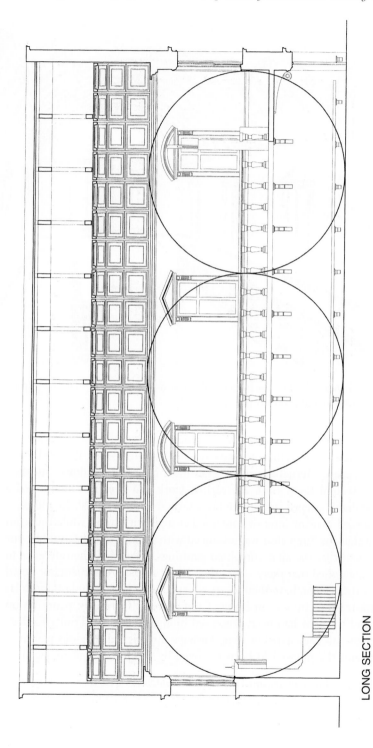

LONG SECTION

Fig. 4: Length-wise section of the reconstructed Jesuit chapel at Kildare Hall (circles indicate the triple cube proportion of the structure)

Fig. 5: Reconstructed view of the interior of the Jesuit chapel at Kildare Hall from the upper balcony looking toward the altar

have 'a chimney, table, or window that any may look out of'. Calling it a 'hall' was the countess's subterfuge to indicate the private rather than religious nature of the space. Actually, Kildare Hall must have had windows, but they were on the second floor. Both the earl of Cork and Brereton mentioned a 'curious', probably carved pulpit, 'richly adorned with pictures'. In addition, the earl observed that the interior contained an altar with steps, while Brereton commented that the 'high altar was advanced with steps, and railed out like our cathedrals', and that the altar contained paintings.[54] Possibly, the reference to the high altar implied that there were other, lesser altars. A commentator noted in 1629 that the Jesuits 'have their altars adorned with images and other idolatrous popish trash as fully as in Rome if not more'.[55] Curiously, paintings on the pulpit and the altar had been preserved by the officials of Trinity College when Brereton saw the chapel in 1635. Perhaps the original religious paintings of the altar and the pulpit had been removed by the Jesuits and replaced by

54 The painting may have been imported from the continent, because the country had very few native painters at this time. A set of imported paintings was seized by government officials in 1617. See A.B. Grosart (ed.), *The Lismore papers* (London, 1886–88), series 1, ii, 116–17.   **55** *Cal. S.P. Ire.*, 1625–32, 442, 2 March 1629, description by Sir John Bingley.

more innocuous non-religious pictures so that they were less likely to be destroyed in case of an intrusion by government or civic officials.

Several other aspects of the Kildare chapel, although not explicitly mentioned in contemporary descriptions, warrant attention. It is very likely that the chapel, because of the Sodality of the Blessed Virgin Mary, had one or more statues of our Lady. Although not mentioned by the witnesses, the chapel's lofty space converges on the altar, its altar cloth, silver chalices, wax lights and a silver pyx for the reservation of the sacrament, all of which became prescribed ornaments in early seventeenth-century liturgy.[56] It is also likely that, in addition to the coffered ceiling, plasterwork decorations were used. The descriptions do not include mention of a tower with bells, but bells may have announced the commencement of sermons and Mass.

The earl of Cork noted four confession boxes 'neatly contrived', placed on each side of the altar, an innovation resulting from the Tridentine reforms, which advocated an environment of splendour suitable to the sacrament. The chapel occupied a two-storey space with a gallery above the ground floor with 'rails and turned' coloured banisters (earl of Cork) that ran on three sides of the chapel (Brereton), substantially increasing the space for worshippers.

The ceiling of the chapel was presumably unlike any other ceiling typical of known Irish churches, which usually had open rafters. The earl of Cork mentioned the organs in the main chapel and that the chapel had a 'compass roof', which the *Oxford English Dictionary* defines as one ' in which the braces of the timbers are inclined so as to form a sort of arch'. The ceiling of Jesuit churches, and eventually Protestant churches, was acoustically adapted to accommodate the sound of sermons and evangelical music. As early as 1535, the builders of San Francesco della Vigna in Venice recommended that 'all the chapels and the choir be vaulted because the word or song of the minister echoes better from the vault than it would from the rafters'.[57] A surviving 'tunnel-vault' ceiling is in the Jesuit church of St Charles Borromeo (known as the St Carolus church) in Antwerp, commenced in 1615, and dedicated in 1622. Neither the Jesuits, nor the countess, or Brereton commented on the overall quality of the chapel and adjoining buildings. However, the earl of Cork stated that the chapel and 'a cloister above with many other chambers, all things most fair and graceful, [were] like the banqueting house at Whitehall'. The comparison with the banqueting hall, designed by Inigo Jones, appears appropriate in that that building was also of two storeys, had windows on the second storey only, and had a gallery on the second storey as well.

It is likely that music, especially organ music, was an important component of religious service at Kildare Hall. The role that the Jesuits played in the creation of sacred music should not under-estimated. For example, the superior

56 Gillespie, 'Catholic religious cultures', 137.   57 R. Wittkower and I.B. Jaffe, *Baroque art: the Jesuit contribution* (New York, 1972), 19.

of the Jesuit residence in Dublin, Robert Nugent SJ, wrote many hymns in Irish to Irish tunes, and he devised the double-strung harp. His colleague, Stephen White (1574–1648), a native of Clonmel, taught arts and music at the Irish college in Salamanca before coming to Dublin.[58] Music was an integral part of the creation of transcendental feelings in a spiritual space.

KILDARE HALL, ST JAMES'S CHAPEL IN LONDON, AND CONTINENTAL SOURCES

The timing of the building and the features of Kildare Hall can be best understood by comparison with a royal Catholic chapel, designed by Inigo Jones at St James's Palace in London and built from 1623 onwards.[59] This chapel was the first semi-public chapel for a Catholic congregation built in London since the Reformation, prompted by the anticipated marriage between the future Charles I of England and the Spanish infanta.[60]

Kildare Hall and St James's Chapel have several features in common. Both were specifically constructed for Catholic religious service. Both were rectangular in plan, and were lighted by windows in the upper rather than the lower storey. Both had a coved, coffered ceiling. The concept of St James's Chapel was that its 'strictly classical character was something new for England'. Jones, who had been to Italy to study classical Roman architecture, used at the Chapel Royal the 'cella of a Roman temple, but with a strong horizontal division as of a Palladian house, the lower part rusticated'. Jones conceived the chapel as a double cube hall with 'a majestic barrel-vaulted canopy of coffered timber adapted from Palladio's woodcut of the Roman Temple of Venus in his *I Quattro libri* (IV, p. 38), first published in Venice in 1570.[61] The interior of Kildare chapel may also derive from Palladio's interpretation of this Roman temple, and probably more directly from Inigo Jones' design of St James's chapel.

Who could have designed Kildare Hall? Little is known about architects working in Dublin during the 1620s, such as the Protestant Sir Thomas Roper, 1st Viscount Baltinglass. Nicholas Pynnar, director-general of the royal fortifications and buildings, had travelled to Italy, and must have been familiar with Roman and Renaissance architecture.[62] There were others in Dublin who made architectural designs, such as the heraldic expert, William Leverett,[63] and the

58 Little, 'Jesuit University', 38.   59 The following details are based on H.M. Colvin, J. Summerson, M. Biddle, J.R. Hale, and M. Merriman, *The history of the King's works, vol. iv 1485–1660* (Part II) (London, 1982), 248–9, 263–5; P. Palme, *Triumph of peace, a study of the Whitehall Banquetting Hall* (Stockholm, 1956), 20.   60 G. Redworth, *The prince and the infanta: the cultural politics of the Spanish match* (New Haven, 2003).   61 J. Summerson, *Architecture in Britain 1530–1830* (London, 1953), 128; J. Harris and G. Higgott, *Inigo Jones: complete architectural drawings* (New York, 1989), 182–5.   62 R. Loeber, *A biographical dictionary of architects in Ireland, 1600–1720* (London, 1981); R. Loeber, 'Architects and craftsmen admitted as freemen to

sculptor Edmund Tingham. However, none of them is known to have been employed by either the countess of Kildare or by the Jesuits. Recent research, however, has revealed that Francis Andrews, as a 'tomb maker' and a pupil of Nicholas Stone (who in turn was a close associate of Inigo Jones in London) lived at Back Lane in 1634, the same street where Kildare Hall was located. He also worked for the earl of Cork during this period.[64] It is not clear, however, whether he resided in Ireland at the time that Kildare Hall was built.

Some architectural historians argue that Jesuits employed architects who were members of their own order, which in Europe had a long history of art patronage, ranging from the building of churches and seminaries to the commissioning of church furniture and paintings.[65] Jesuits employed members of their Society to design and execute churches in Italy and the southern Netherlands.[66] Typically, the design of a planned Jesuit establishment and church was sent to Rome to be approved by the Jesuit general and his staff.[67] The Jesuit mission to Ireland was subject directly to the general of the Society in Rome (Vitelleschi from 1615 onward), and was not under the control of the regional or provincial unit.[68] Therefore, the plans for Kildare Hall are also likely to have needed approval at the highest level in the Jesuit hierarchy.

Several art historians have previously proposed that the Jesuits developed their own distinctive style of architecture, but this has been proven to be wrong.[69] However, the Jesuits in Europe, starting with the building of the Gesù in 1571–2, their mother church in Rome, spear-headed a new interpretation of classical architecture. According to Wittkower and Jaffe,[70] that church and other subsequent Jesuits churches 'represented the perfect answer to the Counter-Reformation demand for spacious naves in churches which would accommodate very large congregations ... [which] offered proper facilities for a new form of preaching and confession as well as many altars for multiple Masses'. It is well known that the Jesuits placed a deeper significance on spiritual growth of the penitent, on the occasion of his/her sacramental confession, and confessionals thus became as indispensable in the furnishing of churches as altars'. These principles were widely accepted by Jesuits in different locations and caused the development of a certain 'measure of

the city of Dublin (1464–1485, and 1575–1774)', unpublished manuscript, vii, deposited in the National Gallery of Ireland; Loeber, *Dictionary*, passim. 63 Loeber, 'Sculptured memorials', 282. 64 Grosart, *Lismore papers*, iv, 45, 133. I am indebted to Amy Harris and Dr Adam White for information about Francis Andrews' apprenticeship to Nicholas Stone, mentioned in the Masons' Company of London records (City of London, Guildhall Library, Ms. 5303/ f. 55v.). For other work by Andrews in 1638, see PRO, SP 46/93, f. 16. 65 Wittkower and Jaffe, *Baroque art*, passim; see also, G.A. Bailey, 'Le style jésuite n'existe pas': Jesuit corporate culture and the visual arts' in J.W. O'Malley, G.A. Bailey, S.J. Harris and T.F. Kennedy (eds), *The Jesuits: cultures, sciences, and the arts, 1540–1773* (Toronto, 2000), 38–89. 66 H. Gerson and E.H. Ter Kuile, *Art and architecture in Belgium, 1600 to 1800* (London, 1960), 17. 67 Wittkower and Jaffe, *Baroque art*, 5–8. 68 T. Corcoran, 'Early Irish Jesuit educators (II)' in *Studies*, 30 (1930), 59. 69 J. Braun, *Die belgische Jesuitenkirchen* (Freiburg im Breisgau, 1907); Wittkower and Jaffe, *Baroque art*, 2. 70 Ibid., 2–3.

conformity' in church architecture. The Jesuits' emphasis on preaching, which required churches that could accommodate large congregations, was common to Jesuit Counter-Reformation and Protestant Reformation churches. Both needed a nave free from encumbrances, such as rood screens and free-standing tombs, so that the congregation could see and hear the sermons. These features also applied to Kildare Hall, which with its gallery, must have been able to house a sizeable congregation.

CONFISCATION AND RE-ESTABLISHMENT

In 1628 Protestant officials became worried about the number of religious houses in Dublin. On 1 April 1629, the lord deputy and council issued a proclamation forbidding the 'exercise of Romish ecclesiastical jurisdictions' and ordered that the owners of the 'public oratories, colleges, Mass houses, and convents' were to expel the friars and resume their property on pain of confiscation. Four days later, Falkland reported that in Dublin there had been no resistance to the proclamation and that all Catholic religious houses were locked up 'with the locks hanging on the doors'.[71] Soon afterwards, however, he reported to Archbishop Ussher that people had 'ordinary recourse' to the religious houses 'by their private passages… [with] those Mass houses being continued in their former use, though perhaps a little more privately, without any demolishing of their altar'.[72]

A possible trigger to the more permanent change in religious tolerance is contained in the instructions to Falkland's successors, the lord justices, the earl of Cork and Archbishop Adam Loftus, issued in July 1629. This document, formulated in London, instructed them to 'suppress all Popish colleges, etc. & all foreign jurisdictions'. The signing of the treaty of peace with France in May of that year removed earlier inhibitions to the execution of such an order.[73]

A pivotal event took place in Dublin on St Stephen's Day 1629 (26 December). News reached the Protestant religious and civic leaders attending religious service in Christ Church that a Mass was being publicly celebrated at the Franciscan chapel. The Anglican archbishop, mayor and sheriffs rushed away from their own service to interrupt the public celebration of Mass at this chapel. They damaged the chapel's interior, but an angry crowd of Catholics ejected the Protestant party. Soon after, the Dublin city government clamped down and seized the 'Houses of Franciscans, Dominicans, Carmelites and Capuchins' for the 'King's use by the mayor and aldermen and the keys delivered to the Lords Justices'. All of this happened without legal proceedings.

71 Steele, *Royal proclamations*, ii, 31; *Cal. S.P. Ire.*, *1625–32*, 446, 5 April 1629, lord deputy to privy council. 72 C.R. Elrington (ed.), *The whole works of the most Rev. James Ussher, D.D.* (Dublin, 1847), xv, 438, 14 April 1629, Lord Deputy Falkland to archbishop of Armagh. 73 Historical Manuscripts Commission, *12th Rep.*, app. I, 398–9; *Cal. S.P. Ire.*, *1625–32*, xxxviii, 471.

Judging by the countess of Kildare's letter to Falkland, Kildare Hall had closed its doors so as not to provoke an intrusion by the Protestants.[74] However, the earl of Cork seized Kildare Hall for the government on 7 January 1630, again without legal proceedings. A day later, the nunnery (probably of the Poor Clares) near Newgate was also confiscated.[75] One of the earl of Cork's justifications for the seizure of Kildare Hall was its location adjoining the town wall and that 'the command of Dublin was in the power of the Catholics, being master of the [town] wall, turrets & flankers …'[76] The Franciscan house, with the approval of the king, was demolished in 1630, and two other former religious houses were turned into houses of correction.[77]

On 19 May 1630, Kildare Hall was granted by the government to Trinity College, because the 'Jesuit house … in regard of the capacitie and manner of building is most convenient for ye education of scollars'.[78] The building was renamed the 'New College', but the term 'New Hall' was also used. Rules were drawn up, dated 17 July 1630, about how it was to be used by its rector, tutor, lecturers and students.[79] The earl and several others contributed funds to pay for a public theological lecture every Tuesday.[80]

Sometime before June 1629, the countess of Kildare had settled at her own house at Kilkea.[81] A painting survives of her nephew, the 16th earl of Kildare, in 1633. Significantly, it has Kilkea Castle rather than Maynooth Castle in its background,[82] and this may have served as a way to pique the dowager countess and to signify to others that Kilkea Castle eventually would revert to the earl of Kildare's estate. The countess's income from the Kildare estate was not yet settled in April 1633, when a proposal was made to assign her an annuity of £500 and the 'town and demesne' of Kilkea and other lands during her life.[83] It is likely that this proposal was realised. The prospect of the countess regaining possession of Kildare Hall, let alone resettling the Jesuits there, must have looked grim in 1634. She was not discouraged by the earl of Cork's activities against her, and changed tactics by donating her dower house, Kilkea Castle in Co. Kildare, to her relative, Father Robert Nugent SJ, in 1634 for the use of the Jesuits.[84] A chalice of this period survives, donated by her to the Society of Jesus.[85] Mass is likely to have been celebrated in the tall hall attached to the

74 BL, Sloane MS 3827, f. 177. 75 Ware MS, f. 198; B. Jennings (ed.), *The Wadding papers, 1614–1638* (Dublin, 1953), 337, 7 Feb. 1630, J.N. Turner [John Roche, bishop of Ferns] to Luke Wadding. 76 PRO, SP 63/250, f. 69, – Jan. 1630, earl of Cork to English privy council; Grosart, *Lismore papers*, series 1, iii, 14. 77 *Cal. S.P. Ire., 1625–32*, 21, 2 March 1630, [earl of Cork to Dorchester]. 78 TCD, MUN/P/25/12. 79 Mahaffy, *Epoch*, 216–18; Ware MS, f. 114. 80 Grosart, *Lismore papers*, series 1, iii, 82. 81 Marquis of Kildare, *Earls of Kildare*, 237; see also PRONI, D 3078/3, 1/5, 48–49, 29 July 1631, dowager countess of Kildare to earl of Kildare. 82 A. Crookshank and the Knight of Glin, *Ireland's painters, 1600–1940* (New Haven, 2002), 9, pl. 6. 83 PRONI, D 3078/3, 1/5, 117–18, 22 April 1633, Richard Talbot to earl of Kildare. 84 P.N.N. Synnott, *Kilkea Castle* (n.l., n.d.), 18, and plates of the castle before its restoration in 1849; Marquis of Kildare, *Earls of Kildare*, 232. 85 W. FitzG[erald], 'Miscellanae. A chalice

medieval hall of this castle. The castle and its estate were the most valuable of her dower lands.[86]

The relocation of the Jesuits to the countryside followed a similar move of other orders whose properties had been seized or surrendered following the events in Dublin in 1630. For example, the Poor Clares, then situated on the Merchant's Quay, were forced in 1631 to abandon the city, transferred to the estate of the family of their abbess, the Dillons of Costello Gallen, near Loughrea, and settled at Bethlehem where they built a convent, the ruins of which survive to this day.[87] Similarly, the Capuchins were driven out of Dublin, and settled on the estate of the Catholic baron of Slane in Co. Meath.[88]

In July 1633, the earl of Cork was replaced as lord deputy by Wentworth. This provided the countess with an opportunity to try to repossess Kildare Hall. She planned to speak with Wentworth at the end of August 1633. That same year, 'diverse lords and gentlemen' petitioned Wentworth for the restitution of the confiscated 'Mass houses'.[89] The countess was able to convince Wentworth that the matter should be reviewed with witnesses at the council board, and a hearing was set in motion in the spring of 1634.[90] According to Wentworth, Lady Kildare in her petition stated: 'that the inheritance of the best of those houses was her Ladyships, and that she let it BONA FIDE, to a tenant for rent, and that if it had been used otherwise then it ought, yet by no justice ought she to loose her rent during the terme, and much less the inheritance after. And the like course was taken by other the owners and inheritors of the residue of those [religious] houses'.

A 'full' hearing was held, witnesses were heard, and it appeared that there was 'noe ground for those seizures', and the rightful owners were restored.[91] Further proceedings must have been equally favourable to the countess, and she was able to reclaim her lease of the Kildare Hall property.[92] Kildare Hall once more functioned as a public chapel. During Wentworth's trial in London in 1640, one of the initial charges was that he 'restored divers Fryeries and Mass-Houses … (two of which houses are in City of Dublin, and had been assigned to the use of the University there) to the pretended Owners thereof, who have since imployed the same to the Exercise of the Popish Religion'. His defence

presented to the Jesuits in 1634 by the Countess of Kildare' in *Journal of the Kildare Archaeological Society*, 5 (1906–8), 60–2. **86** The castle has been rebuilt since, but is fundamentally the old structure; its adjoining village has disappeared. The village counted 107 inhabitants in 1660. The castle appears to have escaped destruction in the aftermath of the 1641 rebellion. See R.C. Simington, *The civil survey AD 1654–1656, vol. 8 County of Kildare* (Dublin, 1952), 118; S. Pender, *A census of Ireland, circa 1659* (Dublin, 1939), 404. **87** Clarke, *Old English*, 62–3; Ware MS, f. 198, 207; Grosart, *Lismore papers*, series 1, iii, 106; Concannon, *Poor Clares*, 11, 18–29. **88** A. Cogan, *The diocese of Meath, ancient and modern*, 3 vols (Dublin, 1862–70), i, 287. **89** PRONI, D 3078/3, 1/5, f. 139, 19 Aug. 1633, dowager countess of Kildare to earl of Kildare; Clarke, *Old English*, 72. **90** TCD, MUN/P/23, f. 41, 6 May 1634, Notice for hearing. **91** Grosart, *Lismore papers*, series 1, iv, 183; BL, Harl. MS 4297, f. 111, 15 Jan. 1634[-35], Petition of the Provost, fellows, and scholars of Trinity College to Lord Deputy Strafford. **92** TCD, MUN/P/1, f. 234, 4 Feb. 1633–4, Summons to six witnesses; Ware MS, f. 124.

was that the earl of Cork had seized the houses 'without Legal Proceedings, which, upon Suits prosecuted at Council Board, were, according to Justice, restored to the Owners'.[93] Cox, the seventeenth-century historian, confirmed that Kildare Hall in Lord Strafford's time 'was disposed of to the former use & became a Mass house again'.[94]

At the outbreak of the rebellion in October 1641, Catholics seized Protestant churches in many parts of Ireland, except Dublin where city and government controls were strong.[95] Before the close of that year, a proclamation was published in Dublin, 'interdicting the exercise of the Catholic religion; a rigorous search was made to discover the priests and religious, and no fewer than forty of them arrested, they were, for some time treated with great rigour in prison, and then transported to the Continent'. However, not all Jesuits were rounded up. Fr Robert Nugent's letters of this time turn from caution into alarm as persecution of Catholics and priests increased. He wrote that Fr Quin 'assumes all kinds of disguises', and that all but a few of the Jesuits had left Dublin 1643. Those left behind were Frs Quinn, Purcell (who was ill), and Lattin (who was imprisoned), all names which had been associated with Kildare Hall in the late 1620s; the remaining Jesuits had left Dublin to live dispersed among Catholics in the countryside.[96]

The countess of Kildare was outlawed in 1642, but probably remained safe by staying at Kilkea Castle, which does not seem to have been besieged during the military campaigns after the rebellion.[97] The earl of Ormond visited her there in the 1640s 'on the pretence of hawking a recreation'.[98] However, after an eight-month illness, she died on 26 October 1645. The Jesuit superior, Robert Nugent, lamented her death, writing to the Jesuit vicar-general that she was 'truly the mother of our Society in this realm'. In her will, she left everything to the Jesuits to fund a novitiate. The will also left the Jesuits as masters of Kilkea Castle. The Catholic nuncio Rinuccini stayed at Kilkea Castle in October 1646, where Generals Preston and Eoghan Rua O'Neill paid him a visit. The Jesuits were wealthy enough to lend the nuncio £800. However, the Jesuit ownership did not last long: they were forced to leave the castle in 1646 when the earl of Kildare, whose principal residence, Maynooth Castle, had been burned and looted by the rebels in 1642, claimed it as his patrimony.[99]

93 J. Rushworth, *Historical collections of private passages of state* (London, 1659–1701), viii, 69, 77; TCD, MS 6404, f. 108r. cited in Flynn, *Irish Dominicans*, 265 n.13, also 265–7. The change is confirmed by the absence of payments for costs related to Kildare Hall in the accounts of Trinity College, and the discontinuation of payments for the lectureship among the diary notes of the earl of Cork. **94** R. Cox, *Hibernia Anglicana: or, the history of Ireland*, 2 vols (London, 1690), ii, 54; *A declaration of the commons assembled* (London, 1642), 6. Cox also mentioned that the lord deputy tolerated a public 'Mass house' at Naas, close to his country house at Jigginstown (Cox, *Hibernia*, ii, 60). **95** O'Donoghue, 'Jesuit mission', 265. **96** P.F. Moran, *Historical sketch of the persecutions suffered by the Catholics* (Dublin, 1884), 34–6. **97** Marquis of Kildare, *Earls of Kildare: addenda*, 360; J.T. Gilbert, *History of the Irish confederation and the war in Ireland 1641–49*, 7 vols (Dublin, 1882–91), iii, 369; *The particular relation of the present state and condition of Ireland* (London, 1642), 5. **98** *Cal. S.P. Ire., 1660–62*, 209. **99** Marquis of Kildare, *Earls of Kildare*,

The Jesuits subsequently moved to Kilkenny, the main headquarters of the Confederates. There, Robert Nugent SJ and the Jesuits, probably with the legacy left them by the countess, established a novitiate at St John's abbey and a school near St Canice's cathedral.[1] The presence of the Jesuits and several other orders in the city, such as the Franciscans, Dominicans, and the Capuchins, recreated the configuration of missionary orders that had been present in Dublin about twenty years early. This centre of Catholic worldly and spiritual power came to an end when the city was besieged by Cromwell's army and surrendered in 1650, after which the Jesuit house and oratory were destroyed.[2]

CONCLUSION

Of all the Jesuit sites patronised by the countess – Kildare Hall, Kilkea Castle, and buildings in Kilkenny – Kildare Hall emerges clearest as a centre of pastoral and missionary activity. Before sliding into oblivion, Kildare Hall had a strong presence that lasted into the end of the seventeenth century. After the restoration of Charles II, the property was leased in 1662 by the dean and chapter of Christ Church cathedral to Wentworth, 17th earl of Kildare.[3] However, soon after, Roger Boyle, 1st earl of Orrery, as guardian of the earl of Kildare, was tenant of the 'hospital, formerly called Kildare Hall' in Rochelle Lane (the old name for Back Lane) for a rent of £12 from Michaelmas 1662.[4] It is ironic that the earl – son of the earl of Cork, who originally seized the property – is later associated with it.[5] In 1671 it was mentioned as the 'great house in Back Lane, commonly called the Hospital' when it was 'much out of repair'. A letter from the king was drafted for setting up a free school, conveying the king's interest in the hospital in Back Lane, 'known as Kildare House' to the lord mayor and the archbishop of Dublin for the use of such a school.[6] After 1698, the history of Kildare Hall is obscure, and the significance of its buildings for the architecture of Dublin was largely forgotten. Only excavations are likely to further clarify its significance as a place of worship and learning in the tradition of the Counter-Reformation.

248; O'Donoghue, 'Jesuit mission', 273, 277, 299; M.J. Hynes, *The mission of Rinuccini* (Louvain, 1932), 111. It was said that she died in 1664 (Marquis of Kildare, *Earls of Kildare. addenda*, 360), but this is clearly mistaken. **1** F. Ó Fearghail, 'The Catholic church in county Kilkenny 1600–1800' in W. Nolan and K. Whelan (eds), *Kilkenny: history and society* (Dublin, 1990), 197–249: 210. **2** Ó Fearghail, 'Catholic church', 213. **3** McEnery and Refaussé, *Christ Church deeds*, no. 1638. **4** Public Library, Pearse St, Dublin, Gilbert MS 69, n.p. **5** Note that the rent was the same as that paid by the countess of Kildare. The site is again mentioned in 1672 when it was vested in Dr John Parry and Dr Thomas Steele for the use of a school, again at the rent of twelve pounds per year (McEnery and Refaussé, *Christ Church deeds*, no. 1762). **6** J.T. and Lady Gilbert (ed.), *Calendar of the ancient records of Dublin*, 19 vols (Dublin, 1889–1944), iv, 522, 535, 543; v, 61; vi, 61, 204; *Cal. S.P. Domestic, 1671*, 146.

Acknowledgments
The authors are indebted to the following individuals for their advice in the preparation of this essay: Amy Harris, Fr Brian Mac Cuarta, Fr Fergus O'Donoghue, Jane Ohlmeyer, and Raymond Refaussé. Anne M. Burnham commented on an earlier draft and gave most helpful advice. The authors thank Niall McCullough and Cathal Curtin for producing the computer-generated reconstruction of Kildare Hall.

Architectural change and the parish church in post-Reformation Cork

EAMONN COTTER

The combined effects of the Reformation and the Tudor wars of the late sixteenth century spelt ruin for many of the country's church buildings, as noted by contemporary observers such as Edmund Spenser and John Davies.[1] It is clear, however, particularly from episcopal visitation records, that many churches were subsequently repaired and reused, usually by Protestant communities. In the diocese of Elphin, for instance, it was recorded by the Catholic bishop in 1631 that 'formerly there were sixty-five churches in the diocese: only five of these remain and are used by Protestants'.[2] Roman Catholic worship in the period was generally practised in private houses, though the construction of 'Mass houses' became more common. While there is abundant documentary evidence for these 'Mass houses', especially in towns and cities, the buildings themselves have generally not survived. In remote rural areas, however, a little-known group of church buildings has survived which appear to belong to this era and represent the presence of an active 'underground' Roman Catholic Church.

This paper looks at the physical evidence for structural alterations to existing church buildings and the construction of new buildings, in Co. Cork, over the course of the seventeenth and eighteenth centuries. It concentrates on the rural churches because they are the ones which, although often badly ruined, still retain some evidence of their appearance at the moment of their abandonment. Urban churches, on the other hand, have generally been either replaced or extensively repaired and modernised, often precluding the identification of earlier changes and additions.

LATE MEDIEVAL CHURCH LAYOUT

The late medieval churches of Co. Cork are almost invariably laid out to a standard blueprint. They consist basically of a long rectangle oriented

---

1 E. FitzPatrick and C. O'Brien, *The medieval churches of County Offaly* (Dublin, 1998), 111.
2 Quoted in F. Beirne (ed.), *The diocese of Elphin* (Dublin, 2000), 85.

east–west, with the altar against the east wall, a piscina at the east end of the south wall, and one or two aumbries nearby. The entrance is usually at the west end of the south wall. Although chancels had generally been added to earlier churches, such as Coole, Ahacross and Brigown, churches built in the later medieval period did not, as a rule, have 'external' chancels, but probably had wooden partitions (timber rood screens) dividing the church space internally. Evidence of such partitions can still occasionally be seen in the form of beam sockets near the east ends of the north and south walls or, as in the case of Ballyhooly, an abrupt end to the internal render which coats the walls at the east end of the church.

A notable feature is the dearth of natural light in the church. Windows are concentrated around the altar area, the standard arrangement being a two-light window in the east wall and a single-light window in the south, and also occasionally a single-light window in the north wall. The altar area would therefore have been relatively well lit, but it is rare to find windows in the nave, west of the chancel screen, though occasionally one finds a single slit window in the west wall.

One of the most obvious features of subsequent alterations to these churches, and one that is frequently found, is the insertion of windows along the south wall. A good example of this can be seen at Ballynacorra, outside Midleton, which has the standard late medieval ground plan with windows at the east end, but with an additional four windows inserted in the south wall (fig. 1).

The purpose of inserting new windows is obviously to allow in more light, but it may have had a liturgical impetus. One of the central changes sought by advocates of the Reformation was that the liturgy was to be a communal celebration with no separation between people and clergy, as had previously been the case. In injunctions of 1551–2, for instance, John Hooper, Bishop of Gloucester and Worcester; gave orders that 'chapels, closets, partitions and separations' in churches were to be taken down, and the churches were to be without 'closures, imparting, and separations between the ministers and the people'.[3] This injunction was clearly followed, in some cases at least, in Ireland, with one commentator complaining that 'the Protestants have broken up the stone altars that were in our churches and altered the arrangement of the church in order that the marks of their original delineation should disappear'.[4] Another, writing of the diocese of Elphin, complained to the pope that 'The Cathedral still stands, but all its altars, chapels and images have been destroyed and a Protestant altar erected in the centre of the edifice in Protestant fashion.'[5]

While such documentary evidence of this process survives for some churches, the actual presence of inserted windows in many surviving ruins

3 G.O. Addleshaw and F. Etchells, *The architectural setting of Anglican worship* (London, 1948) 25.
4 Quoted in R. Gillespie, *Devoted people: belief and religion in early modern Ireland* (Manchester, 1997), 93.   5 Beirne, *The diocese of Elphin*, 84.

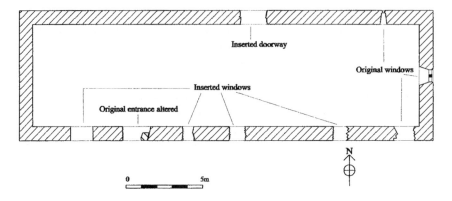

Fig. 1: Ground plan of Ballynacorra church, Co. Cork

could also be regarded as physical evidence of the processes of change and re-ordering. This re-ordering of interior church space probably also involved the destruction of chancel screens and, at least in the case of Aghacross in north Co. Cork, the destruction of a stone-built chancel arch. At Aghacross the original Romanesque church was extended in the later medieval period by the addition of a chancel. The usual method of combining the original church with the new chancel was by breaking an opening through the original east wall and constructing a chancel arch, as was done at nearby Brigown. The east wall of the original church at Aghacross has now been completely demolished, though evidence of its location can still be seen in the internal stonework of the south wall. In the east wall of the chancel, however, most unusually, a moulded limestone arch frames the rear arch of the late medieval window. Comparable arches are not found in this position in other churches, which suggests that the Aghacross example is not in its original location. Its erection in this position certainly predates the construction of the 1749 Massey tomb, which partially obscures it, and was most likely to have been carried out while the church was still in use, which would place it before 1695, according to the diocesan records.[6] It is likely that this arch was in fact originally a chancel arch, which was dismantled in the post-Reformation era and rebuilt in its present position.

It is not clear how widely the practice of replacing the altar with a central table was adopted, but it seems to have been short-lived. The architectural evidence indicates that by the late seventeenth/early eighteenth century the altar had again moved to the east end of the church, presumably following the controversial reforms begun in England by Archbishop Laud in 1617, and new church buildings in that period were furnished with chancels, which were occasionally railed off from the nave. The remarks of Bishop Downes on his

6 W.M. Brady, *Clerical and parochial records of Cork, Cloyne and Ross,* 3 vols (Dublin, 1863), ii, 114.

diocesan tour in 1699/1700 indicate wide variety in the interior furnishings of churches. Murragh church, for instance, was reported as having 'a pulpit and communion table',[7] Aghadown had 'a pulpit, but no communion table',[8] while Inischarra had 'a handsome altar rayl'd in, a pulpit, desk and three large good pews'.[9]

Change in liturgical practice is also indicated at the medieval church at Clonmeen, in the Blackwater valley, west of Mallow. Here, the interior walls were slate-hung, a feature common in Protestant churches of the late seventeenth and eighteenth centuries, and in the process a finely executed late medieval piscina, which clearly no longer had any function, was blocked up.

CONTRACTION OF CHURCH SPACE

Another major change in church buildings in this period was the contraction of the church space in use. This is a phenomenon that has been recorded for other areas of the country also, as in the churches of south Leinster.[10] This contraction was, no doubt, necessitated by a lack of sufficient resources to fully maintain the church, and it frequently involved the maintenance of the chancel only and the abandonment of the nave. Hence we frequently find in the episcopal visitation records entries such as that for Ballynoe in 1615 '*ecclesia ruinata, cancella repata*'.[11]

In other cases, in churches without a structurally distinct chancel, it seems that a section of the church was partitioned off and it alone was kept in repair. This was clearly the case at Kinneigh, north of Ballineen, where, in 1699, according to Bishop Downes 'the partition betwixt that part of the church which is covered and the east end, which is uncovered, is not plastered'.[12]

An interesting insight into this aspect of church architecture, as well as into the tensions that had developed over the use of churches and graveyards between Catholics and Protestants, Irish and English, is provided by the example of Rathbarry, a few miles south-west of Clonakilty. Rathbarry, as its name suggests, was a medieval Barry foundation, with a church and neighbouring castle, which came to the ownership of the Freke family, presumably in the seventeenth century. In her diaries, written between 1671 and 1714, Mrs Elizabeth Freke records that her family was evicted from Rathbarry Castle in 1684 by one John Hull. She was, however, avenged, as she says, when Hull was in turn dispossessed on the accession of James II. Hull subsequently died

7 T.A. Lunham, 'Bishop Dive Downes visitation of his diocese 1699–1702' in *Journal of the Cork Historical and Archaeological Society*, 14 (1908), 66–80, 141–9; 68.   8 Ibid., 142.   9 Lunham, 'Bishop Dive Downes', 168.   10 A. Dolan, 'The larger medieval churches of the dioceses of Leighlin, Ferns and Ossory: a study of adaptation and change' in *Irish Architectural and Decorative Studies*, 2 (1999), 26–65.   11 Brady, *Clerical and parochial records*, ii, 48.   12 Lunham, 'Bishop Dive Downes', 22.

destitute, and, as Freke records, 'lyes buried with one of his children in the open part of the Church of Rathbarry amongst the common Irish, to his eternal infamy'.[13] Her comment clearly points to the division of the church, with one part being roofed and the other remaining open. But it also points to a division of burial space between the Irish and the New English settlers, such as the Frekes themselves who appear from the comment to have been buried within the section of the church still in use. Elizabeth's son, Ralph, was certainly buried in the church, where his tomb still stands, midway along the south wall.

It is impossible to say today how the division of Rathbarry church was effected, or where exactly the partition stood. It may have been a poorly constructed stone wall that has collapsed or been demolished to facilitate burial within the church, or it may have been a wooden partition that has decayed without trace. However, there is some evidence at Rathbarry to suggest that it was the west end which was maintained, as it is clear that much of this end has been reconstructed. This reconstruction work included the building of a slender tower, possibly a bell tower, which is now largely collapsed. West towers are not found in the medieval parish churches of Co. Cork, but they are almost invariably found in Protestant churches of the eighteenth and nineteenth centuries. The Rathbarry tower is a rare example of the addition of such a tower to a medieval church and it seems to be one of the earliest examples of this distinguishing feature of Protestant churches.

CONTINUITY OF USE

A recurring theme in the study of churches of this period is the continuity of use, of buildings, of location and of architectural styles. While it may initially have been a matter of convenience or expediency for a community to repair an existing church, nevertheless, when it came to building anew, Protestant communities rarely moved to new sites. Instead, they built on the foundations of the medieval church or within a few metres of the earlier ruins, or in rare cases, within the ruins.

A number of Protestant churches of the eighteenth century incorporate remains of the medieval building. At Clonmeen a small church was built in the south-east corner of a much larger medieval church, of which only part of the west wall now stands, some 20m from the present church (fig. 2). The new building incorporated part of the south wall of the earlier church, with an original late medieval ogee-headed window near the east end. The late medieval doorway in the south wall probably came from the west wall of the original church. New windows were also inserted, in the south and east walls.

13 Anon, 'Mrs Elizabeth Freke her diary 1671 to 1714' in *Journal of the Cork Historical and Archaeological Society*, 17 (1911), 1–62: 12.

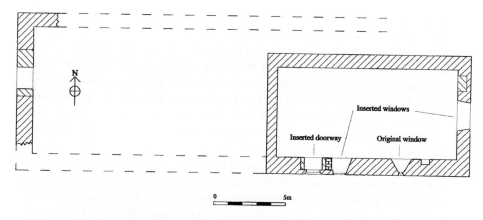

Fig. 2: Ground plan of Clonmeen church, Co. Cork

At Skull in west Co. Cork, the church was extensively renovated in 1721. This was no doubt the church described in 1699 as 'uncovered, the walls standing, well built'.[14] It has the standard features common to almost all of the Protestant churches of the region: a west porch, a high chancel arch, high, wide windows in contrast with the poorly lit buildings of the medieval period, and weather slating on the exterior walls. Meanwhile, at the east end of the north wall a late medieval ogee-headed window and a blocked door survive to indicate its medieval origins.

At Castlelyons the medieval church appears to have been kept in repair well into the eighteenth century, when it was replaced in the 1770s by a new building, which is not alone built on the foundations of the medieval church but is built partially within its remains. The medieval remains at Castlelyons consist of the north and east walls of the high crossing tower of what appears to have been a large cruciform church, more in keeping with the style of a monastic church than a parish church. The 1770s church was built on the foundations of the nave of the earlier building, with its east wall where the west wall of the crossing tower stood and its chancel projecting into the crossing space, dwarfed below the lofty remains of the tower. It has been suggested that the traceried east window in the chancel was removed from the medieval church.[15] However, the moulding profile does not appear to be medieval and the window is almost certainly an eighteenth-century copy, pointing to a common practice of deliberate copying of medieval forms and styles. This is repeated at Rathbarry, where a new Protestant church was built in 1825 within a few metres of the medieval building. A significant feature of the new church is the triple-lancet east window, which is almost a carbon copy of its medieval forerunner.

14 Brady, *Clerical and parochial records*, ii, 170.　**15** P. Power, 'Place-names and antiquities of south-east Cork' in *PRIA* 34C (1918), 184–230, 217.

In the post-Reformation period existing church buildings were adopted by the Protestant Church. Many were subsequently repaired and maintained by Protestant communities, before being finally abandoned and replaced by new churches in the late eighteenth and early nineteenth centuries. The majority of new churches were built either on the site of an existing medieval church, incorporating elements of it, or in close proximity. The new buildings frequently mirrored earlier architectural styles, and in their general layout retained the form and outline of their predecessors, both in their east–west orientation and by the presence of chancels. The interior layout of the buildings was most likely determined by current liturgical rubrics, but the choice of location and the deliberate copying of earlier architectural styles may well have been a reflection of aspects of the theology of the Church of Ireland as enunciated by Archbishop Ussher in the early seventeenth century, which regarded the Church of Ireland as the true successors to the early Church of St Patrick.[16]

CATHOLIC MASS HOUSES

With many existing church buildings having come under the control of the Protestant Church in the post-Reformation period, the Catholic community initially worshipped mainly in private houses.[17] Gradually, however, specific buildings came to be recognised, and tolerated, as places of worship, especially in towns and cities, and by 1624 Cork's first post-Reformation Catholic church had been built.[18] Under the Penal Law regime Mass houses continued to be generally tolerated and had become the norm in much of the country by the time of the 1731 report on the State of Popery.[19] Open-air Masses were not uncommon however, as in the parish of Ballimony in west Co. Cork, where in 1699 Bishop Dive Downes records, the Catholic priest 'celebrates Mass generally in a ditch sheltered with a few bushes and sods, and sometimes in a cabin'.[20]

Little physical evidence of these Penal churches or Mass houses survives today. In the towns and cities they have undoubtedly been demolished to make way for later development, or perhaps incorporated into later buildings. In rural areas, however, many of the sites are indicated on the first edition six-inch Ordnance Survey maps, usually as 'R.C. Chapel (in Ruins)' and in some cases the ruins of the buildings do survive. The most striking aspect of these remains is that they are, with few exceptions, located in remote areas, well away from the

16 A. Ford, 'James Ussher and the creation of an Irish Protestant identity' in B. Bradshaw and P. Roberts (eds), *British consciousness and identity* (Cambridge, 1998), 185–212, 198ff. 17 C. Lennon, 'The Counter-Reformation in Ireland 1542–1641' in C. Brady and R. Gillespie (eds), *Natives and newcomers* (Dublin, 1986), 75–92: 89. 18 E. Bolster, *A history of the diocese of Cork, ii: from the Reformation to the Penal era* (Cork, 1982), 16. 19 P. Corish, *The Irish Catholic experience* (Dublin, 1985), 130. 20 Lunham, 'Bishop Dive Downes', 21.

nearest centre of settlement. A few, as at Ballybrowney near Rathcormac in north Co. Cork, and Coolowen, near Blarney, were located in ringforts, presumably to afford privacy from the authorities, but no standing remains survive. A Roman Catholic chapel at Ballynoe was located in the village, directly across the road from the site of the medieval church and graveyard. This must have been the building described in 1750 by Smith as the 'decayed church'[21], and in 1831 by the Commissioners of National Education as 'an old chapel', part of which housed a school which could accommodate 300 children.[22] It too has disappeared.

The ruins of a number of these churches survive in west Co. Cork. There are no known dates for their construction, but several were in ruins by 1841, when the first edition Ordnance Survey maps were compiled. They were probably built in the eighteenth or perhaps the late seventeenth century and used until their abandonment during the spate of new church building in the early nineteenth century.

In addition to their remote location, Catholic Mass houses are remarkable in their layout and plan for being so completely different to their medieval predecessors, which, as noted above, were laid out to a standard blueprint. In contrast, these churches are distinguished architecturally by a complete lack of uniformity of plan. It is as if, in the disorder and discontinuity caused by the Reformation and the political upheavals of the seventeenth century, the Catholic Church had forgotten the architectural traditions of the past, or, perhaps had deliberately turned its back on them. Alternatively, it may indicate a lack of any centralised direction from Rome as to the proper layout of a church, with individual bishops or priest deciding on their own particular styles.

The most complete of these Mass houses is at Mass Mount, in Kildromalive townland on the Beara peninsula (fig. 3). Like the others in this group it is a plain masonry building with no cut stone mouldings or architectural embellishments. In its ground plan it retains some of the features of earlier churches, in particular the east-west orientation of the nave, with the entrance in the west wall and windows at the east end, lighting the altar area. The T-shaped ground plan is, however, a new departure, as medieval transepts normally formed a cruciform plan. The lack of symmetry is notable, with the doorway off-centre in the west wall, and the northern transept almost twice as long as the southern.

Another church of this group, located at Cooladurragha, near Union Hall in west Co. Cork is poorly preserved but is indicated on the Ordnance Survey six-inch map as being laid out in the shape of a Greek cross, with each arm of equal length.

The chapel at Gurteenroe, west of Ballydehob, is a simple rectangular structure, 18m long and 6m wide with clay-bonded walls. It lies well hidden in a deep cleft between out-cropping rock ridges, remote from any settlement. Its

21 C. Smith, *The ancient and present state of the county and city of Cork*, 2 vols (Cork, 1815), i, 153.
22 Anon., *Ballynoe national schools* (local publication, n.d.), 29.

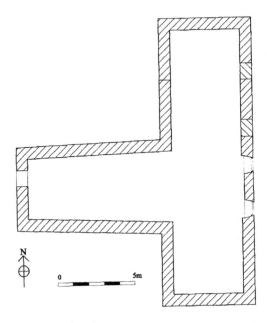

Fig. 3: Ground plan of Kildromalive Roman Catholic church, Co. Cork

north-east–south-west orientation follows the alignment of the surrounding rock ridges rather than adhering to any ideological preference as was the case with medieval churches which are invariably laid out on an east–west axis.

The ruined church at Knockaveale, south west of Bandon, was built in 1680, according to a datestone on the west gable and local tradition. It has several features characteristic of medieval churches, namely the altar and aumbries clustered at one end, but in this case these are at the west end, whereas in medieval churches the altar was invariably at the east end.

Probably the most radical departure from established traditions of church architecture is found in Bandon town itself. At Gallows Hill, to the south-west of the town, and outside the town walls, a Roman Catholic chapel was built in 1796–7.[23] The original building has long since disappeared, replaced by a school, but it is depicted on the 1841 Ordnance Survey map as a rectangular structure aligned south-west–north-east, with a projecting semicircular apse midway along the south-east wall. The traditional east–west alignment has been abandoned in favour of simply following that of the street frontage, with the apse to the rear of the building, hidden from the public road. The impression is of a building maintaining a low profile, as seems to have been the case elsewhere.[24]

Kilbrogan graveyard, to the north of the town, was the location of a medieval

23 P. Ó Flanagan, *Bandon: Irish historic towns atlas*, 3 (Dublin, 1988), 11.   24 Corish, *Catholic experience*, 128.

church, probably the building described in 1615 as being 'in good repair'.[25] It seems to have been abandoned shortly afterwards and its stones reportedly used in the construction of Christ Church, the Church of Ireland church which was built within the town walls at North Main Street *c.*1620.[26] The ruins at Kilbrogan were rebuilt in 1796 as a chapel of ease for the Catholic chapel at Gallows Hill. It was rebuilt in 1802 after it had been burned by government troops in 1798.[27] This unusual building, substantial remains of which survive, was built in a style that has no precursor, and it does not seem to have been repeated. It is a rectangular two-storey structure, 19.4m long and 8m wide, with high, wide doorways at either end of the south wall. Large arched windows, all nearly identical in size, light each floor. Overall the building is notable for its symmetry, in marked contrast to the earlier Catholic churches mentioned above. It is, in essence, a two-storey house with, apart from a stoup inside each doorway, nothing to indicate its function as a church and no clues as to the location of the altar. This may again have been quite deliberate, an attempt to remain discreet, to avoid the attentions of the authorities.

The nineteenth century witnessed what has been referred to as the 'steady infiltration' of Irish Catholics into Bandon town, which, since its foundation in the seventeenth century, had been staunchly Protestant.[28] This process had probably begun in the eighteenth century. The building of churches at Kilbrogan and Gallows Hill suggest the presence of a substantial Catholic population in and around the town, a population not yet confident enough to build within the town walls, instead building in discreet forms around the outskirts. By 1861 the fortunes of the Catholic Church had clearly changed and the present St Patrick's church, built in that year, is a bold Pugin design, carefully located on an eminence dominating the town and overlooking both Church of Ireland churches, in a pattern which was repeated in many towns through the country in the upsurge of Catholic church-building which was witnessed in the nineteenth century.

CONCLUSION

In the aftermath of the Reformation a great many of the surviving medieval church buildings were abandoned and allowed fall into disrepair. Others were maintained by Protestant communities, and they were usually altered to accommodate the demands of the new liturgy. The evidence of these alterations can frequently be traced in the surviving ruins, in the form of inserted windows and demolished chancel arches, which facilitated the placement of the altar in the centre of the church rather than at the east end, and in the contraction of usable space in church buildings whereby only the chancel was maintained, as

25 Ó Flanagan, *Bandon*, 10. 26 B. O' Donoghue, *Parish histories and place-names of West Cork* (Bandon, 1986), 138. 27 Ó Flanagan, *Bandon*, 10. 28 Ibid., 6.

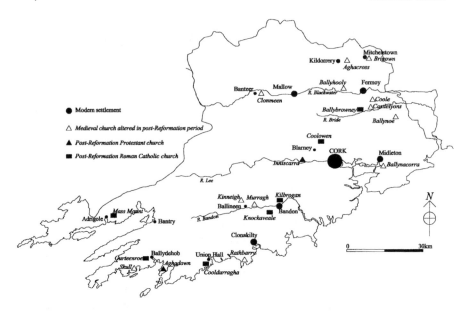

Fig. 4: Distribution map of church sites mentioned in the text

attested to in contemporary documentary references. By the late seventeenth
century new Protestant churches were being built. By this time the altar
appears to have again moved to the east end and the newly built churches were
generally furnished with chancels. In this and in their general layout they
retained the form and outline of their medieval predecessors. They were
usually built on or close to the sites of the buildings which they replaced, and
their architectural features were often direct copies of medieval forms.

Catholic communities generally worshipped in private houses in the
immediate post-Reformation period, though occasionally new churches were
built and were tolerated under the Penal Law regime. A number of these Penal
churches survive in Co. Cork. They are notable for their location, usually
remote from the nearest settlement and for their layout, which marks a
complete break from the standard layout of medieval churches, in contrast to
their Protestant counterparts which retained the traditional east–west orientation, with the altar at the east end. Ground plans of these Catholic churches
include the T-shape, a Greek cross, and the standard east–west rectangle, but
with the altar at the west end.

The number of Catholic churches increased in the closing years of the
eighteenth century and, more dramatically, in the early decades of the
nineteenth century. At Bandon a gradual movement of the Catholic church
closer to the walls of the staunchly Protestant town can be traced through those
decades until, in the late nineteenth century, it achieved its present dominant
position overlooking the town and the nearby Protestant church.

The Dublin parish, 1660–1730

ROWENA DUDLEY

The importance of the role assumed by the urban parish in metropolitan life grew in significance as the seventeenth century progressed. In Dublin the process of exploiting the parish as a unit of local government had begun in the 1620s, but with few legislative demands placed upon the individual parish its participation in local affairs remained largely voluntary.[1] As the century progressed there was, however, a gradual change in emphasis. Slowly the parish's obligations to the local community, as well as to the civic authorities, became more clearly defined and regulated. It became accepted practice for the municipality to involve the parish in the implementation of civic ordinances. This involvement became more sharply defined after 1660, when the requirements of a rapidly expanding city, coupled with the desire to underpin Anglican supremacy, forced the government into a series of measures that directly impacted upon the parish and its role within the community. Duties, which had once been undertaken on a voluntary basis, became obligatory with the onus of implementation resting with the churchwarden and his subordinates. By 1729, numerous laws, affecting all aspects of parish life, had been enacted.[2] One, of particular importance with regard to the parish and its contribution to civic life, was the adverse legislation, passed in 1704, which imposed a sacramental test on Dissenters and Catholics. This measure effectively excluded men of both persuasions from local government and public office.[3] Furthermore, additional legislation also excluded most Catholics from actively participating in parish affairs.[4] So, by the beginning of the eighteenth century, the responsibility for parochial management fell squarely on the shoulders of the Anglican community.

Although the catalyst for much of this legislation was urban expansion, there

1 J.T. and Lady Gilbert (ed.), *Calendar of ancient records of Dublin*, 19 vols (Dublin, 1889–1944), iii, 128–9. The parish was required to maintain specified fire-fighting equipment and was answerably to the city's Treasurer for its upkeep.   2 R. Dudley, 'Dublin's parishes, 1660–1729: the Church of Ireland parishes and their role in the civic administration of the city', unpublished PhD (TCD, 1995), 2 vols , ii, 346–9, appendix 7. In the seventy-one years between 1660 and 1731 sixty-five new laws were introduced which had some bearing upon parochial management. 3 Irish statutes 2 Anne, c. 6.   4 Among the Irish statutes banning Catholic participation were 2 Anne, c. 6; 9 Will. III, c. 1; 2 Geo. I, c. 10; 6 Geo. I, c. 10; 8 Geo. I, c.10; 10 Geo. I, c. 3 and 3 Geo. II, c. 11.

was also a growing awareness that urban living, if it was to be successfully sustained, needed to be regulated in a more structured way. It was the measures taken to safeguard against fire and disease, to improve policing, street lighting and the lot of the urban poor, coupled with the employment opportunities offered by the city, that encouraged migration from the countryside. An additional incentive to urban growth was the enactment of legislation, in 1662[5] and 1692,[6] specifically designed to encourage Protestants to settle in Ireland. Dublin, as the country's single administrative and commercial centre, dominated urban life. More significantly, at a time when the national population growth rate was either static or growing very slowly, the city experienced a period of spectacular, if somewhat sporadic, growth.[7] At the beginning of the seventeenth century Dublin was a small provincial city of some 10,000 inhabitants.[8] By 1744 she had become Europe's eleventh largest city with a population of 112,000 and her topography and demography had undergone a succession of far-reaching changes.[9]

The impact of urban expansion was felt in all aspects of parish life but the most obvious result of its invasive character was the changes it forced upon the city's parishes and their respective boundaries. The development of carefully planned estates by astute entrepreneurs such as Aungier and Jervis, allied with the decision of a cash-strapped Assembly to release large plots of land on both the north and south sides of the city, resulted in city-wide growth. Mid-seventeenth century Dublin was a city of thirteen parishes of varying sizes. For the intra-mural parishes of St Audoen's, St Michael's, St Nicholas Within, St Werburgh's and St John's, confined as they were by the city's walls, expansion was never an option and consequently their boundaries remained unchanged. Elsewhere there were changes, some of greater significance than others. The regaining, by St Andrew's, of its independence in 1665;[10] the designation, in 1680, of St Peter's as the new head of the combined parishes of St Peter's and St Kevin's[11] were the direct result of urban expansion. More significant, because of their impact on all aspects of parochial management, were the boundary changes introduced in 1697[12] and 1707.[13] As a result of the 1697 revision the city's only northern parish, St Michan's, was divided to form three

5 Irish statutes 14 & 15 Chas. II, c.13. For the impact of this Raymond Gillespie, 'Planned migration to Ireland in the seventeenth century' in P.J. Duffy (ed.), *To and from Ireland: planned migration schemes, 1600–2000* (Dublin, 2004), 39–56: 49–55.   6 Irish statutes 2 Will. & Mary, c. 2.   7 S.J. Connolly, *Religion, law and power: the making of Protestant Ireland 1660–1760* (Oxford, 1992), 43–4.   8 L.M. Cullen, 'The growth of Dublin 1600–1900: character and heritage' in F.H.A. Aalen and K. Whelan (eds), *Dublin city and county: from prehistory to present* (Dublin, 1992), 252–77: 277 n. 2.   9 Connolly, *Religion, law and power*, 44.   10 Irish statutes 17 & 18 Chas. II, c. 7.   11 TCD, MSS 2062–2063. The Order in Council reflects the changes of demographic distribution within the parish as it noted that St Kevin's, until 1680 the principal church within the parish, had grown too small and was too inaccessible for the majority of the parishioners. It was therefore deemed necessary to construct a new church on a site more adjacent and convenient for the parish's population.   12 Irish statutes 9 Will. III, c. 16.   13 Irish statutes 6 Anne c. 21.

separate parishes – St Paul's, the new St Michan's and St Mary's. The revision in 1707 created a further three new parishes – St Anne's, St Mark's and St Luke's – as well as dividing St Catherine's into the separate parishes of St Catherine's and St James's. So, by 1707, Dublin had seventeen parishes; a situation that would remain unaltered, despite Archbishop King's proposals for additional new churches in 1711[14] in 1728,[15] until the construction of St Thomas's in 1749.[16]

In every parish, the annually elected parochial officers, charged with the duty of overseeing the parish's affairs, faced a challenging year. Some of the responsibilities they assumed were entirely church-related and highlighted at the visitation through the questions put by the archbishop or his representative.[17] The purpose behind the questioning was to allow the visiting cleric to gain some impression of the physical state of the parish and its church, and to ensure that the spiritual well being of the parish was being maintained in accordance with the canons of the Anglican Church.[18] The questions were also designed to make the incoming officers aware of their responsibilities. For example, the churchwardens were held responsible for the safe keeping of the parish's Bible, Book of Common Prayer and its communion silver. They had to ensure that all baptisms, marriages and burials were conducted and recorded correctly.[19] Most of the duties, however, arose as a consequence of the day-to-day management of the parish. Many of these, such as policing, fire fighting, the care of the poor and scavenging, were assumed in conjunction with the municipal authorities. Although, in Dublin, overall authority for these matters was usually vested in the lord mayor, it was the parish's responsibility to ensure mayoral ordinances were properly implemented.

Despite escalating civic responsibilities, Dublin's parishes were still able to exercise a considerable degree of autonomy within their boundaries. Parochial government was a hierarchical organization led by the minister. Every year, at the Easter vestry meeting, two churchwardens were appointed to assist him in the management of parish affairs.[20] The churchwardens were assisted by sidesmen, much of whose time was spent in the collection of parish cesses,[21] and by overseers for the poor. Theoretically each parish was also obliged to appoint overseers for the highways. In practice, however, only one Dublin

14 R. Kennedy, 'Administration of the diocese of Dublin and Glendalough in the eighteenth century', unpublished MLitt (TCD, 1968), 96. **15** TCD, MS 750/9/125–7, Memorial to George II, 8 June 1728. The changes advocated by King were halted by his death in 1729. **16** M. Craig, *Dublin, 1600–1860* (Dublin, 1980), 179. **17** Dudley, 'Dublin's parishes, 1660–1729', i, 68–71. The annual visitation was held under the supervision of the archbishop's representative. The archbishop, himself, conducted the triennial visitation. **18** *The charge given by Narcissus, lord archbishop of Dublin to the clergy of the province of Leinster, at his triennial visitation, Anno Dom. 1694* (Dublin, 1694). **19** *The charge given by Narcissus, lord archbishop of Dublin.* **20** The incoming churchwardens did not assume their responsibilities until the outgoing churchwardens' accounts had been delivered and passed by the vestry. **21** St Catherine's vestry minutes, i, 1657–1692, RCB, P117/5/1, Memorandum 19 April 1681.

parish, St Peter's, consistently filled this post; a reflection perhaps of the need to oversee a largely rural hinterland.[22] All the posts were unremunerated and held for one year. St Kevin's vestry minutes show that, certainly during the seventeenth century, the appointment of the churchwarden was made by 'lawful succession'.[23] By 1727, the complexities of the job were such that St Catherine's stipulated that no parishioner should be considered for the post of churchwarden without first having served as an overseer for the poor and then as a sidesman.[24] The less demanding nature of the minor offices, such as overseer for the poor, meant that appointments to these offices could be approached more pragmatically. While no parish filled every minor office, and the number of officers elected each year varied according to individual require-ments, each parish always appointed a minimum of four parishioners – two churchwardens and two sidesmen – to oversee the running of the parish.

Although every Protestant parishioner could expect to be called upon to serve his parish, some occupations were legally exempt from service.[25] By claiming 'privilege' peers of the realm, attorneys and members of parliament could avoid parochial office. When nominated to serve as churchwardens in St Peter's in 1687–8 Henry Monck, a patentee, and Joseph Bodin, an attorney, both used their right of 'privilege' to evade their term of office.[26] Conversely, rather than claim 'privilege', Lord Charlemont opted to serve St Paul's as a churchwarden in 1701.[27] Robert Rochford and Alan Broderick, both members of parliament, showed particular commitment to their parish, St Mary's, serving as churchwardens from 1700 to 1704.[28] These men were, however, unusual. Most parochial officers were drawn from among the 'middling sort' – the tradesmen and shopkeepers of the parish. Fortunately, most chose not to shirk their responsibilities. Some, admittedly a small percentage, were even persuaded to serve on more than one occasion. The willingness of parishioners to serve more than once varied from parish to parish. St Michael's relative success can, in part, be explained by the fact that it was an established tradition for a churchwarden to serve for two consecutive years.[29] St Paul's, with no such ready explanation, was also relatively successful whereas St Catherine's and St John's seldom persuaded parishioners to serve more than one term in office.[30] Compliance, however, could never be taken for granted. Resistance was encountered from time to time, obliging the parish to devise ways of enforcing its authority. The most popular sanction for recalcitrance was a fine and the more important the office the greater the fine. In the seventeenth century, those

---

22 St Peter's vestry minutes, i, 1686–1736, RCB P45/6/1. **23** NAI, MS 5136, 'Extracts from St Kevin's Vestry Book 1669–1674', 30 Nov. 1671. **24** St Catherine's vestry minutes, ii, 1693–1730, RCB, P117/5/2, 4 April 1727. **25** R. Burn, *Ecclesiastical law*, 4 vols (7th ed., London, 1908), i, 366–80. **26** St Peter's vestry minutes, i, 1686–1736, RCB, P 45/6/1, 5 Oct. 1687. **27** St Paul's vestry minutes, i, 1698–1750, RCB, P 273/6/1. **28** St Mary's vestry minutes, i, 1699–1739, RCB, P27/7/1, 1 April 1700; 22 April 1701; 30 March 1703; 17 April 1704. **29** St Michael's vestry minutes, i, 1667–1754, RCB, P118/5/1, 2 April 1678. **30** Dudley, 'Dublin's parishes 1660–1729', i, 80–1, table 2: 1.

refusing the office of churchwarden could expect to be fined £5, while those who refused the lesser office of sidesman faced a fine of £3.[31] In the eighteenth century, St Bride's, although not increasing the fines, added the caveat that they must be paid within ten days.[32] Other parishes, such as St Catherine's, did demand higher fines.[33] More importantly, the vestries retained the right to fine as appropriate ensuring that the penalty for non-service could be adjusted, if necessary, to reflect the status of the noncompliant parishioner.

As a 'fine' was the recognized way to avoid office, it was, consequently, never refused, even when a parish was faced by a number of rebellious parishioners. Finding an explanation for these occasional periods of persistent defiance, as for example occurred in St Catherine's between 1679 and 1683, is difficult as the vestry minutes give little indication of any possible cause. St Catherine's had, however, introduced a vestry ordinance demanding every parishioner serve his term of office and this may have prompted the rebellion.[34] On the rare occasion when a parishioner proved especially obdurate, refusing to serve and to pay the fine, then the parish could use its ultimate penalty, prosecution – a remedy employed by St Bride's when faced by one such intransigent parishioner in 1695.[35] Undoubtedly, for many, the onerous nature of the churchwarden's duties was an influential factor in their decision not to serve their parish.[36]

Although the churchwardens and their subordinates were expected to assume overall responsibility for parish affairs, they did receive assistance. Parishioners were regularly co-opted on to the supervisory committees formed to oversee the numerous concerns of parish life. The applotment of cesses, taxes levied on the parishioners to raise money to meet both domestic and civic demands; the annual auditing of the churchwardens' accounts; the building of a watch house and, in new parishes such as St Mary's, the building of the church all required the supervision of parochial committees. It was common practice to nominate more parishioners than required and then to add a qualifying proviso, 'any three' or 'any five', to the end of the list of nominees. Such flexibility was sensible given that every parish tended to rely upon a small group of willing volunteers, most of whom had already served the parish in some official capacity. Very occasionally, usually when financial concerns became particularly pressing, the elite of the parish became involved. The illustrious nature of the committee, nominated by St Mary's in March 1714, to examine the church building accounts reflects the deep concerns felt within the parish

31 St Bride's vestry minutes, i, 1662–1742, RCB, P327/3/1, 16 Oct. 1673. 32 Ibid., 21 April 1701. 33 St Catherine's vestry minutes, ii, 1693–1730, RCB, P117/5/2, 16 Oct. 1696. The new fine was fixed at £10 for a churchwarden and £5 for a sidesman or overseer for the poor. 34 St Catherine's vestry minutes, i, 1657–1692, RCB, P117/5/1, 22 April 1679. 35 St Bride's vestry minutes, i, 1662–1742, RCB, P327/3/1, 28 Oct. 1695. There is no record in the vestry minutes of the outcome of the prosecution. 36 TCD MS 750/8/96, King to the lord mayor of Dublin, Joseph Kane, 10 May 1726. King remarked on the very burdensome nature of a churchwarden's duties.

over the debt. Few parishes would have been able to call upon the services of the lord chief baron of the exchequer, Robert Rochford; the attorney general, George Gore or the lord chancellor, Constantine Phipps, to solve their problems, but wealthy citizens with long standing connections within a parish could sometimes be prevailed upon to help.[37] This happened in St Catherine's when financial problems stemming from the economic uncertainties of the 1720s forced the parish to revive old allegiances and seek the help of Richard Tighe, the grandson of a former parishioner.[38] Although Tighe was no longer a resident his family associations with the parish coupled with his interest, as a member of parliament, in church affairs made him eminently suitable. The family may even have retained property within the parish, which would have entitled him to participate in parochial affairs. His involvement is, however, an example of the trust that could be fostered through service to the parish.

Every parish also appointed a number of paid officers, both ecclesiastical and secular, to fulfill certain parochial duties. Many of Dublin's parishes employed extra clerics, known as lecturers and readers. These men were licensed and undertook specific religious duties within their parish. St Michael's lecturer, appointed in 1681, was paid £30 per annum and expected to 'preach once every Lord's Day'.[39] When, however, a new lecturer was appointed in 1694, it was decided not to raise his salary through public subscription, as had previously been the case. Instead the cost was to be divided between the minister, who was to pay £10, and the parish, which paid the remaining £20.[40] The parish's reader, Josias Chollet, appointed in 1704, received £8 per annum to read Sunday morning and evening prayers.[41] As the eighteenth century progressed, however, fewer parishes bothered to employ a lecturer relying instead on the three men Archbishop William King deemed necessary 'to supply the least parish in Dublin well … a minister an assistant & reader'.[42]

The demands of parish life also led to the employment of a variety of laymen. Each parish employed a parish clerk to record its baptisms, marriages and burials. It also appointed a sexton who was expected to attend throughout divine service so that he could seat people in church according to their rank.[43] He was also expected, among other things, to keep the church clean, maintain church ornaments and clerical vestments, dig graves, protect church property against vandalism, attend all vestry meetings and ensure seemly behaviour within the church and churchyard.[44] The post was generally held for life and

37 St Mary's vestry minutes, i, 1699–1739, RCB, P277/7/1, 5 March 1713[/14]. 38 St Catherine's vestry minutes, ii, 1693–1730, RCB, P117/5/2. Tighe signs the vestry minutes from 29 Feb. 1719[/20] to 20 Feb. 1721[/2]. Richard was grandson to Richard Tighe, an English merchant who had settled in St Catherine's in 1640. The family had then moved to St Michan's where Richard senior was buried in 1673. 39 St Michael's vestry minutes, i, 1667–1754, RCB, P118/5/1, 13 Jan. 1681[/2]. 40 Ibid., 9 April 1694. 41 St Michael's vestry minutes, i, 1667–1754, RCB, P118/5/1, 25 May 1704. 42 TCD, MS 1995–2008/2317, *c.*1693, Section 2, No. 4, Archbishop W. King to Henry Capell. 43 St Michan's Memorial Book, 1725, RCB, P276/12/3 (now in local custody). 44 Ibid., also see St John's vestry minutes, i, 1658–1711,

was often passed down from generation to generation within a family.[45] Another mainstay of parish life was the beadle. The parish messenger, he was also expected to help maintain law and order within the parish. Although each officer received an annual salary the parishes were always prepared to reward an individual for exceptional diligence with a bonus. On the other hand, any misdemeanor earned a sharp reprimand and, as the office was generally held on 'good behaviour', in cases of serious misconduct the offender faced the possibility of dismissal. The employment of a vestry clerk, to record the vestry's dealings, was very much a seventeenth century innovation and one that some Dublin parishes were slow to adopt.[46] The duties imposed upon St John's sexton in 1695, suggest the parish had no vestry clerk.[47] St Bride's first vestry clerk, Stephen Conduit, a Dublin merchant, was not appointed until the eighteenth century.[48]

In addition to these four officers, there were numerous other posts that, from time to time, required filling. Organs, first introduced into the parishes in the 1680s, necessitated the employment of both an organist and a man to work the organ's bellows.[49] The parish school, although a legal obligation since the reign of Henry VIII, did not become a permanent fixture until the early eighteenth century.[50] St Bride's first permanent school was founded in 1711. It provided an education for forty boys, most of whom were Catholic.[51] Other eighteenth-century innovations, such as the foundation of the parish-based fire service, helped to swell the ranks of parish officials. All these employees, including the clerics, were appointed by, and were answerable to, the parish's governing body, the vestry. As the base upon which parish authority was founded, the vestry's power was considerable. Working in conjunction with the minister and church-wardens, the vestry's purpose was to oversee and approve the management of all parish business. Meetings, with the exception of the vestry held during Easter week to elect the incoming church officers, were discretionary and held as business dictated. Although theoretically required to enter all vestry 'acts' into the minutes, the parishes appear to have entered only those that were important or likely to be challenged. This was a sensible precaution given the apathy shown by most parishioners towards parochial affairs. Every parishioner paying church rates was entitled to attend and vote in vestry but, under no obligation to do so, the majority stayed away unless personal involvement forced their attendance. Very occasionally, the odd meeting was well attended –

RCB, P328/5/2, 21 Jan. 1694[/5]. **45** St Mary's vestry minutes, i, 1699–1739, RCB, P 277/7/1, 22 Feb. 1721[/2]. **46** S. and B. Webb, *English local government from the revolution to the Municipal Corporations Act: the parish and the county* (London, 1906), 124. **47** St John's vestry minutes, i, 1658–1711, RCB, P328/5/2, 21 Jan. 1694[/5]. **48** St Bride's vestry minutes, i, 1662–1742, RCB, P327/3/1, 6 April 1702. **49** B. Boydell, 'St Michan's Church Dublin: the installation of the organ in 1725 and the duties of the organist' in *Dublin Historical Record*, 46 (1993), 101–20: 117, n. 5. St Catherine's vestry minutes, i, 1657–1692, RCB, P. 117/5/1, 25 June 1678; 13 April 1680. St Peter's vestry minutes, i, 1686–1736, RCB, P. 45/6/1, 29 March 1687. **50** Irish statutes 28 Hen. VIII, c. 15. **51** Dudley, 'Dublin's parishes, 1660–1729', i, 203, table 4: 11.

when pews were reassigned for example – which raises the question as to whether the Dublin parishes operated 'select' or 'general' vestries? The lack of signatures and the fact that most vestries appear to have been managed by a small number of well-connected parishioners certainly favours the argument for select vestries. On no occasion, however, do any of Dublin's parishes acknowledge a select vestry such as occurred in the parish of St Saviour in Southwark. There, according to a pamphlet printed in 1729, a select vestry of thirty people had taken it upon themselves to manage parish affairs without reference to, or consultation with, the vast majority of the parishioners.[52] It may be that, in Dublin, the increasingly onerous nature of parish affairs persuaded many to avoid such matters at all cost.

A changing religious profile may also have had some bearing on vestry numbers. Although between 1660 and 1729, a relatively short period of sixty-nine years, the influence wielded by the city's various religious communities depended very much on the politics of the day, of more immediate relevance to the parish was the gradual change in Dublin's religious makeup. The growing numbers of Catholics and Dissenters had the potential to disrupt parochial government. Resentment could be, and most probably was, registered through the nonpayment of parish cesses. The implications behind such an action were serious, given the ever-present threat of insolvency that loomed over most of Dublin's parishes. Eighteenth-century Dublin was still, as she had been throughout the second half of the seventeenth century, apart from a brief period during the late 1680s, a Protestant city. Her religious profile was, however, in the process of undergoing a subtle change. The significance of this change is revealed through an incomplete survey undertaken for Archbishop King in 1718 and a remark made by Arthur Dobbs in 1731. Parochial returns showed King that although some parishes – SS Bride's, John's, Nicholas Within and Luke's – had an Anglican majority of three to one, there were other parishes, such as St Michan's, where the religious balance was very different.[53] There King was told there were 'few dissenters, but the papists are 8 or 10 times more than both protestants, Conformists & dissenters'.[54] By 1731, the Anglican community had declined further and, as Dobbs noted, 'catholics and dissenters were equal in number to, if they did not exceed, members of the established church'.[55] Dublin was still a Protestant city but those charged with her governance were, by 1731, in the minority.

No doubt, for the ordinary parishioner, about to begin his term of office, such details would have been of little consequence. Of more immediate concern would have been the day-to-day management of parochial affairs and, in particular, the administration of the parish's finances. Parochial expenditure fell within two broad categories, the ordinary and the extraordinary. The

52 British Library 816 m. 9 (94), Pamphlet 'to the Parishioners of St Saviour in Southwark'.
53 Dublin Public Libraries, Pearse Street Library, Monck Mason Papers, vol. III/69.   54 Ibid.
55 Ibid., vol. I/62, 195.

maintenance of the church, the salaries of its officers and the general care of the parish poor were all 'ordinary' expenses. Parochial income to pay for these everyday needs was derived from the cess, rents, fines, legacies, fees and pew sales. More unusual expenditure, the 'extraordinary', arose with the building of a parish church or the raising of money to alleviate the sufferings of fellow Protestants. These special costs were either met by public subscription or by a parochial cess but, where substantial sums were required, the parish frequently sought government aid. St Werburgh's, for example, sought and received a royal donation of £2,000 – the proceeds from the sale of land in Essex Street – when they embarked upon the rebuilding of the parish church in 1716.[56] The rebuilding of Holy Trinity, Cork was also subsidized by government aid in the form of a parliamentary tax of 1s. per ton on all coals brought into Cork.[57]

In addition to raising money to meet its own needs, the parish was also required to act as a tax collector for the state and the city. Parish officials collected hearth money and poll tax. They apportioned and collected civic taxes raised to maintain the city's infrastructure. During the seventeenth century warrants to levy civic taxes, known as presentments, were approved and granted by the tholsel. In the eighteenth century, however, the lord mayor was obliged to seek authorization in the king's bench court. While never popular, civic taxation in the seventeenth century aroused no overt parochial discontent. Some complaints do, however, emerge in the early eighteenth century when growing civic demands prompted rumblings of discontent throughout Dublin. St Paul's complained in 1702.[58] St Catherine's noted the generally discontent felt by all the parishes in 1716.[59] St Michan's registered the universal displeasure felt in 1725.[60] The authorities were aware of the disgruntlement but did little to mollify the parishes and no effort was made to ease their financial burdens.[61] St Michan's, therefore, took the precaution of ordering their vestry clerk to procure advance notice of all future presentments so that the parish could take 'seasonable' notice of them and so prevent further 'impositions'.[62]

Parochial dissatisfaction with the civic cess did not prevent the parish from exploiting the cess as a method of raising money for domestic needs. Its

56 Permission to rebuild had been granted in 1712 under Irish Statutes 2 Geo. I, c. 24. In 1715, under Irish statutes 2 Geo. I, c. 24 permission was granted to change the site of the church. Also see St Werburgh's Miscellaneous Papers 27.3.173, 1720, RCB, P326/27/3.   57 T.J. McKenna and C. Moore, *The modest men of Christ Church, Cork* (Naas, 1970), 43. On 8 February 1716 men were employed to take down the church. The foundation stone for the new church was laid on St Patrick's Day, 1718. The levy on coal imports was imposed in 1719 and lasted for seven years. In 1726 there was still a deficit of £480, revenues earned from the re-imposed coal tax met this. The parish vestry minutes give a hint of the difficulties the parish experienced with the rebuilding of the parish church see RCB, P527/7/1.   58 St Paul's vestry minutes, i, 1698–1750, RCB, P273/6/1, 16 Dec. 1702.   59 St Catherine's vestry minutes, ii, 1693–1730, RCB, P117/5/2, 17 April 1716.   60 St Michan's vestry minutes, i, 1724–1760, RCB, P276/4/1, 7 Dec. 1725.   61 An effort was made in 1703 to prevent Grand Juries from misappropriating money raised through presentments under Irish Statutes 4 Anne, c. 6.   62 St Michan's vestry minutes, i, 1724–1760, RCB, P276/4/1, 7 Dec. 1725.

popularity, with the civic and parochial authorities alike, lay in the fact that it could be tailored to suit specific requirements, could be levied when needed and was capable of realizing substantial sums. For taxation purposes each parish was divided into wards. Initially these wards were probably coterminous with the civic wards but many were later modified to reflect population changes within a parish. These readjustments were essential as a cess could be levied for a very specific purpose within one particular area of the parish. In 1725, St Michan's cessed the inhabitants of Church Street, King's Street and Stirrip Lane who had any 'dependence' on a new sewer recently constructed in Church Street. Another cess was imposed on fifteen parishioners in Hamon Lane.[63] The occasional revision of parochial wards therefore ensured that only those personally affected would be called upon to pay for any repairs or improvements.

At first the only condition imposed on those charged with determining the cess (also called an applotment), the minister, the churchwardens and a panel of specially elected parishioners, was one of fairness.[64] The introduction, in 1665, of Minister's Money, a tax based on the valuation of all property within the parish and introduced to provide a regular income for the Anglican clergy did, however, allow the parishes to begin to standardize the way applotments were calculated.[65] St Bride's was one of the first parishes to employ minister's money as a benchmark. In 1679, the parish ordered that double the amount usually paid in minister's money was to be applotted upon the parish to pay for church repairs.[66] Thereafter it was used with increasingly frequency. Parishioners were cessed to pay so many pence/shillings per £1 of minister's money, with the rate charged always determined by the overall sum required and the number liable for taxation. By the eighteenth century minister's money had become the recognized way of determining a cess, a fact implicitly acknowledged in 1723 by its use, for the first time, in legislation.[67]

Despite its obvious usefulness the effectiveness of the cess as a means of raising money was hampered by one serious drawback – it was notoriously difficult to collect. Almost every cess, whether civic or parochial, fell into arrears simply because a small proportion of the people levied either could not or would not pay their dues. Generally the individual amounts owed were small and could be recouped by distraint. This allowed the churchwardens the right to confiscate and sell goods owned by the defaulter up to the value of the default. Of course this procedure was resented and the parishes were forced to indemnify their churchwardens whenever they were obliged to distrain.[68]

---

63 St Michan's applotment book, i, 1711–1725, RCB, P276/10/1, 1725.   64 The panel was not allowed to instigate any decision without the presence of the minister and at least one churchwarden.   65 Irish statutes 17 & 18 Chas. II, c. 7. The Act entitled the incumbent to have all the property valued within the parish once every three years. Valuations could be adjusted to reflect improvements made in the intervening years between valuations. The maximum rate that could be charged was fixed at 12*d.* per £1 of yearly value and no house could be rated above £60.
66 St Bride's vestry minutes, i, 1662–1742, RCB, P327/3/1, 2 Feb. 1679[/80].   67 Irish statutes 10 Geo. I, c. 3.   68 St Peter's vestry minutes, i 1686–1736, RCB, P45/6/1, 24 Sept. 1695. The

Circumspection in disposing of the goods taken was essential as defaulters were frequently slow to pay their default but nevertheless expected to have their property returned once the outstanding sum had been paid.[69] A more drastic method of dealing with nonpayment was used by the parish of Holy Trinity, Cork. There parishioners who refused to pay their part of the parish cess were automatically brought before the consistory court.[70] Serious difficulties could arise, however, if arrears were left unpaid. For example, the churchwardens' accounts show that church maintenance was often just a matter of paying for relatively small repairs that were seldom expensive. Major repairs, however, undertaken at some stage by most parishes, were always costly and frequently resulted in long-term arrears. The building of St Mary's church is one such example. Construction on the church began in 1701[71] but a succession of cesses failed to raise sufficient money to pay the contractors.[72] Still in debt in 1711, despite a protracted struggle to pay off its financial obligations, the parish found itself facing legal charges for nonpayment.[73] More legal charges for nonpayment were brought in 1721 when the parish was finally forced to admit it was 'incapable' of paying off the arrears.[74]

St Mary's experiences were not unique. The debts incurred by the rebuilding of St Werburgh's took years to repay.[75] Parochial dissent over taxation for church rebuilding was not just an eighteenth century phenomenon. Similar difficulties had been encountered by St Bride's[76] and St John's[77] when the parishes embarked upon major church renovations during the seventeenth century. Although reluctance on the part of Catholics and Dissenters to pay for church repairs and rebuilding probably helped to push the parishes into debt, there would have been many Anglican parishioners too poor to meet their dues.[78] From the parish's point of view finding additional resources to repay disgruntled tradesmen was not easy given that the value of other sources of parochial income, traditionally used to supplement spending, was slowly being

churchwardens had been arrested when they distrained goods from a Mr Gee who owed Poor Money. The parish promised to indemnify them against any claims made by Gee. 69 St John's vestry minutes, i, 1658–1711, RCB, P328/5/2, 8 Oct. 1688. The parish had had to pacify a number of irate parishioners after distraints taken from them could not be found by promising to buy a trunk in which to hold all future distraints. 70 Holy Trinity, Cork, vestry minutes, i, 1710–1760, RCB, P527/7/1, 15 Jan. 1725[/6] and 11 April 1726. There is no evidence, to date, that the Dublin parishes used this method to enforce payment. 71 Rolf Loeber, *A biographical dictionary of architects in Ireland, 1600–1720* (London, 1981), 95. 72 St Mary's vestry minutes, i, 1699–1739, RCB, P277/7/1, 18 May 1702, 4 March 1703[/4], 3 Oct. 1704, 7 Dec. 1705. 73 St Mary's vestry minutes, i, 1699–1739, RCB, P277/7/1, 23 Jan. 1711[/12]. 74 Ibid., 13 Nov. 1721. 75 St Werburgh's miscellaneous papers, RCB, P326/27/3/ 96–7, 110, 162, 181, 183, 192, 201, 205, 213. 76 St Bride's vestry minutes, i, 1662–1742, RCB, P327/3/1, 2 Feb. 1679[/80], 1 Dec. 1685, 6 Nov. 1691, 9 Dec. 1692. 77 St John's vestry minutes, i, 1658–1711, RCB, P328/5/2, 24 May 1680, 13 April 1681. 78 The introduction of Irish Statutes 12 Geo I, c. 9 in 1726 ended the right of Catholic parishioners to attend vestries called to deal with financial matters. Exclusion from the vestry, however, probably made for more obstinate opposition and an even greater unwillingness to pay any cess levied for church repairs.

eroded. For example, the contribution made by rents to St Catherine's budget dropped from 49 per cent in 1687[79] to 17 per cent in 1702 despite an interim increase in the rents.[80] The money earned from fees and fines was never significant and generally reserved for poor relief. Similarly, the income earned from pew sales was seldom substantial. Major reconstruction within the church, such as the rebuilding of the pulpit or the construction of a new gallery, as well as the redrawing of parish boundaries, did necessitate large-scale re-allocation and the subsequent sale of pews undoubtedly provided a welcome addition to parochial income but such events were rare. Most pew sales were made on an individual basis, prompted by death; a change of parish or improved financial circumstances and the money was generally used to relieve the parish poor.[81] Therefore, with little alternative when it came to meeting their various financial obligations the parishes came to rely, increasingly, upon the cess as their principal method of raising money. Most parishes did manage to contain their day-to-day spending and, where arrears were incurred, provided they were small, they were usually budgeted for in the following year's cess. In particularly difficult times, as the carefully itemized churchwardens' accounts occasionally show, it was even possible to defer a small part of the salaries of church employees. Such methods could not be used in the case of the persistent arrears associated with major projects. These arrears were less easily met and often took years to repay.

Implementing a cess was undoubtedly time-consuming; a fact belatedly acknowledged by St Michan's when, in 1726, £10 was granted to the churchwardens to enable them to employ an assistant cess collector.[82] The struggle to collect arrears and so remain solvent was essential if the parish was to have any chance of meeting its other commitments. Some of these commitments, such as the care of the poor and the maintenance of law and order, had always been part of parish life. Other commitments, however, were only assumed as a result of legislation or in frustration at the ineffectiveness of municipal ordinances. Increasing parochial responsibility with regard to fire fighting, street lighting and scavenging inevitably involved the parishes in additional expense. For example, in the case of fire-fighting equipment, during the seventeenth century, the parish was obliged to maintain a supply of buckets, ladders and fire hooks.[83] Surprisingly, given the high incidence of fire within the city, the parishes were slow to acquire this equipment and lackadaisical about its upkeeping. Rapid urban expansion and a spate of fires during the early part of the eighteenth century galvanised the Assembly into buying two fire engines in

79 St Catherine's vestry minutes, i, 1657–1692, RCB, P117/5/1, churchwardens accounts 1687. Total receipts £36 4s. 4d., rent receipts £17 16s. 4d.   **80** RCB, P117/5/2, churchwardens accounts 1702. Total receipts £140 5s. 0d., rents receipts £24 6s. 4d.   **81** R. Dudley, 'The Dublin parishes and the poor: 1660–1740' in *Archivium Hibernicum*, 53 (1999), 80–94: 84.   **82** St Michan's vestry minutes, i, 1724–1760, RCB, P276/4/1, 1 April 1726.   **83** Gilbert (ed.), *Anc. recs Dub*, iv, 504.

February 1705[/6].[84] Municipal ordinances were also introduced directing how fires should be fought and looting prevented.[85] These ordinances were later endorsed by legislation.[86] By 1719, these measures were no longer effective and legislation was introduced compelling the parish to take a more pro-active role in fire fighting.[87] The result was more expense as each parish was now obliged to purchase a fire engine, employ someone to maintain it and construct an engine house. St John's, for example, spent £69 buying two engines and £10 on the construction of the engine house.[88] St Mary's decided it would need to spend £150 if it were to comply with the regulations.[89]

Although lighting Dublin's streets was the Assembly's responsibility, concerns over the failure of the lamps contractors to meet their obligations finally compelled the parishes to take action. A citywide survey to assess the situation was undertaken in the 1720s.[90] As a result some parishes decided to withhold their lamp tax money until the situation was improved.[91] In other parishes the churchwardens were ordered to take steps to ensure that the lamp contractors met their obligations.[92]

Scavenging was another civic responsibility. A dogged effort was made by the Assembly to ensure the city's streets were kept repaired and clean. It was, however, an impossible task. Finally, in 1730, the parish became directly involved in the struggle when the churchwardens were ordered to perambulate through their parish, on at least four occasions during the year, and then report their findings to the lord mayor.[93] Admittedly, with the exception of the fire fighting equipment, meeting these commitments required only a limited amount of expenditure. Nevertheless they underline the invasive nature of urban life and the mounting burden it placed upon the parish.

Meeting the commitment made to the poor did, however, impose a serious financial burden upon every Dublin parish. The burden was made all the greater by the fact that the municipality offered little practical help. Over a period of almost seventy years the city was responsible for only two major undertakings, the founding of the King's Hospital School in 1669[94] and the Workhouse in 1703.[95] Such caution is difficult to explain, although the experiences of other cities, political instability, economic hardships and a chronic shortage of cash may all have had a bearing on civic attitudes towards the poor. Furthermore the civic authorities were under no statutory obligation to provide

---

84 Ibid., vi, 347. A third engine was acquired in 1712. 85 Ibid., vi, 347. 86 Irish statutes 2 Geo. I, c. 15, § 3. 87 Irish Statutes 6 Geo. I, c. 15, § 8 and § 9. 88 St John's vestry minutes, ii, 1712–1766, RCB, P328/5/3, 1 March 1720[/1]. 89 St Mary's vestry minutes, i, 1699–1739, RCB, P277/7/1, 23 March 1720[/1]. 90 *For the benefit of the publick, An agreement of the Church-Wardens of the several parishes in the city and suburbs of DUBLIN, at a meeting on the 19th November, 1725* (Dublin, 1725). 91 St Michan's vestry minutes, i 1724–1760, RCB, P276/4/1, 7 Dec. 1725. 92 St Mary's vestry minutes, i, 1699–1739, RCB, P. 277/7/1, 23 Jan. 1726. 93 St Paul's vestry minutes, i, 1698–1750, RCB, P273/6/1. A loose, printed advertisement, found in the minutes. 94 L. Whiteside, *A history of the King's Hospital* (2nd ed., Dublin, 1985), 1. 95 Gilbert (ed.), *Anc. recs Dub*, vi, 296.

for the poor. This obligation had been ceded to the parishes in 1665 when legislation was introduced giving the parish the right to assess and levy inhabitants
for the purpose of raising money to help the poor.[96] Instead the city chose to
concentrate its efforts on devising ways of containing the hoards of beggars
who roamed Dublin's streets leaving the parishes to care for the needy, the sick
and, despite the arrival of the Foundling Hospital in 1728, the orphaned.[97]

During the seventeenth century parochial provision for the poor was a
largely self-imposed duty.[98] Charity was dispensed in an *ad hoc* way by the
churchwardens to those in need with preference given to the indigenous poor.
'Strangers' were helped, but always with the intention of ensuring the recipient
did not become a permanent burden upon the parish. For the indigenous poor,
all relief was conditional on good behaviour. Misdemeanors were punished in
accordance with the gravity of the crime, with the ultimate sanction being the
right to withhold monetary or material help. This allowed the parish to exercise
considerable control over the poor; a control it did not hesitate to use. Care was
taken to ensure only the worthy received assistance. For example, parishioners
petitioning St Bride's for the right to become parish pensioners were first
questioned by a parish committee. Their conclusions were then presented to
the vestry where the fate of each petitioner was decided.[99]

The extent to which parochial charity was extended to the poor of other
religions is, however, by no means clear. St Bride's, for example, were willing to
pay Turlogh Burne a pension provided he conformed. When, in 1671, he
refused to acquiesce to their demands, the parish responded by withdrawing his
pension. The fact that Burne was later reinstated suggests that expediency had
persuaded him to capitulate.[1]

With no compulsory poor rate Dublin's parishes were, once again, obliged to
use the cess as a means of raising money for the poor. A comprehensive understanding of the extent to which it was used during the seventeenth century is
hampered by a lack of evidence.[2] It was, nevertheless, an important tool and one
the parishes employed with increasing frequency. In the years 1670–89 St
Bride's implemented 10 cesses; St Michael's 14 and St John's 11.[3] Each cess,
although called a poor cess, was spent at the discretion of the churchwardens to
meet the needs of the parish. Some of the money raised went on church
maintenance but a substantial proportion was always spent on the poor. In
1669, St John's spent 38 per cent of its annual income on the poor.[4] St Michael's

96 Irish statutes 17 & 18 Chas. II, c. 7. 97 Irish statutes 1 Geo. II, c. 27. 98 Statutory obligations towards the poor were introduced in 1542 under 33 Hen. VIII, c. 15 but the Elizabethan Poor
Law of 1601 was never enacted in Ireland. 99 St Bride's vestry minutes, i, 1662–1742, RCB, P
327/3/1, 24 April 1685. The vestry had reserved the right to make the final decision concerning
each petitioner. 1 Ibid., 21 April 1671. 2 The levying of cesses was recorded in the
applotment book and only one seventeenth-century book, belonging to St John's, has survived.
Occasionally the vestry minutes record a decision to levy a poor cess, but by no means every parish
decision was entered into the minutes. It is therefore possible more cesses were levied than the
minutes indicate. 3 Dudley, 'The Dublin parishes, 1660–1729', i, 183, table 4: 2. 4 St John's

raised £82 16s. 1d. in 1680 and spent just over half of this, £45 1s. 0d. on the poor.[5] Seven years later, in 1687, the poor of St Bride's accounted for 70 per cent of parochial budget.[6]

Collections also provided a useful source of additional income. There was no statutory obligation upon a parishioner to contribute but a note in St Bride's vestry minutes indicates that regular Sunday collections were made to help the poor.[7] Once again, understanding how the parishes distributed collections among the poor in the seventeenth century is hampered by a lack of evidence. At least one parish, St Michael's, collected briefs; a single collection made for a named individual suffering temporary hardship.[8] Another parish, St Werburgh's, gave a number of collections to several parishioners who had also suffered from a variety of misfortunes.[9] Other collections, made either in church or at the church door, were given to the churchwardens to spend as they saw fit.

The advent of a new century brought no respite as the poor continued to flock to Dublin. Still forced to rely on the cess and Sunday collections as the main sources of income, the difficulty for every parish was to make its limited resources stretch far enough to care for all those requiring its help. Better poor records for the eighteenth century show the poor relief system in a clearer light. The money allocated from the parish poor cess, for example, was now used throughout the city to maintain parish foundlings and their nurses, whereas the occasional civic 'poor' cess levied on the parishes was used by the authorities to provide relief wherever it was most urgently needed – in the city's jails, or to help destitute Protestants living outside Dublin. On most occasions a parish's share of these civic cesses was modest, but not always. St Bride's, for example, was asked to raise almost £60 towards the relief of the Protestants of Lisburn where a fire had inflicted serious damage in 1707.[10]

Church collections were distributed among the poor throughout the year. It was normal procedure to give a collection to a particular individual, although from time to time, some were assigned towards maintaining the charity school. Morning collections were divided into three categories: briefs – money collected for named individuals; offertory – money collected monthly on a specified Sunday and often given to the churchwardens to spend on the parish poor at their discretion; quarterly – money collected and paid to pensioners. Evening collections, always much smaller, were not allocated but always spent

applotment book, i, 1659–1694, RCB, P328/10/1, poor accounts 1669.   **5** St Michael's vestry minutes, i, 1667–1754, RCB, P118/5/1, churchwardens' accounts 1680.   **6** St Bride's vestry minutes, i, 1662–1742, RCB, P327/3/1, 24 Oct. 1687, 25 Oct. 1687.   **7** Ibid., 7 Nov. 1692. The minutes state that a poor cess of £45 was to be spent on the poor over and 'above what is collected every Lords day for that purpose'. In England, under 27 Hen. VIII, c. 25, alms were to be collected every week and given to the impotent poor.   **8** St Michael's vestry minutes, i, 1667–1754, RCB, P118/5/1, churchwardens' accounts 1681.   **9** St Werburgh's miscellaneous papers RCB, P326/27/3/40, 22 July 1660 – 17 Feb. 1660[/1].   **10** Dudley, 'The Dublin parishes, 1660–1729', i, 198, Table 4: 7.

as and where required. The income each parish earned from the collections varied enormously. Over a four-year period, 1700–3, St Bride's average earnings from collections was £28 4s. 10d. per year.[11] In St Michael's the income was similar – between 1706 and 1713 the parish collected, on average, just under £30 per year.[12] By comparison, St Bride's neighbour, St Werburgh's, collected over £100 between November 1726 and October 1727.[13] Clearly each parish could only collect in accordance with its means; therefore, given the ever-increasing cost of maintaining the poor, it was necessary to safeguard this resource. Any money that was not spent on the indigenous poor inevitably aroused parochial resentment and even, on occasion, open hostility. The antipathy felt towards briefs, for example, finally emerged in 1712 during the archbishop's visitation. In a collaborative complaint the parishes expressed their disquiet concerning the practices surrounding the custom. Much of the dissatisfaction stemmed from the fact that briefs were difficult to collect.[14] There was another reason for the disquiet. Briefs were funded by Sunday collections and this meant they diverted money away from the most needy.[15] Furthermore the money did not necessarily go to the person named in the brief but could be used instead to pay the intended recipient's debts.[16] From a parochial point of view the complaint yielded very little. Some practical advice was offered as to how the difficulties mentioned in the complaint might be overcome, but the custom continued unchanged.[17]

Undoubtedly the motivation behind the complaint was an urge to protect parochial income; a reasonable objective given the demands made by the poor upon the parochial purse. In St Michan's, a densely populated but poor parish, maintenance costs for the indigenous and 'needy' poor were, by the late 1720s, approximately £137 a year.[18] This maintained an average of forty-three parishioners who received monetary help according to their pre-determined status. Parochial practice was to divide the poor into three categories. The elite,

---

11 St Bride's churchwardens' accounts 1663–1704, RCB, P327/4/1. The difficulties encountered by the vestry in finding money to pay for church repairs forced them, on occasion, to divert some of the money received in collections away from the poor towards the maintenance of the church. 12 Dudley, 'The Dublin parishes, 1660–1729', i, 201, table 4:9. The actual average annual collection was £29 16s. 4¼d. 13 St Werburgh's miscellaneous papers, RCB, P326/27/3/213. The full sum collected was £107 8s. 9½d. 14 St Paul's vestry minutes, i, 1698–1750, RCB, P273/6/1, Visitation 1712. The churchwardens complained they were obliged to collect from door to door despite the fact that the rubrics stated they were under no obligation to collect for the poor other than in church. 15 St Paul's vestry minutes, i, 1698–1750, RCB, P.273/6/1, Visitation 1712. 16 St Michan's poor records, i, 1723–1734, RCB, P276/8/1, 18 Dec. 1726. The minister, Dean Percival, received the full brief of 14s. 8½d. collected by the parish for Michael Burchall. 17 St Paul's vestry minutes, i, 1698–1750, RCB, P273/6/1, Visitation 1712. The solution offered by Archbishop King was to advise the minister to give notice of the briefs before the sermon and collection of the offertory. Briefs were then to be collected at the church door after the service was over. Those wishing to contribute to the parish poor could do so by contributing to the collection. Those wishing to contribute to the brief could do so as they left church. 18 Dudley, 'The Dublin parishes, 1660–1729', i, 205, table 4: 12. Average for 1724–8 was £137 7s. 10¼d.

entitled reduced housekeepers, received a weekly pension; the accidental sick received alms for as long as was necessary while the stated poor received a weekly pension, but one that was smaller than that given to the reduced house-keeper.[19] In addition to the parish poor, St Michan's, like every other Dublin parish, was expected to provide for the parish's foundlings and employ nurses to care for them. The costs associated with this very vulnerable group were not necessarily high on an individual level, 9*d*. per child per week in 1724.[20] What drove the costs inexorably upwards was the number of foundlings. Under the weight of numbers many parishes engaged in the dubious practice of 'lifting' – the surreptitious placing of foundlings on another parish – in an effort to alleviate some of the financial burden. Parishioners, who had the misfortune of finding one of these abandoned infants on their doorstep, were forced to swear an affidavit proclaiming their innocence.[21] The considerable efforts often made to reunite abandoned infants with their errant parents were undoubtedly driven by a need to limit long-term financial liability.

Another beneficiary of parochial charity were the badged poor. As licensed beggars they were not in receipt of regular charity but, unlike vagrants, who after 1707 faced the prospect of transportation if caught begging, they were entitled to go about the parish soliciting alms. Most parishes accommodated large numbers of badged poor. St Mary's, for example, had 65 badged poor in 1723, most of whom were women.[22] In St Catherine's, at much the same time, 1722, there were 80 badged poor.[23] St Werburgh's also gave its beggars certifi-cates explaining the cause of their misfortunes.[24] Interestingly, the poor of Holy Trinity, Cork were not badged until 1728[25] although the parish had appointed someone to drive 'Strolers & Vagabonds & Idle beggars' from the parish in 1720.[26]

There were other aspects to parochial charity. Most parishes had their own almshouse where a few pensioners lived. There were parochial charity schools. The parish distributed coal to the needy and bread to the hungry in difficult times. It bound parish orphans out in apprenticeship. The needs of the poor were endless; caring for them one of the parish's most onerous tasks.

Only slightly less onerous was the task of enforcing law and order within the parish. Again this was a duty the parish shared with the civic authorities, although, during the eighteenth century, a greater part of the responsibility for the Watch, the traditional night-time guardians of the peace, was transferred to the parish. The problem facing all those concerning with the administration of

19 Ibid., i, p. 205, table 4: 12.   20 Ibid., i, 207, table 4: 13.   21 Ibid., ii, 344, appendix 5, testi-monies sworn by the parishioners of St Michael's, 1 April 1695.   22 St Mary's vestry minutes, i, 1699–1739, RCB, P277/7/1, 29 Jan. 1723.   23 St Catherine's vestry minutes, ii, 1693–1730, RCB, P117/5/2, churchwardens' accounts 1722.   24 Dudley, 'The Dublin parishes, 1660–1729', ii, 343, Appendix 5, Certificates issued by St Werburgh's.   25 Holy Trinity, Cork, vestry minutes, i, 1710–1760, RCB, P527/7/1, 22 April 1728.   26 Ibid., 18 April 1720. The following year a second person was appointed to perform a similar task, see 6 Nov. 1721.

law and order was the open contempt under which the parish beadle, constables and Watch were held. Fully aware of public dissatisfaction, the authorities regularly reviewed, and occasionally reformed, policing within the city. Caution, however, ruled and no radical changes were made until 1786 when a centralized police force was introduced into Dublin for the first time.[27]

The tradition of keeping the Watch went back to the fourteenth century.[28] At first, kept only in the winter months, the Watch had, by the seventeenth century, become a year-round institution. By then too, instead of one Watch being responsible for the security of a single ward, the individual Watches had been united and given a collective responsibility for the whole parish.[29] The Watch was armed with a mixture of halberts, watch-bills, pikes, poles, lanterns and whistles, all bought at the parish's expense. A dearth of records, however, means little is known of its activities during the seventeenth century. In the eighteenth century, although there are few parochial records to draw upon, a clearer picture does emerge, mainly through civic ordinances and legislation.[30] From 1712 onwards, first the civic authorities, and then the government, introduced a series of initiatives in an attempt to create a more effective system of night-time policing.

The first of these initiatives, a mayoral proclamation, made in 1712, ordering greater vigilance probably did little to improve the situation.[31] Thereafter change came at the instigation of the government. Legislation introduced in 1716 and 1719 gave overall control of the Watch to the civic authorities.[32] The failure of these measures prompted further legislation. In 1721 the responsibility for the Watch was placed in the hands of the parishes.[33] Specially called vestries elected Watch directors whose duty it was to supervise all matters concerning the Watch for the coming year.[34] When these measures proved unsatisfactory, further legislation was introduced designed to strengthen the Watch and give the parishes greater control over policing within their boundaries.[35]

Establishing the Watch as a parochially based organization persuaded many of Dublin's prominent citizens to become actively involved in parish matters, for a brief period, as Watch directors.[36] Why is not clear, but the general

---

27 Irish statutes 26 Geo. III, c. 24. The force was not a success and the responsibility was, temporarily, returned to the parishes in 1795. 28 Gilbert (ed.), *Anc. recs Dub*, i, 223. Twelve constables were appointed to the city's Watch in 1305. 29 J.P. Starr, 'The enforcing of law and order in eighteenth-century Ireland', unpublished PhD (TCD, 1968), 147. The decision was taken by St Andrew's parish in 1672 in response to the lord mayor's urging for greater vigilance on the part of the Watch in its attempts to combat burglaries and robberies. 30 The RCB Library holds two Watch Accounts Books for St John's. 31 *Dublin Intelligence*, 8 April 1712. 32 Irish statutes 2 Geo. I, c. 10 and 6 Geo. I, c. 10 respectively. 33 Irish statutes 8 Geo. I, c. 10. 34 Dudley, 'The Dublin parishes, 1660–1729', ii, 234. The vestry was called in February and elected 15 directors, although only seven were required to form a quorum. The directors appointed the required number of constables and watchmen. They made the bye-laws, fixed wages, bought weapons and uniforms. 35 Irish statutes 10 Geo. I, c. 3. 36 Dudley, 'The Dublin parishes, 1660–1729', ii, 235, 237.

disquiet surrounding law and order may have been a persuasive factor. Once the organization had been put in place it was left to the less affluent members to assume the burden of responsibility. Although many of the duties were fixed by the legislation, the parishes had the right to choose the number of watchmen they employed, what wages they should be paid, where watch stands should be sited and how many rounds should be patrolled each night.[37] The amount of money each parish had at its disposal to pay for the Watch varied throughout the city as it was calculated and raised according to minister's money.[38] A rough estimate, however, indicates that watchmen's wages cost the city's parishes between £1,800 and £1,900 a year.[39] Inevitably there was some resistance to service, especially from those called upon to serve as constables, but once again the parish could do little other than fine the offender and appoint a deputy. As for the watchmen, the quality of those called upon to serve was always a cause for concern especially as many were illiterate and often in bad health.[40]

The conversion of the urban parish into a unit of civic administration took just under seventy years. In 1660, at the beginning of the period under review, the parish's involvement in civic affairs was limited. Its responsibilities to the city and parochial community were undertaken as a matter of tradition and its authority, in all matters except those concerning the parish church, was subordinate to the lord mayor's. By 1729, the year the review ends, a series of legislative measures had transferred much of the responsibility for good governance, at a local level, on to the parish and its annually elected officials. These duties, often onerous, encompassed every aspect of urban living and the ever-increasing responsibility they foisted upon the parish was neither popular nor welcome.[41] For those elected to serve the parish, complying with the mass of regulations that defined urban living required time and dedication. Yet most were prepared to serve their parish indicating that some sense of obligation to the parish and the local community did exist.[42] Importantly too, the concerns

---

37 Dudley, 'The Dublin parishes, 1660–1729', ii, 236, table 5: 3. Wages throughout the city varied very little, the maximum paid was £6 the minimum £5.   38 Dudley, 'The Dublin parishes, 1660–1729', ii, 242. Under the provisions of the 1715, 1721 and 1723 Acts, money to pay for the Watch was levied on every house within the parish at a fixed rate related either to Minister's Money or to the property's yearly rental value.   39 Dudley, 'The Dublin parishes, 1660–1729', ii, 244; NLI, Bolton Ms. 15,926. In 1784 watchmen's wages in Dublin amounted to £3,377 4s. 2d. per annum. The 1730 estimate has been calculated by applying the percentage difference which occurs between the two sets of known wages paid by the parishes to the overall cost as recorded in the Bolton Manuscript.   40 St John's watch account book, i, 1724–1738, RCB, P328/28/2, 5 July 1727 and 2 Oct. 1727, two watchmen replaced because of ill health. At the back of the Watch Book the watchmen have signed acknowledging receipt of their half yearly salary, £3. In 1727, six of the ten watchmen signing were illiterate. In 1729, six of the nine were illiterate. In 1730, half of the ten men were illiterate and in 1733, six of the ten were illiterate.   41 TCD MS 750/8/9, Archbishop W. King to Joseph Kane 10 May 1726. King wrote to Kane concerning the proposed Workhouse and noted in passing its unpopularity among churchwardens, remarking that their dislike stemmed from the fear it would mean additional work for them. He commented that he could understand their reservations, as almost every new act of parliament placed further responsibilities on their shoulders.   42 St Catherine's vestry minutes, ii, 1693–1730, RCB, P 117/5/2,

that preoccupied Dublin's parishes and their inhabitants – taxation, law and order, the poor, fire fighting, dirty and congested streets – were not unique. They were the concerns of all urban parishes. In Dublin urban growth and an expanding population exacerbated the struggle. Had the parishes not been co-opted into the civic administration the struggle to meet the demands of urban dwelling would have severely tested the Corporation. Time, however, was to expose the finite potential of the parish as a unit of civic administration. The demands of an increasingly sophisticated urban society eventually became too complex to be managed in such a dispersed, local manner. Towards the end of the eighteenth century a series of measures were introduced that began the process of removing administrative duties away from the parish and into the hands of independent authorities.[43] The time for relying on unpaid volunteers to shoulder the many of the burdens associated with the management of Dublin had come to an end.

18 April 1708 and 29 Feb. 1719. Finding overt expressions of parochial loyalty is difficult, but the boundary arguments that St Catherine's indulged in with her neighbours St Nicholas Without and St Audeon's do suggest there must have been some sense of parochial pride. **43** These measures included the creation of a paving board under 13 & 14 Geo. III, c. 22 (1774) and the first experiment with a centralised police force under 26 Geo. III, c. 24 (1786).

The eighteenth-century parish

TOBY BARNARD

Three principal aspects of the parish can be isolated: geographical; confessional; and its administrative and legal role. What it meant to its inhabitants changed in the sixteenth and seventeenth centuries. With the Protestant reformation, Ireland (like much of Europe) was contested by rival confessions. The contest turned the parish into a battleground. Most obviously possession of the parish church assumed a new importance both as symbol and for its practical implications. During the Catholic resurgences of the 1640s and between 1689 and 1691, church buildings were seized. The ascendant Catholics tried to put their physical re-occupation of the churches on a more secure legal footing.[1] These attempts failed, and from the 1690s the Protestant Church of Ireland was left in control of almost all surviving pre-Reformation structures. This control did not always mean that the Catholics had abandoned the sites. Some remained sacred owing to their antiquity and associations; others were still used for burials.[2] Moreover, at least notionally, the established Protestant Church claimed a monopoly over certain rites of passage, such as marriage and interment. Understandably, these claims were resented by Catholics and Protestant dissenters, especially when expected to pay for them. Just as the Protestants' control of the space had become a grievance, so too the pretensions to monopolize rites important to civil as well as religious society rankled. In the later part of the eighteenth century, both the persons and property of the Church of Ireland incumbents again became targets for attack, as had happened during the Confederate and Williamite Wars.

The growing resentments owed much to the larger role of the parish. In particular, it was saddled with extra legal and administrative tasks. Yet these new duties are often dismissed as minimal in comparison with the many loaded onto the parish by central government in England and Wales in the later sixteenth and seventeenth centuries. There, the parish was made a vital unit in local government. It served as the basis for increasingly complex and intrusive systems of poor relief and social and economic regulation.[3] The flow of powers

1 T. Barnard, *The kingdom of Ireland, 1641–1760* (Basingstoke, 2004), 22, 37; Tadhg Ó hAnnracháin, *Catholic reformation in Ireland: the mission of Rinuccini, 1645–1649* (Oxford, 2002), 77–8. 2 William Henry, 'Hints towards a natural and typographical [*sic*] history of the Counties Sligo, Donegal, Fermanagh and Lough Erne', NAI, M 2533, pp. 365–6. 3 N.J.G. Pounds, *A*

into the parish encouraged a process already in train. In numerous parishes, small groups emerged which undertook many of the devolved responsibilities. The activist could be motivated by religious zeal – the hope of fashioning a godly commonwealth in their midst. Frequently they were drawn from those already prominent in their neighbourhoods, so that their tenure of parochial offices confirmed and enhanced their existing authority. The offices which they added to their quiver full of other responsibilities included membership of the vestry, or – as it developed – the select vestry, and apparently minor offices such as churchwarden, overseer of the poor, surveyor of highways, and assessor and collector of parish rates. Thereby the petty functionaries added more authority to that which they possessed already.[4]

This situation in England invites comparison with Ireland. Yet, as so often with institutions replicated in the two kingdoms, Irish experience did not necessarily mirror the English. For a start, the parish in Ireland was slower to be turned into an administrative work-horse, and never gained all the powers of its English counterpart. Even so, there can be no doubting that in Ireland too it grew greatly in importance in the course of the seventeenth century. Furthermore, there are clear signs that some of the same structural developments occurred that had been seen in England. Parochial offices had the effect of differentiating an élite from the generality of the inhabitants of the parish. In Ireland, inevitably, the situation was further complicated by the confessional divisions. By the end of the seventeenth century, perhaps no more than 12–15 per cent of the population adhered to the Protestant Church of Ireland. Thus, activism in running the parish became an additional mark distinguishing this conformist minority from the Catholic majority and from the Protestant dissenters.

The parish may seem but a small cog in the increasingly complicated state machine of Britain, Ireland and its expanding empire. Nevertheless, it was the place where most were likely to come into contact with the operations of the massive engine. And indeed participation was seen as positive: a device through which the arts of citizenship could be learnt and practised. This made all the more ironical the exclusion of the bulk of the population from the possibility of full participation, and so from learning the civil and social skills which had long been thought the prerequisite for pacifying and enriching Ireland. The exclusions, although less complete than intended, matched those in many other spheres of public life. Cumulatively, they constituted a considerable grievance

history of the English parish (Cambridge, 2000).   4 N. Alldridge, 'Loyalty and identity in Chester parishes, 1540–1640' in S.J. Wright (ed.), *Parish, church and people: local studies in lay religion, 1350–1750* (London, 1988), 85–124; D. Eastwood, *Government and community in the English provinces, 1700–1870* (Basingstoke, 1997), 26–56; M. Goldie, 'The unacknowledged republic: office-holding in early modern England', in T. Harris (ed.), *The politics of the excluded, c.1500–1850* (Basingstoke, 2001), 153–94; S.J. Hindle, 'A sense of place? Becoming and belonging in the rural parish, 1550–1650' in A. Shepard and P. Withington (eds), *Communities in early-modern England* (Manchester, 2000), 96–114.

to the excluded, especially to the Catholics. Just how greatly they were troubled by the inconveniences of being debarred from running the parish and how far their energies and loyalties were diverted into alternative systems are presently impossible to assess.

Bearing in mind the issues raised by the study of the parish outside Ireland, this chapter will consider the main institutional and statutory developments that have left traces, then ponder their implications and consequences, some of which may have been peculiar to Ireland. Since the situation in late-seventeenth- and eighteenth-century Dublin is the subject of another chapter, this one will look chiefly at parishes outside the capital.[5] Inevitably, coverage is constrained by the patchy survival of records. Despite that constraint, some urban parishes – in Athlone, Clones, Cork, Edenderry (Monasteroris), Wicklow and Waterford – and others with a more obviously rural character will be discussed. Within the second group are Blessington (Co. Wicklow), Devenish in Co. Fermanagh and Powerscourt, again in Wicklow. Given the presently under-developed state of this subject, there will inevitably be more questions than firm answers.

The parish was part of a supervisory system in which the elements often overlapped. Sometimes they competed, but also they could complement one another. The other weapons in the administrative armoury include baronies, boroughs, manors and townlands. Some have recently been explored, so that, for example, the importance of the manor is now better appreciated.[6] The townland, too, has attracted the curious. Its importance to its inhabitants cannot be gainsaid, but its administrative functions remain more shadowy.[7] Parishes were, at least potentially, the most important, because the most numerous and therefore – as the most local – best placed to impinge on the population. Yet immediately a caveat has to be entered: there was a great disparity between the large number of historic parishes, recorded in schedules of ecclesiastical livings, and those which still functioned. In the latter category there was a further divergence between notional parishes with incumbents and the smaller number with usable churches. By the end of the seventeenth century, in the diocese of Meath, of 200 parochial benefices, only fifty enjoyed regular services. Often four or five of the ancient parishes were united in order to provide a competence for the minister, as well as a congregation sizeable enough to be worth servicing.[8] By the early eighteenth century, unions, both *ad hoc* and formal, had been accomplished in many dioceses. Resources were

5 R. Dudley, 'Dublin's parishes: the Church of Ireland parishes and their role in the civic administration', unpublished PhD, 2 vols (TCD, 1995). 6 R. Gillespie, 'Finavarra and its manor court in the 1670s' in *The Other Clare*, 25 (2000), 45–8; R. Gillespie, 'A manor court in seventeenth-century Ireland' in *Irish Economic and Social History*, 25 (1998), 81–7; B. Ó Dálaigh (ed.), *Corporation book of Ennis* (Dublin, 1990), 349–66. 7 W.H. Crawford and R.H. Foy (eds), *Townlands in Ulster: local history studies* (Belfast, 1998); B. Ó Dálaigh, D.A. Cronin and P. Connell (eds), *Irish townlands: studies in local history* (Dublin, 1998). 8 P. Loupès, 'Bishop Dopping's visitation of the diocese of Meath, 1693' in *Studia Hibernica*, 24 (1984–8), 134–44.

concentrated in the parishes deemed worth manning with ministers and supplying with regular worship in properly equipped churches. This slimmed down establishment of functioning parishes is interpreted as sensible realism by historians of a rational and managerial cast.[9] However, it represented a public retreat from conventional expectations of what a state church should do, and as such might be thought something of a humiliation. Moreover, it left a void in those many parishes without either churches or services according to the Church of Ireland rite.

One of the most interesting but intractable puzzles is the degree to which the Catholic Church used that older and more comprehensive parochial system. By the early eighteenth century, the Catholic priesthood outnumbered the Church of Ireland clergy. If regulars are counted among the Catholics, then a total of 2,200 is plausible by the mid-eighteenth century: in comparison, the established Church could muster at most 1,200 ordained functionaries.[10] Of course, the Catholic religious laboured under penalties, making much of their activity clandestine. As a result, it has seldom left clear traces for us to decipher. Moreover, the Catholics were forced into makeshifts, which probably did not need the elaborate bureaucracy springing up around the Church of Ireland parish. Occasional evidence – as from Co. Kerry early in George I's reign – shows an active Catholic priesthood. There the negligence of Protestant ministers made parishioners turn to Catholicism: 'several are buried like swine for want of a parson, and others are forced to get popish priests to baptize their children or suffer 'em to die without baptism'.[11] The relationship between the Catholic clergy and the laity was not free of the friction that frequently abraded the incumbents of the Church of Ireland, especially when they sought their dues. How far Catholic priests cooperated with laypeople to run parishes is unclear, owing to the shadows in which Catholics were obliged to operate. As yet it is impossible to judge whether the parish was the unit through which Catholics directed and distributed charity, disciplined the errant and organized education. Evidence from bequests suggests a preference for the religious orders. Even when moneys were donated to the seculars, who generally manned the parishes, it was often left to discretion of the clergy how the funds were distributed rather than being directed explicitly towards the inhabitants of a particular parish.[12]

9 S.J. Connolly, *Religion, law and power: the making of Protestant Ireland* (Oxford, 1992), 179–80. 10 T. Barnard, *A new anatomy of Ireland: the Irish Protestants, 1649–1770* (New Haven and London, 2003), 81–114, 361; Connolly, *Religion, law and power*, 150–1. 11 R. Lloyd to A.H. Herbert, 15 March 1717[18], National Library of Wales, Aberystwyth, Powis Castle correspondence, no. 846. 12 Will of D. Sarsfield, 25 Jan. 1716[17], TCD, MS 2011/64; W. P. Burke, *History of Clonmel* (Waterford, 1907), 328, 330; W. Carrigan, 'Catholic episcopal wills (province of Dublin)' in *Archivium Hibernicum*, 4 (1915), 66–95: 70, 86; P. Crossle, 'Some records of the Skerrett family' in *Journal of the Galway Archaeological and Historical Society*, 15 (1931–3), 33–72: 39, 45; R. Hayes, 'Some old Limerick wills' in *North Munster Antiquarian Journal*, 2 (1940–1), 71–2; G. Rice, 'Four wills of the Old English merchants of Drogheda, 1654–1717' in *County Louth*

II

The parish meant most to those who ran it, but impinged on the many who paid towards its upkeep. By this measure, it was valued by the small band among whom the offices rotated. However, the principle of annual rotation ensured that a sizeable contingent among the respectable male householders would share the responsibilities. In addition, the difficulty of filling the posts, if restrictive confessional qualifications were imposed, meant a degree of latitude. A pragmatic permissiveness ensured that the oaths sworn by the church-wardens and sidesmen contained no doctrinal hurdles. The incoming officer undertook simply to execute the charge faithfully and truly.[13] In themselves the oaths need not exclude Catholics, and there are tantalizing suggestions that they did indeed serve: for example, in Co. Dublin and in Co. Louth.[14] If there was cooperation rather than friction across the confessional frontiers, this brings a new perspective to relationships in provincial communities. Furthermore, it schooled Catholics in administration.

Protestant dissenters, although similarly free to hold the posts for a year, often preferred not to. In particular, the Scottish Presbyterians, strong in Ulster, applied the template taken from their colleagues in Scotland. In consequence, the kirk session assumed many of the duties of the Church of Ireland parish.[15] The survival of the minutes from a few kirk sessions in the late-seventeenth and early-eighteenth centuries enables us to be reasonably confident about some of the financial, charitable and regulatory tasks of these Presbyterian organizations.[16] Often the Presbyterian system of classes and synods existed alongside the parishes of the Established Church. It constituted an alternative and – frequently – a rival outlet for the energies and resources of Presbyterians. Church of Ireland vestries and even its bishops connived at informal deals which allowed Presbyterians, when selected as churchwardens or sidesmen, to name deputies. These unofficial arrangements were regularized by statute in 1719.[17] In the case of Quakers, it seems that they remained liable to

Archaeological and Historical Journal, 20 (1981–4), 96–105: 101–2; J.D. White, 'Extracts from original wills formerly preserved in the consistorial office, Cashel' in *Journal of the Kilkenny and South-East of Ireland Archaeological Society*, new series, 2 (1858–9), 317–20: 319. **13** E. Bullingbrooke, *Ecclesiastical law*, 2 vols (Dublin, 1770), i, 300, 302. **14** D. Mac Íomhair, 'Clergy and churchwardens of Termonfeckin parish' in *County Louth Archaeological and Historical Journal*, 17 (1969), 84–6: 84; Sheila Roe, 'The Roe family of Arthurstown, Charlestown, Glack and Tallanstown, County Louth' in *County Louth Archaeological and Historical Journal*, 24 (2000), 241–52: 547. **15** For the functioning of the kirk, see: R. Mitchison and L. Leahman, *Sexuality and social control: Scotland 1660–1780* (Oxford, 1989); Margo Todd, *The culture of Protestantism in early modern Scotland*, (New Haven and London, 2002). A start for Ireland is made by Patrick Griffin, *The people with no name: Ireland's Ulster Scots, America's Scots Irish, and the creation of a British Atlantic world, 1689–1764* (Princeton and London, 2001). **16** Minutes of Route Presbytery, 1701–6, pp. 8, 68–9, Presbyterian Historical Society, Belfast; Minutes of Connor Session, 1693–1735, s.d. 12 Dec. 1705, 22 April 1711, ibid.; notebook of Samuel Boyce, PRONI, MIC/1, p. 44; J.M. Barkley, *The eldership in Irish Presbyterianism* (Belfast, 1963). **17** 6 Geo I,

selection as churchwardens. In the King's County parish of Monasteroris, which coincided with the township of Edenderry where Quakers were numerous and prosperous, on at least two occasions (in 1716 and 1740) the nomination of a Quaker was refused. It was the local bishop, not the members of the vestry or the nominees themselves, who intervened to prevent the Quakers from serving.[18] Elsewhere, at Blessington, Colonel Richard Eustace refused to act as churchwarden in 1698. Eustace may have wished to escape a potentially onerous obligation. Alternatively, his refusal could have indicated an uncertain attachment to the established Church. Some Eustaces retained affection for the Catholic Church.[19]

The formality that attended the entry of churchwardens onto their annual chore varied. The greatest appears to have been in Waterford, where the office-holders were required to be sworn in the bishop's consistory court. The requirement may have told of no more than the zeal of the eccentric bishop in building parish churches in the city to escape the jurisdiction of his enemy, the dean of the cathedral, and of the convenient proximity of the bishop's court.[20] In Galway, a simple oath was tendered to the incoming wardens.[21] Since the job rotated each year, it might prove difficult to find suitable candidates. Eustace's refusal caused particular alarm lest it serve as a precedent for others to dodge their turns. As with other administrative posts, like service as sheriff in the county or on the grand jury, so with church wardenships, the irritations could be balanced by the opportunities for influence and extra status in the local community. On occasion, those not functionally literate were elevated to the role.[22] This could be a disadvantage, since printed instruments had to be understood for the proper discharge of the office. A yet greater drawback would be innumeracy. The principal task of the churchwardens was to keep accounts of moneys received and spent over the year. Only when their accounts had been presented and approved by a meeting of the vestry were the wardens free from their duties. Failure to produce accounts promptly was a frequent failing. How far it resulted from simple casualness and how far from frauds is hard to tell. In 1727, Edward Forster, outgoing warden at Powerscourt, was reprimanded for accounts deemed 'very defective and faulty'.[23] Vestry meetings had frequently

c5. It followed an English statute (1 William and Mary, c. 18).   **18** Vestry Book, Monasteroris, s.d. 2 April 1716, 7 April 1740, RCB, P 484/1/1; D.M. Beaumont, 'The gentry of the King's and Queen's Counties: Protestant landed society, 1690–1760', unpublished PhD, 2 vols (TCD, 1999), ii, 43–4.   **19** Register, Blessington, s.d. 25 April 1698, RCB, P 651/1/1; E.F. Tickell, 'The Eustace family and their lands in County Kildare' in *Journal of the County Kildare Archaeological Society*, 13 (1958), part i, 307–44, part ii, 364–413.   **20** Vestry Minute Book, St Patrick's, Waterford, 1721–1772, s.d. 15 April 1723, RCB, P 640/5/1; Charles Smith, *The antient and present state of the county and city of Waterford* (Dublin, 1746), 180–1; J. Walton, 'The Boltons of County Waterford' in *The Irish Genealogist*, 7 (1987), 197–8.   **21** St Nicholas, Galway, NA, M 6947; T.C. Barnard, 'Parishes, pews and parsons: lay people and the Church of Ireland, 1647–1780' in R. Gillespie and W.G. Neely (eds), *The laity and the Church of Ireland, 1000–2000: all sorts and conditions* (Dublin, 2002), 70–103: 83.   **22** Vestry Book, St Mary, Athlone, 1750–91, s.d. 5 May 1756, RCB, P 392/5/1; Vestry Book, Devenish, 1739–1828, s.d. 8 April 1776, RCB, P 811/5/1.   **23** Vestry

to be adjourned when wardens and sidesmen did not appear to render their accounts.[24] Repeated delays in presenting accounts at Blessington and in the town of Wicklow led to threats from the vestry that the negligent wardens would be pursued. How best to bring them to book also varied. One method was to report them to the bishop; another was to have them indicted in the bishop's court. A third option, and maybe the most efficacious, because most threatening, was to proceed against them in the secular courts, such as the quarter sessions. In 1740, the Blessington churchwardens for the two previous years were warned that they faced prosecution.[25] Whether the threat sufficed to bring them to heel or whether they were tried is not recorded.

The weakness of the ecclesiastical jurisdiction, either to compel attendance or payment, probably reduced use of this blunt weapon. The ultimate punishment that the consistory could impose was excommunication. For the recalcitrant, who did not belong to the Church of Ireland, being deprived of its salves might please more than it dismayed. The ineffectiveness of the sanctions at the disposal of the established Church was acknowledged with the passage of an act of the Irish parliament in 1751. The statute was devised to try to ease the collection of the contentious tithes, but it also applied to the levies for paying the salaries of the parish clerks. The new procedure was laborious: it involved a pair of local justices of the peace, and a petition to the county assizes, after which the miscreants might be sued in the Dublin courts of exchequer and chancery.[26] Vestry records for the mid-eighteenth century do not suggest that the cumbersome and potentially costly procedure was used in order to recover what in most cases would be small sums of money. Nevertheless, the introduction of the processes suggested not only lay suspicion and dislike of the Church courts, but also the overlap in the local agencies of the state, notably parish, borough and county. Other activities, relating to street-lighting, maintaining watches, dealing with vagrancy and the poor, and repairing roads, reinforced the links, as will be shown below. Sometimes they brought cooperation; sometimes, competition; occasionally obstructionism.

Negligent officials inevitably attract more attention than the dull and dutiful. Errant churchwardens were very few in comparison with the many who duly proffered acceptable accounts and then demitted from office. Most wardens, already prominent within their parishes, did the necessary, and may have grasped the chances to direct modest contracts towards their chums and to seat themselves and their families more conspicuously within the church.

Book, Powerscourt, 1660–1760, s.d. 22 May 1727, RCB, P 109.1.1. **24** Vestry Book, St Olave, Waterford, s.d. 30 July 1788, P 637/1/1; Vestry Book, Devenish, 1739–1828, s.d. 27 March 1769, RCB. P 811/5/1; Vestry Book, St Mary, Athlone, 1750–91, s.d. 5 May 1784, 18 Oct. 1786, 1 Nov. 1786, 20 June 1787, RCB, P 392/5/1. **25** Vestry Book, Wicklow, s.d. 8 Oct. 1729, 6 Sep. 1754, 31 Oct. 1759, RCB, P 611/ 5/1; Register, Blessington, s.d. 7 June 1740, RCB, P 651/1/1; Vestry Book, Devenish, 1739–1828, s.d. 2 March 1773, RCB, P 811/5/1. **26** 23 Geo II, c. 12; .

III

The administrative and financial tasks handed to the parish obliged it to raise money. In its efforts to do so it intruded into the lives of those who lived within its confines. In 1698, the parish was chosen as the unit through which the land tax, recently authorized by the Irish parliament, was to be collected.[27] The tax, despite threats that it would be renewed, was not, and so the parish's role lapsed. In the same year, the Dublin parliament made the parish responsible for implementing a scheme to plant trees, sorely needed for timber, fuel, shelter and ornament.[28] The Fermanagh assizes, for example, awarded the parish of Clones a quota of 275 saplings to nurture. In the first flush of enthusiasm for this improving project, during Queen Anne's reign, parishes attended to the matter, but the ardour soon cooled.[29]

Other statutory powers vested in the parish carried financial implications. The parish oversaw the provision of night watches, the construction and repair of roads, policing the quarter and the lighting of some towns. It was also required to employ and pay a parish clerk, who had canonical duties to assist with religious services. Indeed, where the majority of parishioners spoke only Irish, and the incumbent knew nothing but English, the parish clerk was required to perform parts of the liturgy in the Irish language. He might also be expected to sing.[30] In addition, the parish had to pay its immediate expenses: the elements of bread and wine used in the celebration of the sacrament; cleaning and embellishing the church; providing service books, bible and surplices. Most onerous – in time and sums of money expended – was the relief of the poor.

All parishes were required to obey the laws, but each vestry had liberty to decide how best to assess and collect the money, and indeed how to disburse it. By the early eighteenth century, in many places, the needs of a minority quickly burdened a majority. In 1733, one prosperous Catholic was obliged to pay nearly £2 each year in taxes, half of which financed the operations of the Protestant parish in which she lived. Yet this householder paid £6 to the local priests for mass to be celebrated on the anniversary of her husband's death.[31] Catholics as householders rated to contribute towards parish levies were in the habit of turning up to defeat proposals for which they might have to pay. As the main authority on the law as it affected the parish stated in 1770, the vestry 'properly speaking, is the assembly of the whole parish'.[32] Alarm at this form

27 Vestry Book of St Catherine's, Dublin, 1693–1730, RCB, P 117/5/2, pp. 80, 105. 28 10 William III, c. 12. 29 Vestry Book, Clones, s.d. 27 July 1702, 14 Oct. 1703, 8 June 1704, RCB, P 804/1/1; Register, Blessington, s.d. 25 Jan. 1702[3], RCB, P 651/1/1; Vestry Book, Wicklow, s.d. 23 Sep. 1713, P 611/5/1; T.C. Barnard, *Making the grand figure: lives and possessions in Ireland, 1641–1770* (New Haven and London, 2004), 194. 30 Bullingbrooke, *Ecclesiastical law*, i, 292. 31 Accounts of Jane Lattin, 1733, NLI, Mansfield Mss, Ms 38,378/2. 32 Bullingbrooke, *Ecclesiastical law*, i, 301.

of Catholic militancy prompted Church of Ireland leaders to promote a bill which, in 1726, ended the attendance of Catholics when issues with financial implications were to be decided by the vestry.[33] Parish taxes were equally irksome to Protestant dissenters. The act of 1726 confined votes to 'the Protestant parishioners there assembled'.[34] So, the dissenters, by virtue of being householders and rate-payers, remained – at least notionally – members of the vestry. In this capacity, they could decide votes, especially when extra money was to be raised, usually to pay for improvements to the church fabric. Signs of coordination, notably in Ulster, alarmed Church of Ireland incumbents, and were sometimes hard to outwit.[35] Only in 1774 did new legislation debar the Protestant dissenters from voting at vestries by confining their operations to those 'that are of the communion of the Church of Ireland by law established'.[36] In the next session of parliament, this statute was repealed, but it is not clear whether or not the practice of excluding Protestant dissenters from voting in the vestry, nevertheless, continued.[37]

Important issues drew in crowds. The humdrum meetings of the vestry – by far, the majority of occasions – held less allure. What is often hard to gauge is whether the signatories to the minutes of vestry meetings represent all present. In at least one parish, after eleven parishioners had signed the minute, it was added, 'with several other of the parish being present'.[38] Although there are uncertainties, clearly attendance fluctuated. The largest gatherings, at least as measured by the signatories, occurred when decisions that might compromise the distinct identity of the parish had to be taken. In 1748, a vestry was summoned in St Nicholas's parish in Cork, in order to debate a possible union of several poor parishes in the south of the city. All the parishioners of St Nicholas were exhorted to come. At least seventy-two did, including eleven women and many with names that suggested Old Irish ancestry.[39] St Nicholas's had been erected recently – in 1720 – in order to supply the populous southern districts of the city with places for worship. The active parishioners maintained the incumbent through their contributions. The church, said to be 'neat' and 'well pewed', had thirty-nine pew-holders.[40] Accordingly, it may be that most of the interested adult householders of the parish did attend in 1748, not least because of the monetary impact of the proposal. But they were a small fraction of the total population. An estimate of 1720 had reckoned the number of houses in the three southern parishes of the city – of which St Bridget and St Nicholas was one – to be 3,739.[41]

33 12 Geo I, c. 9. 34 Vestry Book, St Nicholas, Cork, s.d. 13 Nov. 1721, RCB, P 498/5/1; Vestry Book, St Mary, Athlone, 1750–91, 20 April 1750, 17 April 1751. 35 Barnard, 'Parishes, pews and parsons', 81. 36 13 & 14 Geo III, c. 10. 37 15 & 16 Geo III, c. 14. 38 Vestry Book, St Patrick, Waterford, 1721–1772, s.d. 22 Dec. 1721, RCB, P 640/5/1. 39 Vestry Book, St Nicholas, Cork, s.d. 1 Aug. 1748, RCB, P 498/5/1. 40 Charles Smith, *The ancient and present state of the county and city of Cork*, 2nd edn, 2 vols (Dublin, 1774), i, 380; Vestry Book, St Nicholas, Cork, s.d. RCB, P 498/5/1. 41 Houses and hearths in Cork, 10 Jan. 1719[20], Marsh's Library, Dublin, MS Z3.1.1, xxvii.

At Clones in 1715, a scheme to construct a new chapel to serve part of the parish provoked an unusual concourse. At least 135 parishioners recorded their presence. The number of Easter communicants in the parish was said to be 160 to 180. The project in Clones again had potentially serious financial consequences for the existing parish, and seems as a result to have been opposed by its leaders.[42] Similarly in the Co. Cork parish of Innishannon, the plan to build a church resulted in larger attendances at the vestry in 1760 and 1761.[43] At the other extreme, occasions abounded, both in rural and urban districts, when advertised meetings had to be adjourned for want of a quorum. The records suggest that this may have become more of a problem in the 1770s and 1780s – times when the Established Church and its clergy were entangled in controversies – than it had been earlier in the century.[44] Usually, between four and a dozen are recorded as attending the vestry. A meeting had to include either the incumbent or a curate.[45] Usually one churchwarden – if not both – was also present. Other officers, such as the overseers of the poor, applotters of cesses, sidesmen and surveyors of highways, would be required to attend when the business with which they dealt was discussed. These parochial functionaries constituted an inner group, but its size was not so restricted as at first might appear, simply because the occupants of the posts changed each year. Over any decade, a high proportion of the adult male householders who were communicants of the established Church could expect to be involved in the institutional life of the parish.

To many, maybe even to the majority, that dwelt within the parish, the institution was felt as a device for control and for financial exactions. Connected with these tasks were enquiries, instituted from on high, into the confessional affiliations of the households within parishes. Twice in the eighteenth century – in 1731 and 1766 – the authorities in Dublin decided to count how many belonged to the distinct denominations.[46] An easy way to do so was to command Church of Ireland incumbents to compile returns of the inhabitants in their cures. That they were able to furnish plausible figures reflected the frequency with which the functionaries of the parish routinely assessed the standing and resources of its people.

Although some parishes straggled across too many acres and too varied terrain for it to be possible to know the identities and worth of all, more were susceptible to minute analysis. In 1700, the vestry of Clones in Monaghan responded to the bishop's visitation by reporting that the parish was inhabited by 665 families. The information was not innocent of propagandist purposes.

42 Vestry Book, Clones, s.d. 25 Aug. 1715, RCB, P 804/1/1.   43 Vestry Book, Innishannon, s.d. 2 Oct. 1760, 11 May 1761, RCB, P 142/1/1.   44 Vestry Book, St Olave, Waterford, s.d. 30 July 1788, 15 Nov. 1790, P 637/1/1; Vestry Book, St Nicholas, Cork, s.d. 5 May 1778, 17 Feb. 1779, RCB, P 498/5/1; Vestry Book, Devenish, 1739–1828, s.d. 2 June 1772, 25 May 1779, RCB, P 811/5/1.   45 Bullingbrooke, *Ecclesiastical law*, i, 303–4.   46 B.F. Gurrin, *Pre-census sources for Irish demography* (Dublin, 2002), 17–18, 21.

It was stated confidently that the numbers of conformist Protestants far exceeded those of Protestant dissenters and Catholics. Veracity was lent to the claim with the detail that between 160 and 180 had taken communion in the parish church the previous Easter.[47] Occasionally bishops, notably Edward Synge in Elphin, or beneficed ministers, like Daniel Beaufort in Navan, initiated investigations to quantify the numbers and confessional affiliations of the inhabitants in their territories.[48]

Less ambitious, but more common, were the returns made by parochial office-holders and committees to establish liabilities to the assorted levies. Statutes of the Irish parliament prescribed how these investigations should be conducted. Again they revealed potentially widespread involvement in the minutiae of local administration. Vestries were empowered to authorize churchwardens and others specially appointed to apportion rates. In the matter of levying local taxes for the purpose of lighting the district, more complicated provisions governed the process. All heads of families who paid £5 (or more) annually in rent could attend a meeting to decide the details of the new illuminations. A minimum of five valuers, 'discreet and judicious persons', would then fix liabilities. A further meeting of substantial householders scrutinized and might amend the assessments.[49] So long, as the minimum obligations of collecting money were met, it does not seem that the authorities in Dublin worried too much about the precise strategies. They did, however, stipulate that rates for lighting should not exceed six pence in each £ at which a property was valued. Relatively compact and largely urban parishes were more easily surveyed than the capacious countryside in which few Protestants dwelt. In Edenderry, the directors of the Church of Ireland parish decided to divide contributors to a parish rate between 'farmers and able tradesmen' and 'poor tradesmen and cottiers'. The former paid at three times the rate of their poorer neighbours. Yet these arrangements were provisional ones. Within forty years, the criterion on which payments towards parish rates were to be levied had been simplified. In 1739, it was decreed that 'solvent inhabitants of the parish' would be taxed.[50] At Athlone, when, in 1761, a belfry was to be added to St Mary's, contributions were to be reckoned according to the rents of houses. On another occasion in the same parish, it was decreed that owners of pews, even when they lived on the more distant Connacht side of the River Shannon, must contribute annually to the repairs of the fabric. In Cork, too, holders of pews in St Nicholas's were obliged to pay towards renovations.[51] Indeed, the select who owned or rented pews – normally there were between two and three dozen in

47 Vestry book, Clones, s.d. 9 May 1700, RCB, P 804/1/1. **48** Census of Elphin, 1749, NA, M. 2466; B.F. Gurrin, 'The Union of Navan in 1766' in *Ríocht na Midhe*, 14 (2003), 144–67. **49** E. Bullingbrooke, *The duty and authority of a justice of the peace and parish officers for Ireland*, revised by J.G. Butler (Dublin, 1788), 500–4, 588. **50** Vestry Book, Monasteroris, s.d. 25 April 1698; 23 April 1739, RCB, P 484/1/1. **51** Vestry Book, St Nicholas and St Bridget, Cork, from 1712, s.d. 20 June 1748, RCB, P 498.5.1; Vestry Book, St Mary, Athlone, 1750–91, s.d. 25 Feb. 1761, 1765.

each building – had a permanent stake in the church. Often it attested to and
even enhanced the local standing of the proprietors; in return, they were
expected to finance many of the operations of the parish.[52]

Ability to pay could be gauged by the applotters and collectors of parish rates
on the basis of their intimate acquaintance with the locals. Willingness to pay
was a different matter. In most parishes outside Ulster and a few in Dublin, the
bulk of householders were Catholic. Furthermore, throughout much of Ulster,
the Protestants divided between adherents of the Established Church and of
dissenting congregations. Despite their detachment, merely by virtue of living
within a district, Catholics and dissenters might be expected to contribute
towards the expenses of the state cult. In Clones in Co. Monaghan, those who
failed to pay the annual cess were to be prosecuted in the diocesan court. Again,
whether this was more than bluster may be doubted. It told, perhaps, of an
assertiveness of the Church of Ireland officials in an area which had seen
serious confessional strife. Back in 1688, during the reign of James II, when
Catholic hopes had revived strikingly, there had been widespread refusals on
the part of Catholics to pay towards the Protestant parish. In order to overcome
this non-compliance, the authority of the constables and the justices of the
peace had been invoked. At this juncture, the magistrates were also Catholic
and so unsympathetic to the cause.[53] By 1708, the parish officers in Clones had
reverted to the ecclesiastical courts to try to coerce defaulters.[54] However,
because the bishops' courts were increasingly ineffective, the trend was towards
greater use of the secular ones. A series of laws passed in the reigns of George
I and George II allowed churchwardens faced with non-payment of their cesses
to apply for help from the justices of the peace. Ultimately, the recalcitrant
could be sued at the assizes or, for outstanding sums of more than £20, in the
Dublin courts.[55] The realities of the situation were recognized even more
explicitly in 1751, when a statute abandoned the threats of the ecclesiastical
courts and excommunication, and instead applied the sanctions of lay courts to
those who refused to pay parochial dues. How far aggrieved churchwardens, as
distinct from clergy seeking to extract their tithes, used the cumbersome and
divisive procedures is not clear. Vestry records and churchwardens' accounts
suggest that they were reluctant to increase their difficulties and unpopularity
by bringing such suits. What the statutes did emphasize was the continual
blurring of the boundaries between ecclesiastical and secular matters, and the
legal privileges accorded to the functionaries of the Church of Ireland parish.
Such special treatment can hardly have increased its appeal for the Protestant
dissenters and Catholics excluded from many of its activities and benefits.

52 Barnard, *New anatomy*, 239–43. **53** Vestry Book, Clones, s.d. 19 April 1688, RCB, P
804/1/1. **54** Vestry Book, Clones, s.d. 6 April 1708, RCB, P 804/1/1. **55** Bullingbrooke,
Duty and authority of justices of the peace, pp. 587–9; 3 Geo II, c.11; J. Brady, 'Remedies proposed
for the Church of Ireland, (1697)' in *Archivium Hibernicum*, 22 (1959), 163–73: 172; *Letters written
by his excellency Hugh Boulter ...*, 2 vols (Oxford, 1769–70), i, 212–13; Connolly, *Religion, law and
power*, 176–8.

Further elision of the spheres of the civil and Church authorities was revealed in the town of Wicklow when the functionaries of the borough, in the persons of the portreeve (or mayor) and two burgesses, were to applot the cess which would finance parish obligations. Another example comes from Kinsale in 1713. There, £35 raised by the corporation of the borough was passed to the churchwardens of the parish church for disbursement to the poor of the town. Furthermore, the officials of the corporation undertook acts of charity and punishment that in settlements without borough status fell entirely to the parish.[56] Clearly, at Kinsale and Wicklow – as in numerous other towns – the routines of the corporation and of the Church of Ireland parish overlapped.[57] The taxes irritated those who, owing to their confession, were denied full participation in either the municipality or the parish. The mulcts were hardly more welcome to the communicants of the established Church. Yet it was the members of the congregations that were most likely to be harried for unpaid contributions, because most susceptible to the pressures that the parish could exert. An embarrassing example was the earl of Meath, who failed to pay his church tax at Powerscourt in 1722.[58] Before this, during the reign of Charles II, the Cork parish of Holy Trinity tried to keep track of those who had not paid the cesses. Some were evidently too poor to do so; others had left the parish. The churchwardens resorted to the bishop's court, where they presented 11 parishioners for failing to pay one rate, and another 21 for non-payment of a second. Some defaulters were figures of consequence in the parish, including a lieutenant, a butcher and a former churchwarden.[59]

Elsewhere, there were suggestions that churchwardens, confronted with resistance on the grounds of unfairness in the assessments, did not proceed with great vigour. Indeed, some, anxious to avoid trouble, omitted to set rates for possibly contentious purposes, such as the rebuilding of churches.[60] In 1749, the Dublin parliament intervened to remove one cause of contention within the parish when it stipulated that each parish clerk must be paid between £5 and £20 annually. A vestry was to be held each year specifically to apportion the rate to raise the salary. Before this, the clerks had extorted dues for routine services from parishioners, claiming custom as the justification.[61] In some parishes, funds had been diverted from the poor rate to pay the parish clerk.[62] A further sign that churchwardens backed away from antagonizing neighbours by struggling to collect sums of money, the size of which hardly justified the labour, came from Athlone in 1786. There it was decided to limit liability to the

56 M. Mulcahy (ed.), *Calendar of Kinsale documents*, 7 (Kinsale, 1998), 5, 17, 23–4, 26–7, 51–2, 64, 79, 93, 96–8. **57** Vestry Book, Wicklow, s.d. 19 April 1756, RCB, P 611/5/1. **58** Vestry Book, Powerscourt, 1660–1760, s.d. 26 March 1722, RCB, P 109/1/1. **59** Accounts, Holy Trinity, Cork, 1664–1709, RCB, P 527/7/1, pp. 18–19, 26, 39–40. **60** Bullingbrooke, *Ecclesiastical law*, i, 258. **61** Vestry Book, St Patrick, Waterford, s.d. 29 March 1725, 26 March 1751, RCB, P 640/5/1; 23 Geo II, c. 12. **62** Vestry Book, St Nicholas and St Bridget, Cork, from 1712, s.d. 20 April 1733, RCB, P 498/5/1.

parish tax to householders worth a minimum of £10 each year.[63] This was a
high threshold that exempted most within the Protestant community. Its introduction may suggest a wish to avoid the demeaning and destructive
controversies over compelling those who did not worship in the Established
Church to finance it and its members. It may also signal a retreat by the 1780s
from many of the larger ambitions previously entertained by the state Church.
During this decade there are other indications that fewer energies were directed
into the humdrum workings of the parish, despite the fact that the state had
added fresh and topical duties to those of the parochial drudges.

The busiest functionaries were likely to be in the largest towns. The latter
faced the most visible problems of poverty and destitution. During the
eighteenth century, as the duties of the parish multiplied, so rates increased. At
the same time, the number of householders liable to the charges grew, but so
too did the lists of the parish poor. At Easter 1733, the parish of Wicklow set a
rate of £60; by 1747, it needed to collect £163. However, the cess for 1752 was
£120.[64] Worries about disorder and crime also produced initiatives in policing,
several of which were linked with the work of the urban parishes, first in
Dublin itself but eventually – by the 1780s – in populous places such as Cork
and Waterford. Linked to the anxieties was an interest in improvements that
might simultaneously discourage criminals and please the respectable.
Important among the projects was the provision of street-lighting. Laws were
passed that authorized the erection of lights in Dublin, Cork and Limerick.
Soon this provision was extended into Galway and Waterford.[65] Again responsibility for this enlightenment was split between the civic authorities and the
city parishes. The former initiated the schemes; the latter decided how much
each householder should pay towards the costs. By 1738, Dublin parishes were
to summon vestries specifically to apportion the taxes for lights.[66] In large
towns like Cork and Waterford, the desire for better illumination obliged the
parish to oversee raising the house-by-house taxes to provide the money. By
1780, in the Waterford parish of St Olave, a special vestry did indeed decide on
the arrangements for lighting during the winter nights. It awarded a contract
and employed a lamp-lighter.[67] In the Cork parish of St Nicholas and St
Bridget, there is evidence that this matter was occupying the vestry in the
1760s. By 1765, the thoroughfares to be lit were extended southwards beyond
the South Bridge of the city. At the same time, five valuers were appointed by
the parish to decide the rates to be paid by each house. In 1778, the vestry stipulated that the contractor (Richard Fuller) should supply 100 globes 'of the best

63 Vestry Book, St Mary, Athlone, 1750–91, Vestry Book, St Mary, Athlone, 1750–91, s.d. 28
Aug. 1786, RCB, P392/5/1.   64 Vestry Book, Wicklow, s.d. 26 March 1733, 22 July 1747, 18
Oct. 1752, RCB, P 611/5/1.   65 N. Garnham, *The courts, crime and the criminal law in Ireland,
1692–1760* (Dublin, 1996), 27–32.   66 8 Geo I, c. 16; 3 Geo II, c. 22; 11 Geo II, c. 19; 15 Geo II,
c. 11.   67 Vestry Book, St Olave, Waterford, s.d. 11 Aug. 1780, 10 Aug. 1781, 27 and 31 July 1784,
P 637/1/1.

white glass free of defect', and specified the dimensions and weight.[68] These might seem wearisomely trivial concerns. Yet, the need to raise money justified the minute enquiries which reminded of the intimate spaces of the urban parish, in which it was feasible to evaluate properties, enumerate householders and distinguish strangers from locals. Moreover, the lights marked out these few urban spaces from the darkness or simple moon- and star-light that fell over most places during winter nights.

Illumination was advocated as a method to lessen crime. Further apprehensions about restlessness made extra work for city parishes. From the requirement to appoint watchmen developed more ambitious attempts at policing, again based on the parish. The parishioners of St Patrick's, Waterford, were required first to arrange the police in their quarter and next, in 1795, to provide two men for the newly raised militia.[69] What was possible in a sizeable town, whether increasing the physical attractions or reassuring the respectable about their security, was seldom possible in rural parishes. Moreover, the duty to arrange for night watches was shared between the parish, manor and jurisdictions like liberties. Although the vestry, or a special committee appointed by it, might make the arrangements, oversight remained with the magistrates.[70]

Another chore that occasioned work for the parish – until 1760 – was the maintenance of roads within its precincts.[71] At the annual election of officers, overseers or surveyors of highways were chosen.[72] So complex was the task in the parish of Wicklow that overseers were appointed for specific roads: in all, twelve individuals were named.[73] To them – and to their counterparts in other parishes – fell the duty of organizing labour among the parishioners to complete the necessary repairs. There survived an obligation among male inhabitants to provide six days' labour each year. This had been given statutory backing in James I's reign. Again, the responsibility seemed another instance where a self-selecting few imposed burdens, either physical or fiscal, on the humbler inhabitants of the parish. In 1740, a proposal for a new road in the parish of Clones drew an unusually large confluence to the vestry. The same parish had chosen the curate, the Reverend Adam Nixon, as its director of high roads in 1737.[74] Just what powers of compulsion and what penalties were at the

68 Vestry Book, St Nicholas and St Bridget, Cork, from 1712, s.d. 28 June 1762, 15 May 1765, 26 Aug. 1778, 9 Nov. 1778, RCB, P 498/5/1. 69 Vestry Book, St Olave, Waterford, s.d. 27 July 1784, 1 July 1786, 1 July 1787, 8 Sep. 1788, 6 Oct. 1789, 24 April 1795, 24 Jan. 1798, P 637/1/1. 70 M. Dutton, *The office and authority of a justice of peace for Ireland*, 2nd edn (Dublin, 1727), 434–6. 71 33 Geo II, c. 8. 72 Vestry Book, Clones, s.d. 19 April 1688, 30 Sep. 1746, 15 Oct. 1755, RCB, P 804/1/1; Vestry Book, Powerscourt, 1660–1760, s.d. 13 April 1696, 3 April 1727, 31 March 1729, 3 Oct. 1733, RCB, P 109/1/1; Register, Blessington, s.d. 26 March 1706, RCB, P 651/1/1; Vestry Book, Devenish, 1739–1828, s.d. 30 Sep. 1740, 2 Oct. 1744, 2 Oct. 1745, 2 Oct. 1751, 6 Oct. 1756, 3 Oct. 1758, 3 Oct. 1764, RCB, P 811/5/1; Vestry Book, Monasteroris, 2 April 1716, 30 March 1719, 10 April 1721, 16 April 1723, 3 Oct. 1732, 2 Oct. 1738, 3 Oct. 1749, RCB, P 484/1/1. 73 Vestry Book, Wicklow, s.d. 1 Oct. 1729, 1 Oct. 1735, RCB, P 611/5/1. 74 Vestry

parish's disposal are unclear. The deficiencies of the system led to its being supplemented by turnpikes, for which trusts were established by parliamentary statutes after 1729, and then to the transfer of the obligation from the parish to the county in the shape of its grand jury.[75]

IV

In the course of the seventeenth and eighteenth centuries, parishes were expected to oversee the population more closely. Notwithstanding the additional duties, varied problems long identified as sources of unrest consumed the most time and resources of the parish functionaries. The chief were the poor and vagrants.[76] Here, as in other matters of regulation, the parish worked sometimes in parallel and sometimes in conjunction with the municipalities and county administrations. In sizeable communities that lacked the status of incorporated boroughs, such as Clones and Edenderry, the parish could offer the most convenient mechanism through which to regulate the locality. In Edenderry, and elsewhere, it functioned alongside the manor.[77]

By the eighteenth century, most parishes accepted a degree of responsibility for relieving some within their precincts. Often, the annual cesses were supplemented by bequests administered by the incumbent, churchwardens and other trustees. The readiness of testators, such as Mary Clotworthy and James Lambly at Athy, Jacob Peppard, a burgess of Wicklow town, or Sergeant John Stokes and Alderman Austin in Cork, to channel charity through a particular parish may suggest not just continuing affection for a place but some recognition of the institutional continuities offered by the parish.[78] Often benefactors were prominent in the parish. This was the case with Sir Francis Blundell, effective owner of much of Edenderry, the Vaughans in Co. Donegal, the Handcocks and Dodwells of Athlone, Francis Adderley and a former rector at Innishannon in Co. Cork.[79] They – or their descendants – owned pews, donated silver utensils and bespoke funerary monuments. In some cases, painted boards advertised their generosity lest any overlook it. Tables of this

Book, Clones, s.d. 4 Oct. 1737, 1 Oct. 1740, RCB, P 804/1/1. **75** Barnard, *The kingdom of Ireland*, 94–5; D. Broderick, *The first toll-roads: Ireland's turnpike roads, 1729–1858* (Cork, 2002), 34–83. **76** Vestry Book, St Olave, Waterford, s.d. 1, 8 and 22 July 1784, 1 July 1786, 1 July 1787, 24 April 1795, 24 Jan. 1798, P 637/1/1; Vestry Minute Book, St Patrick's, Waterford, 1721–1772, s.d. 16 May 1764, 8 Oct. 1766, 15 July 1767, 20 Oct. 1767, RCB, P 640/5/1. **77** Misset to Blundell, PRONI, D 607/A/12, 16 Nov. 1723, 1725. **78** Vestry Book, Athy, 1669–1714, s.d. 6 March 1676[7], 30 Aug. 1698, RCB, P 630/1/1; Vestry Book, St Nicholas and St Bridget, Cork, from 1712, s.d. 22 July 1757, 15 July 1761, RCB, P 498/5/1; Vestry Book, Wicklow, s.d. 8 Oct. 1729, RCB, P 611/5/1; C. and M. Jackson, 'The Vaughan charity, 1763–1934' in *Clogher Record*, 12 (1986), 171–80: 171–2; J.C.T. MacDonagh, 'A seventeenth-century Letterkenny manuscript' in *The Donegal Annual*, 3 (1956), 139–41. **79** Vestry Book, Monasteroris, s.d. 5 April 1743, RCB, P 484/1/1; Vestry Book, Innishannon, s.d. 16 Aug. 1739, 26 Nov. 1757, RCB, P 142/1/1; Vestry Book, St Mary, Athlone, 1750–1791, s.d. 18 April 1780, 14 June 1780, RCB, P 392/5/1.

sort were displayed in Holy Trinity, Cork, early in the eighteenth century, and were to be set up in the parish church of Wicklow in 1729.[80] Affection of an individual for a parish eased the lot of the indigent. In 1761, Alderman Austin's benefaction to St Nicholas's, Cork, was divided among thirty-nine poor tradesmen and housekeepers.[81] Yet, the generous intentions of testators were not always realised. Executors and trustees regularly disregarded their duties. Even without such dishonesty and negligence, the bounty of individuals hardly lightened the burdens shouldered by most parishes.[82] As yet, the paucity of evidence from Ireland and the absence of systematic study of what survives prevent the posing, let alone answering, of questions that have interested historians of philanthropy and the parish in England.[83] In time, it may be possible to sketch the changing patterns of giving, the proportions of charity raised respectively by parochial rates and benefactions, and the differences (whether merely alleged or real) in Catholic and Protestant habits.

Rate-payers and those then charged with distributing the rates wished to direct the emoluments towards those whom they adjudged deserving. Conventions existed as to who fell within this category. But they were conventions rather than immutable rules. A merit of the system of parochial relief was that much power resided in the locals chosen to administer and dispense the funds. The system in Ireland followed the outlines of that in England. But England was not always the most pertinent rule. In particular, whereas in an English parish, overwhelmingly the inhabitants could be counted, at least nominally, as adherents of the state Church, the reverse was true in all Irish parishes outside parts of Ulster and Dublin. From this arose the fundamental conundrum about the parish in Ireland: to what extent its residents who did not observe the rites of the Established Church were obliged to pay towards its upkeep and received its benefits. The trend throughout eighteenth-century Ireland, susceptible to variations from place to place, was to require non-communicant residents to contribute to the expense of the state Church while denying them aid.

The criterion of sectarian affiliation was an easy way to reduce obligations to a manageable size. Even this limit, however, did not suffice. In order to ensure

80 Accounts, Holy Trinity, Cork, 1664–1709, s.d. 19 Jan. 1707[8], RCB, P 527/7/1, p. 84; Vestry Book, Wicklow, s.d. 22 Oct. 1729, RCB, P 611/5/1. **81** Vestry Book, St Nicholas and St Bridget, Cork, from 1712, s.d. 15 July 1761, RCB, P 498/5/1. **82** Vestry Book, Wicklow, s.d. 28 Oct. 1729, RCB, P 611/5/1; Vestry Book, St Nicholas and St Bridget, Cork, from 1712, s.d. 31 May 1775, RCB, P 498/5/1. **83** I.W. Archer, 'The charity of early modern Londoners' in *Transactions of the Royal Historical Society*, 6th series, 12 (2002), 223–44; J. P. Boulton, ' "Going on the parish": the parish pension and its meaning in the London suburbs, 1640–1724' in T. Hitchcock, P. King and P. Sharpe (eds), *Chronicling poverty: the voices and strategies of the English poor, 1640–1840* (Basingstoke, 1997), 19–46; J.P. Boulton, 'The poor among the rich: paupers and the parish in the West End, 1600–1724' in P. Griffiths and M. Jenner (eds), *Londinopolis: essays in the cultural and social history of modern London* (Manchester, 2001), 197–225; P. Slack, *From reformation to improvement: public welfare in early modern England* (Oxford, 1999).

that small resources were spent carefully, it proved necessary to distinguish between Protestants. Discriminations between the deserving and undeserving, familiar in England, were used in Ireland. In both poor and well-populated parishes, charity had to be confined to those known to be regular in their church attendance. In 1763, St Nicholas's parish in Cork, short of funds, voted to limit regular parochial relief to a dozen recipients. Within three years, the list had lengthened to sixteen. In 1765, the vestry decided to strike from the list of the parish poor any who failed to attend divine worship twice each Sunday and to receive communion each month. Ten years later, one recipient of the parish's limited charity was dropped because she was a Catholic. Soon this unfortunate was re-instated, presumably because she had disproved allegations – malicious, no doubt – that she had lapsed from orthodox Protestantism.[84]

The instinct in most Church of Ireland parishes, understandable remembering the limited funds, was to restrict the numbers eligible for financial help. Occasionally, in response to directives either from the privy council or the bishops, help was given to more distant places, like Lisburn, Castle Lyons and Carlingford, that had suffered a disaster such as fire.[85] Willingness to assist outsiders seldom arose spontaneously. Even among those deemed deserving within the immediate locality, further distinctions were drawn. In Dublin and elsewhere, three different kinds of eligibility for charity were defined.[86] In Wicklow town, the three sorts of poor were designated simply as 'classes'.[87] There, the impression of careful grading was rather spoilt when an investigative committee complained how badly the lists were maintained.[88] Nevertheless, the belief was strong that the poor should be sorted into grades of merit by the not poor. It may be suspected that rankings coincided more closely with perceptions of moral worth than with exact measurement of degrees of poverty. Several parishes graduated what was given. In Cork, the favoured received a weekly dole of 1s. 1d.; others, half the sum.[89] Again, it is unlikely that the help coincided exactly with need. As in the higher branches of the civil establishment – pensions on the civil list, places in the revenue and excise – allocations reflected the degree of interest that had been made by patrons on behalf of the recipients and how long they had queued for help.[90] In many parishes, the overseers, knowing the annual budget, set totals for what was to be spent on maintaining the poor, nursing foundlings, educating the young and apprenticing the apt.

84 Vestry Book, St Nicholas and St Bridget, Cork, from 1712, s.d. 3 May 1763, 15 May 1765, 30 May 1766, 17 April 1775, 1 Sep. 1775, RCB, P 498/5/1. 85 Vestry Book, Wicklow, s.d. 6 April 1711, 15 May 1717, RCB, P 611/ 5/1. 86 Poor book, St Michan's, 1723–34, RCB, P 276/8/1; Dudley, 'The Dublin parishes and the poor', i, 80–94. 87 For the early uses of this term, see: P. Corfield, 'Class by name and number in eighteenth-century Britain' in P.J. Corfield (ed.), *Language, history and class* (Oxford, 1991), 101–30. 88 Vestry Book, Wicklow, s.d. 8 Oct. 1729, RCB, P 611/5/1. 89 Vestry Book, St Nicholas and St Bridget, Cork, from 1712, 23 Feb. 1769, RCB, P 498/5/1. 90 *A dialogue between Dean Swift and Tho. Prior, Esq; in the Isles of St Patrick's Church, Dublin … October 9th, 1753* (Dublin, 1753), 95.

The ability of the charitable to control those whom they assisted within the parish was further helped by the system of badging those licensed to receive alms or to beg. The habit seems to have started in Dublin, where it was authorized in the parish of St John's as early as 1644. Badging was resumed there and in other central Dublin parishes during Charles II's reign.[91] Slowly it spread from the densely packed quarters of the capital: for example, to Clones and Cork early in the eighteenth century.[92] Although attempts to identify more exactly fit objects for charity had not always originated with the parish, it was the last that often had to implement orders from county quarter sessions or the privy council. This was particularly the case in places that lacked a municipal corporation: the other principal organization to which care and control of the poor might reasonably be delegated. In 1700, the Monaghan town of Clones decided to enter into the vestry book the names of the licensed beggars of the parish. Those then authorized to beg locally were to wear either badges or tickets of 'brass, copper [or] pewter' embossed with the name of the parish. The unlicensed were to be whipped from the district. The regulations belonged to a larger scheme, stimulated by the justices and grand jurors at the quarter sessions in the town. The authorities sensed an increase in begging. In the countryside, the high and petty constables were to tackle the problem; in the town of Clones, the matter was referred to the parish vestry. Linked with the threat were others, notably the need to mount effective night-time watches, to punish the parents of bastards and to apprentice the deserving young.[93] The very poverty that increased the numbers begging reduced the ability and willingness of parishioners to help the indigent. The following year, the vestry was keen to reduce the number which it helped: it totalled seven individuals.[94]

These priorities persisted in Clones: detecting the parents of abandoned children who became a charge of the parish, listing the children, teaching orphans to read and apprenticing them into the weaving trade, and regulating the poor.[95] Orders for badging the licensed beggars were repeated in 1735. They were designed as a prelude to a more determined drive to rid the parish of the unlicensed. Those who did not sport the official badges were to be treated as 'strollers' and whipped to the next market town. During the famine of 1740–1, parishioners were instructed not to give to any, 'at our doors', who were not holders of the parochial badge. Yet, in the face of adversity, more names were added to the list of the parish poor, so that it totalled thirty-eight. In at least one case, the vestry was prepared to accept the testimony of the Catholic priest about the desserts of one whom it licensed to beg.[96]

The scale of the problem that faced many parishes obliged the authorities to

91 Barnard, *New anatomy*, 319; R. Gillespie (ed.), *The vestry records of the parish of St John the Evangelist, Dublin, 1595–1658* (Dublin, 2002),18, 167. 92 Vestry Book, St Peter, Cork, NLI, MS 764, p. 1. 93 Vestry book, Clones, s.d. 9 May 1700, RCB, P 804/1/1. 94 Vestry book, Clones, s.d. 26 April 1736, April 1741, RCB, P 804/1/1. 95 Vestry book, Clones, s.d. 24 May 1733, 30 Aug. 1733, RCB, P 804/1/1. 96 Vestry book, Clones, s.d. 4 Sep. 1701, RCB, P 804/1/1.

look beyond small-scale solutions. In 1676, a Cork city parish entrusted its funds for poor relief to a local goldsmith, in order to raise an income. The goldsmith, Robert Goble, was also paid for making a chalice and pattens for the parish. His employments reminds of the smallness of the overlapping communities of Protestant freemen, municipal notables and parochial functionaries. With commissions directed to the favoured, inevitably suspicions were aroused that the same jobbery that affected the state and civic bureaucracies occurred also in the parishes.[97] A century later, another Cork parish, St Nicholas's, had accumulated a fund of £130 from which the poor were to be relieved. It was invested to generate an income. A special committee was established by the vestry to deal with the matter.[98] If parishes were ingenious in trying to rise to the challenge of an increasing burden of the impoverished in their midst, they were assisted by external developments. Parliament legislated to erect workhouses in each county. By 1774, a house of industry had been constructed at Enniskillen. As a result, nearby parishes, such as Devenish, were required to send a return of the vagrant poor within their own precincts to the clergyman who presided over the committee that ran the Enniskillen workhouse. Institutions of this kind, coupled with foundations of hospitals and schools in Dublin, might free the parish of some obligations, but necessitated surveys of the local situation to satisfy distant inquisitors.[99]

In 1776, the churchwardens and sidesmen in the Athlone parish of St Mary were to round up all the beggars who had arrived in the town during the previous three years and to expel them. This drive to restrict relief to locals was to be assisted by borough officials.[1] In Cork, too, the standing committee of St Nicholas's parish instituted enquiries in 1773 to ascertain which helpless poor had lived in the district for a year or more. The investigations went beyond this simple matter. The return was also to include information about the 'characters' of the unlucky, how they had been reduced to their present condition, and details of their children. Those who managed to satisfy these exacting researches would be issued with licences and badges and so permitted to beg within the confines of the parish.[2] The act of removing the unlicensed, although in the longer term, it lessened the financial burden on the parish, required money. Indeed, the parishes of Kells (Co. Meath) and Kilshannig (Co. Cork) enlarged their retinue of officials by employing whip beggars during the 1740s and 1750s.[3]

97 Accounts, May 1676, 1677, Accounts, Holy Trinity, Cork, 1664–1709, RCB, P 527/7/1, pp. 65, 71.   98 Vestry Book, St Nicholas and St Bridget, Cork, from 1712, s.d. 12 Aug. 1767, 2 Oct. 1770, 6 and 27 April 1779, RCB. P 498/5/1.   99 Vestry Book, Athy, 1714–1768, s.d. 2 Oct. 1744, 27 Nov. 1745, RCB, P 630/1/2; Vestry Book, Devenish, 1739–1828, s.d. 19 Oct. 1774, RCB, P 811/ 5/1.   1 Vestry Book, St Mary, Athlone, 1750–91, s.d. 9 April 1776, RCB, P 392/5/1. 2 Vestry Book, St Nicholas and St Bridget, Cork, from 1712, s.d. 12 May 1773, RCB, P 498/5/1. 3 Vestry Book, Kells, s.d. 30 Sep. 1741, 13 July 1742, 5 April 1743, 26 April 1748, RCB, P 192/5/1; Vestry Book, Powerscourt, 1660–1760, s.d. 23 May 1743, RCB, P 109/1/1; A.B. Wilson, 'Licensed beggars' in *Journal of the Cork Historical and Archaeological Society*, 2nd series, 4 (1898),

The modest system may have been strained to the verge of collapse by the increasing numbers of the destitute. Parishes were also emboldened to shuffle some of the responsibilities onto others as larger scale and centralized institutions, such as the nurseries of the Incorporated Society, the hospitals and schools of Dublin, infirmaries and workhouses in county towns, opened. The availability of more distant helps weakened the ties between parishes and their own. But the links were never sundered completely. Alongside the more impersonal systems of help, centred on the capital and the county, there survived the parochial. St Nicholas's in Cork further refined its treatment of the parish poor in 1778. Along with the aged, young foundlings, abandoned in the parish, burdened the ratepayers. In 1779, the costs of keeping the foundlings amounted to more than £18 of an annual expenditure of £54. Predictably, the vestry wished to limit its obligations. Also, it insisted that the infants should be nursed in the countryside, at least five miles distant from the city. The injunction may have spoken of a disinterested care for the foundlings' health; alternatively, the vestrymen may have been trying to sever the links between the children and their surviving kindred still in Cork.[4] Certainly the Incorporated Society for Protestant schools practised a policy of removing its charges far from the district in which they had originated.

A minority among the poor might identify with the parish since it distributed their dole. In Cork, for example, the parish poor had been selected for help because of their previous loyalty to the Protestant Church. Continuing attendance at worship qualified them for further aid. Other devices turned the parish into something more than an abstraction or intrusion. Some parishes owned a pall to drape over the coffin at a funeral. Thereby greater dignity was lent to the solemnity. At both Athy and Edenderry, the parish possessed a pall that it hired out. The cloth at Athy had been presented by a local squire: the fees from its hire were used to assist the parish poor. In 1747, the Edenderry vestry spent £4 on a new black pall made of hair shag. Money was thereby generated. Organizers of funerals were charged on a sliding scale that was graduated according to the dead person's degree of involvement in the parish.[5] Blessington also had a pall cloth. Here the privilege of using it was connected yet more explicitly with ideas of who did or did not belong to the parish. In 1701, it was decreed that 'foreigners' must pay one shilling to use the cloth. 'Foreigners' in this context were defined as those who did not contribute to the levies for the repair of the church. In this way, assorted degrees of membership were emphasized.[6]

Liability for church repairs was frequently linked with possession of a fixed

318–20.   **4** Vestry Book, St Nicholas and St Bridget, Cork, s.d. 21 Jan. 1772, 16 May 1775, 20 Jan. 1778, 20 Jan. 1779, 3 Feb. 1779, RCB, P 498/5/1.   **5** Vestry Book, Athy, 1669–1714, s.d. 17 Dec. 1707, RCB, P 630/1/1; Vestry Book, Monasteroris, s.d. 29 March 1703, 9 April 1705, 20 April 1747, RCB, P 484/1/1. RCB, P 484/1/1; Vestry Book, Powerscourt, 1660–1760, s.d. 26 May 1740, RCB, P 109/1/1.   **6** Register, Blessington, s.d. 22 April 1701, RCB, P 651/1/1.

pew within the body of the church. Owning or renting a pew was one of the clearest indicators of identification with the parish and its church. Pews were sources of income for the parish. In addition, they embodied and accentuated the desire for order and decency in the internal arrangements of the building. The overriding principle, stated in Cork city in 1681, was 'that all parishioners of the ... parish should be seated in seats suitable to their qualities'.[7] Allocating the seating also made more work for the vestry. However, the rankings decided by the vestrymen might not always correspond to individual parishioner's self-assessment. An extreme example of the proprietorial arrogance towards the parish, or at least to its physical centre the parish church, was the gift from a local squire and magistrate, Gershon Herrick, of a silver flagon to Innishannon. This coincided with his being ritually invested in the pew that he had had built for his family's use in the church.[8] More usefully, at Powerscourt, the vestry reserved a seat in the church gallery for the inhabitants of a particular townland in the parish.[9] In the church at Blessington, two common pews were provided for the parishioners.[10] At Innishannon, the vestry placed benches around the walls of the chancel, perhaps to accommodate humbler worshippers.[11] Not all who owned pews used them, because absent or indifferent. At Athlone in 1786, the vestry, conscious that the church could not accommodate all parishioners, decreed that the pews belonging to non-residents be sold. The churchwardens were authorized to auction them publicly. Presumably, the owners would be recompensed. Even so, it was a potentially worrying invasion of the property rights of the laity. The enforced sales hardly overcame the shortage. Within two years, it was proposed to add two new galleries.[12] Yet, possessing a seat distinguished a few both from the commonalty forced to use benches or to stand and from the many unmoved to enter the state Church to the church.[13] The extent to which ownership of pews coincided with regular attendance at the vestry and appointment to the more prestigious parish offices has yet to be demonstrated.

The business of assigning seats could occasionally provoke contentions.[14]

---

7 Accounts, Holy Trinity, Cork, 1664–1709, s.d. 14 Feb. 1680[1], RCB, P 527/7/1, p. 81. 8 Vestry Book, Innishannon, s.d. 15 April 1700, RCB, P 142/1/1. Five years later he became a justice of the peace: H. F. Berry, 'Justices of the Peace for County Cork' in *Journal of the Cork Historical and Archaeological Society*, 2nd series, 3 (1897), 61. 9 Vestry Book, Powerscourt, 1660–1760, s.d. 27 April 1736, RCB, P 109/1/1. 10 Register, Blessington, s.d. 18 April 1720, RCB, P 651/1/1. 11 Vestry Book, Innishannon, s.d. 6 Jan. 1712[13], RCB, P 142/1/1. 12 Vestry Book, St Mary's, Athlone, s.d. 28 Aug. 1786, 21 May 1788, RCB, P 392/5/1. 13 Vestry Book, Clones, s.d. 10 July 1694, 28 July 1735, 26 April 1736, RCB, P 804/1/1; Vestry Book, Powerscourt, 1660–1760, s.d. 5 April 1708, 9 May 1709, RCB, P 109/1/1; Vestry Book, Athy, s.d. [ ] March 1706, 3 May 1714, 6 Jan. 1725[6], RCB, P 630/11; Vestry Book, Monasteroris, s.d. 19 Oct. 1720, 23 April 1739; RCB, P 484/1/1; Vestry Book, St Nicholas and St Bridget, s.d. 13 Sep. 1722, 2 Oct. 1722, 16 Jan. 1726[7], 20 April 1733, 19 July 1753, 2 Aug. 1753, RCB, P 498/5/1; Vestry Book, Innishannon, s.d. 29 July 1762, 5 Jan. 1763, RCB, P 142/1/1; R. Odlum to Lord Digby, 3 Nov. 1765, Dorset County Record Office, D/SHC, 3C/81. 14 Barnard, *New anatomy*, 239–43; K.B. Dillow, 'The social and ecclesiastical significance of church seating arrangements and pew disputes, 1500–1640', unpublished DPhil (Oxford University 1990); C. Marsh,

Pews also represented the growing enthusiasm for decency and respectability. Church buildings responded to other manifestations of the enthusiasm. Some were fitted with pulpit, altar, reredos and board on which the ten commandments were inscribed.[15] Pernickety vestrymen decreed the colour that pine pews and woodwork had to be painted: 'a dark mahogany colour' in Cork; 'Spanish brown' at Wicklow; and to simulate Danzig oak in Athlone. At Devenish, the seats were to be finished 'regularly and uniformly'.[16] More exacting still was the commission that the vestry for Edenderry entrusted to Thomas Smallwood in 1720. Smallwood was to make a new communion table, 'with twisted feet', and rails around it, with 'twisted balusters'. All were to be 'of well-seasoned oak' and 'strongly and neatly turned and fitted'. Articles such as a dozen brass candlesticks or pegs on which to hang hats were procured. In 1757, St Peter's Cork required sixty brass candlesticks.[17] The varied prescriptions indicated a pride in the setting for the communal worship of a minority, and the pressures towards decorum. Windows were regularly broken and had to be re-glazed. Especially in urban parishes, the churchyard was treated as an amenity for the respectable. It, in common with the approach to the church, was to be invested with greater dignity.[18] In several towns, trees were planted, the sward tidied up and maintained as a place where worshippers could promenade. Indeed, this area was often the most central in a scattered parish and might accordingly be chosen as the venue for military exercises when volunteer bands of militiamen were mustered and drilled in emergencies.[19]

The prominence given by architecture and setting to some Church of Ireland buildings contrasted strikingly with the reticence into which the Catholics were forced and which the dissenters generally preferred. In so far as the church itself embodied the reality of the parish, it once more reminded of the confessional as well as economic and occupational fragmentation of the inhabitants. In a few places, seating also segregated men from women. The Waterford churches of St Olave and St Patrick separated the sexes. However, this disposition was uncommon, and may have arisen from the idiosyncratic notions of

'"Common Prayer" in England, 1560–1640: the view from the pew' in *Past and Present*, 171 (2001), 66–94; C. Marsh, 'Sacred space in England, 1560–1640: the view from the pew' in *Journal of Ecclesiastical History*, 53 (2002), 286–311. **15** Carlow Vestry Book, 1669–1762, RCB, P 317/5/1, pp. 68, 69, 118, 124; Vestry Book, St Catherine's, Dublin, 1657–1692, s.d. 16 Jan. 1663[4], RCB, P 117/5/2, p. 190; Smith, *Waterford*, 181. **16** Vestry Book, St Mary's, Athlone, s.d. 2 Oct. 1770, RCB, P 392/5/1; Vestry Book, St Nicholas and St Bridget, Cork, from 1712, s.d. 12 July 1769, RCB. P 498/5/1; Vestry Book, Wicklow, s.d. 22 Feb. 1709[10], P 611/5/1; Vestry Book, Devenish, 1739–1828, s.d. 15 May 1744, RCB, P 811/5/1. **17** Vestry Book, St Nicholas and St Bridget, Cork, from 1712, s.d. 13 Oct. 1768, 6 Feb. 1770, RCB. P 498/5/1; Vestry Book, St Patrick, Waterford, s.d. 21 April 1735, RCB, P 640/5/1; Vestry Book, St Peter, Cork, NLI, MS 764, p. 5. **18** Vestry Book, Devenish, 1739–1828, s.d. 31 March 1761, 10 June 1761, RCB, P 811/5/1. **19** Vestry Book, St Nicholas and St Bridget, Cork, from 1712, s.d. 11 Sep. 1775, 20 Jan. 1779, RCB, P 498/5/1; Vestry Book, St Patrick, Waterford, s.d. 30 March 1730, RCB, P 640/5/1; Athlone, 1780s. Further examples occur in Barnard, 'Parishes, pews and parsons', 79–80.

Bishop Thomas Milles, who had had the churches constructed.[20] Stratifications were deepened when churches served as the settings for municipal, quasi-military and political ceremonies. Church services were incorporated into the regular celebrations of the Protestant state in Ireland. A special liturgy was devised to commemorate the Protestants' sufferings and eventual deliverance in and after 23 October 1641 when Irish Catholics had risen. In Dublin, through attending the special service, the lord lieutenant or his surrogates set an example to be imitated by underlings throughout the provinces.[21] More regularly, the office-holders in boroughs, justices of the peace and grand jurors at the start of the assizes and quarter sessions, officers and troopers in the numerous garrisons and the freemen of trading or craft guilds were required to participate in Church of Ireland rituals in their parish churches. In some, seats were reserved for the mayor and civil worthies and for the regimental officers.[22] Although these ostentatious reminders of the links between membership of the Church of Ireland and full citizenship in Ireland between 1690 and 1783 related most to what happened within the churches themselves, they may have affected perceptions of the wider parish. In a few places, notably Dublin, but also Kinsale, the boundaries were ridden or trodden each year. At Kinsale, the limits may have been coterminous with the ecclesiastical parish, but for those who traced the bounds it was less a sense of the parish than of the liberties of the town that they acquired. Furthermore, as with the pompous parades of the robed and uniformed to Church of Ireland places of worship, so with the cavalcades around the edges of Dublin or Kinsale, few of the poor or of the Catholics would join other than as bemused onlookers or butts for the derision of the privileged.[23]

Heroic efforts were required when churches were built, rebuilt or given substantial additions. Again, concern with this work tended to separate a minority who identified strongly with the parish from an unconcerned

20 Accounts, Holy Trinity, Cork, 1664–1709, RCB, P527/7/1, pp. 12, 67; A. Crookshank, 'Eighteenth-century alterations, improvements and furnishings in St Michan's Church, Dublin' in *Studies*, 64 (1975), 386–92; Walter Harris, *The antient and present state of the county of Down* (Dublin, 1746), 61; J.J. McKenna and C.V. Moore, *The modest men of Christ Church, Cork* (Naas, 1970), 31; Samuel McSkimin, *The history and antiquities of the county of the town of Carrickfergus* (Belfast, 1811), 49; Smith, *Waterford*, 180–1. 21 T.C. Barnard, 'The uses of 23 October 1641 and Irish Protestant celebrations' in *English Historical Review*, 106 (1991), 889–920, reprinted in T.C. Barnard, *Irish Protestant ascents and descents* (Dublin, 2004), 111–42. 22 'Schedule of seats', 1724; entry s.d. 8 Oct. 1729, in Wicklow, Vestry Book, RCB, P611/5/1; Vestry Book, St Mary's, Athlone, s.d. 2 Sep. 1768, 25 Sept. 1782, 6 July 1785, RCB, P392/51; T.C. Barnard, 'The cultures of eighteenth-century Irish towns' in P. Borsay and L. Proudfoot (eds), *Provincial towns in early modern England and Ireland; change, convergence and divergence*, Proceedings of the British Academy, 108 (2002), 195–22: 207–8; M. Mulcahy (ed.), *Calendar of Kinsale documents*, 3 (Kinsale, 1994), 24; 6 (Kinsale, 1998), 15; R.M. Young (ed.), *The town book of the corporation of Belfast* (Belfast, 1892), 52–3. 23 Barnard, 'The cultures of eighteenth-century Irish towns', 215–19; Barnard, *Making the grand figure*, 361–72; G.L. Barrow, 'Riding the franchises' in *Dublin Historical Record*, 33 (1980), 135–8; Mulcahy (ed.), *Calendar of Kinsale documents*, 6, 53.

majority. In a few special instances, mostly in Dublin and Cork, the Irish parliament allowed taxes to be levied towards the provision of new churches. Such measures copied English ones. In Queen Anne's reign, zealous churchmen, worried at the inadequate provision of places of worship and fearful that it explained the stampede into dissent and irreligion, vowed to make good the deficiency by building fifty new churches. In the event, only twelve were erected. Nevertheless, the scheme served as a precedent for concerned clerics in Ireland, such as Archbishop King in Dublin and Dean Henry Maule in Cork. At least one new church in King's archdiocese, that in Wicklow, occupied the vestrymen.[24] At St Nicholas's in Cork, it was necessary for the vestry to impose a levy of first £40 and then £45 to supplement what had been provided by parliament.[25] Elsewhere, works were paid for by subscription or by special cesses.[26] By 1744, the church at Blessington, consecrated some sixty years earlier and paid for by the owner of the adjoining estate, Archbishop Michael Boyle, had fallen into disrepair. Indeed, its dilapidated condition was said to keep some parishioners from worship and to endanger those who did come. The vestry set up a committee to consider the necessary renovations.[27] At Innishannon, a new building was wanted urgently by 1761, since the walls of the old one were bulging. Also, the vestry planned to add a gallery to seat the pupils of the charity school and a vestry room for the more decorous conduct of parochial business. The French Society in Dublin gave £40 towards the structure. Innishannon, with its incipient − but in the end unsuccessful -silk industry had sought Protestant refugees from France. The major burden, nevertheless, fell on the parishioners. Subscriptions were headed by Thomas Adderley, member of parliament for the nearby borough of Bandon and the local landowner who was promoting the silk project, and the patron of the parish. Adderley gave £40; the patron, £20.[28] Neighbourly pressures may have impelled subscribers to make generous donations, but at least the method of subscription freed those who did not use the parish church from financing its erection. Levies on the whole parish were a different matter, and caused resentment that led to obstructionism from Catholic and nonconformist house-holders. As has been shown, the first group was disenfranchised at vestry meetings called to set rates in 1726, but not the Protestant dissenters for another fifty years.

Enlargement and embellishment of buildings arose sometimes from

24 Vestry Book, Wicklow, s.d. 22 Feb. 1709[10], 10 April 1710, 27 Feb. 1711[12], 13 Feb. 1713[14], RCB, P 611/ 5/1. **25** Vestry Book, St Nicholas and St Bridget, Cork, from 1712, s.d. 13 Nov. 1721, 16 Dec. 1723, RCB. P 498/5/1. **26** Vestry Book, Athy, 1669–1714, s.d. 6 March 1676[7], RCB, P 630/1/1; Vestry Book, Clones, s.d. 7 Aug. 1740, RCB, P 804/1/1; Vestry Book, Monasteroris, s.d. 10 April 1721, RCB, P 484/1/1; Vestry Book, Devenish, 1739–1828, s.d. 30 Sep. 1740, RCB, P 811/5/1. **27** Register Book, Blessington, s.d. 17 Sep. 1683, 14 Jan. 1743[4], RCB, P 651/1/1. **28** Vestry Book, Innishannon, s.d. 28 May 1758, 2 Oct. 1760, 11 May 1761, 26 April 1762, RCB, P 142/1/1; Johnson-Liik, *History of the Irish parliament*, iii, 56–9; Smith, *Cork*, i, 211–12.

necessity: a decrepit fabric unsafe and unfit for use; buildings too cramped to accommodate all who came. More commonly, physical improvements reflected changing notions of comfort and decency among the leading parishioners. The undertakings frequently proved troublesome to the vestries, and not only because of the reluctance of parishioners to pay their contributions. There remained suspicions of trickery in the award of contracts when ambitious works were in prospect. The inner clique within the vestry was sometimes viewed as an oligarchy akin to those that were thought to dominate trading guilds and municipal corporations. Renovations and additions were suspected of being inspired less by need than by a wish to benefit craftsmen and suppliers within the parish.[29] An extreme if somewhat puzzling example of the resulting contentions comes from Devenish in 1779. The rector noted, in the parish vestry book, that he had been warned not to oppose the re-roofing of the church with Irish fir. If he did so, 'the whole church would be in the most imminent danger'. Consequently, the incumbent, although he regarded 'Irish fir [as] the most unfit for the work', in order 'to keep down present disputes', reluctantly acquiesced. It is unclear from the cryptic memorandum whether the hostility was sectarian, from local Presbyterians or Catholics, commercial (from putative suppliers of the timber), or patriotic and intended to stop the use of imported wood.[30] In comparison, other setbacks were more straightforward. In 1696, the vestry at Clones contracted with John Golphine to mend the church steeple. Within four years, Golphine was to be taken to court because of his failure to complete the contract. In the end, the suit was dropped owing to Golphine's poverty, and instead a new agreement for the steeple was made with a joiner in Monaghan town.[31] The spire of St Mary's, Athlone, proved equally troublesome to its vestry. The contractor who was to complete the structure and add a golden ball delayed the work so long that the vestry threatened to award the job to another. The threat sufficed to make the original undertaker, William Kelly, finish the commission, for which he was paid forty guineas.[32] Clocks were rare on public buildings outside Dublin. Archbishop Boyle's foundation at Blessington boasted one. Soon it gave the vestrymen extra worries. By 1721, they planned to sue the clockmaker for failing to attend to the church clock.[33] But once more, in pressing and paying for the work, and often in overseeing it through the vestry and its committees, this minority of activists showed a higher degree of engagement with the parish than did the bulk of their neighbours.

The parish, like other institutions – the municipality, trading corporations

29 J. Devereux, *Mr Devereux's letter to the inhabitants of St Catherine's parish* ([Dublin], 1740). 30 Vestry Book, Devenish, 1739–1828, s.d. 25 May 1779, RCB, P 811/5/1. 31 Vestry Book, Clones, s.d. 13 April 1696, 9 May 1700, 25 April 1701, 4 Sep. 1701, 22 June 1710, 31 July 1711, 22 April 1712, RCB, P 804/1/1. 32 Vestry Book, St Mary, Athlone, 1750–91, s.d. 29 May 1789, 19 Aug. 1789, 14 Sep. 1789, 24 March 1790, 10 May 1790. 33 Register, Blessington, s.d. 11 April 1721, RCB, P 651/1/1.

and voluntary groups – with which it sometimes overlapped, reflected and accentuated notions of hierarchy. Pews in particular displayed the inequalities in status, wealth and regard. A sense of solidarity may have been encouraged among the householders, rate-payers and vestrymen by the parish. But it excluded more than it included, and might expose and aggravate divisions within the community. The prebendary of Devenish alluded to such tensions in 1779. Before this, in 1736, it was thought necessary in Blessington to establish a committee of five 'to settle and adjust all affairs and disputes depending in this vestry'.[34] Acrimony may have arisen simply from assessments thought to be unfair. Alternatively, more deep-rooted issues could divide the parish. The very intimacies that permitted houses to be valued and collections made from door to door could occasion feuds.

In the absence of copious evidence, it would be foolhardy to portray the parish as a scene of constant friction. Yet, at the very least, the potential for tension existed both within an internally differentiated Church of Ireland community and between that privileged minority and the bulk of the population. The parish was a space as well as an institution. Feelings towards each of its aspects depended on the degree to which inhabitants were caught up in the operations of the parish. Its boundaries seem to have been less clearly demarcated than, for example, those of the borough. Parish bounds were not customarily beaten, whereas the liberties of a town like Kinsale or the franchises of Dublin would be ridden annually. However, there were frontiers between Dublin parishes which led to rivalry between the watchmen from separate quarters; in the countryside, there are also signs of these identifications with a precise locale. For a fortunate few, the parish may have functioned as a nursery in civic duties; for rather more, it was irksome and intrusive. The strongest signs of the vitality of the parish come from Dublin and the largest towns: a reflection of a larger conforming population and of the pressing social and economic problems to which the parish was obliged to attend. Of necessity, more were drawn into the work of the parish than into that of the county grand jury or Dublin parliament. William Molyneux, a member of parliament who defended the historic rights of Ireland against England, was a member of the emerging Church of Ireland ascendancy. Molyneux, in the tradition of his family, had an allocated seat in St Catherine's church on the edge of the Liberties in Dublin. Throughout 1696 and 1697 he is to be found frequently at meetings of the vestry, and signed among the auditors of the churchwardens' annual accounts.[35] It would be extravagant to contend that Molyneux was schooled in his constitutional thinking more by his work in the parish than as a barrister or member of parliament. Instead, it can be emphasized how neatly the activities interlocked. Through the parish, the locality was overseen.

34 Register, Blessington, s.d. 27 April 1736, RCB, P 651/1/1. 35 Vestry Book of St Catherine's, Dublin, 1693–1730, RCB, P117/5/2, pp. 30, 47–51, 67.

Alongside and above it rose the higher tiers of government: manor, municipal corporation, barony and county. Of the institutions, the parish was most the ubiquitous, and required the most participants. In consequence, between the 1690s and 1780s, it advertised most blatantly – and perhaps offensively – the Church of Ireland ascendancy.

The role of the parish in building and maintaining Anglican churches in the north of Ireland, 1660–1740

WILLIAM ROULSTON

All buildings require regular maintenance. Missing slates need to be replaced; clogged gutters require cleaning; dry rot calls for attention. If such problems are ignored the building will start to decay. The decline will be gradual at first, but will accelerate to the stage where the structure is no longer usable. However, if initial defects in the fabric of the building are detected at an early stage and remedied quickly, the more serious problems will never be given the opportunity to develop.[1] Despite regular maintenance, there may come a time when, for a variety of reasons, reconstruction is considered more appropriate than repair. This essay examines the relationship between parishioners and Church of Ireland parish churches in the north of Ireland between 1660 and 1740. It considers the different types of building work relating to churches, how the work was financed and also how it was organised.

The affairs of the parish were governed by the vestry. In theory, membership of the vestry was open to all those who were liable to parish rates. In practice, however, judging from the number of signatures and marks in the surviving vestry minute books, it would appear that most meetings of vestry were attended by the rector or his curate, who presided, and the leading parishioners – the landowners, if resident in the parish, and the principal farmers or merchants if the parish contained a significant urban settlement. At the more important meetings, such as those to decide whether or not to build a new church, attendance was much higher. At one meeting in the parish of Knockbreda, Co. Down, in 1733 around three hundred persons were present.[2]

---

1 R. Morris, *Churches in the landscape* (London, 1997), 316. 2 Connor and Down and Dromore Diocesan Offices, Belfast, notebook kept by Bishop Francis Hutchinson, *c.*1729–39 (hereafter Hutchinson notebook), 121. This has recently been transferred to PRONI.

CHURCH MAINTENANCE AND REPAIR

The officers of the parish in both civil and ecclesiastical matters were the churchwardens. There were two to a parish and they were elected on an annual basis, although the post could be held by one man for several years at a time. To help the churchwardens many parishes appointed assistants known as sidesmen. The churchwardens had a wide range of responsibilities. Their duties with regard to the fabric of the church building were set out in Canon 93 of the Irish Canons of 1634:

> [The churchwardens] shall take care and provide that the churches be well and sufficiently repaired, and so from time to time kept and maintained; that the windows be well glazed, and that the floors be kept paved, plain and even; and all things there, in such an orderly and decent sort (without dust or any thing that may be noisome and unseemly).[3]

The maintenance of the fabric of the church was a major concern for the parish vestry. The surviving vestry books indicate that money was raised every year to keep the church in repair, the roof and windows generally requiring greatest attention. Periodic inspections were carried out to ensure that the church was structurally sound. In 1703 the vestry of Raphoe parish, Co. Donegal, issued instructions that the foundation of the cathedral church be inspected for its strength and depth and also the roof examined for its soundness.[4] Contemporaries were well aware of the need for regularity in the upkeep of a church. Bishop William King of Derry pointed out to the parishioners in his diocese that they ought not 'to allow those [churches] that were falling into decay to go to utter ruin, as that would be the cause some time of great expense to themselves, which a small expenditure could now prevent'.[5]

In addition to regular maintenance, church repairs were required in other circumstances. In 1710 the vestry of Raphoe was forced to act with some haste when it was discovered that the roof of the cathedral church was 'in danger of falling and coming to ruin unless speedily prevented or helped by the repair thereof'.[6] Vestry books record several instances of high winds damaging churches. In 1698, for example, as a result of 'an extraordinary violent storm' the church in Clones parish, Co. Monaghan, was 'so damnified that it could not be made use of for divine service'.[7]

During periods of warfare churches were damaged or suffered neglect. In 1660 most of the churches in the north of Ireland were in ruins following the

---

3 *Constitutions and canons ecclesiastical treated upon by the archbishops and bishops and the rest of the clergy of Ireland* (Dublin, 1816), 434.   4 PRONI, MIC/1/95, Raphoe parish vestry minutes. 5 C.S. King (ed.), *A great archbishop of Dublin, William King D.D., 1650–1729* (London, 1906), 34.   6 PRONI, MIC/1/95, Raphoe parish vestry minutes.   7 PRONI, MIC/1/147, Clones parish vestry minutes.

1641 rebellion and the ensuing decade of destruction. There followed in the 1660s through to the 1680s a major programme of reparation work. It is recorded that in this period most of the churches in the diocese of Armagh were 'rebuilt or repaired'.[8] Again during the period 1689–91 many churches were damaged and had to be repaired or in a few cases rebuilt.[9] In at least one instance a church had to be entirely rebuilt following its destruction by fire during peacetime. In 1707 the town of Lisburn, Co. Antrim, including the castle and cathedral church, was accidentally burnt to the ground. The following year the foundation was laid for a new church and this was completed about 1712.[10]

Aside from absolute necessity, the cost and the level of commitment required meant that there had to be good reasons for wanting to build a new church. In some cases the condition of an existing church had been allowed to deteriorate to the stage where a new church was necessary. By 1722 the 'small timber chapel' used as a place of worship in the parish of Ballinsacreen, Co. Londonderry, had become so dilapidated that the parishioners were afraid to meet in it.[11] They, therefore, set about building a new church. In 1735 the vestry of Kilbarron parish church in Ballyshannon, Co. Donegal, decided that the church had become ruinous to the extent that it was unsafe to continue meeting in and ordered a new church to be built.[12]

On a few occasions a new church was required because a decision had been made to move the site of the church to a new location.[13] This was usually to accommodate the needs of the Protestant inhabitants of the parish. Through petitions and the support of the bishop of the diocese the parishioners argued their case. In 1670 it was said that the church in Dunboe parish, Co. Londonderry, was:

> situate with great inconveniency to the inhabitants of the said parish, especially in the best planted parts thereof, for their attending the public worship of God, being in the utmost part of the said parish and under the skirt of the great mountains without any house or shelter for the relief of the inhabitants in ill weather, which is there very frequent by reason of the nearness of the sea and bleakness of the place.[14]

8 PRONI, T/505/1, visitation books, Armagh and Derry dioceses, 1693. 9 Ibid. 10 PRONI, MIC/1/4, Blaris parish vestry minutes. 11 PRONI, D/3632/A/352, deed of July 1722 relating to the grant of a plot of land for a new church in Ballinscreen parish, Co. Londonderry. 12 H. Allingham, *Ballyshannon: its history and antiquities* (Londonderry, 1937), 51. 13 Of the 215 or so Anglican parish churches in use in the north of Ireland in 1740 more than two-thirds occupied the sites of pre-Reformation parish churches. Once a pre-Reformation site had been settled upon for a new Protestant church it was unusual to change it. Changes in the location of a parish church nearly always occurred when the parish was initially being provided with a Protestant church. See W.J. Roulston, 'The provision, building and architecture of Anglican churches in the north of Ireland, 1600–1740', unpublished PhD (QUB, 2003), ch. 3. 14 T.W. Moody and J.G. Simms, *The bishopric of Derry and the Irish Society of London, 1602–1705*, 2 vols (Dublin, 1968–83), i, 429.

Soon afterwards official permission was granted to have the site of the church relocated to a better planted part of the parish.[15] Those seeking the removal of a parish church often couched their request in terms of the benefits that relocation could bring to the Established Church. In 1733 the parishioners of Termonmagurk, Co. Tyrone, argued that building a new church in a more convenient place would provide the people with 'an opportunity of hearing evening service on Sundays and in all probability greatly increase the number of our congregation'.[16]

In most cases the proposal to relocate the parish church was formally brought to the attention of the parishioners at a vestry meeting usually held at the existing church whether or not it was in actual use at that time. Sufficient notice of this meeting was to be given to the parishioners, in writing if need be.[17] At this vestry meeting the incumbent of the parish and bishop of the diocese would be present as would the patron of the parish, or his or her representative. Those in attendance would be given the opportunity to discuss the proposed relocation. On at least one occasion the parishioners were given the opportunity to vote on the matter.[18] Undoubtedly many of these vestry meetings were called for the sake of appearances. Those with power and influence in the parish had already decided on the need to relocate the parish church and on where it should be built. In parishes where Protestants were in the minority a proposed relocation could be thwarted. In response to this the Irish parliament passed a law in 1723 which stated that only the consent of a majority of the Protestant, that is, Anglican, parishioners was needed before a new church was built.[19]

The relocation of a parish church to a new site did not always run smoothly and on occasion proved extremely divisive. For example, Knockbreda parish was the scene of an intense dispute in the early 1730s over whether or not the site of the parish church should be changed. Knockbreda combined the former parishes of Knockcolumcille and Breda. The parish church was built on the site of the pre-Reformation church at Knock. Lady Midleton offered to build a new church at her own expense on another part of the parish and on 21 May 1733 the parishioners voted by a majority of 279 to seven in favour of moving the church to the townland of Breday (pl. 1).[20]

However, this move was opposed by Lady Ikerin and Charles Echlin of Portavoe, neither of whom actually lived in the parish of Knockbreda. They unsuccessfully sought the intervention of the bishop of Down and Connor, Francis Hutchinson, who viewed both sites and considered the new site to be the more convenient. Ikerin and Echlin then took the matter to the archbishop

15 PRONI, DIO 4/5/7, Unions that have passed since the making of the Act for Real Union and Division of Parishes, 1662–82. 16 PRONI, DIO 4/32/T/4/2/1. The request of the parishioners to have the church relocated was rejected by the archbishop of Armagh. 17 8 Anne c.13, s.4. 18 Hutchinson notebook, 121. 19 10 Geo. I, c.6. 20 Hutchinson notebook, 121.

Pl. 1: Knockbreda parish church, Co. Down, designed by Richard Cassels and built 1733–7

of Armagh, claiming that at the above meeting the parishioners had been 'influenced' to move the church to a 'remote part' of what had been the old parish of Breda, which would be 'very inconvenient to the majority of the parishioners'.[21] However, their objections were again overruled and the construction of the new church went ahead (pl. 1).[22]

21 PRONI, DIO 4/26/7/2/1, petition of Lady Ikerin and Charles Echlin to Lord Primate, n.d. [1733]. 22 PRONI, DIO 4/26/7/3.

FINANCING CHURCH-BUILDING WORK

Building a new church or carrying out extensive alterations and repairs to an existing one was a major financial undertaking by any parish. Money raised for building or repairing churches had to be properly managed and spent wisely. Misuse of parish funds was a serious offence. By law, all those who possessed land in a parish, whether as owners or tenants, were obliged to contribute to the repair of the nave of the parish church, even if they did not live in that parish.[23] It was usual for the rector of the parish to maintain the chancel of the church and the parishioners to look after the nave. When there was no structural chancel this usually translated into the eastern third of the church building.[24] The amount of money required for the construction, repair and maintenance of a church was usually decided by the parish vestry. Before levying the sum of money needed to pay for the work, the vestry required an estimate of the expected total cost of the project. The churchwardens may have done this themselves or the undertaker who was going to be responsible for the work might have done it. On 22 May 1727 a mason, John Cox, estimated that it would cost £36 to add 21 feet to the length of Loughguile parish church, Co. Antrim, raise the walls 18 inches higher, rebuild one of the corners of the church and slate the roof.[25] On 6 November 1727 the Loughguile vestry accepted his estimate and ordered the sum of £36 to be levied off the parish to carry out the work.

Parish levies or applotments were generally sufficient on their own to pay for minor repairs or alterations to a church. However, a major program of repairs or the construction of a new church usually required additional sources of funds. In a few cases churches were built entirely at the expense of a local landowner. In the 1730s, for example, Lady Midleton built Knockbreda parish church and Acheson Moore built Carnteel parish church in Aughnacloy, Co. Tyrone.[26] Usually, however, the landlord contribution supplemented money raised off the parishioners.

The usual method of raising the funds for church-building work was for a levy to be collected off every townland in the parish. This usually varied

---

23 H. Bullingbrooke, *Ecclesiastical law; or the statutes, constitutions, canons, rubricks and articles of the Church of Ireland*, 2 vols (Dublin, 1770), i, 262. When a church needed to be rebuilt, 'upon a general warning to the parishioners, the major part meeting may make a rate for pulling it down and rebuilding it on the old foundation'; see G. Jacob, *A new law dictionary* (London, 1762), n.p., note under 'Church'. **24** It was possible for the rector to abrogate his responsibility to maintain the chancel in return for committing himself to other building work. For example, in 1700 the rector of Aghaloo parish church in Caledon promised to pay half the cost of building a wall around the churchyard in return for which the parishioners agreed to keep the chancel in repair (PRONI, D/2602/1, p. 3). For how long this arrangement was to remain in place is not clear. **25** PRONI, DIO 1/24/3/13, extracts from the Loughguile parish vestry minutes. **26** W. Harris, *The antient and present state of the County of Down* (Dublin, 1744), 72; PRONI, DIO 4/32/A/2/2/2, draft of an act of consecration of Carnteel parish church in Aughnacloy, 1740.

according to the size and value of the land in each townland.[27] Assessors were appointed to go around each townland and place a value on it. In July 1725 the vestry of Derriaghy, Co. Antrim, ordered that money be levied off the lands in the parish 'considering their several conditions and circumstances'.[28] The churchwardens were then to collect the money from each townland. A slightly different approach can be seen in Moira parish, Co. Down (pl. 2), where in 1728 the vestry issued instructions that money for the new church was to be applotted at the rate of 3¼d. per Irish acre, seemingly without distinction as to the quality of the land. If the money raised in this way did not come to the required amount, the applotters were allowed at their discretion to raise the figure per acre to cover it. In Derrynoose parish, Co. Armagh, the vestry issued instructions in April 1710 that the churchwardens were to give the assessors a week's notice of when they wanted to collect the money.[29]

Money was also borrowed to pay for church-building work. When in 1728 the vestry of Ballintoy decided that the whole church and new aisle were to be 'ceiled' plastered and 'decently seated' they also realised that the parishioners were too poor to pay for this in one year.[30] The minister and churchwardens, therefore, decided to borrow £60 to have the work finished. In May 1740 the rector of Enniskillen, Co. Fermanagh, was authorised by the vestry to borrow £50 'upon the legal interest' to slate part of the parish church.[31] The money was to be repaid over four years. Money was also borrowed to help pay for a steeple to Derriaghy parish church in the early eighteenth century.[32]

Subscription was another means of raising money to pay for building work at churches. The use of subscriptions can be shown in the case of Clones parish. On 15 April 1692 the rector of Clones returned to his parish following his flight from there with his Protestant parishioners on or about 19 March 1689 at the beginning of hostilities with the supporters of James II.[33] He found the roof, glass and seats of the church destroyed and immediately called a vestry meeting for 2 May 1692. At this meeting nearly forty individuals subscribed £10 0s. 9½d. towards the repair of the church, the sums ranging from more than £1 to less than two shillings. The money was used to slate the roof, glaze the windows, replace the door and plant a hedge round the churchyard. In 1696 the vestry decided to repay the money subscribed through a parish applotment.

27 In 1668 draft directions for vestries in Derry diocese included the instruction that every person over sixteen and capable of being a communicant should pay one penny quarterly in lieu of all assessments towards the repair of the church and churchyard and for providing books, utensils and ornaments for the church (Moody and Simms (eds), *Bishopric of Derry*, i, 419). Where the church was not roofed or glazed the sum of two pence (2d.) was to be collected and this was to continue until this had happened when the figure would be reduced to one pence. Whether these directions were ever actually put into effect is not known. 28 PRONI, MIC/1/32, Derriaghy parish vestry minutes. 29 PRONI, MIC/1/14, Derrynoose parish vestry minutes. 30 PRONI, T/679/68, Ballintoy parish vestry minutes. 31 PRONI, D/1588/6, p. 36, extracts from Enniskillen parish vestry minutes. 32 PRONI, MIC/1/32, Derriaghy parish vestry minutes. 33 PRONI, MIC/1/147A/1, Clones parish vestry minutes.

Pl. 2: Moira parish church, Co. Down, built *c.*1728–32

A number of parish vestries were imaginative the way they raised money for church-building work. In 1733, for example, the vestry of Hillsborough parish, Co. Down, ordered that several ash and sycamore trees growing in the churchyard be cut down and sold by public auction to the highest bidder.[34] The

34 PRONI, MIC/1/62A, Hillsborough parish vestry minutes.

money raised in this way was to be applied towards putting a roof on the steeple and repairing the roof of the church. When a church was being rebuilt the materials from its demolished predecessor could have been sold and the money raised applied to the new work of construction. It may have been for this reason that the vestry of Down parish ordered the churchwardens on 1 October 1734 to 'take an account of the timber, glass, tile and other materials of the old church' and retain the account for the next vestry meeting.[35] In 1722, during the rebuilding of Shankill parish church in Lurgan, Co. Armagh, the vestry requested that £100 bequeathed by Mrs Jane Brownlow towards buying bells for the new church be used instead to finish the work of building the new church.[36] This sum would then be applotted over a four year period towards buying the bells.

Money needed to build a new church or carry out a major program of repairs or renovations was raised off the parish over a number of years. The vestry book of the parish of Down, Co. Down, illustrates this well.[37] In April 1723 Down parish vestry ordered £20 to be levied for 'building and raising' the walls of the church. The following year the same amount was applotted, but this time it was for 'building *or* raising' the walls of the church, suggesting that the vestry may have been considering something more than enlargement of the church. By 1728 the vestry minutes record that this annual levy of £20 was to be used for 'rebuilding' the church. The money raised was invested at a good rate of return.

In April 1732 the accounts were inspected by the vestry and it was agreed that the sum of £264 3s. 7½d. was to be immediately called in and placed in the hands of the Rt Hon. Edward Southwell, the principal landlord of the town and parish, who had promised to pay 6 per cent interest on it in order to encourage the rebuilding. In 1733 the vestry ordered that £30 be levied towards the building work and that this would be continued for four years provided that the 'directors and managers of the building' found it necessary. Southwell then advanced £100 to allow the building work to commence that year.

The size, population and relative wealth of the parish had a bearing on the sums raised each year towards building work. In the rural parish of Ballintoy, already noted as not having major financial resources at its disposal, money for building a tower was raised over a six-year period between 1733 and 1738 in annual amounts ranging between £10 and £15.[38] On the other hand the parish of Shankill, Co. Armagh, with its large Anglican population and thriving market town of Lurgan was able to afford to raise £50 a year over a four-year period towards the cost of building a new church.[39] The piecemeal nature of some of the repairs carried out to a church is reflected in the vestry book for

35 PRONI, MIC/1/38, Down parish vestry minutes.   36 PRONI, MIC/1/18, Shankill parish (Co. Armagh) vestry minutes.   37 PRONI, MIC/1/38, Down parish vestry minutes. 38 PRONI, T/679/68, Ballintoy parish vestry minutes.   39 PRONI, MIC/1/18, Shankill parish (Co. Armagh) vestry minutes.

Culdaff parish, Co. Donegal, where the vestry decided on 9 April 1716 to levy £3 for slating one quarter of the roof of the church.[40] This sum was to be raised every year until the roof had been completely slated.

Raising sufficient funds to finance church-building work was fraught with difficulties. In some cases the parishioners were simply too poor to afford to contribute to the repair or rebuilding of a church. This was particularly evident in the aftermath of war. In Derry diocese, for example, Bishop Mossom noted that the lingering effects of the 1640s meant that parishioners, 'such was their extreme poverty', were unable to build or repair their churches 'so that holy offices of God's public worship were for the most part, administered either in a dirty cabin or in a common alehouse'.[41] It was a similar story after the events of 1689–91. In 1693 it was found that Creggan church, Co. Armagh, which had been burnt by supporters of King James a few years before, was:

> now out of repair and no divine offices celebrated in it, and by reason of the wastness of the parish and the poverty of those who are in it is like to continue so if some more than ordinary means be not found to repaire it.[42]

Aside from poverty, the main obstacle to the construction and maintenance of churches was the reluctance of parishioners to contribute towards the costs. This was a particular difficulty when the majority of the inhabitants of a parish refused to conform to the Established Church, because they were either Presbyterians or Roman Catholics. In the diocese of Down and Connor, where there was a large Presbyterian majority, the shortage of suitable candidates for the position of churchwarden was a major problem in some parishes. In 1693 it was found that in consequence of this the churches 'go out of repair and the decayed ones are not repaired'.[43] In Finvoy parish, Co. Antrim, it was reported in 1711 that the only two people who could be found to collect the money for the proposed new church were Ambrose O'Neal, a Roman Catholic, and William Galland aged seventeen and a half.[44]

The Church had certain powers to deal with those who refused to co-operate with church-building work. Parishioners who refused to contribute to the cost of repairing or rebuilding a church could have a case brought against them in the ecclesiastical court.[45] It may have been through this process that Bishop King was able to claim in 1702 that three churches in the diocese of Derry were being built through enforced contributions from parishioners.[46] In 1667 an earlier bishop of Derry had excommunicated a number of inhabitants of

---

40 PRONI, D/803/1, Culdaff parish vestry minutes.   41 R. Mant, *History of the Church of Ireland from the Reformation to the Revolution* (London, 1840), 667.   42 PRONI, T/505/1, visitation books, Armagh and Derry dioceses, 1693.   43 PRONI, DIO 4/5/3, no. 23.   44 TCD, MS 1995–2008/1412, Mrs Elizabeth Crumy [Cromie] to Archbishop William King, 5 November 1711.   45 Jacob, *New law dictionary*, under 'Church'.   46 TCD, MS 750/2/3/89, Bishop William King to Bishop Thomas Smith, 16 January 1701[2].

Balteagh, Co. Londonderry, for refusing to repair the parish church.[47] In April 1722 the vestry of Derrynoose parish decided to levy 10s. for 'suing the nonsolvents that do not pay their church cess'.[48] At the same time, vestries did take on board genuine grievances about excessive applotments. For example, in July 1710 the parishioners of Derrynoose complained to the vestry of the 'wrong done them by the public assessments'.[49] The vestry responded by ordering a new assessment to be made of the value of the parish.

When several parishes were united in one union and where there was only one church there were occasionally problems with ensuring that the parishioners in all the parishes in that union contributed to the repair of that church. In 1698 Bishop King of Derry advised the bishop of Down and Connor that:

> in general you may where any church is already built oblige the parishioners to put them in good repair …; where several parishes are small and one church will serve you may force all the parishioners to contribute to that one.[50]

In 1729 an act was passed by the Irish parliament to ensure that all the inhabitants of an ecclesiastical union contributed to the repair of the designated parish church.[51]

While the gentry were generally regarded as upholders of the Established Church, on at least one occasion one of their number used his influence to the detriment of a parish church. In the late 1730s there was a dispute in Artrea parish, straddling the Londonderry-Tyrone border, over the levying of money for work on the church at a time when it was 'very much out of repair'.[52] On 13 July 1739 the churchwardens of the parish stated their case at Armagh, accusing George Conyngham Esq. of Artrea parish, who served as a justice of the peace, of being the 'opposer and preventer of said church's being repaired'. The reason for Conyngham's obstreperous behaviour is not made clear, but in the end he was forced to capitulate. The churchwardens of Artrea argued their case successfully and the following year the vestry instructed them to collect the money levied for that year as well as what was in arrears.[53]

In Moira it was not so much opposition to the work as organisational chaos that delayed the construction of a new church in the 1720s. The need for a church was occasioned by the creation of the new parish of Moira out of the parish of Magheralin in 1722.[54] Three years later, on 8 September 1725, the vestry met and agreed to applot £150 off the parish, in three equal amounts over the course of the next three years, towards the cost of building the church.[55]

---

47 PRONI, T/552/ii.   48 PRONI, MIC/1/14, Derrynoose parish vestry minutes.   49 Ibid. 50 TCD, MS 750/1/238–9, Bishop William King to Bishop Edward Walkington of Down and Connor, 31 May 1698.   51 3 Geo. III, c.11.   52 PRONI, DIO 4/32/A/7/6/1.   53 PRONI, MIC/1/319, Artrea parish vestry minutes.   54 *Liber munerum publicorum Hiberniae*, 2 vols (Dublin, 1852), ii, part v, 124.   55 PRONI, MIC/1/79, Moira parish vestry minutes.

The legality of this act was later questioned with the result that the bishop of Dromore himself was forced to intervene and order a vestry to be held 'on the ground where the church of the said parish is building' on 8 July 1728. At this vestry meeting, with the bishop presiding, it was agreed that the sum of £50 be levied by the following Michaelmas and 'applied to the building of the church'. For unknown reasons the amount applotted in 1728 was never collected and so the vestry met again on 10 August 1730 and decided to levy the originally agreed £50. Yet again this sum was never collected necessitating a further vestry meeting on 5 July 1731 at which the amount was applotted. The church was finally completed and consecrated in May 1732 (pl. 2).[56]

THE ORGANISATION OF CHURCH-BUILDING WORK

Once it had been agreed to build a new church or undertake some work on an existing one and the money needed to pay for it secured or at least in the process of being raised, attention could then be focused on the building work itself. If a new church was being built some consideration had to be given to its design. None of the deliberations over the design of a church have survived. The architect in the modern sense of the word was all but non-existent in the period covered by this study and the design of most churches seems to have been left to the master mason with perhaps some suggestions from an informed landlord or cleric. It was said that the Reverend Philip Skelton's father had 'some knowledge of architecture being employed to superintend the building of the present church of Derriaghy'.[57] Derriaghy parish church was built in the 1690s. The 'some knowledge of architecture' possessed by Skelton senior – we are not told how he acquired it – was probably the height of the qualifications of most of those who designed churches in the seventeenth and early eighteenth centuries.

In any case, the simplicity of most churches meant that the services of a skilled architect were not required. The only church known to have been designed by someone with proven skills in the field of architecture was Knockbreda, consecrated in 1737. This was the work of Richard Cassels, the principal architect working in Ireland at that time.[58] At the same time, the detailed requirements contained in the specifications given to the builders indicate that careful thought had gone into the design and layout of the church. Ideas were copied from other churches. In 1715, for example, the vestry of Carnteel parish ordered that the new pulpit was to be of exactly the same dimensions as that in the church in nearby Caledon.

There were different approaches to the building work. These depended to a large extent on the nature and scale of the task in hand. Some work, particularly

56 Ibid. **57** S. Burdy, *The life of Philip Skelton*, ed. N. Moore (Oxford, 1914), 15. **58** Harris, *Antient and present state … Down*, 72.

if it were minor, could be left entirely to the supervision of the churchwardens who were authorised to select workmen at their own discretion. Alternatively a group of individuals could be appointed by the vestry to organise the work. When the vestry of Tynan parish, Co. Armagh, decided to proceed with the construction of a steeple in 1709 they appointed four men to 'treat with workmen for building the said steeple'.[59] Larger projects, such as the construction of a new church, were more demanding on time and resources and required a different approach. In some cases the vestry and churchwardens took an active role in organising and supervising the construction of a new church. On other occasions they delegated the work to a committee composed of representatives of the parish. An example of the former approach can be illustrated in the case of Derrynoose parish in the early eighteenth century.

By the beginning of the eighteenth century the parish of Derrynoose had been without a Protestant church for at least sixty years. In 1682 it had been united to the neighbouring parish of Tynan.[60] About 1700 Bishop King of Derry recommended that Derrynoose again be provided with its own church on the grounds that the parish was 'now planted with Protestants'.[61] In 1709 the union of Tynan and Derrynoose was formally dissolved by an act of parliament.[62] The vestry minutes for Derrynoose survive from the date of the dissolution and cover the period in which the new church was built.[63] These reveal the vestry to have taken quite an active role in overseeing the construction of the new church. What becomes apparent is that there was a lack of forward planning in the early stages of the building work.

For example, in 1710 the vestry agreed that the new church was to be 40 feet long and 20 feet wide. However, by the following year it had realised that this church was going to be too small and proposed that an extra 10 feet be added to its length. The year after that the vestry came to the conclusion that 'upon more mature consideration we do find that the place fixed on in Lisglen is very inconvenient and "defickelt" to build a church on' and instead decided to build the church on Madden glebe. How far the building work had progressed by this stage is unclear, but presumably an attempt had been made to dig the foundations for the parishioners to know that the original site was unsuitable for building on. Captain Henry Richardson, the lessee of several thousand acres in the Derrynoose area from Trinity College, Dublin, played the major role in overseeing the construction of the new church.[64] Money raised for building the church was forwarded to him and he was to pay the workmen out of this for the work they had completed.[65] Initially there seems to have been no formal agreement between Richardson and the vestry, but in May 1712 he was

59 PRONI, MIC/1/18, Tynan parish vestry minutes. **60** PRONI, DIO 4/5/7. **61** PRONI, DIO 4/29/2/1/2. **62** 8 Anne, c. 13. **63** PRONI, MIC/1/14, Derrynoose parish vestry minutes. **64** TCD, MUN/P/24/258. **65** PRONI, MIC/1/14, Derrynoose parish vestry minutes.

appointed overseer of the construction of the new church in the parish. This church was completed in 1713.

A different approach was adopted by the vestry of Down parish when the task of rebuilding the church came before them. In April 1733 Down vestry appointed nine individuals, including Major General Price and the dean of Down, to act as 'directors and managers' of the new church.[66] These men were 'to do everything necessary towards building and finishing the same'. Any three of the directors could form a quorum with notice of an intended meeting to be announced on the Sunday before it was due to take place. The responsibility of rebuilding the church seems to have been left entirely to this panel of directors as there is scarcely any other mention of it in the vestry minutes. It would have been up to them to have hired the workmen, paid for materials and supervised the actual building work. The inclusion of Major General Price among the directors is interesting. He was not a native of the parish, but had a short time previously been a major contributor to the refurbishment, if not rebuilding, of the parish church in nearby Saintfield.[67] The success of this approach is shown by the fact that in October 1734 it was reported that there would be a balance of £37 19s. 2½d. remaining after the building expenses had been paid off. The vestry resolved that this money would be applied to completing the interior of the church. Again 'directors and trustees' were appointed to supervise this work.

The agreement to build a church or carry out repairs to an existing building usually took the form of a written contract by which the workman, known as the undertaker or the contractor, bound himself to perform certain tasks. Contained in the building contracts could be specific instructions that the undertaker was required to follow. The specifications included the dimensions of the church, the materials to be used in its construction, the number, form and positioning of the windows. Failure to honour the terms of his contract would result in a financial penalty. Contracts were not simply drawn up when a new church was being built or a major program of works was being undertaken. Vestry minutes record agreements between the churchwardens and workmen relating to the maintenance of certain parts of the fabric of the church. For example, in 1719 John Kelly was contracted to keep in good repair the roof and windows of Comber parish church, Co. Down, for a period of twenty-one years.[68]

When it came to building a new church the work could be contracted out to one or more men who would be responsible for the entire project. An example of this is the agreement of 1710 for a new church in Arboe parish, Co. Tyrone. This was made between Stewart Blacker and William Latham, both of Bonetroan and both styled esquire, on the one hand, and Dr Christopher

66 PRONI, MIC/1/38, Down parish vestry minutes.   67 Harris, *Antient and present state ... Down*, 71.   68 PRONI, MIC/583/36, Comber parish vestry minutes.

Jenney, rector of Arboe, and five members of the local gentry acting on behalf of the parishioners.[69] The work of building the church was left entirely to Blacker and Latham. As far as is known neither man was a mason or builder. Both could be classified as members of the minor gentry, and therefore for the work to have been carried out they would had to have hired the necessary craftsmen. How they organised this work was left to their own discretion. So long as they fulfilled their part of the agreement the other signatories were not concerned with how they did it.

In other instances it seems that workmen were hired to carry out specific building activities. For example, a bond (undated, but probably from the 1720s)[70] relating to the construction of Gartan parish church in Co. Donegal reads: 'I do "oblidg" my self to build the stone work of ye church of Gartan, furnishing all materials to my hand & "rufcast" it for eleven pence a pearch.'[71] In this case the agreement relates purely to the construction of the walls of the church.

There were several methods of paying undertakers and workmen. In the first instance the undertaker could be paid in one lump sum when his work had been completed and approved. The second option was to pay the undertaker in instalments in the course of his work. A third option was to advance the undertaker a sum of money towards his work and then pay him the remainder when he had finished. When William Hare was contracted to slate the south side of the roof of Tickmacrevan parish church, Co. Antrim, in 1726 he was paid £2 up front and £3 10s when he had completed his work.[72] Payment followed, at least in some cases, the presentation of a written invoice to the church-wardens.[73]

Contracts were secured by a bond, which was usually double the expected cost of the work. Under the terms of his contract James Kinseallagh was to be paid £50 for his work at Clones parish church in 1710 and he was to provide a bond for £100. The value of the bond of 1710 between Blacker and Latham and the rector and the other parties to the agreement for a new church in Arboe parish was £500, suggesting that the anticipated cost of building the church was £250. One or more individuals guaranteed the bond. These so called bondsmen were often members of the local gentry. For example, the bondsman for Hugh and William Glass, when they were contracted to repair and maintain the roof of Comber parish church, was Simon Vane of Ballywalter styled 'esquire'. The bondsman for James Kinseallagh, when he contracted to repair the steeple of Clones parish church in 1710 was James Stanous, a merchant in the town of Monaghan.[74]

If the undertaker failed to finish the building work the bondsmen were

69 PRONI, DIO 4/32/A/5/2/1. **70** RCB, GS/2/7/3/34, Visitations of Raphoe diocese, 1729 and 1733. **71** TCD, MS 1995–2008/2420. **72** PRONI, T/3054/B/4A, Tickmacrevan parish vestry minutes. **73** PRONI, MIC/583/36, Comber parish vestry minutes. **74** PRONI, MIC/1/147A/1, Clones parish vestry minutes.

expected to ensure its completion themselves. The vestry considered the provision of security important. When Robert Hamilton was contracted to keep the windows of Tynan parish church in repair, the vestry insisted that he was not to be paid until he had given security to do this for eight years.[75] This bond was to be void on the completion of the work set out in the agreement. The contracts usually contained a specified time period for the work to be completed. Blacker and Latham were to have the new church in Arboe 'at the end of four years from Easter last in as good condition and repair as the old church is at present'.[76] Kinseallagh was given four months to complete the repairs to Clones parish church in 1710.[77]

Until the work had been completed the undertaker was responsible for any problems that may have arisen. This placed him at some financial risk. It meant, for example, that the builders were reluctant to work in unfavourable conditions. In December 1691, John Leslie, the rector of Urney parish (pl. 3), Co. Tyrone, informed his bishop that money had been assessed and a workman contracted to carry out repairs to the church.[78] However, despite having drawn slates and timber to the church, the workman was unable to finish roofing the church because of the weather. Because of this the work was being delayed until the following February and in the meantime if any slates were blown from the roof it would be to the cost of the workman and not the parish.

When the work was completed it was inspected either by the churchwardens or men appointed by them. Upon completion the new church in Arboe parish was to be approved 'according to the judgement of two persons indifferently chosen'.[79] In 1739 in Kildress parish, Co. Tyrone, when the roof had been shingled by James Rodgers it was to be 'viewed by knowing workmen'.[80] Of the three men appointed to do this, at least one had previously been employed by the vestry to carry out work on the church. In the agreement between Neile Kar and the vestry of Donagh parish, Co. Monaghan, for keeping the church in repair, the former was to be paid his fee at the end of each year, but only if his work had been to the satisfaction of the parishioners.[81] The undertaker's involvement with the church did not necessarily end when he had completed the building work. Following the completion of his work on the roof of Kildress parish church, James Rodgers bound himself to keep the roof water-fast for five years. James Kinseallagh was bound by his contract to uphold his work to the steeple at Clones for seven years.[82]

A workman who failed to complete his task or who carried out his work unsatisfactorily could be sued. The vestry minutes of Derriaghy parish of 20

75 PRONI, MIC/1/18, Shankill parish (Co. Armagh) vestry minutes. 76 PRONI, DIO 4/32/A/5/2/1. 77 PRONI, MIC/1/147A/1, Clones parish vestry minutes. 78 TCD, MS 1995–2008/191, Rev. John Leslie to Bishop William King, 5 December 1691. 79 PRONI, DIO/4/32/A/5/2/1. 80 PRONI, MIC/1/107, Kildress parish vestry minutes. 81 PRONI, MIC/1/127/D/1, Donagh parish vestry minutes. 82 PRONI, MIC/1/147A/1, Clones parish vestry minutes.

Pl. 3: A keystone bearing the name of the builder (S. Murray 1734) of Urney parish church, Co. Tyrone

February 1712 hint at a problem with a workman.[83] At this meeting it was noted that a 'misfortune' had happened to the church bell requiring its repair. The churchwardens were instructed to take 'what methods the law will advise for arresting Salem Bickerstaff for the mending of this bell'. It seems likely that Bickerstaff had been employed to carry out some work to the church and in the process had damaged the bell.

If the defaulter could not be brought to account for his defective workmanship, the vestry was left with having to make alternative arrangements to have the work completed. This happened in Clones parish at the beginning of the eighteenth century.[84] An agreement to build a steeple had been made with John Godolphin in the latter part of the seventeenth century. However, by May 1700, with the work still not completed, the vestry decided that the minister and churchwardens should take legal action against Goldolphin over

83 PRONI, MIC/1/32, Derriaghy parish vestry minutes. 84 PRONI, MIC/1/147A/1, Clones parish vestry minutes.

his failure to fulfil his obligations in the contract. Godolphin pleaded poverty and pointed out that both of the original bondsmen to the contract were dead. The vestry was then forced to make its own arrangements to have the tower finished.

The necessary materials for the building work could be provided to the workmen by the churchwardens or alternatively the workmen would have to provide them themselves. If the vestry decided on the latter, the expense of the materials could be part of the agreement between the vestry and the workmen. If not the workmen would be recompensed for the materials they had used. In the aforementioned agreement between the Clones vestry and James Kinseallagh, the latter was to 'furnish, buy, and draw and provide all the stone, lime timber boards, nails and other materials for the work at his own expense'.[85] When the bishop of Raphoe proposed building transepts to the cathedral, the dean and parishioners offered to draw the materials to the church and furnish the lime.[86] In 1712 James McCamon, carpenter, was paid £8 11s. for putting on rafters on the entire church, all materials being provided to him 'which he is to reduce to proper scantline for the said work'. The Raphoe churchwardens were ordered to buy as much bog fir as would be required for this work and ensure that it was delivered to the church.

The means by which building materials were transported to the church was also an important consideration. The minutes of the cathedral church in Raphoe contain a number of references to this.[87] In September 1676, when 400 deal boards had to be brought to the church for the purpose of seating it, the vestry ordered that every quarterland was to send two horses and men to transport the boards or pay two shillings in lieu. Similarly, in September 1685 the vestry ordered that two horses from each quarterland were to draw freestone from a quarry on the far side of Strabane in Co. Tyrone to floor the chancel of the church, a round trip of some thirty miles. Much more onerous was the order in July 1693 that seventy-two horses were to be sent to Burndouglas, near Lifford, in Co. Donegal, to collect building stone, 'each horse [was to be] well loaded with stones consisting of twelve score weight'. The owners of the horses were only to be given two days' notice to be ready to make the trip.

Other parishes followed the same practice. In the vestry book of Donagheady parish, Co. Tyrone, we also read in 1700 of an order that sixteen men and thirty men and thirty horses were to be provided for repairing part of the churchyard wall.[88] About 1730 the vestry of Saintfield, Co. Down, ordered every townland to send four horses and three men to draw stones to the church or instead pay one shilling for every man and horse.[89] While horses were the principal means

85 Ibid. 86 PRONI, MIC/1/95, Raphoe parish vestry minutes. 87 Ibid. 88 PRONI, MIC/1/35, Donagheady parish vestry minutes. 89 PRONI, MIC/1/69, Saintfield parish vestry minutes. A precise date cannot be put on this because of the illegible nature of the vestry minutes.

of drawing materials, river transport was also used where practicable. In Co. Fermanagh building materials were transported by boat through the lakes and rivers. Near Belcoo was a good slate quarry. The slates from it were carried through Lough MacNean and the River Arney into Lough Erne and from there throughout the county.[90] Shingles for re-roofing the church in Ballyshannon in 1692 were brought from Enniskillen, probably by boat via Lower Lough Erne and the River Erne.[91]

Vestries were concerned that suitably qualified masons and craftsmen were employed to carry out the work. Shoddy workmanship had resulted in the collapse of one church in Co. Tyrone in the 1680s.[92] About 1713 the vestry of Carnteel instructed the churchwardens to employ 'proper workmen' to make alterations to the windows.[93] In 1729 the churchwardens of Artrea were instructed to employ an 'honest workman or workmen' to repair the roof of the church.[94] How the builders were recruited is not recorded in any of the surviving vestry books. The placing of advertisements in newspapers did not become commonplace in the north of Ireland until the latter part of the eighteenth century. It is likely that word of mouth and recommendations from satisfied clients were the main way of identifying potentially suitable builders and craftsmen.

Most of the men employed to carry out building work at churches were probably local, from the same parish or within a short distance from it. Alexander Mitchell, for example, who was responsible for most of the routine maintenance work at Donagheady parish church, lived at Leitrim, less than a mile away from the church.[95] A Mr Middleton, who was employed in making seats in Aghaloo parish church in Caledon in 1707, was possibly from Dublin since he had to send to there for his tools when the workmen had failed to appear as promised.[96] Alternatively he may have been working on another job in Dublin. He may have been the same as the Robert Midleton who was employed in 1728 to make a new door to the steeple of nearby Tynan church and paint the woodwork in the interior of the church.[97] James Kinseallagh, who carried out alterations to the tower at Clones, was from Monaghan, about twelve miles away. William King who was responsible for maintaining the roof of Derrynoose parish church was from Armagh, about ten miles away.

Whether the specialist craftsmen were able to derive a sufficient living from their profession to avoid having to find additional sources of income is unclear. Many of them probably leased small farms to supplement their incomes from

90 PRONI, T/2521/3/1, 'The Rev'd Mr Henery's account of the county of Fermanagh, written anno 1739'. 91 Allingham, *Ballyshannon*, 50. 92 PRONI, T/505/1, visitations of Armagh and Derry dioceses, 1693. 93 PRONI, MIC/583/31, Carnteel parish vestry minutes. 94 PRONI, MIC/1/319, Artrea parish vestry minutes. 95 PRONI, MIC/1/35, Donagheady parish vestry minutes. 96 TCD, MSS 1995–2008/1278, John Hamilton, Caledon, to Archbishop William King, 15 November 1707. 97 PRONI, MIC/1/18, Shankill parish (Co. Armagh) vestry minutes.

building work. Despite being labelled under a particular occupation, a workman could carry out several different building tasks at a church. In 1723 the vestry of Derrynoose employed their slater, probably William King of Armagh, to build and hang a new gate for the churchyard, and to keep it in repair for so long as he was responsible for maintaining the roof of the church.[98] There is some evidence that individual craftsmen carried out work on more than one church in their locality. The man responsible for the reconstruction of Leckpatrick parish church, Co. Tyrone, in 1693 was a Mr Mitchell.[99] He may have been the same as the aforementioned Alexander Mitchell of Leitrim in the neighbouring parish of Donagheady.[1]

CONCLUSION

This essay has provided a survey of the role of parishioners in building, repairing and maintaining churches, casting some light on a hitherto neglected subject. Gaps in the documentary record mean that there is much that we do not know about the relationship between parishioner and church. Nonetheless it is clear that the ordinary parishioners played a crucial role in the provision of Anglican churches in the north of Ireland during this period. To its members and adherents, the importance of a Church of Ireland parish church cannot be overstated. It gave physical form to the Established Church in a locality. In most parts of Ireland in this period the Anglican parish church was the most important public building and in many places it provided the focus for settlement. For the curious, the legacy of these buildings can still be explored, either through those churches still in use or, as is more usually the case, through edifices in varying stages of ruination. Here among the tombstones and the ivy it is possible to appreciate the level of commitment and resourcefulness that brought these structures into being and then kept them, generally speaking, in a satisfactory state of repair for as long as they were needed. As such they provide a powerful link with the past.

98 PRONI, MIC/1/14, Derrynoose parish vestry minutes.   99 TCD, MS 751/1, account book of Bishop William King of Derry.   1 PRONI, MIC/1/35, Donagheady parish vestry minutes.

Index of personal and collective names

Index of places